*When a Woman Becomes a Religious Dynasty*

# When a Woman Becomes a Religious Dynasty

## THE
## *SAMDING DORJE PHAGMO*
## OF TIBET

Hildegard Diemberger

Columbia University Press
*New York*

Columbia University Press
*Publishers Since 1893*
New York   Chichester, West Sussex
Copyright © 2007 Columbia University Press
All rights reserved
Library of Congress Cataloging-in-Publication Data
Diemberger, Hildegard.
When a woman becomes a religious dynasty : the Samding Dorje Phagmo of Tibet /
Hildegard Diemberger.
p.   cm.
Includes bibliographical references and index.
ISBN 978-0-231-14320-2 (cloth : alk. paper)
1. Chos-kyi-sgron-ma, 1422–1455. 2. Dorje Phagmos (Vajravārāhī incarnations)—Biography.
3. Bsam-lding dgon-pa (Tibet, China)—History. I. Title.
BQ946.O756D54   2007
294.3'923092—dc22

2007000291

∞

References to Internet Web sites (URLs) were accurate at the time of writing. Neither the author
nor Columbia University Press is responsible for URLs that may have expired or changed since
the manuscript was prepared.

# CONTENTS

# ILLUSTRATIONS

# FOREWORD

## *Marilyn Strathern*

*From time to time anthropologists unearth surprises that would rank on anyone's* register as "discovery." At the center of this fascinating account is just such a discovery: the copy of a rare fifteenth-century text found in an archive in Beijing and shown to Hildegard Diemberger in New York. The narrative concerned a famous Tibetan princess who, against all expectations of her gender, founded an incarnation lineage higher than that of most male reincarnation lines. The text was the story of her life. It was a discovery in this sense more for the anthropologist than for the world, but Dr. Diemberger has turned her realization of what she was looking at into a discovery of another kind. She has uncovered just what a remarkable tale that manuscript tells.

Dr. Diemberger has made her own translation of the biography the center of this book, and it is absorbing reading. She brings it alive though the directness of her language; she also brings it alive through a device that would not be foreign to her Tibetan counterparts: by providing an account first of what is known of this princess's life and times, and then of just what it means that this lady, Chokyi Dronma, can also be thought of as the founder of a dynasty, a lineage of majestic dimensions with an unbroken succession until the present day. Chokyi Dronma was also known as the Dorje Phagmo of a notable monastery, Samding.

Dr. Diemberger turns to social anthropology to disclose facts about her subject in a manner that mirrors the way the biography itself was written. This makes her translation a very special book within a book—in short, a discovery within a discovery.

For the original manuscript was itself an act of discovery. It was written in order to disclose to the world a series of untoward facts about this young woman who had forsaken her royal marriage to become a nun. The details—about her thoughts, her exploits, her unusual powers—build up to a picture almost unique in Tibetan religious writing. So what did the biography uncover? It revealed that Chokyi Dronma was successor to a tantric master, itself a matter of considerable remark for a woman; it also reveals that she was the emanation of a deity that gave her the title Dorje Phagmo, and was written in the knowledge that the deity in the form of Chokyi Dronma would be reborn in a woman who would succeed her. So she lived again in what became a whole line of women, from the fifteenth century to the present.

The Tibetan author of this biography (its compilation may have involved more than one hand), thought to have compiled the account very shortly after Chokyi's early death (she was only thirty-three), was doing more that reporting on the discovery of her identity that had been made during her lifetime. He was reenacting that discovery in the way he arranged his narrative and in the events he emphasized, in order to guarantee the continuing effect of her recognition. And he did so by depicting her experiences with the detail that still makes such compelling reading. The very manner in which her life as a human being unfolded was what revealed her divine identity.

The book around this book is also a reenactment of sorts. Dr. Diemberger's identification of the manuscript did not stop with the find. The commentary that she adds is intended to reveal to a now modern world exactly what she thought she had discovered. Chokyi Dronma/Dorje Phagmo is a well-known historical figure, already familiar to Western scholars of Tibet, of great renown to visitors from Europe who sought audiences with her successors, and at times coupled with the Dalai Lama in the care with which she has been treated by foreigners. Dr. Diemberger discloses two further dimensions.

The first underlines Chokyi Dronma's gender. It was known that she was a remarkable woman, and that in the Tibetan tradition few women have aspired to discipleship and been accepted in the way she was. What was less clear—and the fact that the biography contains what seem to be fragments from her own voice or hand is key here—is just how much of an issue that was, or was not, for her. Her self-knowledge and her self-belief, her persistence and her resignation, all reveal something of the inspiration she must have been.

The second emphasizes the extent to which she lived in a world of change, of cultural innovation and technological invention on the one hand and continually shifting religious and political identities on the other. The reader is made aware just how Chokyi Dronma's own person becomes multilayered, not least through her diverse titles and the claims made in turn of what her own spiritual antecedents were, and learns of a labile and constantly reconfigured web of allegiances across groups and regions. She was a significant patron and political figure who clearly was able to manage different identities to great effect. The skill is discovered again in the most recent Dorje Phagmo, who has weathered the changing fortunes of life under a Chinese identity, being now a prominent communist cadre, now the spiritual rebuilder of the Samding monastery.

However, this book shows that the subject of the biography exists not just in a world of multiple religious and political identities that make it so important to have her specific and particular life rehearsed again: she also lives in a changing world of multiple texts. It was crucial that there should be a text. Yet, when the biography was first being written, it must have existed alongside numerous others discovering deities and proclaiming true discipleship, and it was destined to be passed on in diverse forms, open in turn to people's readings and interpretations. Among other things, this is a compelling contribution to understanding the social practices of writing.

We are left with what history itself discloses. Chokyi Dronma endures in the continuing emanation of Dorje Phagmo's presence in the world through the line of women who followed, living, physical embodiments of her. You might meet one walking down a road, as Hildegard did. This original and earliest of her biographies, at once more fragile and more robust than these many women, has survived to tell the beginning of the tale.

Scholars in and of Tibet will be grateful that a further facsimile of this precious relic has been returned to its place among what remains of the stupendous literature of Tibet. Other readers will be grateful to the author for bringing Chokyi Dronma/Dorje Phagmo to view. I think of the way a roving searchlight catches shapes and contours before it fully illuminates its object. In turning some of our contemporary concerns on her, Dr. Diemberger has discovered a figure, ahead or behind but not so very far away, walking in time with us.

# CHOKYI DRONMA'S JOURNEYS

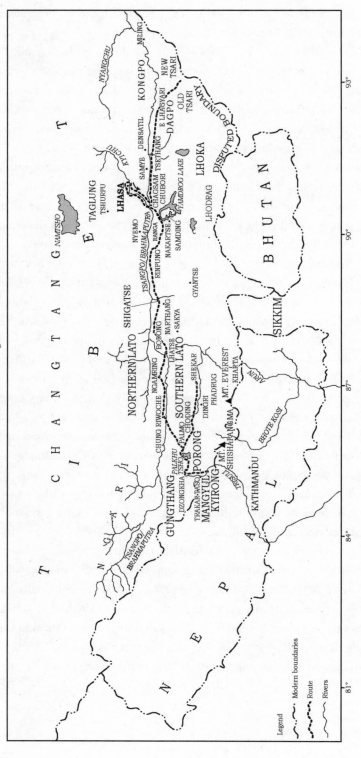

Map showing Chokyi Dronma's homeland, Mangyul-Gungthang, and the itinerary of her journeys: as a royal bride from Gungthang to Shekar in Southern Lato; as a prospective nun from Shekar to Porong Palmo Choding monastery; as a *yoginī* on her final journey from Gungthang to Chung Riwoche in Northern Lato, to Lhasa, and eventually to Tsari, where she died. The map includes the most important place names that appear in the biography.

Legend

- – · – Modern boundaries
- ● ● ● Route
- ——— Rivers

# PREFACE

*In 1920, as he was traveling through Tibet on a diplomatic mission, Sir Charles* Bell stopped at the monastery of Samding, where he met "the holiest woman in Tibet." Like many other travelers, he was captivated by the aura of sanctity surrounding the woman who embodied the tantric deity Vajravārāhī, known in Tibetan as Dorje Phagmo. "The standing modern example" of Tibetan women who had devoted their careers to religion, he wrote,

> is to be found in the monastery of the peaceful hill overlooking the "Lake of the Upland Pastures" (*Yam-dro Tso*) and facing the eternal snows of the Himalaya. Not inaptly is this monastery called "The Soaring Meditation" (Samding). Both the situation and the character of its occupant justify the name. For here resides the holiest woman in Tibet, the incarnation of the goddess Dor-je Pa-mo. The present is the eleventh Incarnation. When one dies, or "retires to the heavenly fields," her spirit passes into a baby girl, and thus the succession goes on. . . . It was my privilege to visit her on my way to Lhasa. . . . We were the first white men to be received by her, indeed the first she had seen. (Bell 1994 [1928]:166)

In the eyes of the Tibetans the human embodiment of Dorje Phagmo is endowed with a particular form of sacredness, seen as a powerful spiritual entity linked with the cults of Avalokiteśvara and Cakrasaṃvara, and, at times, is considered a symbolic female counterpart to the Dalai Lama. In the 1970s two leading Tibetan scholars described her as "the only female reincarnation spiritually and officially recognized in the whole of Tibet and famous throughout Central Asia as Samdhing Dorjee Phagmo—the Thunderbolt Sow of Soaring Meditation" (Dhondup and Tashi Tsering 1979:11). Research since then has shown that other, less famous female reincarnation lines had existed in Tibet over the centuries (Tashi Tsering 1993; Chayet 2002), but the Samding Dorje Phagmo was the first female line to be established and remains the only one most Tibetans know of and relate to. "The powers attributed to the institution of Dorje Phagmo," wrote Dhondup and Tsering,

> [have] held considerable spiritual and mystic sway over the Tibetan mind. The very mention of Samdhing inspired a longing for solitude and peace. Popular songs in Tibet idealised Yamdrog Samdhing as a spiritual heaven of solitude and eulogised Dorje Phagmo as a special spiritual force. (Dhondup and Tashi Tsering 1979:12)

Just as the Dalai Lama, the physical manifestation of Avalokiteśvara, is seen as the defender of Tibetan Buddhism, so is the Dorje Phagmo entrusted with this task. In addition, she seems to have had a particular significance for women and is especially invoked by those who are unhappy in love or unhappily married. A popular song goes:

> Oh! Divine Dorje Phagmo,
> I do not want to get married!
> I am not in love with the world.
> Ordain me as a nun
> And take me into your fold!
> (DHONDUP AND TASHI TSERING 1979:12)

These verses reflect the sorrow of women, repeatedly found in Tibetan history, who have to struggle against social obligations to fulfill their wish to renounce the world. But they have a special resonance and appeal in the case of the lineage of Dorje Phagmo: the actual life of the princess who first established the tradition in the fifteenth century was dominated by such struggle. Chokyi Dronma renounced her royal life to become a nun and in due course came to be seen as an emanation of the deity Dorje Phagmo. She died while still a young woman, and a young girl was recognized as her reincarnation, thus beginning the first and most famous line of female reincarnations in Tibet. Over the centuries that lineage has become not only a religious institution but also a powerful symbol in the Tibetan landscape and a prominent feature in prophecies, long an important part of Tibetan culture and politics. Sarat Chandra Das, the Bengali scholar who traveled secretly through Tibet in the nineteenth century, allegedly on a mission for the intelligence service of the British Empire, wrote of an encounter at Samding with the tenth Dorje Phagmo and of the prophetic accounts of her power and importance to the country. He had been taken gravely ill as his party approached the monastery, and in his account he recalls the powerful mythology of lakes and threatened inundations surrounding this holy woman:

> It is due, by the way, to the Dorje Phagmo's spiritual influence that the waters of the inner lake or Dumo tso ("Demon's lake") of the Yamdo tso are held in bounds, for otherwise they would overflow and inundate the whole of Tibet. It was for this that the Samding lamasery was originally built. . . . My eyes fell on the Dumo tso, and on the place where the dead are thrown into the lake, and I shuddered as I thought that this had come near being my fate. (Das 1988 [1902]:136–138)

Samding lay not far from the shortest route taken by travelers hoping to reach Lhasa from India, and later British explorers and military campaigners also found their way there. Edmund Candler, one of the reporters who accompanied the British invasion force that ravaged Tibet in 1903–04, chose from the stories surrounding the Dorje Phagmo the one that most closely mirrored his own position as part of a foreign conquering force, and wrote an account that was to become famous in the West of the miraculous powers she displayed when faced by earlier invaders:

> The wild mountain scenery of the Yandrok Tso, the most romantic in Tibet, has naturally inspired many legends. When Samding was threatened by the Dzungarian invaders in the early eighteenth century, Dorje Phagmo miraculously converted herself and all her attendants into pigs. Serung Dandub, the Dzungarian chief, finding the monastery deserted, said that he would not loot a place guarded only by swine, whereupon Dorje Phagmo again metamorphosed herself and her

satellites. The terrified invaders prostrated themselves in awe before the goddess, and presented the monastery with the most priceless gifts. . . . I quote these tales, which have been mentioned in nearly every book on Tibet, as typical of the country. Doubtless similar legends will be current in a few years about the British to account for the sparing of Samding, Nagartse and Pelthe Jong. (Candler 1905:178–179)

Mythical and human at the same time, embodied deity and living person, the Dorje Phagmo intrigued and charmed foreign visitors; the sacred woman captured their imagination and their orientalizing gaze. Other Asians were not immune: four decades later, Mao seemed not indifferent to the charm of a subsequent reincarnation. The Twelfth Dorje Phagmo was invited to Beijing along with her sister after both young women had escaped from Tibet during the 1959 uprising and had decided to return a few months later. The sister described their being positioned on the high rostrum near Mao and General He Long at a giant celebration to mark China's national day, October 1, and the tenth anniversary of the founding of the PRC. "In the evening we had a banquet," she recalled, "and when the Chairman Mao met with Dorje Phagmo he kept praising her as the 'female living Buddha' (Ch. *niu huofu*)."[1]

Subsequently the Twelfth Dorje Phagmo was given a high position as an official in the administration of the Tibet Autonomous Region, combining her religious role with a secular one conferred upon her by the Chinese government. Such personal vicissitudes and paradoxical positionings have made the current Dorje Phagmo a somewhat mysterious and disputed figure in contemporary Tibetan religion and politics, and first attracted me to her as a subject of study. I had heard of the Samding Dorje Phagmo relatively early in my studies of Tibetan culture and history; she is mentioned in numerous books about Tibet, especially where issues concerning gender and religion are discussed. I was intrigued by this deity-woman who has been reincarnating generation after generation for centuries, and I soon discovered that despite her popularity, information about her was slight and often confused, as Tashi Tsering (1993) and Anne Chayet (2002) have pointed out. At first, perhaps on account of her fame and the controversies surrounding her current position, I felt shy about engaging in any research about her. Only much later did I come across her again, as a result of studying the scarcely known religious tradition to which she belongs.

I first visited the monastery of Samding in 1996, while on a journey to some of the monasteries and shrines belonging to the obscure and eclectic Bodongpa school of Tibetan Buddhism.[2] I was studying the life and the work of the main scholar of this tradition, Bodong Chogle Namgyal (1375/6–1451), a great polymath who taught many of the masters of his time. During the long evenings at Samding, the monks told me that this great scholar had been the main teacher of the princess Chokyi Dronme (also called Chokyi Dronma) and described how she had miraculously founded the monastery and become the first of the famous line of female incarnations associated with it. They showed me her image among the mural paintings that decorated the newly reconstructed monastery and told me of other monasteries where much older portraits of her could still be found.

Two years later, in New York, as I was looking for further sources on the Bodongpa tradition, the legendary scholar of Tibetan studies, Gene Smith, showed me a copy of the biography of the same princess. It was an astonishing discovery: Leonard van der Kuijp, then newly appointed as the Professor of Tibetan and Himalayan Studies at Harvard, had been able to reproduce this rare text from an archive in Bejing; later he generously provided me with a copy and encouraged me to work on it. Coming across the life of this extraordinary woman was like finding a missing link in the tradition. It is a fascinating narrative, vibrant and unexpectedly human, that became the basis for innumerable other stories, genealogical accounts, myths, and rituals.

This unique text has now been returned to Tibet, to be available for the people and the monasteries that currently embody the Dorje Phagmo's tradition. Witnessing their efforts and realizing the significance for them of texts that have survived the Cultural Revolution induced me to look at the living tradition as well. The first and second parts of this book are devoted to the life of the princess as described in her biography and the third part to her tradition: how her reincarnation line was established, how it developed over the centuries, and how it is currently lived among the Tibetans. The questions I try to answer are not abstract philosophical issues, but largely practical inquiries about how a woman came five hundred years ago to occupy an important position in a largely male-dominated spiritual hierarchy, and how she is viewed today. Who was this princess in the first place? Why and how was she reincarnated? How could she be both a woman and an embodied female deity transcending space and time? What is her significance for her followers, for Tibetans, and for religious women in general? I use texts, visual materials, and such oral accounts as I have been able to collect, along with some anthropological methods of investigation into social practices. To allow the reader to get a feel for the original narrative, I decided to render it in English and include it here. This is a literary translation with a minimum of explanatory notes, since the material is likely to be interesting for a readership broader than the academic audience of Tibetologists. A more technical annotated translation will be provided, in due course, in a specialized publication, in which the original Tibetan text will be reproduced (Diemberger and Pasang Wangdu forthcoming).

Tibetan terms are given according to their pronunciation, except where the transliteration is particularly significant for the context, in which case it is given in brackets according to the Wylie system. Chinese terms are given in pinyin.

I have transposed the Tibetan system of reckoning age to the international convention; hence when texts say that Chokyi Dronma (1422–55) died aged thirty-four, I give the age as thirty-three.

# ACKNOWLEDGMENTS

*This book reflects research involving many people and institutions over a number of years, who would be impossible to mention in a comprehensive way.*

I am grateful to the British Arts and Humanities Research Council (AHRC), the Mongolia and Inner Asia Studies Unit of the University of Cambridge (MIASU), the Austrian Sciences Fund (FWF), and the Italian Ev-K2 CNR Committee for their support, without which this project could not have come to fruition. I am particularly grateful also to the Tibetan Academy of Social Sciences in Lhasa for its precious assistance and collaboration that made research in Tibet possible and fruitful.

I wish to thank Gene Smith and Leonard van der Kuijp for making the text of the biography of Chokyi Dronma accessible to me; Pasang Wangdu, who has assisted me through fieldwork and through the laborious process of translating the Tibetan text; and Burkhard Quessel for his help in retrieving Tibetan sources. I thank Per Sørensen and Karma Phuntsho for their help in finalizing the text of the translation as well as Robert Barnett, who has provided invaluable assistance in dealing with modern Tibetan issues and in tackling issues of style and organization of the narrative. I am very grateful also to Mary-Elisabeth Cox and Libby Peachey for their editorial help, to Leslie Kriesel for copyediting, to Do Mi

Stauber for the index, to Milenda Lee for the design, and to Anne Routon for her understanding and support throughout the process of producing this book.

A special thank you goes to Dawa Dargyay, the late Gangkar Dondrub, and the Porong community in Kathmandu; Gangkar Tsultrim Kesang, Geshe Pema Dorje, and his collaborators of the Bodong Research Center; Zenkar Rinpoche Tubten Nyima and his collaborators; Dawa of Porong; Thrinley Namgyal; Dikey Drokar; Denlhun Tsheyang; Kesang Dronma; the late Thubten Namgyal; the Twelfth Dorje Phagmo; and the Bodongpa communities in Tibet. I am also indebted to the late Tsering Damchoe and Marlies Kornfeld for the crucial role they played in the initial phase of my research.

Special thanks go also to Marilyn Strathern, Stephen Hugh-Jones, Caroline Humphrey, Yael Navarro Yashin, Alan Macfarlane, James Laidlaw, Andre Gingrich, Jonathan Mair, and Jo Cook for their encouragement and for providing very precious methodological and comparative ethnographic information. Peter Burke was a providential source of information on the Italian Renaissance, which I know mainly from my personal Italian background but had not dealt with before academically. Molly Andrews and Jens Brockmeier provided enormous help while dealing with the study of narratives cross-culturally, while Charles Ramble, Ernst Steinkellner, Deborah Klimburg-Salter, Jill Sudbury, Kurtis Schaeffer, Helmut Eimer, Franz-Karl Ehrhard, Tsering Shakya, Hanna Havnevik, Janet Gyatso, Clare Harris, and many other friends in the field of Tibetan Studies provided a wealth of useful information concerning Tibetan sources. I am particularly grateful to Cyrus Stearns for making available a copy of his forthcoming book on Thangtong Gyalpo, which was a precious source of information concerning the period in which Chokyi Dronma's life intersected with that of the famous bridge builder.

I am indebted to the Pitt Rivers Museum, University of Oxford, for giving me access to the photographs of the Charles Bell collection and allowing publication of some—and to Philip Grover, who was very helpful in finding them; to Roy Barlow and Owen Tucker for technical assistance in dealing with photographs and maps; to Carlo Meazza, my mother, Maria Antonia Sironi, and my partner, Bruce Huett, for their own photographs; to my sister, Karen Diemberger, and my daughters, Jana Diemberger and Yancen Diemberger, for their drawings; and finally to my father, Kurt Diemberger, for support and inspiration. I am particularly grateful to them also for sharing some of the salient moments of the research and the completion of the book.

# INTRODUCTION

*This book is about a woman born five hundred years ago in southwestern Tibet,* recognized by two of the greatest scholars of her time as the embodiment of the ancient Indian tantric deity Vajravārāhī, and known in Tibetan as Dorje Phagmo or "the Thunderbolt Female Pig." Chokyi Dronma was a princess of an important kingdom in southwestern Tibet in the fifteenth century who, after the death of her first and only child, a daughter, insisted on renouncing her royal status and her family obligations in order to become a Buddhist nun. She rapidly became famous as a dynamic and inspirational follower, possibly a tantric consort (*phyag rgya ma*), of three of the outstanding religious tantric masters of the era. She was also recognized as a master in her own right and as the spiritual heir of her main teacher. She contributed to some of the most significant works of art, architecture, and engineering of her time and had seminal influence in the development of printing. Furthermore, she expressed a particular commitment toward women, promoting their education, establishing nunneries, and even creating new religious dances that included roles for them. Chokyi Dronma died at the age of thirty-three, leaving a tangible mark on history not only through her own deeds but even more through what happened after her death: her disciples searched for the girl in whom she had reincarnated and thus initiated a line of female reincarnations that became the first and most famous in Tibet. Over the centuries these women have embodied a tradition of female leadership in religion, and sometimes politics, that has continued to the present day. The twelfth of this line, each of whom is known as the Samding Dorje Phagmo, is currently the head of Samding monastery in Tibet and a high government cadre in the Tibet Autonomous Region.

Hence this book is about a woman who was the embodiment of a deity—a female *tulku* or "emanation body"—as well as, in the words of Charles Bell, "the holiest woman in Tibet." She stands in the minds of most Tibetans both as a human being and as a spiritual entity who has existed for many centuries. Any attempt to understand her in her cultural context necessarily questions conventional notions of both deity and woman and has to dispense with assumptions about the singularity and temporality of human life. She is both one and many. Different women have embodied her over the centuries and have constituted a lineage in which the continuing element is some sort of spiritual principle or mental continuum that reincarnated within each of them, combined with the memory of the lives of each of the predecessors. This line of reincarnations, called in Tibetan a *thrungrab* (*khrung rabs*) or genealogy, has been associated for the last five centuries with the throne of Samding monastery. It has political and social implications that make it comparable to a dynasty or succession of related rulers.[1] However, the transmission of a spiritual principle rather than kinship as commonly understood relates one generation to the next, an idiom of relatedness distinctive to Tibetan Buddhism.

The Dorje Phagmo is known not only through the accounts of the few foreign travelers who passed through southern Tibet or Lhasa in recent centuries, some of which are described in the preface, but also, more importantly, through a number of Tibetan narratives, images, and ritual practices that date from the fifteenth century to the present. Foremost is the biography of Chokyi Dronma, the princess who established this tradition. The English translation of the main events of that narrative forms the core of this study. Written and oral narratives were read and reconstructed in multiple ways in successive generations, producing readings that in turn influenced the construction of her genealogy and the process through which the Samding Dorje Phagmo emerged as one of the highest religious institutions in Tibet. She was listed among the highest-ranking reincarnations at the time of the Fifth Dalai Lama, recognized by the Tibetan government and acknowledged by the Qing emperors. After the absorption of Tibet within communist China in the 1950s, the Dorje Phagmo survived and adapted to the paradox of being a prominent religious figure in a radically secular state.

Looking at the rise and the transformations of the Samding Dorje Phagmo through some five hundred years of history provides a unique diachronic view of the Tibetan social and cultural fabric. It also raises questions about some ways the terms "gender," "individuality," "religion," and "politics" are used and conceptualized. Study of the later narratives about Chokyi Dronma and comparison with her biography, written just after she died, reveals a powerful example of a phenomenon that has been often described in feminist historiography (see Scott 1988:28–50; Gyatso and Havnevik 2005:3): the loss or effacement of a woman's contribution to culture in later, more conventional accounts. Reading her projects and social initiatives back into the historical narrative of the period in which she lived recasts that time from conventional descriptions of political struggles and fragmentation to a period of unique social and cultural innovation and creativity.[2] The models of periodization according to which Tibet was "traditional" at some previous time and "modern" in some current moment, like the construction of a "middle age" (see, for example, Snellgrove and Richardson 1968) that preceded a climactic epoch of national consolidation, a characterization often found in descriptions of the seventeenth-century rule of the Fifth Dalai Lama, lose their solidity when the life stories of their protagonists cross historical periods and override conventional divisions of historiography. As Gyatso showed in her study of Jigme Lingpa, the Tibetan division of the biographies of those protagonists into "outer," "inner," and "secret" versions creates further difficulties with common assumptions about individuality: Chokyi Dronma had many selves while living, and was a single entity embodied by many different women over the centuries. Biographies, genealogical accounts, and oral life histories thus disclose the transformation of words and concepts over time, the social dynamics of innovation or orthodoxy, and a fabric of complex subjectivities that contrast with any holistic image of Tibetan culture.

The biography of Chokyi Dronma reflects the initial stage of a process through which the story of the Gungthang princess was merged with that of the Dorje Phagmo deity and was told and retold over the centuries. The core of her story acquired an iconic character as part of narratives that circulated widely among the practitioners of her tradition and as part of more widely shared Tibetan knowledge about history and religion. The importance and the distinctive character of the biography are indicated by its opening words, in an unequivocal language of revelation: a highly esoteric invocation by the writer to the female deity Dorje Phagmo, or Vajravārāhī as she is known in Sanskrit. The biographer requests her protection as he embarks on his literary project:

Homage to Vajravārāhī!
Ultimate giver of pleasure to Heruka![3]
Head of innumerable *ḍākinīs,*
*Vajra* queen, mother of all Buddhas,
Protector of the living beings of the auspicious eon, protect me!

Although she is still, in the peace of Dharmakāya,
Her bodily emanations appear in many forms to suit the minds of the followers;
I write the biography of the *vajra* beauty
who performs and enjoys the multiple magic dance.

The text then moves from verse to a prose statement in which, after paying respect to the writer's teacher and to the highest female principle in the Buddhist pantheon, the writer requests permission to reveal what is described as the "highest secret": "Through the blessings of His Eminence the Lover of the Goddess of Divine Melody [the famous lama, Bodong Chogle Namgyal], the embodiment of the wisdom of all the buddhas, and through the blessings of Vajrayoginī, the mother of all buddhas, may I be granted permission to write the highest secret."[4] Was the biographer referring to Chokyi Dronma's esoteric achievements and relationships or to the fact that she was simultaneously a human being and a deity? Or just to the events of her life as such? Who gave him permission to write—the princess as an embodied deity or the spiritual entity itself?

Beyond the more esoteric and complex issues of tantric secrecy, which will be dealt with later in this book, the act of writing the biography in itself appears to be highly significant. Perhaps it is here that a first clue to the highest secret can be found. Writing meant capturing and codifying a pool of oral narratives and fragmentary notes that had surrounded the life of this exceptional woman. The idea of writing her secret implied disclosure: narrating Chokyi Dronma's life in a manner that would reveal her secret identity as an embodiment of the Dorje Phagmo in a consistent and authoritative way, qualitatively different from verbal statements and rumors. The written account, in the form of a single coherent narrative, represented textual authority in itself, through which the biographer consciously addressed a readership that included not only those with direct knowledge of the deceased princess but also a wider contemporary audience and future generations. This transmission of a secret was thus linked to the construction of a tradition and to its continuity over time.

The life of Chokyi Dronma thus became embroiled with the temporality of texts and the centuries-long Buddhist tradition of preoccupations with textual authority and multiple readings. On a local and limited scale, it reflected some of the issues inherent in the relationship between the life of the Buddha and the Buddhist scriptures. Donald Lopez (1988:1) locates the roots of Buddhist hermeneutics in the final words of the Buddha himself. According to the Pāli canon, the Buddha said, "The Doctrine and the Discipline, Ānanda, which I have taught and enjoined upon you is to be your teacher when I am gone."[5] With these words the Buddha instructed Ānanda that his teaching should be the teacher. After the teachings had been written down, they were passed on in the form of texts, in which they were open to multiple readings and discussions concerning authenticity. Lopez saw in this instruction an effort by the Buddha to address the problem of continuity and authority that faced the religious community upon the death of its founder by linking continuity to textual tradition, thus highlighting a dilemma that recurs in all discussions about the authoritativeness of texts and their interpretations. In Chokyi Dronma's case, as in many other such instances in Tibetan religious history, the source of authority was not only the doctrinal assemblage of rules, insights, and teachings that she had received from her masters but also her own narrative—a story of a life and its celebration of individual persistence and ability. Even though Buddhism was already well established in Tibet by Chokyi Dronma's time, the story of this life, cut short by her early death, acquired a foundational character for the community of her disciples. She became a narrative that held them together. As time passed, that narrative was incorporated into rituals, genealogies, and landscape mythologies that reenacted aspects of Chokyi Dronma's life, keeping her memory, and that of the continuing Dorje Phagmo principle, alive for over five hundred years. She became an icon of sacred femininity, a protectress of the Tibetan landscape deeply linked to some of its most sacred lakes, and an exemplar for other extraordinary religious women.

This book is a journey in which I explore the story of Chokyi Dronma, whose life as the incarnation of the deity Dorje Phagmo has become particularly meaningful for generations of Tibetans right up to the present day. The first part focuses on Chokyi Dronma herself, with four chapters that describe the background to her life and the period in which she lived. The second part is a translation of the Tibetan biography. The third part outlines her tradition from the fifteenth to the twenty-first centuries.

Chapter 1 outlines the historical context in which Chokyi Dronma was born and lived. It describes the kingdom of Gungthang and her royal family; the principality of Southern Lato into which she married; her spiritual masters, Bodong Chogle Namgyal, Thangtong Gyalpo, and, more marginally, Vanaratna and Pal Chime Drupa; the religious conflicts between Buddhists and Bonpos; and the cult of the Indian tantric female deities Vajrayoginī and Vajravārāhī. It also discusses notions that were fundamental to the political and religious practices of that time, such as the donor-donee relationship and, most importantly, the effort in fourteenth- and fifteenth-century Tibet to revive the legacy of the imperial era some seven hundred years earlier. This is a key element in understanding the sense of sacred leadership that can be perceived throughout the biography, for Chokyi Dronma was (and saw herself as) a direct descendant of the ancient Tibetan emperors who had controlled much of the heart of Asia between the sixth and the ninth centuries.

Chapter 2 summarizes the key events in Chokyi Dronma's life. It uses the biography as the main source but situates these events within the landscape through which I traveled while researching her story. The passes and lakes, arid plateaus, snow-capped mountains, and nomadic and agricultural areas feature significantly in the narrative, and the reading of the text is often informed by the specificities of place.

Chapter 3 examines the technical difficulties involved in interpreting the manuscript and its origins, since the text is incomplete and does not give any explicit information about its compilation. On the basis of evidence from the narrative and other sources, I suggest a hypothesis for its dating and authorship and reconstruct the circumstances of its compilation. I show how the writing of the biography was closely linked to the author's aim to reveal Chokyi Dronma as an important incarnation, probably in order to establish a basis for the legitimate identification of her successor. Through a critical examination of the text, I then explore general questions: the idea of authorship, the multiplicity of voices that can be perceived in the narrative, and the role of Buddhist narrative models. In particular, this analysis leads me to conclude that the writer was a man, a disciple and companion of Chokyi Dronma. The text, however, presents a remarkable combination of a male biographer with voices, details, and views that distinctively reflect the lives of Tibetan women, which can be attributed to the multiple sources of input in the compilation process, involving female disciples of Chokyi Dronma.

Chapter 4 explores some of the religious and social themes arising from the study of Chokyi Dronma's life. The initial section focuses on the socioeconomic context and on cultural production in Chokyi Dronma's time, a process to which she contributed significantly. This was a period in which political fragmentation and multifarious forms of patronage accompanied an extraordinary development of new forms of arts and crafts, writing and printing. Chokyi Dronma's homeland, the kingdom of Gungthang, became one of the main hubs for the development of printing, which had an important impact on knowledge and knowledge practices. In this region, in the fifteenth and sixteenth centuries, the earliest prints of works on Tibetan medicine, classics such as the *Maṇi bka' 'bum,* and masterpieces of Tibetan literature such as the *Life of Milarepa* were produced with the patronage of the ruling elite, first and foremost the Gungthang royal family. At the same time, the ancient Tibetan empire and Buddhist India had increasingly emerged as models of lost civilizations that needed to be revived. Chokyi Dronma thus can be seen as an agent of what, leaning upon a powerful image of European historiography and extending a notion that has been recently used in relation to the revival of Buddhism from the tenth to the thirteenth centuries (Davidson 2005; Kapstein 2006:95), I call a "Tibetan Renaissance."[6] I use this term more as an evocative metaphor than as a cross-cultural historical theory, mainly in contrast to conventional terms such as the "Middle Ages," which is often used to define this period of Tibetan history, in order to suggest that the use of different "historical lenses" might reveal otherwise invisible processes.

In this chapter I also explore issues of gender and relatedness, the role of crisis and illness in religious experience, and the extraordinary fact that Chokyi Dronma achieved full ordination even though she was a woman. She was indeed one of the very few known cases of Tibetan female full ordination, a practice that has often been claimed by later writers not to exist. In the final section I discuss the many names and epithets that define her in the biography, which are highly significant and point to the many forms in which she was viewed. Three names in particular frame her identity according to a classical Tibetan threefold model: as a royal princess she was called Queen of the Jewel (Konchog Gyalmo), her "outer" name; when she took her vows she became known as Lamp of the Doctrine (Chokyi Dronma), her "inner" name; as a divine incarnation she was called Thunderbolt Female Pig (Dorje Phagmo), her "secret" name. The names that she progressively acquired during her life also marked three different modes of being in the world: the worldly, the monastic, and the esoteric. Thus she positioned herself in different ways within hierarchies and conventions. Ultimately, however, she transcended them in the light of her experience of Buddhism.

The core material of the book is an annotated translation of the Tibetan text. I included it in full because it is an important and previously unknown source in Western literature as well as an engaging narrative. The description of Chokyi Dronma's successful surmounting of countless obstacles gives a unique insight into the social fabric of her day, portraying a woman of intense emotions and exceptional will power. A multilayered historical and religious document based upon oral materials from Chokyi Dronma herself and her direct disciples, it is unique in its genre. I have rendered the Tibetan text as a relatively free, literary translation, giving a literal version of the original only when details of idiom and construction appeared particularly significant. In those instances I added vernacular terms in brackets and footnotes to help readers understand these particular features.[7] Given the richness of the narrative, it will undoubtedly elicit more readings and interpretations than I can provide within the confines of this book.

Chapter 5 looks at the events around and after the death of Chokyi Dronma, exploring the questions of why and how she was reincarnated and was inscribed in a sort of "genealogy." Relying on sixteenth-century sources, I analyze the issues of succession and the principal factors involved in the establishment of the reincarnation line.

Chapter 6 examines how the Dorje Phagmo institution was consolidated in the succeeding centuries and inscribed in Tibetan landscape mythology. This chapter focuses on the transformations of the institution, outlining the sequence of women who occupied this position from the sixteenth to the twentieth centuries. I review the Dorje Phagmo's increasing social and symbolical significance and her interaction with the main religious and political leaders of the time: the Karmapas, the Dalai Lamas, the Panchen Lamas, the Qing empire, and, eventually, representatives of the British Empire. In addition to textual sources, I relied on a number of hitherto unknown mural paintings that reproduce the lineage of the Dorje Phagmo.

Chapter 7 explores the life and the experiences of the current Dorje Phagmo, whom I had the chance to meet on several occasions. Born in Tibet when it was still under the rule of the Dalai Lama, she was recognized as the reincarnation of Dorje Phagmo when she was a child of six. During her life she has experienced the radical transformations and upheavals that affected her country as a result of the Chinese takeover in the 1950s. She is now, in the post-Mao era, not only the head of her monastery but also a high-level cadre in the Chinese administration in what is now the Tibet Autonomous Region. This chapter is based on Tibetan and Chinese published materials and on interviews with her and her elder sister conducted between 1996 and 2005.

Chapter 8 outlines Chokyi Dronma's legacy within the living tradition. It highlights how the moral and religious authority of the past is deployed in the context of late socialist, contemporary Tibet. This view sees Buddhism, in its Tibetan form, as part of a particular history in which the religion has been revived or disseminated in different waves or phases. Some Tibetans define the revival of Buddhism in the post-Mao era as the *yangdar* (*yang dar*), "the further spread" of the doctrine, following the *ngadar* (*snga dar*), the "early spread" of the doctrine in imperial times (from the sixth to the ninth centuries), and the *chidar* (*phyi dar*), the "later spread" that started in the tenth and eleventh centuries. Thus history appears as the continuum of the development of Buddhism that encompasses modern and postmodern technologies and forms of sociality. Accordingly, the Dorje Phagmo tradition and the story of the princess act as powerful referents for both women and men who engage in the reconstruction of the tradition under the challenging circumstances of contemporary Tibet. A short epilogue touches on the unpredictability of the Dorje Phagmo lineages and manifestations, as she appears in a surprising, somewhat postmodern, encounter.

Although largely based on textual sources, my work is informed by a particular attention to social practices that relate to the texts. I therefore looked at what the Dorje Phagmo means for contemporary Tibetans and for Tibetan women in particular. Janet Gyatso and Hanna Havnevik have pointed out how both the Dorje Phagmo deity and famous religious women of the past such as Khandro Yeshe Tshogyal, Maṇḍāravā, and Machig Labdron[8] have had a significant impact on the lives of a number of Tibetan women by acting as powerful exemplars: "To have authorizing referents for women is extremely important in the context of Tibet's entrenched system of *tulku* (reincarnation) recognition, and outstanding women, both inside Tibet and in exile, still have recourse to these and other figures in crafting their identity and position" (Gyatso and Havnevik 2005:22).

Chokyi Dronma herself was apparently aware of her significance for other women: the concept of "women," or even "all the women," appears often in her biography and in its later interpretations. Much has been written about the most common Tibetan word for woman, *kyemen* (*skye dman*), since it is said to have originally meant "low birth" and thereby to inscribe in gender terminology what is seen as the negative karma of women that caused them to be born in a female body (Aziz 1988:25–34; Gyatso and Havnevik 2005:9). Even though this etymology has been occasionally disputed, the very fact that it has been read into the term (at least since the eleventh century) is telling. What may have been overlooked are the many different connotations and the possible strategic uses of this language, of which Chokyi Dronma's biography provides very interesting examples. Chokyi Dronma and the biographer used the word *kyemen* (*skye dman*), apparently endorsing its derogatory connotations, but they also used another, more honorific and positive term for woman, *bume* (*bud med*), in contrast to it. Chokyi Dronma thus announces her explicit commitment to women at the time of her ordination: "In general there is no significant difference between those who succeed and are born as male and those who fail and are born as female (*skye rgyal pham*). However, from now on, I will focus on supporting Buddhist practices for women (*bud med*), the source of trust (*blo gtod pa*) for all women (*skye dman*)" (folio 46a).

The statement refers to the subtext of the word *kyemen* (*skye dman*) deliberately, but the purpose is to emphasize the limits of the term—to indicate, by contrast, the possibility that the condition of *kyemen* can be transcended. The general term *bume* in the context of Chokyi Dronma's life refers to the positive and honorific side of womanhood—thus, for example, she is called the "most precious among women" (*bud med kyi mchog*). In contrast, Chokyi Dronma is quoted as using *kyemen* when, for example, she conceded that her project to benefit all women by opening a religious avenue for them had not produced all the expected results: "In general I did everything I could for the doctrine and living beings, and in particular I wished to help all women (*skye dman*). It seems, however, that no great benefit has resulted" (folio 72b).

This strategic use of language is clear in a number of other statements concerning religious women and resonates with passages that reflect Chokyi Dronma's critique of social customs. For example, Chokyi Dronma is described at one point as a young bride criticized by her mother-in-law for showing extreme respect toward a monk who was a simple water carrier, while at the same time deliberately neglecting to show the deference expected of her toward secular people of high rank. Chokyi Dronma's approach is also reflected in the descriptions of the social position that nuns acquired as a result of her endeavors, which contrasted with widely held and continuing assumptions in Tibet about their

10

marginality. According to the biography, for example, at that time people in her region would pay particular respect to nuns when encountering them. It also notes that they had become very prosperous. This is in sharp contrast to a statement attributed to Thangtong Gyalpo about the common difficulties that nuns faced in sustaining themselves through donations. The comment by this spiritual master from Northern Lato undoubtedly reflected the more widespread perception and is consistent with the findings of a number of studies concerning the status of nuns in Tibetan Buddhism (see, for example, Havnevik 1990).

The narrative of the biography repeatedly mentions women as a distinctive category and as a major concern for Chokyi Dronma. She had declared this a principal task for herself at the time of her ordination, a key point in her life, and pursued her objective with a distinctive, sometimes idiosyncratic approach. She was remarkably different from other female religious practitioners whose history we know, such as the seventeenth-century nun Urgyen Chokyi (Schaeffer 2004), who chose a religious life but lamented the plight of women as one of inescapable misery. Chokyi Dronma, perhaps in part because of her elite status as a princess, was militant. She shifted strategically between gendered and gender-neutral behaviors, and often tried to manipulate the social and religious system to the advantage of her peers and herself. Her commitment to women, however, was always located within the context of other relationships that shaped the society of her time, primarily that between Buddhist monasticism and the lay community. Accordingly, the particular use of gender terminology in the biography reflects social hierarchy but at the same time refers to the possibility of women transcending that hierarchy by taking a religious route. Buddhism could thus express a "counternarrative" to worldly, gendered conventions: these could be transcended, at least potentially, through a religious life choice.[9]

What is perhaps particularly remarkable is not that Chokyi Dronma sought expressly to promote the cause of women with the Buddhist framework, but that her male teachers specifically endorsed this project, despite considerable opposition. In so doing, her masters were following the counterhegemonic tradition in Buddhist history of the "crazy yogins" who engaged in social critique and alterity. But they were also building on a particular Buddhist attitude toward gender present already in the earliest Buddhist scriptures that Alan Sponberg has termed "soteriological inclusiveness" (1992:8)—that is, the attitude that one's sex, like one's class or caste, presents no barrier to attaining the Buddhist goal.[10] However, Chokyi Dronma always had to obtain permission from her father and her father-in-law in her enterprises, and she encountered serious resistance among other

Buddhist practitioners, so that her position had to be defended by her spiritual masters. She also experienced mixed outcomes of her ambitious projects. These inevitably complicate the picture: it is not a story of successful social transformation, still less of feminist reform. A passage in which she rebukes a group of prostrating monks for being too devout to her clearly illustrates her priorities:

> The Venerable Woman said, "Monks! You have too much faith in me!" The monks replied, "Do not speak like this! If we did not have faith in your great deeds, how would we be able to develop compassion?" She said, "As a wife and a mother I had not taken the vows. Since being ordained, I have behaved like an ordinary member of the monastic community." (folio 54a)

Chokyi Dronma's statements and behavior counter any temptation to read her story as what Lila Abu-Lughod (1990) calls a "romance of resistance" in proto-feminist terms. Rather, they show the complexities of the society and the religious world in which she was operating as an elite woman, thinking about women and trying to transcend gender-specific constraints through Buddhist practice. Chokyi Dronma's vision that ordination be an avenue open to all women remained unfulfilled in spite of the fact that she was defined as "the Spring of all fully ordained women (*bhikṣuṇī*)." In the event, she was the only one to be fully ordained, which might have been related to her royal status. This is also reflected in the biography by the title "Great Lady," *dagnyi chenmo* (*bdag nyid chen mo*), in contrast to other pious women, who are referred to at most as "great woman," *kyemo chenmo* (*skye mo chen mo*), endorsing social and religious hierarchy. It is thus important to keep in mind that the overall framework of Chokyi Dronma's statements about women is that of Buddhist soteriology, even when it encompasses worldly sociality. It would be misleading to interpret her position in a different way: her project was primarily religious, not social, and this defined her priorities. Undeniably, Chokyi Dronma's views resound with what are now seen as feminist agendas, and it is not surprising that her story, along with that of the other Dorje Phagmos, has often been read in this perspective. It serves as an illustration of the debate by feminist critics over the tensions between feminist analytical and political projects (Mahmood 2001; Butler 1990; Strathern 1987, 1988; Rosaldo 1983) and is a powerful rejection of any claims that modern Western feminism has a prerogative over gendered strategies of power geared toward changing the conditions of women or of other human beings more generally. Like the Muslim women described in Saba Mahmood's study of piety in contemporary Egypt (2000:202–236), Chokyi Dronma was engaged in a project that was focused on women but was inevitably predicated on her historically and culturally situated self-fashioning, morality, and strategic priorities, which do not necessarily reflect the normative liberal assumptions, the notions of female subjectivity, or the teleological orientation of contemporary Western feminism.

That proto-feminist agendas can to some extent be read into the lives of Tibetan women of past centuries is thus dubious (although not entirely inconceivable). In the twenty-first century, however, the story of Chokyi Dronma's story and her lineage is certainly read within a framework of feminism-informed perspectives. Even though "the feminist movement has roots so clearly in Western society that it is imperative to contextualise its own presuppositions" (Strathern 1988:xii), it made waves that penetrated very different contexts, cutting across religious, political, and ethnic boundaries. The honorific term in Tibetan for woman, *bume,* used in Chokyi Dronma's biography to indicate religious women and women of high rank, is today relatively common, used with a modern, political, and feminism-informed connotation. *Bume* and not *kyemen* has been chosen to render in Tibetan, both among exiles and within the People's Republic, terms such as "Woman's Day" (*Bume duchen*),[11] "Woman's Rights" (*Bume wangcha*), and the "Women's Federation" of China (*Bume nyamdrel lhentsog*).[12] It is also used in the subtitle of *Yumtso,*[13] or "Turquoise Lake," a periodical published by the Amnye Machen Institute in Dharamsala, where the Tibetan government in exile resides, which describes itself as "a journal of Tibetan women's studies" (*Bokyi bume rigpe dudeb*).[14] Tellingly, the first issue included an article on the Dorje Phagmo.

A number of different and sometimes competing narratives on the subject of "women" speak of a number of different "feminisms" that have informed the current readings of the Dorje Phagmo. The Twelfth Dorje Phagmo is currently a high-level cadre in the administration of the Tibet Autonomous Region, part of a cohort of "patriotic" members of the former religious and political elite who were co-opted by the Chinese government to endorse the legitimacy of its rule. They are considered to have renounced the "old society" and welcomed the reforms that transformed Tibet and gave way to the "new society." The Dorje Phagmo was particularly celebrated in a number of accounts that expressed the communist agenda of promoting the emancipation of women as revolutionary subjects while celebrating "unity among nationalities" (Ch. *minzu tuanjie*).[15] A sort of state feminism was indeed part of the modernist argument legitimizing the Chinese presence in Tibet as the indispensable modernizing agent, in contrast to the oppression and backwardness of the traditional society. This perspective was, at least as far as one could tell from their public statements and actions, endorsed by the Tibetans who operated within that system. But it was also used strategically in different ways at different times.[16] The article written in 1995 by the Twelfth Dorje Phagmo herself, together with the senior monk from her monastery at Samding, Thubten Namgyal, can be read in this light: it presents a genealogy of the Dorje Phagmo reincarnation line that culminates with the celebration of the Twelfth Dorje Phagmo and the reconstruction of her monastery in the post-Mao era. It declares continuity with the premodern past by emphasizing how everything has been reconstructed as it used to be, as well as successful adaptation to the modern context by highlighting the political bodies and policies that enabled that restoration.

Two important articles concerning the Dorje Phagmo published by Tibetan scholars in exile (Dhondup and Tashi Tsering 1979; Tashi Tsering 1993) present an opposite view concerning gender, religion, and ethnicity. They highlight the institution and the lineage of female reincarnations as the most prominent example of religious women but are critical of the current Dorje Phagmo. This is part of a wider effort to celebrate, positively, women in traditional Tibet as to some degree modern without undermining or excoriating "traditional values," and at the same time to challenge claims that women's emancipation was an innovation justifying the specifically Chinese modernization of Tibet. Tibetans in exile have sometimes criticized the reading of women's emancipation as something that was brought to Tibet through its "peaceful liberation" by China, or by its more recent successor, Chinese modernization, and a number of scholars in exile have written about famous Tibetan women of the premodern era such as the Dorje Phagmo in this light. Such a position may also endorse the feminist project of bringing to light women who have been neglected by local and Western scholarship. Without denying the misogynisms that have often been described in Tibetan culture and society, this approach shows a sensitivity and receptivity toward new issues and views, including those informed by transnational feminism that have penetrated and developed within the Tibetan community in exile (see, for example, Tatun Wangpo 2006). This sort of position, by no means the only one, is reflected in the two articles mentioned above and, more generally, in *Yumtso,* the journal published to encourage attention to women's issues by Tibetan scholars in exile.

This very rough outline of two diametrically opposed views on Tibetan women expressed in modern Tibetan works on the Samding Dorje Phagmo is an example of the many ways gender and ethnicity interact and are deployed in the particular context of Sino-Tibetan relations. It is never just an issue of "women" alone, for these readings reflect "intersecting" issues of ethnicity, religion, and politics according to contrasting and shifting alignments (Mackley 1999:343).[17]

The Samding Dorje Phagmo has also been present in various strands of international scholarship, for the relationship between women and Tibetan Buddhism has been the object of increasing attention. This scholarship has emerged against the background of the twentieth-century interest in Buddhism as an important religion in Asia, within which women have increasingly claimed new spaces. The debate has become not just scholarly but also practical and controversial for women Buddhists: it centers on the question of women's access to full ordination as *bhikṣuṇī,* an issue currently being discussed among the higher authorities of Tibetan Buddhism in response to pressing requests from female Buddhist practitioners.[18] The scholarly discussion includes people writing within the Buddhist tradition, those writing according to research methods developed in the West, and some combining the two approaches. Their studies have been informed by feminism, reflected in a variety of contrasting ways. On the one hand are works in reaction to male-biased views of established scholarship (for example, Shaw 1994) and to what has been perceived, in Alan Sponberg's terminology, as Buddhist "institutional androcentrism" (1992:13); on the other hand are critiques of feminist or romanticized interpretations (for example, Huber 1994:350ff.; Simmer-Brown 2002), which often reflect the widespread assumption that "the deployment of feminist issues constitutes an obfuscating projection of the modern, 'Western' concerns on the object of study" (Gyatso 2005:3). The debate ranges from issues of textual interpretation to studies of society to political-religious debates about the access of women to religious resources. The many readings of the Dorje Phagmo and other Tibetan women reveal different, sometimes competing, viewpoints in which the issue of gender is deployed contextually at local, national, and global levels. Accordingly, any study of the Dorje Phagmo that tries to look beyond specific agendas begs for a historically situated approach, relying on a wide range of resources.

Given the position of Tibetan Buddhism in the Buddhist world and of the Samding Dorje Phagmo within Tibetan Buddhism, many authors writing on the subject of Buddhist women or Buddhist female deities have referred to her, even when she was not the central focus of their argument (Willis 1989; Havnevik 1990; Schaeffer 2004:52–53; Chayet 2002:65ff.; Herrmann-Pfandt 2001:134; Simmer-Brown 2001:185–186; English 2002:xxvii). However, they often have pointed out how the complexity of her religious position and the scarcity of sources made any in-depth treatment difficult. The biography of Chokyi Dronma is therefore an important discovery, for it makes an initial historically situated study of the subject possible. It also offers an invaluable starting point for an analysis of the subsequent reinterpretations and transformations of the Samding Dorje Phagmo.

The biography of Chokyi Dronma tells much more, however, than a story of "women" or of an individual whose greatness was primarily in having been an extraordinary woman. It outlines the life of someone who became a prime agent in an important cultural and social development of the time, providing unique insight into a little-known period of Tibetan history, a high point of innovation and skill in technology, art, and crafts that had momentous consequences. In particular, the biography of Chokyi Dronma captures the unique moment in which printing was about to emerge as a new means of reproduction of texts in the kingdom that would host some of the most important early printing houses. Chokyi Dronma indeed seems to have directly or indirectly contributed to what can be called the Tibetan "printing revolution," borrowing a term from Elisabeth Eisenstein (1983), who suggested that the advent of printing technology was a main agency of change in the European Renaissance, the Reformation, and the rise of modern science. Even though in Tibet the printing of books was always done with wooden blocks, its introduction in the fifteenth century[19] had a significant, often underestimated impact on the development of Tibetan culture. It facilitated access to textual resources, promoted the circulation of standard works, and contributed to the creation of shared standards and editing criteria. Although the spread of literacy remained limited, printing ultimately reshaped the relationship to knowledge in terms of access and control, informing subsequent historical developments, including the rise of clerical power.[20]

Considering Chokyi Dronma's profile and influence, it would thus have been reductive to consider her only or primarily in the light of her gender. Her commitment to women stood in direct relationship to her more general religious views. In any case, she made a remarkable contribution to Tibetan culture irrespective of the fact that she was a woman. I have therefore tried to take into account both the gendered aspect of her life and her broader engagement with the world she experienced. Considering how these were intertwined, I think it likely that there are specific relationships among the lack of a hegemonic polity, competing patronage, and cultural innovation that gave rise to the social and conceptual spaces that Chokyi Dronma was in the position to carve out for women in the name of Buddhism. This remains a possible avenue for further Tibetan and cross-cultural research.


The biography of Chokyi Dronma comes from a tradition that has a centuries-long preoccupation with states of mind, and this text, written close to the actual experiences and events, renders them with a distinctive concreteness. At the same time it also resonates with my own experiences as a reader, and in retelling the story I have been drawn toward projecting my sensibilities into the narrative. This raises a fundamental issue: how do I relate to a text so distant in terms of culture and time? How is it possible that I could feel it so close to my own twenty-first-century interests and predispositions?

The story of Chokyi Dronma, like that of the Buddha, aims at an audience that transcends cultural and historical boundaries. It is one example of a rich Tibetan literary genre that goes generally under the name of *namthar*, meaning literally "liberation from everything," the account of the life of a highly achieved personality who is seen as an exemplar on the way toward spiritual liberation. This genre has similarities to Western hagiography but reflects a distinctive religious and philosophical tradition that placed a particular emphasis on the self. Janet Gyatso (1998) has demonstrated that Tibetan biographical and autobiographical writing reflects a kind of notion of the self that dominant theories of Western literature usually see as a prerogative of Western modernity. Chokyi Dronma's biography, especially in the description of personal reflections and emotions such as regret,[21] definitely adds material that supports this view.

What makes Chokyi Dronma's story unique and particularly appealing is not only that this is one of the few examples of a biography of a Tibetan woman[22] but also that it was composed when many of the people who had direct contact with her were still alive. In addition, it is written in a plain style that seems to have been popular in her region at that time. The descriptions of common experiences and everyday details, use of reported speech and thoughts, and frequent quotations from contemporary notes and letters render Chokyi Dronma in a particularly human way, different from the tropes common to this genre. Taking into account the blurred boundaries between Tibetan biography and autobiography, the biography of Chokyi Dronma presents features that come close to the "individualistic self-conception" characteristic of autobiographical writing (Taylor 1989; Gyatso 1998:112). It has a distinctive character that to some extent diverges from the predictable "script of life" inspired by Buddha's *Life* (Weintraub 1978:xv, Gyatso 1998:111) and reaches beyond the didactic purpose of more conventional biographical projects. The narrative is unusually personal, sometimes idiosyncratic, reflecting intense emotions that occasionally contradict Buddhist exemplary behavior. Yet it also reveals Chokyi Dronma as the incarnation of a deity, placing her beyond and in contrast to ordinary human experience. The narrative is thus caught in a pervasive, sometimes contradictory tension between two perspectives, the human and the divine, which at first sight would seem irreconcilable. A second protagonist, Deleg Chodren, who emerges at the beginning of Chokyi Dronma's monastic life as her attendant and friend, intervenes as a providential figure with whom the reader can identify, especially in the later part of the text. She takes care of Chokyi Dronma, asks straightforward questions, and often speaks common sense. She is a sort of second exemplar, one with which the ordinary reader can identify more easily. The biography thus presents a twofold religious model, the extraordinary and the ordinary, which allows for different aspirations, moralities, and forms of identification. Deleg Chodren "leads" the reader through the transformations of the princess and the revelation of her identity as incarnated deity. In contrast to the ambiguous features of Chokyi Dronma/Dorje Phagmo, she is consistently human. The public disclosure of Chokyi Dronma as an incarnated deity was the process that empowered Deleg Chodren as the attendant and spokeswoman of the Dorje Phagmo, and eventually led her to play an important part in the identification of her reincarnation. I shall argue in chapter 3 that the narrative itself was conceived in connection with the search for a reincarnation of the princess shortly after her death, as if the text and her human rebirth were together regenerating, in a form of codified and reenacted memory, the person she had been, in order to continue her mission. Ultimately, the biography bears witness to how the princess's life had become narrative and the narrative in turn laid the foundation for the process of her "ritualization" (Humphrey and Laidlaw 1994): the definition of a set of actions that disjoined this woman from day-to-day life experience and revealed her as the deity she represented.

A set of ritual acts directly related to the narrative of Chokyi Dronma's life became a distinctive aspect of her persona as it reincarnated over the centuries. George Bogle, who in 1775 met a later reincarnation of Chokyi Dronma, gave this description of the young woman:

According to the belief of the people [she] is animated by the spirit of a holy lady who died many hundred years ago. . . . The Dorje Phakmo . . . was attired in a Gelong's [monk's] dress. Her arms bare from the shoulders, and sitting cross-legged upon a low cushion. . . . She is about seven-and-twenty, with small Chinese features, delicate though not regular, fine eyes and an expression of languor and melancholy in her countenance, which I believe, is occasioned by the joyless life that she leads. She wears her hair, a privilege granted to no other vestal I have seen; it is combed back without any ornaments and falls in tresses upon her shoulders. (Lamb 2002:183–185)

His description of her long hair recalls the passage in the biography that describes how it was decided that in contrast to the female monastic tradition, she should keep her hair long in the manner practiced by *yoginīs*. The distinctive monastic robe symbolizes the princess's full ordination, recalling her unique spiritual attainment and displaying a status that seems to have been normally reserved only for men. Similarly, the prescribed ritual sleeping postures of Chokyi Dronma's later reincarnations (Dhondup and Tashi Tsering 1979:11–17) evoke a number of passages that describe her nocturnal meditation practice. The narrative of her life seems thus the background against which the ritualization of her persona as an incarnation of Dorje Phagmo took place. The actual biography represents an early and crucial phase of this process, as it was compiled when many of the people who had experienced her could provide direct testimony to the events. In comparison to later accounts, it combines her divinity with her humanity in a much more striking and vibrant way. Chokyi Dronma's story speaks from another age and another culture, yet it has such an expressive power that it touches the intimate sensitivities of very different people, including its twenty-first-century readers, like the classical epics or the grand works of literature that have been read and re-read over the centuries under different lights and in different translations.

Samding Dorje Phagmo narratives have been told again and again for over five hundred years, building on one another, but the original text of the biography must have vanished from wider circulation relatively early. So far I have found only one other text that seems to have been directly informed by it, the 1609 biography of Thangtong Gyalpo, one of the spiritual masters of Chokyi Dronma. Also, in spite of the fact that Deleg Chodren was a key figure in ensuring the survival of Chokyi Dronma's legacy, she seems to have disappeared from all other known sources. Another indication that the text has not been widely circulated for several centuries is that Chokyi Dronma's biography gives an un-equivocal statement that she received full ordination. Yet it has been consistently claimed that the tradition of *bhikṣuṇī* never arrived in Tibet, or that if it did arrive it was soon lost (Willis 1987:96ff.; Havnevik 1990; Chayet 2002:65ff.) and that therefore full ordination was not an option for Tibetan women.[23] This view could hardly have persisted if this biography had been widely known. Paradoxi-cally, the narrative that was closest to the life of the holy princess seems to have disappeared at the same time that her story was becoming increasingly popular. When, why, and how a text that referred to such a prominent figure disappeared from wider circulation was probably part of a new layer of its "highest secret." Was it perhaps hidden among the numerous texts withdrawn from circulation in the seventeenth and eighteenth centuries as a consequence of political and religious reforms, which are currently coming to light in Tibet?[24] Like any secret, it contains not only what it obscures but also the magic of its real or potential disclosure: what is made possible by avoiding the public eye, what it evokes with-out stating, and what is eventually communicated. This book, in itself, can be viewed as a new disclosure of the biography in an open-ended process that will doubtless elicit further readings among different interpretative communities.

Last but not least, this book is an account of a Tibetan reincarnation. This historical and ethnographic exploration that starts in fifteenth-century Tibet is thus strangely topical at a time when the institution of reincarnation, with competing claims of authenticity and legitimacy, is at the center of one of the main controversies within Sino-Tibetan politics and of China's policy toward its Buddhist nationalities in general. On account of the delicate position of Tibet on the chessboard of China's foreign policy, this also became an issue of interna-tional politics, as witnessed by the headlines repeatedly made in the international media by Tibetan reincarnations such as the Dalai Lama, the Panchen Lama, and the Tshurphu Karmapa. More broadly, the issue of the reincarnation of Tibetan Buddhist authorities can be seen as one of the many intricacies in the relation-ship between religion and secular states, in a context in which the state seeks to control mechanisms that rest on a form of authority—that associated with reli-gion—that exceeds its own foundation. The paradox is bluntly revealed anytime a state official presides over the ritual selection procedures of a reincarnation or needs to ratify the validity of decisions founded on divination and prophetic vi-sions from a holy lake that are based on beliefs he is not supposed to hold.[25] Para-dox, however, does not prevent things from happening, as numerous political and religious practices in contemporary Tibet and the rest of the world show. It is possible to see parallels between controversial issues surrounding the selection of Tibetan Buddhist reincarnations and the appointment of bishops in China, in relation to the principle of apostolic succession as an essential legitimizing factor. These issues will certainly emerge the day the current Samding Dorje Phagmo moves to the heavenly spheres to be further reincarnated, adding new layers to her "highest secret."

*Part I*

1

# THE WORLD OF CHOKYI DRONMA

*Nyemo, central Tibet, July 1996. Climbing a steep dirt road on foot, my daughter and* I reach a small, somewhat decrepit monastery. The once-white walls rise from a mound overlooking a small stream and a grove of willows, surrounded by a flat sandy area. As we enter through the gate of the enclosure around the main building, a young monk, seemingly unused to foreign visitors, comes toward us. I ask him whether this is Nyemo Chekar. Surprised both by our arrival and by the question, he replies yes. The monastic compound is indeed surrounded by the *chekar* (*bye dkar*) or "white sand" to which it owes its name.

We have come from Samding monastery, where the head lama, Thubten Namgyal, told me about the Dorje Phagmo, the Princess of Gungthang who founded the lineage of female reincarnations in the fifteenth century; about the current reincarnation, who is the head of his monastery and a government cadre; and about how much of Samding and the tradition survived the Cultural Revolution. From the start of the monastery restoration, he has painstakingly pieced together salvaged manuscripts, ritual items, statues, relics, people, and memories. He even designed a set of mural paintings representing the various Dorje Phagmo reincarnations, based on his own recollections and a few ancient murals that had survived. A similar room, an old one at Chekar in Nyemo, has

FIGURE I.I  Nyemo Chekar monastery as it appeared in 1996. *Jana Diemberger*

been his source of inspiration. Thubten Namgyal told us that the sixteenth-century Bodongpa monastery survived the Cultural Revolution because it had been transformed into a granary, so the mural paintings had been protected from major damage.

My eleven-year-old daughter and I have been traveling along the Tsangpo, the Brahmaputra river, and through the lush and fertile valley of Nyemo while I try to complete a long overdue study of Bodong Chogle Namgyal and his tradition.[1] In what would turn out to be an extraordinary coincidence, I had made the difficult decision to leave my one-year-old daughter at home with her grandmother.[2]

A group of welcoming and somewhat bewildered monks have gathered around us by the time we reach the porch of the temple. There we find what I have been searching for: portraits of the reincarnations of Dorje Phagmo, freshly painted in bright colors. We are told that the old paintings had been so damaged that the monks decided to repaint them. I am growing anxious. Perhaps it is too late, perhaps everything that was left has been covered by these pleasant but decidedly new images. I ask whether there are any other paintings of the Bodongpa tradition in the monastery. The monks show us into a dark altar room full of dust, broken statues, and ritual items in disarray, witnesses to a tragic history.

As our eyes become accustomed to the darkness, we discern that the walls are fully decorated with remarkable portraits. With the help of a flashlight, I identify Bodong Chogle Namgyal, the deity Dorje Phagmo, and the blue horseman who is the protector of the Bodongpa tradition, Tashi Ombar. But there are no signs of anything that could represent the human forms of the Dorje Phagmo. After leading us through the dark rooms of the ground floor, the monks take us to the upper floor, where, over tea, they recount the history of the monastery, founded by an incarnation of the Dorje Phagmo called Nyendra Sangmo and by the Bodongpa spiritual master, Chime Palsang. We talk about my year-long research on the monasteries, shrines, and people of the Bodongpa tradition and the journey that led to Thubten Namgyal at Samding.

After tea, the monks lead us through the upper rooms. Piles of loose folios of manuscripts, probably recovered after the Cultural Revolution and still waiting to be sorted, speak of the current state of the monastery; the monks make no secret of the difficult conditions under which they are operating. One room, however, looks much better and seems to be where the small community practices rituals on a regular basis. There is a new statue of Bodong Chogle Namgyal, and a copy of the Buddhist canon neatly arranged on the bookshelves. Gradually we realize that this room is fully decorated and that there is a beautiful painting of the blue horseman just behind the door. I can make out small, somewhat rough and damaged images of Bodong Chogle Namgyal and Chokyi Dronma on the wall, but these are standard representations, not the historic, realistic images I have heard exist in this monastery. However, half hidden behind the books are numerous other images of all types: famous spiritual masters such as Bodong Chogle Namgyal and Chime Palsang, various Karmapas, and a number of women. One of them seems to be peeping out from behind the books; she has remarkably realistic features, full monastic robes, long black hair hanging loose over her shoulders, and earrings of gold and turquoise. Next to her are other, similar women, each with a distinctive outfit and expression. In the middle there seems to be a large image of the Shamar, the Red Hat Karmapa. The monks confirm that these are the paintings that the monks of Samding have recently used as models for their representations of the lineage. No names are written beside them but by comparing them with the new ones reproduced in the porch, which include the names, I can identify most of the women as different reincarnations of the Dorje Phagmo. The age of the monastery, the emphasis given to the Red Hat Karmapa and to Chime Palsang, and the number of Dorje Phagmo incarnations suggest they date from the late sixteenth or early seventeenth century. On this basis, the image of

*The World of Chokyi Dronma*

the woman we first saw through the books seems to be that of Chokyi Dronma, the Princess of Gungthang. At last we have found her—at least provisionally, since not all the mysteries of this painting are fully unraveled.

I returned to the monastery several times in later years and came to know the monks as part of the network of Bodongpa monasteries and nunneries that have tried to revive this tradition. Many of the great masters who led the early stages of its reconstruction, including Thubten Namgyal, have since died. But the 1996 visit to Samding and Nyemo remains one of my earliest and most remarkable direct encounters with the princess and her tradition. The picture of Chokyi Dronma with her royal jewels, the long hair of a *yoginī,* and the monastic robes of a nun seemed to epitomize the distinctive and conflicting features of her personality, which I would later come to know through her biography.

But where did she come from originally? At the western edges of the Tibetan plateau, the mountains rise to form a ridge surrounding a high, mostly arid expanse that provides a livelihood for nomadic herders and pastoralists. This area is intersected by deep river valleys inhabited by farmers. It is the region known to Tibetans as Ngari Khor Sum, after the three areas that constitute it and that touch what was, until the mid-nineteenth century, the independent Tibetan Buddhist kingdom of Ladakh to the west. In the easternmost of these three areas, in a fertile valley alongside one of the rivers that thread through the lower half of the plateau on their way to become the principal rivers of South Asia, Chokyi Dronma was born. Her father was the ruler of Gungthang, a separate kingdom that had been founded by a splinter of the ancient dynasty that ruled the Tibetan empire from the sixth to the ninth centuries. Therefore, in the eyes of her contemporaries and of later generations, she has represented not only Buddhist female sacredness but also the Tibetan imperial legacy.

## A Glance at the Broader Historical Picture

Human presence on the Tibetan plateau dates back several thousand years (the most ancient finds, so far, suggest habitation some 40,000 years B.C.E.), but the archaeology of the region is still in its infancy and hardly anything is known of the people who lived there in prehistoric times (Chayet 1994:21ff.). At the dawn of recorded Tibetan history, around the sixth century C.E., the sources speak of a number of local polities that were unified under the kings of a side valley of the Brahmaputra river south of present-day Lhasa, known as Yarlung.

A royal myth—told in the most ancient of the extant Tibetan chronicles[3] and in many later documents—tells how the first king descended from heaven by a rope of light and was welcomed by the representatives of these small kingdoms. He married a *lumo* (*klu mo*), a female deity of the underworld, and became the legitimate ruler of "the black-headed people," as the Tibetans then called themselves. Each of the early kings returned to heaven after his mission on earth was completed, until one of them became involved in a fight that led to this rope of light being severed. The kings thenceforth became mortals: they died on earth. The custom of celebrating royal funerals and building royal tombs thus began. The Tibetan kings used to wear white turbans that recalled the rope of light and so reflected their divine origins and their special powers,[4] upon which the prosperity of the whole country was thought to depend. Large tombs were established during this period in the ancestral region of the Tibetan kings, the Yarlung valley, south of the Brahmaputra River. This was where these kings ruled before relocating their capital to Lhasa around the middle of the sixth century.

Songtsen Gampo, who died in Lhasa in 649, is the most famous of the early Tibetan kings. He vastly expanded his domain through a series of conquests and is usually considered the dominant figure in the story of the Tibetan empire. He also acquired a highly symbolic importance: the invention of the Tibetan script, the legal code, and the introduction of Buddhism are traditionally attributed to him and his ministers, even though these were in reality lengthy and complex processes that stretched over a long period of time and involved other members of his dynasty. But there is no doubt that between the sixth and the ninth centuries the kingdom expanded to become a powerful empire that controlled much of Inner Asia and competed with the Chinese empire of the Tang dynasty farther north and east. Tibet's foreign policy shifted back and forth between marriage alliances and war. Songtsen Gampo's own marriage with the Chinese imperial princess Wencheng, in particular, became the most celebrated in later histories and epic cycles,[5] and more recently, under Chinese influence, has been featured in innumerable songs, dances, plays, and films.

During the time of Songtsen Gampo and his immediate successors, Tibet experienced what is known as the *ngadar* (*snga dar*), "the early diffusion"—the introduction of Buddhism under the patronage of the king and other members of the ruling elite. The first Buddhist monastery was established at Samye in 779 at the orders of King Thrisong Detsen (742–797?), and many Buddhist texts were translated into Tibetan, mainly from Sanskrit, during his reign and

*The World of Chokyi Dronma*

those of his successors. In the ninth century the Tibetan empire began to disintegrate as a result of clashes among the ruling clans, especially between pro- and anti-Buddhist factions, which had increasingly come into conflict as Buddhist institutions had become steadily more powerful. When the extremely devout Buddhist King Ralpacen was murdered, Langdarma, who strongly opposed Buddhism, ascended the throne and initiated a persecution of Buddhist institutions that led to his own death in 842 at the hands of a now famous monk called Lhalung Palkyi Dorje, who has been identified by an eminent Tibetan historian as the abbot of Samye monastery (Karmay 1988:76ff.). Civil war erupted and the kingdom rapidly fragmented.

Very little is known of the subsequent period of internal conflicts and political fragmentation, which lasted about a century. A number of local polities, some of which had emerged from splinter groups of the former royal dynasty, gradually came to power, and their rulers became the new supporters of Buddhism. In the eleventh and twelfth centuries a significant number of scholars and translators, both Indians and Tibetans, traveled back and forth across the Himalayas, bringing about what is usually known as the *chidar* (*phyi dar*), "the later diffusion" of Buddhism. Indian and Tibetan religious masters like Atiśa, Rinchen Sangpo, Khon Konchog Gyalpo, Marpa, Milarepa, Phadampa Sangye, and Machig Labdron, to name but a few of the most renowned, together with their disciples, established religious centers that gained increasing cultural and political importance. During this period many practices were transmitted from India to Tibet that belonged to the tantric or later form of esoteric Buddhism, including the *Anuttarayogatantra* cycles centered on the cult of Cakrasaṃvara and Vajravārāhī. These were to have an important bearing on Chokyi Dronma's life.

After the collapse of the empire, Tibet underwent a radical political and social change that saw the almost total eclipse of the ancient clans, some of which had originated from the confederation of small polities that had preceded the empire and continued to dominate the political scene during dynastic times.[6] The religious centers that had emerged around the masters of the eleventh and twelfth centuries acquired a higher social and political profile, creating their own distinctive traditions and becoming influential among the competing interests that supported them. Eventually some of the religious schools forged or tried to forge alliances with Tibet's powerful neighbors, the Mongols, who, by the thirteenth century, under Chinggis Khan and his successors, had become the major political force in Inner Asia.

One of the most important religious centers at this time was located at Sakya in southern Tibet, and it became the first to create a successful alliance with the Mongols when Sakya Paṇḍita (1182–1251) and his nephew Phagpa (1235–1280) joined with the Mongol emperor Kubilai (1215–1294) to establish what is known as the "Yuan-Sakya rule" over Tibet. This lasted approximately a century and brought about a reunification of Tibet as a single polity administered by a governor based at Sakya within the framework of the Yuan empire. Important administrative reforms, such as the reorganization of the population into "myriarchies" (groups of 10,000 people), were introduced, and the establishment of a postal service significantly improved communications. This period saw an extraordinary blossoming of Tibetan Buddhism that helped to unify Tibetans and Mongols in a common religious endeavor. Politically, however, there were ambivalent feelings about this arrangement in which Tibet was unified but subject to an outside power, even though the relationship between the Yuan court and Sakya was seen as that between a donor and a spiritual preceptor. These feelings were exploited by some of the Tibetan local rulers, who pleaded for a return to Tibetan customs; these ideas were strongly reflected in some of the contemporary literature.[7]

In 1352 Phagmodrupa Changchub Gyaltshen (1302–1364), the ruler of one of the administrative units located in the Brahmaputra valley southeast of Lhasa, was able to assert himself against the Sakya government, overthrow its rule, and gain supremacy over Tibet. Some scholars, such as Tucci, saw him as a sort of early nationalist:

[Phagmodrupa Changchub Gyaltshen] is undoubtedly one of the most remarkable men Tibet ever produced. . . . It was his aim to give Tibet a political consciousness, to pacify internal struggles which had turned it asunder so long, to free it from subjection to China. He aspired to restore the ancient kings' monarchic ideal, to revive national law and customs, and he enacted a code by which up to our days justice is administered in Tibet.

This conscious rebirth of ancient traditions, this humiliation for present misery, appearing all the greater as compared with past glories now evoked, was attended not only by a renewal of historical studies and a vast production of chronicles, but also by research for documents, real or presumed, which might revive, as a reminder, the age of the kings. (Tucci 1999 [1949]:23)

Although this view is considered somewhat overstated in light of more recent research (Petech 1990) and was apparently informed by notions that emerged in modern European history, it is clear that during this time Tibet experienced a blossoming of cultural activities that aimed at searching for its ancient roots and reviving the memory of its imperial greatness. Under Phagmodrupa Changchub Gyaltshen, Tibet again became the center of its own power, but he had to face a complex constellation of competing polities. His descendants gradually lost political control, and in 1434 the rule passed to the lords of Rinpung[8] for 130 years, until the King of Tsang in turn wrested power from them. Except for Phagmodrupa Changchub Gyaltshen himself, none of these rulers was able to establish firm, unified control over the Tibetan areas beyond their immediate domains. Some supported an important Buddhist school, the Karma Kagyu, a subsect of the Kagyu school that had been established by the disciples of Marpa and Milarepa in the twelfth century. Meanwhile, thanks to Tsongkhapa (1357–1419), another powerful Buddhist school had emerged: the Gelugpa. The strife between these two schools continued until 1642, when an army of Hoshuud Mongols, who supported the Gelugpa hierarchs, defeated the King of Tsang and installed the Fifth Dalai Lama as the ruler of Tibet, allowing it to be unified for the first time in almost 300 years.

Considering Tibet in general, scholars usually construct a linear sequence of rulers—Sakyapa, Phagmodrupa, Rinpungpa, followed by the King of Tsang (this latter period is sometimes described as one of Karmapa rule, in reference to the dominant religious school at that time) and eventually the Gelugpa. However, from the middle of the fourteenth century to the middle of the seventeenth century Tibetan rulers rarely had full control. They had their main strongholds in different areas of central Tibet, and when they lost power they usually just became more localized and remained supporters of the leading religious figures. A more decentralized model may offer a more appropriate way to think of these conditions, such as Geoffrey Samuel's use of Tambiah's notion of a "galactic polity" within which "regional administrations drift between periods of attachment to one or another centre and periods of autonomy. What is a centre at one period . . . may be a subordinate entity at another period . . . without undergoing a drastic change of identity" (Samuel 1993:62). Imagining these polities and their rulers as systems of stars and satellites, whose light or power of attraction could increase or fade, gives a sense of the fluidity of the political landscape within which figures like Chokyi Dronma moved.

The sponsorship of important Buddhist leaders was not only meritorious but also a means to assert political power. The support of Buddhism enabled the sovereigns to increase their majesty and bolster their claims of legitimacy by fulfilling the role of *Dharmarāja,* the Sanskrit term for the legendary tradition of a king acting as a protector of the Buddhist *Dharma*. This support, rooted in both worldly and religious motivation, had an enormous impact on the lives and deeds of the Buddhist masters. Even though the fourteenth and fifteenth centuries were complex and shaped by conflicts and political fragmentation, this period led to extraordinary and seminal achievements: the edition and distribution of the Buddhist canon, first assembled at Narthang between 1310 and 1320; the introduction of the practice of holding debates over numerous doctrinal subjects; the introduction of wood-block printing, enabling increased standardization and wider distribution of texts; the production of innumerable masterpieces of religious art and architecture; feats of engineering like the construction of iron-chain bridges over major rivers and new systems of irrigation; and a deliberate promotion of trade.

There were some parallels between this fragmented but intellectually productive Tibet and Italy in the same period, with its political fragmentation into city-states and its extraordinary artistic and scientific productivity. Patronage of the arts and sciences became an important factor for the competing polities, leading to the so-called "campanilismo"[9] of the Italian Renaissance and bringing to the fore figures like Leonardo da Vinci, sometimes compared by Western scholars of Tibetan history to a Tibetan spiritual master, inventor, and artist of the same period named Thangtong Gyalpo (Kahlen 1993:138ff.), famous for his construction of iron-chain bridges over the Brahmaputra River as well as for his support of arts and drama. In both cases, artists and scholars had to act strategically in accepting or refusing patronage, collaborating, and negotiating constantly shifting allegiances. However, they also enjoyed the relative freedom from a hegemonic power, which, as Peter Burke has pointed out, had an important effect on creativity (Burke 1999:123).[10] A scenario of this kind featured significantly in the life of Chokyi Dronma and of other great religious figures of her time. The record of the invitations they received from rulers and whether they were accepted, postponed, or declined bears witness to this. The plurality of patronage constituted an important background for daring religious choices and innovative cultural production, some of which would have decisive influence on her life.

## The Kingdom of Mangyul-Gungthang or Ngari Me

Chokyi Dronma was the eldest daughter of Thri Lhawang Gyaltsen (1404–1464), a descendant of the ancient Tibetan royal house, who ruled over an area known as Mangyul-Gungthang or Ngari Me (Lower Ngari). This kingdom is often considered part of the "upper regions" (sTod phyogs), the term used for the western and higher regions of Tibet, even though it was often more like a buffer zone in the shifting alignments between western and central Tibet. It stretched roughly from Mount Sishapangma and the Palkhu/Pekhu Lake in the east to the pass called Mayum La in the west, from the Brahmaputra River in the north to the Himalayan valleys in the south (see map). The areas under its jurisdiction varied greatly over time as the power of the local rulers expanded and contracted. "Gungthang" and "Mangyul-Gungthang" refer to the core areas of the kingdom, which appears under both names in historical sources.

Over the centuries, Mangyul-Gungthang has been an important gateway between the north and the south of the Himalayas, traversed by the main route between Tibet and Nepal, which passed through the Kyirong valley and led to Kathmandu. This was, at times, also an important route between China and India. The area is known from documents and inscriptions that go back to the imperial period (the sixth to ninth centuries). On an overhanging rock not far from the ruins of the royal palace is a Chinese inscription left in 658 by Wang Xuance, a diplomat of the Tang imperial court who passed through on his way to and from India.[11] According to the *dBa' bzhed* (folios 5–10) and other sources, this was also the route taken by Padmasambhava and Śāntarakṣita in the eighth century on their way from India to Tibet. During the imperial time this area was considered part of the kingdom of Shangshung and subsequently of Ngari, as western Tibet later became known.[12]

In the thirteenth century, under Sakya rule, the kingdom of Mangyul-Gungthang was founded by Bumdegon (1253–1280) (Everding 2000:391ff.), who, like the kings who had founded Guge and Purang in western Tibet some two hundred years earlier (see Petech 1988:369–394), was a descendant of the ancient Tibetan royal house. The name Ngari Me or "Lower Ngari," which is used in Chokyi Dronma's biography, relates this polity closely to the western Tibetan kingdoms, emphasizing their shared ancestral links and ancient royalty. Despite this idealized affiliation, the kingdom was more closely associated with central Tibetan politics. Under Sakya rule and for some time afterward, it became part of a complex network of local political domains that included Sakya, Northern and Southern Lato, and various nomadic groups. The relationships among these powers alternated between collaboration and hostility; marriage alliances and religious patronage were important integrating factors until the Gungthang kingdom was destroyed in 1620 by the King of Tsang. An eighteenth-century source, the Royal Genealogy of Gungthang (*Gung thang rgyal rabs*),[13] casts some light on the situation of the Mangyul-Gungthang kingdom at the time of Chokyi Dronma. The collapse of Sakya rule had left the kingdom somewhat independent but also at greater risk of involvement in local conflicts. Partly building on the Sakya legacy, the region had experienced a period of relative prosperity through enhanced communications, an increase in cultivated areas, and promotion of trade. It had regained the position of international trading post and gateway between cultures that it had enjoyed during the Tibetan empire; this is reflected in the distinctive local architecture.[14] The discovery of gold in the western areas in the late fourteenth century had also increased the affluence of the country and its rulers. The new capital, Dzongkha, a fortified citadel at the center of a large fertile area in the middle of the Gungthang, had become important within the network of trans-Himalayan trading routes and had acquired some of the character of a cosmopolitan commercial center. Like the *Gung thang rgyal rabs,* the biography of Chokyi Dronma highlights this prosperity. It mentions goods such as silk and tea that came through long-distance trade with China[15] as well as other goods and tools that came from trade with Nepal. Chokyi Dronma, as she appears in her biography, was very much a princess of this little city. She had a considerable amount of wealth at her disposal, including gold and gems, that she used generously to pay for services and materials not covered by the donations she was able to collect as a begging nun. She made a point of promoting not only religion but also the agricultural development of rural communities, for example by building water channels in nomadic areas. Together with ancient Indian cities she knew about through her reading of Indian texts and legends, the capital of the Gungthang kingdom was in many ways her model of civilization and inspired her vision (see folio 110b).

Despite the general affluence, Chokyi Dronma's father, Thri Lhawang Gyaltshen (1404–1464), had ascended the throne at a difficult time. Mangul-Gungthang was torn by succession disputes, the murder of some of its kings, divided loyalties between Sakya and other allegiances, and some local aspirations toward independence that had emerged in the Phagmodrupa period (see Vitali 1996:1029). In addition, the two sons of Chokyi Dronma's grandfather Thrigyal Sonam De (1371–1404) by his wife Gugema Chokyong Gyalmo had died prematurely, leaving him without a legitimate heir. However, just before his own death at the age of thirty-three, he had an affair with a woman called Jamyang who became pregnant.[16] Her son was later enthroned as Thri Lhawang Gyaltshen and became Chokyi Dronma's father. After the death of the king, his widow ruled as a regent for several years. Since the young Thri Lhawang Gyaltshen was the only heir apparent, fearing intrigues and hostilities, his mother took him to her homeland, Nubri, an area only loosely integrated into the kingdom. She became a nun at her uncle's monastery, Nubri Lhamdun, which followed the Sakya tradition. When she was ordained she was given the name Changsem Sangye Wangmo, and she is mentioned as Changsem in the biography of Chokyi Dronma: she is the grandmother described as having supported the 1452 reproduction of the collected works of Bodong Chogle Namgyal initiated by her granddaughter (folio 95a) and as having lamented her departure for the east a few months later (folio 107b).

From 1404 to 1418 Jamyang-Changsem and her son lived in Nubri, sheltered by the monastery and by the relative distance from Gungthang proper. Under the regency of the widowed queen, there were no major crises in the kingdom even though it lost control over part of its territory. At the age of fifteen, Thri Lhawang Gyaltshen was invited to the capital of Gungthang as the legitimate successor to the throne; he was crowned there in 1418/19. This could not have happened without substantial support from within the kingdom, and it is likely that his being seen as descended from the imperial line was decisive.[17]

Shortly after his enthronement Thri Lhawang Gyaltshen married Chokyi Dronma's mother.[18] This woman might have been close to the former regent, the wife of Chokyi Dronma's grandfather, since Chokyi Dronma is said to have expressed as a child very positive views about Guge, the homeland of the regent. Perhaps the marriage with Thri Lhawang Gyaltshen was a strategic move to help secure his claim to the throne.

The delicate question of succession had troubled the kingdom since the untimely death of Chokyi Dronma's grandfather and the regency of his widow. According to the *Gung thang rgyal rabs* (125), Thri Namgyal De, the brother of Chokyi Dronma, seems to have been enthroned when he was fifteen, although this is not directly confirmed in his sister's biography. Apparently power shifted back and forth between father and son several times; their relationship was difficult. The biography of Tsunpa Choleg (1437–1521), a spiritual master from Gungthang who was a few years younger than Chokyi Dronma, describes how Thri Namgyal De became blind in 1461 as a consequence of the conflict with his father (Everding 2002:536). This may have been due to an actual punishment inflicted by the king after he discovered a conspiracy, as suggested by Everding, but it is also possible that his blindness was seen as karmic retribution for his wrongdoing, a metaphorical punishment. In any case, the conflicts were certainly serious and had an important bearing on Chokyi Dronma's life, informing many of her views and decisions.

During the regency of her grandfather's widow and the reign of her father, Thri Lhawang Gyaltshen, the kingdom of Gungthang lost control over many peripheral areas, and this affected its revenues from trade levies. The domain was reduced to its core regions, Mangyul, Gungthang, and, more loosely, Nubri, the home of Thri Lhawang Gyaltshen's mother. Mustang in particular managed to detach itself completely under the rule of Ama Pal (1388–1440?), a descendant of the dynasty established there in 1375, with the support of some of the local nomadic groups (Vitali 1996:1031; Everding 2002:525ff.). Attacks by so-called robbers from Mustang and uncertain control over the pathways are mentioned several times in Chokyi Dronma's biography, although the narrative does not give the impression of a serious decline in the kingdom's wealth and prosperity. In order to compensate for the territorial losses and the vacuum left by the end of Sakya overlordship in terms of mediation of local conflicts, the kingdom had to rely more on a system of marriage alliances with the other regional rulers—including those of areas like Mustang that formerly had been under its control. This system continued for the next two hundred years, with alternating conflicts and alliances. There were repeated tensions with Southern and Northern Lato. Both the *Gung thang rgyal rabs* and the biography mention that around 1444 the capital of the kingdom was seized by the army of Southern Lato and suffered severe damage. According to Chokyi Dronma's biography, this was directly related to the fact that she had left her husband, the son of the ruler of Southern Lato, to take her monastic vows. The collapse of a marriage alliance that was vital to her father's kingdom brought her heavy criticism from the people of both regions.

Southern Lato was located directly east of Gungthang and was ruled by a family that had risen to power under Sakya protection and had produced three Sakya governors (Petech 1990). In Chokyi Dronma's time, the ruler's seat was located in Shekar, where Situ Chokyi Rinchen (d. 1402), the grandfather of Chokyi Dronma's husband, had established the new capital of the domain. In 1385 he founded Shekar monastery just after the construction of a spectacular fortress that can still be seen there today. The *History of Shekar* (*Shel dkar chos 'byung*),[19] a work compiled in 1732 on the basis of preexisting sources, recounts how he also built new irrigation systems, expanded the cultivated areas, increased livestock in the pastoral areas, encouraged pastoral productivity by reducing the tributes owed by subjects who had a large number of animals, reduced trade levies, and opened new passes to promote commercial relations. All this is described as having increased his standing as a ruler in a way comparable to that of another successful ruling family of the time, the lords of Gyantse. An urban center developed at the foot of the fortress and became an important station in trans-Himalayan trade; for geographical reasons, it never attained the same importance as Gungthang, but both were part of a network of trade routes that linked growing cities. The *Shel dkar chos 'byung* also describes Situ Chokyi Rinchen and his son Lhatsen Kyab[20] as great supporters of Buddhism; lists a great number of monasteries, nunneries, and collective rituals established under their rule; and celebrates Bodong Chogle Namgyal and his predecessors, who were born in the area and became leading spiritual masters with their support. Although genealogical records link them to the ancient Wa (dBa') clan, this ruling house represented an emerging political leadership, committed to asserting its profile but liable to be considered of a lesser rank, as Chokyi Dronma often explicitly declared them to be. Despite the perceived difference in status, marriage alliances between Gungthang and Southern Lato were particularly important and were often repeated: both the biography of Tsunpa Choleg (folio 45–46) and that of Tsangnyon Heruka (folio 86–87) refer to Gungthang princesses marrying out to Southern Lato.

The lords of Northern Lato ruled over the adjacent area, north of the Brahmaputra River, and included several important Sakya governors in their genealogy (Petech 1990). They had regular marriage alliances with both Southern Lato and Gungthang and competed with them for control in the region. The mother of Tshewang Tashi, Chokyi Dronma's husband, came from this family, and Northern Lato is mentioned occasionally in Chokyi Dronma's biography as a potential threat to Gungthang.

During this period, the nomadic area of Porong, located between Mangyul Gungthang and Southern Lato, developed as an almost independent cushion state.[21] This was one of a number of lesser nomadic polities that played an important part in regional power relations. The kingdoms of Gungthang, Southern and Northern Lato, and Sakya were the most significant players in a complex network of marriage alliances, trade, and political pacts. The rulers were often also the patrons of the same spiritual masters, who would sometimes act as mediators in cases of conflict. It is significant that Thangtong Gyalpo built one of his famous iron-chain bridges over the Brahmaputra River, and that he constructed the *stūpa* of Chung Riwoche where the "pathways between Northern Lato and Southern Lato and Gungthang meet" (Biography of Thangtong Gyalpo 270). He first met Chokyi Dronma in this locality and he acknowledged her, first of all, as a descendant of the ancient kings of Tibet, reflecting the increasing popularity of the Tibetan imperial legacy.

## Mangyul-Gungthang and the Significance of Tibetan Royalty in Fifteenth-Century Tibet

At the time of Phagmodrupa Changchub Gyaltshen a conscious regeneration of ancient traditions had led to the revival of the imperial legacy in the post-Sakya political era. In Tibet and Mangyul Gungthang in particular, a new wave of *terma (gter ma)* or "treasure" literature—religious or historical texts considered to be discovered and interpreted by specially endowed spiritual masters several centuries after they were written—appeared, and many of them referred to people and events of the Tibetan imperial period in ways that alluded to the contemporary situation.

Tucci points out how many of the *terma* reflected that particular political moment:

> A master was glorified who now for the first time was considered the greatest apostle of Lamaism, an implacable foe of the enemies of religion, the king's wise counselor, i.e. Padmasambhava, but through his glorification Tibet's golden age was recalled, when the Land of Snows sent its armies into all surrounding countries and fought China victoriously. . . . It was an awakening of national consciousness, from which the P'ag mo gru pa's ambition has sprung; their ambition was supported and justified, prophecies recognized it as an unavoidable event, fixed in the course of time by the fatal maturing of destiny. This literature, either by truly discovering and publishing forgotten documents, or by attributing to old masters texts compiled in this spirit, prepared and accompanied the new movement of Tibetan history. (Tucci 1999 [1949]:23–24)

The imperial legacy was undoubtedly used in a variety of different contexts, not merely within a simple binary opposition between Tibet and the Chinese empire; it is disputable whether to speak of "national consciousness" is appropriate—the term "proto-nationalism," as suggested by Dreyfus[22] (1994:205–218), is probably more suitable. However, Tucci highlighted, in a seminal way, the important link between cultural production and the particular political context, a point that has been reiterated in different ways by later scholars studying this period.

One of the greatest "treasure finders" in fourteenth-century Mangyul-Gungthang was Rindzin Godem (1337–1409), a spiritual master affiliated with the Nyingma school of Buddhism, which claims to have descended from the earlier spread of Buddhism. The language of his prophecies symbolically linked the destiny of Tibet to that of Gungthang.[23] Similarly, the kings of Gungthang are mentioned in another, related form of literature describing the *beyul* (*sbas yul*) or "hidden valleys" to be sought at a time of crisis, much of which he revealed or inspired.[24]

In 1403, just before the death of Chokyi Dronma's grandfather, Thrigyal Sonam De (1371–1404), Rindzin Godem had revealed the *bSam pa lhun grup ma,* a text that would become extremely popular.[25] It described the ninth-century Tibetan King Muthri Tsenpo, the son of King Thrisong Detsen, who after the death of his father was extremely concerned about the future of the Buddhist doctrine and of the Tibetan royal line. He had therefore asked Padmasambhava for advice in these words: "My successors will dwell close to the Snow Mountains of Mangyul Gungthang. When they will have become like common people and will experience great suffering, and the Tibetan royal house will be an object of pity, in what will the hope of my successor rest?" (Everding 2000:619, my translation). He then described the troubles and the intrigues of his own times. Padmasambhava replied with a prophecy that concerned Muthri Tsenpo's successor in the seventeenth generation—identified by Everding with Thrigyal Sonam De, Chokyi Dronma's grandfather:

> The future successors of yours who will appear among the snow-mountains of Mangyul Gungthang will protect without doubt the Buddhist doctrine.
> With my compassion I will care for them.
> Do not be sad, Son of God, King of Tibet. (Everding 2000:619, my translation)

By mentioning intrigues, murder, deceitful lamas, and treacherous ministers, the text addressed the contemporary situation, setting it in contrast to past glories and calling on the kings of Mangyul-Gungthang to fulfill their role as *Dharmarājas* (kings of the *Dharma*) as the ancient Tibetan monarchs had done. The message was clear, but how much impact did this kind of literature have? Was this the talk of a single visionary or did he represent a broader and more widespread view? Certainly not everybody was a follower of Rindzin Godem and the Nyingmapa school of Tibetan Buddhism; in many ways he was a rather controversial figure. The Sakya ruling elite, though weakened, was still a power in the region and could have viewed his influence over the Gungthang royal house with anxiety and irritation. Everding (2002:481–496) even suggests that since the predecessors of Chokyi Dronma's grandfather had a close relationship with this treasure finder, this might have been a reason for their murder. Gungthang was in a difficult position, caught between allegiances to the former Sakya overlords whose protection had enabled its rise and its aspirations to a distinctive Tibetan greatness rooted in royal ancestry. Despite some hostility from the pro-Sakya people, Rindzin Godem's prophecies found a receptive audience and his teachings spread quickly throughout the region; one of Chokyi Dronma's masters, Thangtong Gyalpo, was a follower of his tradition.[26] From a local perspective the fortunes of Tibet must have seemed linked, in an almost messianic way, to the Gungthang kings, as descendants of the ancient empire who had thus been invited to fulfill their role. They were the offspring of "the Gods of Clear Light,"[27] the lineage that had descended from heaven or, according to other myths, originated in the Śākya race of the historical Buddha himself and had unified Tibet. They had inherited from their glorious ancestors, the Tibetan emperors, the title of *lhase* (*lha sras*), "Sons of the Gods," and the sacred power to rule.

Even though she did not inherit the throne, the theme of Tibetan royalty appears often in Choki Dronma's life, through epithets, social positioning, and symbols. For example, in the biography she is repeatedly defined as the queen of Ngari and as a descendant of the Gods of Clear Light. She is also explicitly addressed with the title *lhase* (*lha sras*) in the passage (folio 63b) that immediately precedes the public acknowledgment of her as an incarnation of the deity Dorje Phagmo. She appears in a vision of one of her followers as "a red woman with a red turban dwelling in the sky in the middle of rainbows" (folio 54b). The turban had been worn by the ancient Tibetan kings and their high ministers as a symbol of their sacred power and status; the red color evoked her tantric sacredness.[28] There was no doubt that she was from a lineage of leaders, but her position as a spiritual and a female leader raised unusual complications.

## The Politics and Morality of Patronage

In Tibetan, those who provide material support for activities either for the sake of the Buddhist religion or for the common good, or both, are called *jindag* (*sbyin bdag*). In the biographies of great Buddhist personalities, this term appears very often in relation to people of different ranks who provided support for spiritual teachers and adepts. Donors have always been central to the Buddhist tradition and have made it possible for the monastic community to survive. When Buddhism was introduced into Tibet, the term *jindag* was used to translate the Sanskrit term *dānapati,* referring to "the householder who, in the Buddhist structure of society, offers alms . . . to a monk" (Seyfort Ruegg 1997:858). Chokyi Dronma had to deal with the politics and the morality of patronage throughout her life. Her biography gives great emphasis to donors and donations as well as to the ideal of the begging monk and nun who renounce worldly concerns and rely on the support provided by lay followers.

The notion of *jindag* describes an act of giving that transcends norms of reciprocity and exchange. According to Buddhist thought, "what the donor is deemed to receive for his alms is in fact not the Dharma but something rather different, namely religious good (*puṇya* = *bsod nams* 'merit')" (Seyfort Ruegg 1997:862). At least in principle, the act of giving must transcend any self-centered individual strategy and aim at a higher good for the community of believers and all living beings. The donor's personal benefit comes indirectly through the merit accumulated in this way. Thanks to the concept of karma, the results of one's deeds are ripened and come to fruition in the current life or future lives.

Tibetan texts often refer to Indian Buddhist models in describing lay support for religious figures and their achievements. The relationship between the Buddha and Anathāpiṇḍada, a munificent householder and merchant from Śrāvastī, is a model for the relationship between Buton Rinchen Drub and the prince of Shalu in fourteenth-century Tibet (Seyfort Ruegg 1997:863, 865). The concept of *jindag,* however, acquired a range of meanings broader than the original designation used in Indian sources. The term appears in texts from the Tibetan dynastic period and has been used in Tibetan society to describe a wide range of relationships that imply providing material support for something collective, usually but not exclusively with a religious connotation. The honorific form, *yondag,* is used more commonly for royal or princely donors supporting a religious person or activity. Most importantly, this term appears in the compound *choyon* (*mchod yon*), which Seyfort Ruegg translates as "donor and chaplain." This is a key politico-religious idea that has often been translated into English, not without problems, as "patron and priest."

In the framework of the donor-chaplain relationship, Tibetan lamas received donations, and sometimes hospitality, from the rulers of certain areas or even from emperors. By supporting spiritual teachers and religious deeds, a ruler not only accumulated merit but also acted as a *Dharmarāja* or even a *cakravartin* (Ruler of the World), and thereby fulfilled his role as a good and legitimate sovereign. The link between the spiritual teacher and his princely or royal donor expressed the connection between spiritual and temporal powers. In the Tibetan context, these appeared as two orders within one system of legal and moral rules, called the "the twofold law" (*lugs gnyis gyi khrims*). This system was frequently described by the double metaphor of "the golden yoke" and "the silken knot." The two orders were often embodied by distinct figures such as the lay ruler and the spiritual master who related to each other but sometimes overlapped in the same institution, as in the case of the Dalai Lama and of certain local rulers who were renowned Buddhist masters. However, as pointed out by Seyfort Ruegg (1997:857), even though a distinction between the spiritual and the temporal is found in Tibetan thought, such concepts do not rely on binary oppositions like the distinction between the sacred and the profane common in Western traditions.

The terms referring specifically to the donor-chaplain relationship do not appear in Indian sources. They were developed within the Tibetan context and were probably partly shaped by earlier beliefs and ideas. The use of the term *ngathang* (*mnga' thang*), which can be glossed as "majesty," in relation to the performance of religious and worldly deeds points in this direction. The *Shel dkar chos 'byung*, for example, describes the acts of one of the rulers of Southern Lato thus: "The deeds listed so far were of a religious nature. A lord who rules according to the system of both laws (*lugs gnyis*) needs a perfect majesty (*mnga' thang*), and thus the outer majesty consisting of horses, yaks, goats, and sheep had to be increased as well" (folio 33a). A ruler had to accomplish deeds that represented both his "outer majesty" and his "inner majesty," in other words, deeds that reflected both the prosperity of the country and the spread of Buddhism. The sponsorship of Buddhist activities presumably added to a set of pre-Buddhist ideas about what constituted the ruler's "majesty."[29]

*Jindag* and *yondag* thus referred to donors in a broad spectrum of relationships that included donors and donees, disciples and spiritual advisors, and rulers and priests. These concepts could be deployed in a range of religious, political, and economic interactions that implied different hierarchical relations. The negotiation of the relationship was a delicate matter involving careful strategic considerations. For example, a single lama or monastery could be supported by a number of donors, and a donor could support numerous lamas and communities. Merit could be accumulated not only through deeds specifically related to the promotion of Buddhist teachings but also through worldly actions for the common good; the biographies of great Buddhist personalities often list among their accomplishments the construction of bridges and water channels, the taming of robbers, or the control of epidemics, just as many rulers are credited for their religious acts.

Women were recognized as donors in the Buddhist sense in the earliest accounts of Buddhist history (see Willis 1985:59ff.) and are found throughout recorded Tibetan history. In imperial Tibet, for example, several queens are described as having provided important support for Buddhist figures of their time (Uebach 2005:29ff.). Women's names often appear in the colophons of texts among acknowledgments to benefactors, in the lists of donors who funded the production of statues and paintings, the renovation of religious shrines, and other such deeds. For women of the aristocracy, for whom access to a full religious life was often especially difficult, the role of a donor represented a viable and less controversial way to fulfill spiritual aspirations and to participate in the great deeds of spiritual masters. In some cases, women had a particular role as distributors of food and often as managers and key holders of storerooms and treasure chambers—this seems to have been the kind of position that Chokyi Dronma's mother held. Chokyi Dronma herself, however, seems to have felt that being a lay donor was not enough for her, and thus became both a nun and a *yoginī*. But she nevertheless maintained her role as a royal donor who supported her spiritual masters throughout her life.

## Gurus and Religious Schools of Chokyi Dronma's Time

Even though by Chokyi Dronma's time all the major schools of Buddhism had already appeared in Tibet, the relationships among them were quite fluid. Many practitioners received teachings from masters belonging to different schools and many lamas were supported by a variety of donors with different religious and political allegiances. Thus the vacuum left by the diminishing political power of the Sakya was gradually being filled by a variety of other schools. In particular, the Gelugpa, established by Tsongkhapa Lobsang Dragpa (1357–1419), was strongly on the rise even in the eyes of those like Chokyi Dronma who were not directly connected with the tradition.

The royal house of Gungthang experienced a number of different, often contrasting, religious influences. Some members had a close, if controversial, relationship with Rindzin Godem and the Nyingmapas, while the widow of Thrigyal Sonam De (1371–1404), who had ruled the kingdom after his death, had been close to representatives of the Kadampa and the emerging Gelugpa school (Everding 2000:512). More central were the influences of Sakyapa and Bodongpa teachers: Chokyi Dronma's grandfather, Thrigyal Sonam De, had established links with the Bodongpa family of translators, and the Bodongpa school had become the dominant tradition in Mangyul-Gungthang during the reign of Chokyi Dronma's father. He had been brought up in the Sakya monastery of his maternal grand-uncle, and his court chaplain, Chopel Sangpo, who celebrated Chokyi Dronma's name-giving ceremony, was a renowned lama of the Bodongpa school related to the Sakya masters by kin (Everding 2000:517).

Of the four religious masters who were especially important to Chokyi Dronma, Bodong Chogle Namgyal (1375/6–1451) was clearly the most significant. This eclectic polymath was, according to her biography, the first person to have explicitly stated that she was an emanation of the Dorje Phagmo, and it was in order to become his disciple that she renounced secular life around 1442; she stayed with him until his death nine years later. He had disciples from all the Tibetan schools but is associated with one particular tradition, the Bodongpa, named after its original seat, Bodong E, founded in 1049. Bodong Chogle Namgyal is considered the formal founder of this tradition because his extensive writings together formed a body of texts called the *dPal de kho na nyid 'dus pa,* meaning literally "Collected Suchness" (*Tattvasaṃgraha* in Sanskrit), presumably a reference to the canonical texts with the same name, which can be glossed as "compendium of reality." According to the biography of Bodong Chogle Namgyal (221–222), this corpus of teachings, a compendium of all branches of knowledge and religious practice, was composed under the inspiration of the deity Dorje Naljorma (Vajrayoginī). These scriptures are also referred to repeatedly in Chokyi Dronma's biography as the texts that first captured her mind, the tradition she practiced, and the works she edited and reproduced after her master's death. Bodong Chogle Namgyal had inherited his ideas from a number of predecessors. He was born into a family of great translators from Surtsho, a seminomad area of Southern Lato, and was the spiritual heir of the great translator Dragpa Gyaltshen (1352–1405), who was his maternal uncle and who had been initiated by his own maternal uncle, the great translator Changchub Tsemo (1315–1394), the nephew of the great translator Pang Lotsawa Lodro Tenba (1276–1342). The mothers and sisters in this lineage, which appears to have been matrilineal to some extent,[30] were considered accomplished *ḍākinīs* or female deities, although little is known about them. Like his maternal uncle, Bodong Chogle Namgyal took over the position of abbot at a number of monasteries that had been established in the late fourteenth century by various members of this emerging tradition. His own preferred seat was the one he established at Palmo Choding in the nomad area of Porong, not far from the eastern shore of Palkhu/Pekhu Lake, just north of the Himalayas and what is now Nepal. He is renowned for his broad knowledge and for having introduced the practice of holding debates on a large number of subjects. He reckoned among his disciples the greatest spiritual masters of his time, including Gendun Drupa (1391–1474), who was recognized posthumously as the first Dalai Lama; Khedrubje Geleg Pel Sangpo (1385–1438), posthumously recognized as the first Panchen Lama; Taglung Ngawang Dragpa (1418–1496); and many other important figures belonging to different schools of Tibetan Buddhism. The Bodongpa tradition itself flourished during this period, especially in the south and southwest of Tibet, but waned with the fights that led eventually to the Gelugpa's grasping political control over Tibet in 1642.

Another very important figure in Chokyi Dronma's life was the great *siddha* or adept, the famous bridge builder Thangtong Gyalpo (1361?–1485). He was a follower of both the Nyingmapa and the Shangpa Kagyupa traditions. He is known from a variety of sources but especially through the biographies written about him (see chapter 3). He is popularly renowned even today for the iron-chain bridges he constructed across the Brahmaputra and for many other deeds. For example, he is considered to have initiated Tibetan opera as a means to collect funds for his enterprises (though this claim has been difficult to substantiate). He was a unique and multifaceted figure, of whom Cyrus Stearns wrote, "His life and his teachings are intertwined with the themes of divine madness, visionary revelation, demon exorcism, the quest for immortality, the relationship of man with his environment and the process of ultimate enlightenment" (1980:2). He was a great innovator in religion and technology, as well as a great traveler with a vast array of relationships. He established a large number of monasteries and shrines all over Tibet and Bhutan, including the monastery of Menmogang at Tsari, where Chokyi Dronma died in 1455. Chokyi Dronma spent much of the years 1452–54 with him in Northern Lato. She received a number of teachings from him, and after he sent her to the east, relied heavily on people who were close to him. He also is said to have recognized her as Dorje Phagmo and to have associated her with this deity's prophecies, and later to have identified her reincarnation. He had a complex, at times strained relationship with the teachers of the Bodongpa school and was close to the Phagmodrupa rulers, the rivals of the Sakyapa. This tension features prominently in Chokyi Dronma's biography and is the background against which her attempt to steer a middle course among competing networks of politico-religious power must be seen.

The third great influence on Chokyi Dronma was Vanaratna (1384–1468), the last of the Indian *paṇḍita* or scholars to have traveled to Tibet. He was born in Chittagong in what is today Eastern Bengal, and the story of his life is narrated in the Kālacakra chapter of the famous Tibetan history known as the *Blue Annals* (*Deb ther sngon po*), written by his contemporary Go Lotsawa Shonnu Pal (1392–1481), as well as in a number of biographies. He traveled to Tibet three times: in 1426, from 1433 to 1436, and from 1453 to 1454. These journeys were made at the invitation of the Phagmodrupa rulers, and he was acknowledged by Dragpa Jungne (1414–1446), the Sixth Neudong Gongma, as his personal tantric guru. He was also hosted by numerous local rulers such as the lords of Yamdrog and the lords of Southern and Northern Lato. In 1436 Vanaratna visited the King of Gungthang, Thrigyal Lhawang Gyaltshen, Chokyi Dronma's father, and first met the princess, then fourteen years old. According to her biography, he was to recall that initial encounter when they met again in Rinpung in the autumn of 1454. He was then on his way back from Neudong, heading toward Nepal, and she was traveling toward Lhasa. That meeting seems to have been short but intense (folio 131b–134a), with Chokyi Dronma apparently aware of his historic stature: when Deleg Chodren asked her whether he or Bodong Chogle Namgyal was the greater master, she replied that she was not in a position to judge such a high matter (folio 134b).

According to later sources, the fourth of the great masters who were particularly influential in Chokyi Dronma's life was Pal Chime Drupa. He was close to her for a number of years and was probably with her when she died at Tsari. He is the least known of the spiritual masters with whom she had direct interaction but probably the most important in terms of the survival of her tradition, and there is strong evidence that he was her biographer (see chapter 3). According to sixteenth- and seventeenth-century sources, he was considered an emanation of the deity Cakrasaṃvara and a reincarnation of the King of Oḍḍiyāna Indrabhūti and of the Kagyupa master Phagmodrupa Dorje Gyalpo. He was seen as one of the male counterparts to Chokyi Dronma in practical terms and

FIGURE I.2  Vajrayoginī, after a mural painting at Samding monastery. The pig head on the side of the head indicates its identity with Vajravārāhī. *Jana Diemberger*

FIGURE I.3  (right) Vajravilāsinī with tantric partner, after English 2002. Vajravilāsinī, a rare form of Vajrayoginī, is referred to in the biography of Chokyi Dronma. *Jana Diemberger*

to Dorje Phagmo in symbolic terms, a relationship that is discussed more fully in chapter 5.

## Vajrayoginī, Vajravārāhī, and Chokyi Dronma

Dorje Phagmo is the Tibetan translation of the name of the Indian deity Vajravārāhī, whose name became linked to a number of places and rituals as the cult was introduced into the Tibetan context. Vajravārāhī is a special form of the deity Vajrayoginī (known as Dorje Naljorma in Tibetan), whose cult originated among tantric practitioners in northern India and flowered there

FIGURE I.4 The tantric couple Cakarasaṃvara and Vajravārāhī, after a *thangka* that Chokyi Dronma ordered based on instructions from Bodong Chogle Namgyal. *Jana Diemberger*

FIGURE I.5 (right) Cakarasaṃvara and Vajravarāhī, after an illustration from Herrmann-Pfandt 2001. *Jana Diemberger*

especially between the tenth and twelfth centuries (English 2002). Vajrayoginī and Vajravārāhī are associated with what is known as the supreme tantra (*anuttarayogatantra*) and are considered to embody enlightenment, especially when it is achieved through esoteric transgressive practices. Like many tantra of the supreme class, the practices centered on this deity were developed among Indian wandering *yogins* and related to non-Buddhist traditions. In particular, nondual Śaivism had a formative influence upon the Vajrayoginī cult as it later developed in the Buddhist context. Elisabeth English observes that "as in the esoteric Śaiva systems, *kāpālika* and sexual practices in the Buddhist tantras are grounded on a metaphysics of non-duality. Its purpose is to counter the ordinary, conventional dualism of the mind that naturally perceives aspects of the world as either 'pure' or 'impure.' . . . The underlying method of this soteriology is that of 'transgressive discipline'" (English 2002:41). By confronting what a human being would normally avoid, fear, or despise, the practitioner becomes able to transcend all conventional perceptions and to attack the innate dichotomy of subject and object. Cremation grounds, polluted by death, were privileged places for these practices. Human bones, especially skulls, were an essential component of ritual instruments, and polluting bodily fluids such as menstrual blood were ingredients in the rituals. These practices overturned sexual regulations: the female partners of the *yogins* were often outcast women, involved in rituals while menstruating.

As cycles of the *anuttarayogatantra* were adopted into Tibet, the cults of Vajrayoginī and Vajravārāhī entered all schools of Tibetan Buddhism, albeit in different forms and along different pathways, according to the practice of the various masters. In Tibetan ritual texts and iconography this deity appears both on her own and as a part of a couple, in conjunction with a male deity such as Cakrasaṃvara or Padmanarteśvara, a form of Avalokiteśvara. Several different practices centered on Vajrayoginī or Vajravārāhī were transmitted into the numerous traditions of the Kagyupa school and became particularly prominent there. Rituals concerning this deity in her various forms were also adopted into Sakyapa tradition, and the Gelugpa focused on Vajrayoginī/Vajravārāhī in her role as the consort to Cakrasaṃvara, one of their main meditational deities. The Nyingmapa incorporated practices of Vajrayoginī/Vajravārāhī by reading them back into the life of Padmasambhava, identifying his consorts as emanations of this deity. They also consider Vajrayoginī an equivalent of the wrathful female deity at the center of the Machig Labdron cycle of practices (see chapter 4).[31]

Vajrayoginī and Vajravārāhī practices were already widespread when Bodong Chogle Namgyal and Thangtong Gyalpo identified Chokyi Dronma as an emanation of the deity, and a *thangka* painting of Cakrasaṃvara embracing Vajravārāhī that was made according to Bodong Chogle Namgyal's instructions has survived. Vanaratna probably also played a role in the identification of Chokyi Dronma with Vajravārāhī, although less directly. He was a practitioner of the Vajravārāhī cult and of rituals in which she was propagated in a form known as Vajravilāsinī.[32] Among his disciples was the ruler of Yamdrog, who compiled the biography of Bodong Chogle Namgyal and was influential in developing the Dorje Phagmo reincarnation line (see chapter 5). The opening verses of Chokyi Dronma's biography, which begin by invoking Vajravārāhī, go on to refer to "the *Vajra* Beauty" or Vajravilāsinī (folio 2b), the peaceful and compassionate form of Vajravārāhī regarded, in this "secret" form, as highly sensual and erotic (English 2002:86ff.). The meditation practice associated with her is Mahāmudrā, and this is mentioned in the text immediately afterward.

Vajrayoginī and Vajravārāhī were not only aspects of a meditational deity to be visualized by the practitioner during meditation and rituals. In India Vajrayoginī had been one of the female deities associated with holy places, especially charnel grounds, who could possess women (English 2002:43; Sanderson 1988:671). This tradition seems to have existed also in Tibet, since Vajrayoginī is mentioned as possessing Tibetan women there in the fourteenth century (Germano and Gyatso 2000:239ff.). She was also "read" into the Tibetan landscape. In particular, the famous Himalayan mountain of Tsari, in southeastern Tibet, became one of the main sacred sites associated with the tantric couple Cakrasaṃvara and Vajravārāhī.[33] This was part of a larger movement among Tibetan religious groups that identified the traditional twenty-four Buddhist holy places of India (*pīṭhas*) with places in Tibet. The thirteenth-century polemic between the Ka-gyupa masters and Sakya Paṇḍita,[34] who disputed the legitimacy of this wide-spread practice, bears testimony to both its importance and its controversial character.

Like many other places regarded as sacred in Tibet, Tsari is seen as a maṇḍala, with a gate in each of the four cardinal directions giving access to the central, ho-liest area. Tsari's inner sanctum is known as the Pure Crystal Mountain (Dag pa'i shel ri), where celestial entities are said to be accessible to their devotees. Much of the secret symbolism associated with this mountain identifies the body of Vajravārāhī, particularly her sexual organs, in the features of the landscape. Per-haps because of this, women are not allowed access to the innermost sanctuary and are only supposed to participate in the lesser part of the pilgrimage (Huber 1994:350–371); a number of extant narratives describe women—especially reli-gious women—who challenge this ban but are invariably defeated, a theme to which I shall return in chapter 3.

The term "Tsari" is used to refer to an area that is far larger than the circuits followed by pilgrims around the Pure Crystal Mountain and includes a number of other religious sites. It is subdivided into Old Tsari, now part of the mod-ern county of Lhuntse in the southeast of today's Tibet Autonomous Region and including parts of neighboring areas of India, and New Tsari, farther east. The latter was particularly important for Thangtong Gyalpo, because there were located the mines from which he obtained the iron for some of his bridges. In New Tsari he established the monastery of Menmogang and appointed Rigsum

Gonpo, one of his main disciples, as its abbot. Chokyi Dronma spent the last months of her life based at this monastery involved in the production of iron chains (Biography of Thangtong Gyalpo 283).

Over the centuries, the area of Tsari has attracted wandering *yogins* and pilgrims from all traditions who visited, went into retreat, or took up residence in a more permanent way. These people mingled with the local communities and interacted with the so-called Lhopa, the people who lived on the southern slopes of this Himalayan region. The Tibetans going to Tsari established retreats, shrines, shelters for pilgrims, monasteries, and nunneries as well as village communities of various sorts. This area became an increasingly complex interface among different communities and different religious traditions with relations that were not always friendly.

By the time of Chokyi Dronma, Tsari was already well established as a pilgrimage site linked to Vajravārāhī. It is therefore not surprising that she visited it, especially after she had become identified with the deity herself. Whether she went there to join the ultimate sanctuary of the deity, to support Thangtong Gyalpo in the construction of iron-chain bridges, or both, her death shortly after reaching the sacred site fitted perfectly into the framework of prophetic narratives that already surrounded her and added a tantalizing veil of mystery and importance to her story.

# 2

# THE LIFE OF CHOKYI DRONMA

*Chokyi Dronma was born in the year of the tiger, or, by the Western calendar, 1422,*[1] at a moment when an heir to the throne of Mangyul-Gungthang was keenly awaited. The court chaplain, Chopel Sangpo, considered her to be a divine incarnation and gave her the name that, according to a prophetic dream by her mother, she had already given herself: Queen of the Jewel (Konchog Gyalmo)— a title that reflected both her commitment to become a royal supporter of the *Dharma* and the prospect that she would be "victorious in all directions." This name concurs with the representations in the biography of Chokyi Dronma as a tantric deity, but the implication that she had an extraordinary sacred role may also have been an attempt to present her as a potential royal heir in case no son was born to the king.

The scenario changed radically a few years later: when Chokyi Dronma was about five,[2] a son was born to a junior queen. This is said to have deeply troubled Chokyi Dronma and her mother, and is the first point at which she is supposed to have expressed a wish to renounce the world and be ordained. The birth of the male heir apparent not only meant that she faced the prospect of being sent away as a daughter-in-law but also caused great anxiety for her mother, the main

FIGURE 2.1 The palace of Gungthang with its citadel, after 1945 photographs and sketches of the ruins by Peter Aufschnaiter (Aufschnaiter and Brauen 2002), photographs of the Mustang royal palace, and personal experiences of the ruins. The pagoda in the middle is the Droma Lhakhang, a temple in Nepalese style of which the first floor is still extant. *Karen Diemberger*

queen, since she had produced only girls while a junior queen had produced the desired male heir.

Despite these considerations, Chokyi Dronma enjoyed a happy and lively childhood, dividing her time between the capital of the kingdom and the lush valleys of Kyirong, which she loved (many mentioned places are identifiable near Trakar Taso monastery). She would go there often, especially in the winter when the upper areas were frozen and stricken by blizzards. She seems to have been an energetic and adventurous child; the biography also describes her as compassionate toward animals, aware of worldly impermanence, and daring in her choices. She is said to have shown a strong character early on, perhaps a prelude to the fact that throughout her life she never shied away from physical hardship or risky enterprises. Nevertheless, she suffered some health problems in her early childhood and illness seems to have marked difficult periods in her life.

Chokyi Dronma appears to have been a clever and precocious child, but of course it is difficult to read beyond the biographical conventions according to which extraordinary qualities are an indication of an exceptional previous life. At around the age of three she is said to have learned to read and write, activities that she pursued with dedication throughout her life. She is also said to have been able to speak Sanskrit, a claim that would have been related to her "secret" identity as Vajravārāhī/Vajrayoginī. She had easy access to the Buddhist classics, and these became an important source of inspiration and are mentioned in some detail. Her mother seems to have taken special care of her education, and the biography describes how Chokyi Dronma fondly used to read books to her. Throughout her childhood she was beloved by her family and, apparently, by the citizens of the kingdom. Her mother and sister were particularly close to her; she also enjoyed an affectionate relationship with her father, although it was somewhat more distant and formal. Her paternal grandmother also seems to have been very fond of her since, much later, she supported her religious deeds and expressed great sorrow when she decided to leave Gungthang to go to the east.

In about 1438 Chokyi Dronma turned sixteen and thus was of marriageable age. As a child she had expressed a wish to be married out to Guge; this was probably influenced by her mother and by the former regent, who was from the house of Guge, in an area that was seen as pleasant and wealthy and that also had long-standing genealogical links with the house of Gungthang. However, the court decided that she should be married out to the rulers of Southern Lato. Gungthang's strategic relationship with Southern Lato was more crucial than that with Guge, so Chokyi Dronma's father accepted the marriage request from these important allies, who were also potential enemies. A very detailed description is given in the biography of both the grand celebrations held in honor of the marriage and the great sorrow felt at her departure from her homeland. The epic of grand marriages is a popular theme in Tibetan literature, and some resonances can be seen with Songtsen Gampo's marriage to the Chinese imperial princess Wencheng as told in earlier histories, such as the *Maṇi bka' 'bum* and the *rGyal rabs gsal ba'i me long,* that were popular at that time.[3]

The lords of Southern Lato sent a grand procession from Shekar, their capital, to fetch the future bride; they were welcomed in the royal palace by Chokyi Dronma's father and brother, seated on their thrones, with all the people of rank sitting in rows. The princess was seated in the middle of the crowd, absolutely still and shedding tears, as is required by Tibetan marriage customs. The sorrow

FIGURE 2.2 The palace and the monastery of Shekar, built by the grandfather of Chokyi Dronma's husband, after photographs of the early twentieth century. *Karen Diemberger*

in this case seems indeed to have been deep, as she was parting from her beloved mother and from all the people who had great affection for her. The text describes everyone as brokenhearted and lists the gifts with which she was showered. Her brother gave her one of his precious earrings; others offered jewels, rosaries, and precious stones. The sense of loss affected not only the human population but also all the other beings in the area and the features of the landscape: "All the living beings of Ngari [i.e., Gungthang] felt as if they had lost their protector. It was as if the whole essence of the earth had been taken away (*bcud phrogs pa*) and the earth had turned bleak" (13a).

The weeping marriage procession left the royal palace and climbed the steep pass that leads toward the Porong plains and eventually to Shekar. According to the biography, at the top of the pass, Chokyi Dronma prostrated toward her home, more than 3,000 feet below, taking a last look at the royal palace. She would have seen it surrounded by the lush fields of the Gungthang plain and overlooked by the snow-capped peak of Jowo Kula, the ancestral mountain of her family and her kingdom, and she would have been able to make out the deep

FIGURE 2.3 Porong landscape with nomad tents, after photographs from the 1990s. *Jana Diemberger*

gorge leading south, across the Himalaya, to her beloved Kyirong and beyond it to Nepal. She offered a white scarf, a *khatag,* with flowers toward the palace; her people, seeing this, could not control their tears.

After crossing the Gungthang La pass the party reached the Palkhu lake, the Palkhu Palthang plain, and the Porong region, a vast area inhabited by nomads and surrounded by snow peaks. It was a long journey, with the constant threat of attacks by bandits. At first the princess was very withdrawn and shy about meeting the bridegroom's retinue that had been sent to receive her, but eventually she accepted their request to be introduced. Leaving the shore of the lake, the procession passed near Porong Palmo Choding monastery; when she sent some messengers to Bodong Chogle Namgyal asking if she could visit him, he suggested, instead, that they meet on the way. Eventually the party from Gungthang took its leave and she proceeded, escorted by a large number of people who had come from Southern Lato to greet her.

The marriage procession presumably crossed the Surtsho area, north of the Bong-chu river[4] and the holy Tsibri range,[5] and proceeded to Shekar, the "White Crystal," the capital of Southern Lato. From afar they would have seen the mountain rising from the plain with the forbidding fortress on its ridge, and near it the white and

*The Life of Chokyi Dronma*

red of the monastery. Both had been built by the great lord of Southern Lato, Situ Chokyi Rinchen (d. 1402), the grandfather of her bridegroom.

As the procession approached the capital, a group of Bonpo priests came out to meet it, to celebrate some customary marriage rituals: Chokyi Dronma's bridegroom was particularly keen on the local ancestral cults, even though his parents were great supporters of Buddhism. As a committed Buddhist, Chokyi Dronma had very strong views on such practices; she was openly jubilant when the Bonpo priests were driven away by her retinue, dropping their ritual instruments as they made a hasty retreat.

Once in the palace, she further intimidated the Bonpo priests by meditating and empowering herself as Vajrayoginī. This episode and a number of other details introduce a slightly dissonant note in what otherwise seems to have been the perfect fulfillment of her role as a royal daughter-in-law. She behaved very respectfully toward her parents-in-law and her husband and was generally seen as a bringer of prosperity, beautiful and well behaved, even though she sometimes challenged conventions of royal protocol. For example, she sometimes dealt with secular dignitaries without the expected deference and made a point of showing maximum respect to members of the monastic community, whatever their standing. The early stages of her married life are described in an utterly glorious light, although the real situation could not have been easy for her as a young bride in an unfamiliar place. Her father-in-law was particularly fond of her, but her mother-in-law was somewhat more critical and her husband suffered from goiter, a widespread health problem in the region even in modern times, as well as from various character disorders. These more human and realistic details are revealed in the biography only incidentally and much later, when things had started to become difficult. At first, she seems to have adapted reasonably well.

Following tradition, after a period in the new home she was allowed to make a visit to her family. The biography reports that she was welcomed with great affection by her parents and by the whole kingdom. However, she only stayed for three months since her husband kept sending messengers asking her to come back, and eventually she returned to Southern Lato with another splendid celebration that resembled her first journey there as a new bride. According to Tibetan marriage customs, this sealed her acceptance of her new status.

The biography states that she became pregnant in her nineteenth year, which would have been about 1440, and gave birth to a girl. No difficulties are described concerning the delivery of the child, and at first everything seemed to proceed serenely. She enjoyed being with her little daughter, living in a very comfortable residence and assisted by several nannies. When her husband expressed his wish to appoint a Bonpo teacher for the child, she was able to negotiate that the girl should be educated according to Buddhist principles. When her daughter was about one year old, Chokyi Dronma went to the hot springs with her retinue. There she fell so gravely ill that she almost died; her eventual recovery was ascribed to a miracle. Meanwhile, a major dispute had broken out in her father's kingdom and she decided to help in mediating the conflict. She left for Gungthang escorted by 100 horsemen, leaving her little daughter behind with her parents-in-law, her husband, and the nannies. While she was away the child died, and her parents-in-law sent a message informing her. She took the news calmly and replied that there was no reason to worry since the child would soon be reincarnated. However, she also said that the child would have lived longer, but deeds against the doctrine had brought about her untimely death. The biography says that this episode gave her much to think about. Before leaving Gungthang and returning to Shekar she formally announced her wish to take religious vows as a nun. Predictably, her father argued strongly with her and refused to approve it, saying that at the age of twenty she had just started her life and expressing his hope that she would postpone this decision. Chokyi Dronma remained resolute. This marked the beginning of her long and momentous struggle to free herself from her secular obligations. It is difficult to glean from the biography whether her decision to pursue her long-standing spiritual aspirations had been precipitated by her own illness and near death experience, by the death of her daughter, or by her family disputes. Whatever the cause, the biography marks this moment as an important threshold in her life, when she radically changed her outlook.

A short while after returning to Shekar she announced her wish to take religious vows to her parents-in-law and sent a letter to this effect to her father. Neither of the parties agreed. Meanwhile, she had started to take care of the property and the interests of the Porong Palmo Choding monastery at Shekar. She read the collected works of Bodong Chogle Namgyal (*dPal de kho na nyid 'dus pa*), and when this great lama was invited to Shekar she was entranced by his teachings. After his departure she missed him deeply; she felt that her life had become pointless and she had to devote herself to his doctrine. She then read the biography of the Buddha (*Lalitavistara*) and felt a strong wish to emulate Prince Siddhartha, giving up her royal life to strive for enlightenment. She repeatedly requested permission from her father and her father-in-law to become ordained, but to no avail. Eventually she decided that she had to take some action. At first she tried to escape from the castle, without success. Eventually she unbound her hair and started to chop it with a knife, injuring herself in the process. When her shocked parents-in-law found her in this condition, she threw the hair at their feet. The sight of her, standing in the middle of the royal fortress covered in blood and with hair disheveled, led them to allow her to leave and to renounce her secular obligations. Her father-in-law calmed her down and promised to agree to all her wishes provided she would not present herself in this state to her husband, who had recently suffered some kind of mental crisis. She therefore arranged a makeshift wig to cover her hair and dressed in her best clothes to meet him. At first he did not understand the situation, but finally he went along with the decision that he should marry another woman. Chokyi Dronma's feigning or experiencing mental instability in order to achieve a radical change in her life places her in a long tradition of sacred women in Tibet who had to resort to this option, whether nuns, tantric practitioners, or oracles. She may have been the most prominent to do so, but she was not the first: the act of unbinding the hair as an expression of madness and transgression features prominently in the life of Mahāsiddha Lakṣmīṅkarā, the mad Indian princess of the eighth century who was her spiritual ancestor, and has wide resonances throughout the Buddhist world.

Eventually her husband's family allowed the princess to leave. The biography describes her riding off in the rising sun toward the high pastures and the monastery of Porong Palmo Choding, delighting in her newly acquired freedom. At the monastery she was welcomed by Bodong Chogle Namgyal, who ensured that she had arrived with proper permission from her family before admitting her formally. After he had received the confirmation from both Shekar and Gungthang, she was allowed to take part in her first ritual as a member of the monastic community. She dressed sumptuously for the ceremony, had the remains of her hair arranged by an attendant, and took her vows as a novice. She was then given the name under which she became famous, Chokyi Dronma, "the Lamp of the Dharma" (Dharmadīpa).[6] She used the occasion to announce her commitment to support religious practices for women.

Bodong Chogle Namgyal was later to face some sharp criticism for having admitted a woman into a monastic institution, but he always defended his choice staunchly. Chokyi Dronma's life revolved around him from around 1442 until his death in 1451. During this time she moved between Palmo Choding monastery and her homeland, to which she loved to return from time to time. In the monastery she pursued her religious training and eventually was fully ordained

FIGURE 2.4 Deleg Chodren.
*Jana Diemberger*

as a nun. This makes her one of the rare known instances of a fully ordained woman in Tibet, although the biography seems to imply that this practice was more widespread than is currently assumed on the basis of the surviving records, an important and controversial issue to which we shall return later.

In an effort to follow the example of the Buddha, Chokyi Dronma also spent a great deal of time traveling around as a begging nun. Although this was an established practice, seeing their princess in this guise provoked a great deal of surprise in the local population. From simple herdsmen to aristocrats, most became great supporters, and she was extremely successful in collecting all sorts of donations with which to fund the religious activities carried out by her master. She was often joined in her begging by a nun called Deleg Chodren, who became her closest friend and followed her for the rest of her life. This woman was probably one of the key figures in the compilation of the biography.

Throughout the period during which her life was centered around Bodong Chogle Namgyal and Palmo Choding monastery, Chokyi Dronma devoted herself to the recruitment and training of nuns. Often these were inexperienced young girls, and the biography underlines the point that since they were "free from worldly concerns" Chokyi Dronma had to consider all their practical needs. It appears that she even took care of the weaving and sewing of their clothes, while at the same time being deeply committed to their education. She

*The Life of Chokyi Dronma*

apparently taught them proper reading skills and introduced a very effective system of teaching the Buddhist doctrine. The biography is less explicit about the teaching of writing skills, and it is unclear how widespread these were among the nuns. Chokyi Dronma herself was able to write and compose verses, and some members of her retinue are described as having taken notes of teachings and as having edited them. However, it is not uncommon even nowadays, especially among rural members of the monastic community, to encounter a marked discrepancy between reading and writing skills. Bodong Chogle Namgyal himself was particularly sensitive to women's issues and was a great innovator in this respect. Just as he had insisted on bestowing the full ordination on Chokyi Dronma, he established new rituals for women as a conscious revival of lost Indian Buddhist traditions. He encouraged Chokyi Dronma to initiate their performance of ritual dances at a time when female roles were usually performed by monks. The biography gives a very vivid description of the social and cultural challenges that this innovative enterprise entailed and of her skills in successfully overcoming them.

As long as her master was alive Chokyi Dronma seems to have been constantly torn between her wish to be with him and her desire to return to Mangyul-Gungthang. Even though the closeness to her master made bearable the harsh, high nomadic areas where Palmo Choding was located, she apparently preferred the more hospitable agricultural environment of her homeland and the hermitages in the lower, forested valleys of the Himalayas. In Mangyul-Gungthang she was also more effective in mobilizing networks of support for religious enterprises and was able to count on the availability of skilled craftsmen. In the last period of Bodong Chogle Namgyal's life, she seems to have spent most of her time in Mangyul-Gungthang. However, she returned to Palmo Choding whenever her master's health deteriorated. The biography gives a striking description of how she rushed back after having been summoned by Deleg Chodren with the news of the master's fatal illness. The two women, together with Chokyi Dronma's father, rode in great haste by day and night through icy storms over the 5,200-meter pass that separates Gungthang from Porong. The pace that the two young women set was too fast for the father, and he allowed them to ride ahead so that Chokyi Dronma could see Bodong Chogle Namgyal before he died. In the event, they all succeeded in reaching Palmo Choding before his demise, and Chokyi Dronma's father was able to receive important teachings from him before returning to Gungthang, while Chokyi Dronma remained to nurse her master. Eventually, at the end of the third month in the year of the sheep (1451),[7] she was

FIGURE 2.5 Climbing the pass between Gungthang and Porong on horseback, after photographs from the 1990s.
*Jana Diemberger*

summoned from a brief rest to interpret signs that those around him were unable to comprehend. She understood immediately that her master wished to practice meditation and joined him so as to be with him at his passing.

After Bodong Chogle Namgyal's death, she and the most important people of his retinue took care of the funeral rituals. Once his body was cremated, people were divided over what should be done with his relics, a dispute in which she acted as the mediator. Eventually she distributed the bone fragments among all members of the monastic community and had little figurines (*tsha tsha*) made of clay mixed with his ashes and given to the lay disciples and patrons. She felt that he thus belonged to the multitude of his followers rather than being embodied in one precious relic that could be owned and fought over. In many ways this faithfully represented the legacy of a lama whose teachings had been directed to all sects and disciples of all political alignments, rather than being exclusively associated with one place, patron, or tradition.

The events surrounding the death of Bodong Chogle Namgyal are mentioned in several sources, notably in his own biographies. These tend to provide descriptions that conform to the Buddhist ideal according to which death is no reason for grief and emphasize his glorious passing into celestial spheres. Chokyi Dronma's biography instead reveals more of the deep emotional tension and the sense of bereavement among Bodong Chogle Namgyal's disciples at the loss

FIGURE 2.6 Monk writing.
*Jana Diemberger*

of their master. Chokyi Dronma herself was deeply disturbed by the event and spent several months wandering around the hills of her homeland and practicing meditation. The faithful Deleg Chodren accompanied her; she is described as having felt distress and helplessness at seeing her mistress in extreme disarray, covered in lice and randomly praising her master to anyone she encountered, even if these were people who would not understand what she was talking about. In due course she recovered and was able to take care of other disciples of Bodong Chogle Namgyal.

After a while, sometime in 1452, she mobilized her whole retinue, all the disciples of Bodong Chogle Namgyal and the people of Mangyul-Gungthang, in order to fulfill her pledge to have the entire writings of her master edited and reproduced. In doing so Chokyi Dronma possibly played an important part in instigating some of the earliest examples of printing produced in Tibet, second perhaps only to the printings of the collected works of Tsongkhapa and Buton's *dhāraṇīs* just a few years earlier (see Ehrhard 2000:11).

Eventually Chokyi Dronma grew weary of staying in her own region, for reasons that are not completely clear. The biography reports that the people of Palmo Choding wanted her to stay at their monastery, and she agreed on the condition that her vision would be fulfilled: she wished to build water channels so as to create fields that could support a center of learning, similar to the ancient

FIGURE 2.7 Monks carrying books. *Jana Diemberger*

Buddhist cities of India, where a gathering of scholars could reside so as to bring peace to the whole region. Construction was begun and the details of the work are described in the biography; some of the Porong people attribute surviving traces of channels and ruins to these efforts. However, the plan was not carried out as well as she envisaged and she eventually gave it up. Meanwhile, she had started to make contact with Thangtong Gyalpo. She had already heard of this extraordinary *siddha,* who had become famous both for his religious deeds and miracles and for the production of iron-chain bridges over the Brahmaputra River, and she decided to ask him for advice on her situation. So she sent De-leg Chodren as a messenger and, sometime after she had received his reply to her request for guidance, she decided to visit him, leaving Gungthang for what would be the last time. Chokyi Dronma had wished to take her mother with her, but this was not permitted by the court. However, her mother and sister were allowed to escort her up to the pass that leads to the Porong plains, where they had a moving farewell.

After staying at Porong Palmo Choding for a while, she left for Northern Lato, where Thangtong Gyalpo was residing. She probably arrived sometime in 1452 or 1453, and met the great *siddha* at Chung Riwoche, where with her support he would later complete the famous *stūpa.* She stayed near the master

FIGURE 2.8 Thangtong Gyalpo's *stūpa* and bridge at Chung Riwoche, after photographs from the 1990s and sketches by Peter Aufschnaiter (Aufschnaiter and Braun 2002). *Karen Diemberger*

until the autumn of 1454,[8] less than two years in all. The biography devotes much space to her visit, probably because of Thangtong Gyalpo's role in the survival of the tradition. He also appears to have had a decisive impact on her life and is said to have delivered famous prophecies according to which she would enjoy a long life but have few disciples if she remained in her region, but would have an uncertain lifespan and a multitude of followers if she were to leave for the east. This prophecy is mentioned several times in the biography and is considered the reason for her final journey to southeastern Tibet and the holy shrine of Tsari.

Like Thangtong Gyalpo, Chokyi Dronma was an adept of the tradition of the "crazy saints" and used transgressive behavior to convey essential spiritual messages. The biography reports, for example, the story of a hermitess, teacher of Thangtong Gyalpo, who was meditating in a cave in Northern Lato and was visited by a scholar who was utterly shocked by the way she looked:

> She had a frightening appearance with disheveled gray-blue hair standing up on her head. He prostrated to her and asked for blessings. She did not pay much

FIGURE 2.9 The castle of Shigatse, where Chokyi Dronma met the Rinpung lord, Norbu Sangpo, after a 1951 photograph taken by Peter Aufschnaiter (Aufschnaiter and Braun 2002). Although it was destroyed and rebuilt in the intervening centuries, Norbu Sangpo's residence was located in the same position. *Karen Diemberger*

attention to him and gave him her blessing with her hand that looked like the foot of a black crow. Having lost all devotion, he thought, *Who brought me to this? Perhaps I was blessed by a demon.* (117a, b)

Eventually, by elaborating on his first reaction, she taught him the importance of not depending on appearances and conventions in assessing spiritual value. Her appearance clearly recalls that of Lakṣmīṅkarā, who smeared herself with ashes in a charnel ground and thus appeared light blue.

After the rainy season of 1454 Chokyi Dronma set out toward central Tibet. A number of letters sent to the local rulers and a letter of introduction that she carried enabled Thangtong Gyalpo to activate his large network of followers and provide her with adequate support on her way. In particular, some of his disciples from the monasteries of Baru Namtshel and Menmogang in New Tsari set out to meet her.

From Northern Lato she went to Shigatse and Rinpung, and crossed the Gampala pass to reach Lhasa. During her journey she encountered several political and religious personalities of her time, such as the Lord of Rinpung, Norbu

FIGURE 2.10 Thangtong Gyalpo's iron bridge at Chagsam Chubori, after a photograph by Austin Waddell. *Karen Diemberger*

Sangpo, and the Indian *paṇḍita* Vanaratna. In Lhasa she visited the Jokhang temple, paid respect to the holy statue of the Jowo, and had complex interactions with the local rulers, who were utterly surprised by some of her informal behavior, especially since she was wandering around on her own. At the time of Chokyi Dronma's visit to Lhasa the fame of Tsongkhapa, later to be celebrated as the founder of the Gelugpa sect, was rapidly spreading in central Tibet; this deeply impressed the princess and her retinue.

After leaving Lhasa she visited Ushangdo, the temple established by her ancestor, King Ralpacen, in the ninth century. She then went to Chagsam Chubori, where she stayed for a few days next to the iron-chain bridge built by Thangtong Gyalpo. Here she received an extraordinary visit from a lama called Rigsum Gonpo, a disciple of Thangtong Gyalpo who had been appointed as the first abbot of the Menmogang monastery in New Tsari. He told her the astonishing story of how he had come to be there and was then welcomed by Chokyi Dronma and her retinue as a prophetic guide on the way to Tsari. She continued her journey along the southern bank of the Brahmaputra River. The biography follows her up to this point. From other sources we know that she died at New Tsari in her thirty-fourth year—that is, in 1455 or early 1456.[9] Thangtong Gyalpo's biography says that she spent the very last period of her life there participating in the production of chains for the Nyago Bridge. During her sojourn at the Menmogang monastery she composed a prayer in honor of Thangtong Gyalpo wishing long life to the old master,[10] either not knowing or not revealing that she would die shortly afterward, predeceasing him by roughly thirty years. Her sudden, untimely demise seems to have had an impact on the construction of the bridge, which was completed only in 1485, the year of Thangtong Gyalpo's death, by his son, who had taken over the management of his premises at Tsari.

Deleg Chodren reported Chokyi Dronma's death to Thangtong Gyalpo in the hope that he would pronounce whether there would be a reincarnation. The great *siddha* responded by reassuring the concerned nun that her mistress would indeed be reborn as a human. Some three years later, in 1459, a girl called Kunga Sangmo was born and was identified by Thangtong Gyalpo and by the community of Chokyi Dronma's disciples as the reincarnation of the princess.

3

# THE MANUSCRIPT AND ITS ENIGMAS

*When the package arrived, I opened it with palpable excitement and not a little* trepidation, knowing that it contained the copy of the biography of Chokyi Dronma kindly sent to me by Leonard van der Kuijp. I was deeply moved to be holding in my hand an ancient story I had so far known only from the princess's traces in other texts, mural paintings, and oral narratives. The minute calligraphy of the title, the illuminated first page with the portraits of Bodong Chogle Namgyal and Chokyi Dronma, the opening verses in fine Tibetan *dbu med* characters were beautiful . . . but on the title page a tag in Tibetan script was merciless: 146 FOLIOS, INCOMPLETE.

The original manuscript kept in the archive of the Nationalities Palace in Beijing apparently did not include the final part. So I did not find any colophon, the concluding paragraphs that usually give information about the author and the circumstances of compilation. On closer inspection I saw that something else was also missing: the end of the narrative. I was therefore holding not only a remarkable text but also a bundle of difficult questions that had to be answered in order to set this text in relation to Chokyi Dronma's actual life and to other narratives. Was it a story retold over centuries or an account by direct witnesses of her deeds? Why was it written?

FIGURE 3.1 Drawing from the front page of Chokyi Dronma's biography. *Karen Diemberger*

Searching for some solutions to the riddles posed by Chokyi Dronma's biography, especially by its missing part, I have looked at other sources that refer to her or to the people to whom she was linked. These include the biographies of Chokyi Dronma's spiritual masters, later histories of the tradition she belonged to, and histories of the places she inhabited (which have also informed chapter 1). Since reference to these sources is essential to my tentative answers, I provide here a brief outline of the most important works, particularly for those not familiar with the Tibetan historical literature of the period.

## Relation of the Biography to Other Sources

Chokyi Dronma had two main spiritual masters, Bodong Chogle Namgyal and Thangtong Gyalpo, who were described concisely in chapter 1. Their biographies are thus the most important parallel sources I have referred to.

Several biographies of Bodong Chogle Namgyal were written; not all are extant. I was able to get hold of two. The most important is *Feast of Miracles* (*ngo mtshar gyi dga' ston*), completed in 1453 by Bodong Chogle Namgyal's disciple Amoghasiddhi Jigme Bang.[1] Since this is the work I usually refer to, as "the

*The Manuscript and Its Enigmas*

FIGURE 3.2 Chokyi Dronma, drawing from the illumination in her biography. *Karen Diemberger*

biography of Bodong Chogle Namgyal," I will specify the author and title only when referring to the other biographies or where confusion may arise. The second is *Ocean of Miracles* (*ngo mtshar gyi rgya mtsho*), compiled by Karma Mikyo Dorje[2] (1507–1554).

Chokyi Dronma knew Bodong Chogle Namgyal during the final years of his life, between 1442 and 1451. Both biographies draw on the biography in verse by his nephew[3] and on a set of notes compiled by Konchog Gyaltshen, the secretary of Bodong Chogle Namgyal, who was also occasionally involved with Chokyi Dronma. For example, he appears as one of the main scholars in charge of the edition of the collected works of Bodong Chogle Namgyal (*dPal de kho na nyid* 'dus pa) prepared under the auspices of the princess (folio 90b). *Feast of Miracles* is particularly useful, as it was completed before Chokyi Dronma's death and is therefore an independent source that helps in understanding how she was thought of during her lifetime.

There are also several biographies of Thangtong Gyalpo, and I was able to refer to the three that are currently available: one by Sherab Palden, completed by Thangtong Gyalpo's spiritual son shortly before the death of his master in 1485; one by Thangtong Gyalpo's disciples Konchog Palsang and Monpa Dewa Sangpo; and the most famous, completed in 1609 by Gyurme Dechen (1540–1615), which draws upon the older biographies and other preexisting works. This text was recently translated into English by Cyrus Stearns, who also provides a detailed discussion of the relationships among the biographical sources (see Stearns 2007).

Chokyi Dronma appears in all known biographies of Thangtong Gyalpo, especially in passages concerning their encounter in 1453/54 during the completion of Chung Riwoche *stūpa* and his prophecies about her.[4] However, Gyurme Dechen's biography refers most extensively to her, speaking of many events and people that appear in her biography[5] and frequently mentioning Deleg Chodren, who played a central role in Chokyi Dronma's final years but is otherwise unknown from other texts. This version is thus particularly important, as it seems to have used Chokyi Dronma's biography as a source.[6] In particular, several verbatim correspondences show that Gyurme Dechen drew on the preexisting biographies of Thangtong Gyalpo and added passages from the biography of Chokyi Dronma.[7] Most importantly, this text (Biography of Thangtong Gyalpo 283–284) mentions Chokyi Dronma's last journey to Tsari and her death in a passage that follows a verbatim quotation from Sherab Palden's biography. Given Gyurme Dechen's pattern of compilation, it is plausible that he may have quoted or paraphrased the missing part of Chokyi Dronma's biography. He also provides an account of the recognition and the life of Kunga Sangmo, the immediate reincarnation of Chokyi Dronma (Biography of Thangtong Gyalpo 308–309). This passage also seems to be based on materials from or related to Chokyi Dronma's biography.[8] The biography by Gyurme Dechen is the one I usually refer to, as "the biography of Thangtong Gyalpo"; I will specify further details only when referring to the other biographies or where confusion may arise.

There are more biographical sources relevant to Chokyi Dronma's life, such as those concerning Chopel Sangpo (1371–1439), Vanaratna (1384–1468), Taglung Thangpa Ngawang Dragpa (1418–1496), Tsunpa Choleg (1437–1521), and

Tsangnyon Heruka (1452–1507), spiritual masters who lived at the same time as or shortly after Chokyi Dronma. These provide important additional evidence of encounters, views, religious environment, and politics of the time. Since I refer to them only occasionally, I will provide their details in the bibliography and give some contextual information where I mention them.

The *History of Bodong* (*Bo dong chos 'byung*) is a further crucial source. It was compiled by the main disciple of the fourth Dorje Phagmo, Urgyen Tshomo (that is, the third successive incarnation of the deity, starting from Chokyi Dronma), in the late sixteenth or early seventeenth century at the latest. The date is not explicitly mentioned but can be deduced from the fact that the text mentions that Urgyen Tshomo was still alive. This account traces the lineage of a dual system of human emanations of the deities Khorlo Dompa (Cakrasaṃvara) and Dorje Phagmo (Vajravārāhī), who keep reincarnating in male and female historical figures. Even though the text is consistent, in terms of dates and main events, with Chokyi Dronma's biography and with the passages concerning her life in Gyurme Dechen's biography of Thangtong Gyalpo, there are remarkable discrepancies that I will discuss in chapter 5.

General works from the period such as the *Blue Annals,* a famous Tibetan history compiled in 1476 by Go Lotsawa Shonnu Pal, are useful to sketch the historical context and the major figures of the time (like Vanaratna) involved with the princess. However, this work makes little mention of people and teachings belonging to the Bodongpa school.[9] I have also used some information from texts such as the sixteenth-century historical work by Pawo Tsuglag, *Scholar's Feast of Doctrinal History* (*mKhas pa'i dga' ston*), and the early seventeenth-century *History of Taglung* (*sTag lung chos 'byung*), which describe the transmission of the teachings of Bodong Chogle Namgyal and the activities of the Bodongpa school. In addition, historical works from the eighteenth century, such as the *Royal Genealogy of Gungthang* (*Gung thang rgyal rabs*) and the *History of Shekar* (*Shel dkar chos 'byung*), based on earlier documents, are also important sources of information concerning the genealogies of the local rulers and the history of Gungthang (Lower Ngari) and Southern and Northern Lato. The details of these works are given in the bibliography. Finally, I have drawn on various materials located in the monasteries of Samding, Bodong E, Nyemo, and Palmo Choding: ritual texts, genealogies, relics, mural paintings, statues, and even a particular *thangka* of Cakrasaṃvara and Vajravārāhī made under the auspices of Chokyi Dronma herself in honor of Bodong Chogle Namgyal. The painting includes a short explanatory text mentioning the history of this sacred object

FIGURE 3.3   Chokyi Dronma as depicted in the biography of Bodong Chogle Namgyal.
*Karen Diemberger*

that proved particularly helpful in unraveling some of the mysteries surrounding the princess.

## Tentative Dating of the Biography

With no extant colophon at the end of the text, any tentative dating can rely only on elements in the narrative and other texts. Below I demonstrate that the biographer was almost certainly a contemporary of Bodong Chogle Namgyal and Chokyi Dronma, and this is the strongest argument that locates the compilation of the work close to the events. This is also supported by the richness in

*The Manuscript and Its Enigmas*

details that are not immediately relevant to the soteriological design of a Tibetan biography (*rnam thar*) and by the fact that all references to known historical figures appear to be consistent with what is known from other sources of the period.[10]

From the text it can be deduced that the biography was definitely compiled after 1453, since the biography of Bodong Chogle Namgyal—completed in the summer of that year—is explicitly mentioned (folio 78b). It cannot be ruled out completely that the text may have been written in the final years of Chokyi Dronma's life, but there are good reasons to believe that her untimely death may have been the catalyst for its compilation. In particular, the emphasis given to Thangtong Gyalpo's prophetic words concerning her journey to the east and her lifespan—repeated three times in different forms[11]—suggests that the biography was written after her death at Tsari, perceived as a fulfillment of this prophecy. This, together with the assumption that the author was a contemporary of Chokyi Dronma and a direct disciple of Bodong Chogle Namgyal (see below), allows us to narrow down the presumed time of the compilation to a period most likely between 1455, the death of Chokyi Dronma, and 1496, the death of Taglung Ngawang Dragpa. He was the longest surviving disciple of Bodong Chogle Namgyal who was also directly involved in the continuation of the Dorje Phagmo tradition (see below and chapter 5). In addition, Chokyi Dronma's brother is mainly acknowledged as a difficult young man and not as the great Buddhist supporter described in later sources. Another hint that the writing must have taken place soon after Chokyi Dronma's death lies in the passage concerning her journey toward Tsari. As she arrived at Tsethang she was invited to meet the Neudong Gongma, the "supreme ruler of Neudong," whose predecessors had controlled the whole of Tibet and still had great influence in the region. She is described as not being particularly interested and as having continued her journey without meeting him (folio 143b). In the report of this event there is not even a suggestion of any sort of relationship. However, during the time of the next reincarnation, Kunga Sangmo, the Neudong Gongma would become one of the most important patrons of the Dorje Phagmo (see chapter 5).[12] Had the biography been written after this important relationship had been established, it is unlikely that the biographer would have avoided putting any emphasis on the Neudong Gongma and on his potential encounter with Chokyi Dronma. Another useful clue lies in the passage mentioning the two encounters of Chokyi Dronma[13] with the great Indian scholar Vanaratna.

During their second meeting in 1454 he mentions his future plan to go to Nepal. Neither the main narrative nor the other dialogues commenting on the event give any intimation about his death there in 1468 (the death of Vanaratna was known to Go Lotsawa and the people around him by the time the *Blue Annals* were completed in 1483; see also van der Kuijp 2006:24. This is the kind of news that spread quickly, especially among the disciples of a master). In brief, it is possible to locate, tentatively, the process of compilation at around 1460 or shortly afterward, as a rough estimate.[14]

## Authorship: One Biographer, Many Voices

Although the text indicates one biographer, the reader can perceive many voices in the narrative, especially that of the lifelong attendant and friend of the princess, Deleg Chodren. For this reason it is probably more appropriate to consider authorship as likely to have involved Chokyi Dronma's closest companions and disciples as a group. But whose hand compiled the text as it is? Until the missing part of the text turns up to give a more definitive answer, we can make some provisional deductions by looking closely at the biography and at other texts that refer to the same events and people.

### THE IDENTITY OF THE BIOGRAPHER

The author mentions himself (albeit not by name) in the first person right at the beginning of the text, where he gives the reasons for his undertaking:

> In order to complete the deeds of our (*bdag chag*) great Lama, the omniscient Jigdrel (Bodong Chogle Namgyal), Vajravārāhī, the female Buddha, took a human body and enjoyed the magic dance of Mahāmudrā in this world. I (*kho bo*) am therefore writing a short biography of her. (folio 2a)

The use of the male pronoun *kho bo* to indicate "I," in contrast to the feminine *kho mo* used by female speakers in the reported dialogues, allows us to infer that the biographer was male. The reference to "our lama" as *dag chag bla ma* suggests that the biographer was a direct disciple of Bodong Chogle Namgyal like Chokyi Dronma; so he was presumably one of her peers.[15]

A number of other indications can be gathered from the text and its character:

a) The narrative reads, over long stretches, almost like a film script giv-ing—and sometimes implying—the physical and human landscape in which the events are *mis-en-scène*. In particular, it can be inferred from the text that the biographer was quite familiar with the geography, the people, and the internal dynamics of Ngari/Gungthang, the homeland of Chokyi Dronma, as well as with her journeys, of which he must have had either firsthand experience or firsthand accounts.

b) The biographer also seems to reflect the local pride of the people of Ngari in their relations with their neighbors, which suggests a sense of belonging to the Ngari community. For example, in passages relevant to the marriage alliance and kinship relations, the people of Ngari are always treated as the insiders, the people of Southern Lato as the others. Even if this attitude may have come directly from Chokyi Dronma or Deleg Chodren, the biographer endorses it.

c) The biographer was also familiar with the biography of Bodong Chogle Namgyal written in 1453 by Amoghasiddhi Jigme Bang, as he explicitly refers to it. This supports the fact that he was a close follower of Bodong Chogle Namgyal's tradition; he may even have taken the master's biography as a model and source of inspiration. The biographer, however, also reveals, very explicitly, some of the tensions that existed between the princess and the people residing at Palmo Choding, the main seat of this master. It is therefore unlikely that he was one of them; he may even have been part of a group beginning to develop their own tradition on the basis of Bodong Chogle Namgyal's legacy. His allegiance and loyalty appear to lie primarily with Chokyi Dronma.

d) Even though the biography is dedicated to Bodong Chogle Namgyal, the narrative emphasizes in a particular way Chokyi Dronma's relationship with Thangtong Gyalpo,[16] often seen in contrast to her more unstable relationship with the people of Palmo Choding, and by extension Bodong E.[17] This indicates that the biographer probably came from a group of disciples of Bodong Chogle Namgyal who also had allegiances to Thangtong Gyalpo.

e) From the portion of the narrative describing Chokyi Dronma's stay in Lhasa—in particular her dialogue with Deleg Chodren (folio 138b)—the bi-ographer seems to be aware of the growing importance of Tsongkhapa and his teachings and uses the narrative to emphasize Chokyi Dronma's admiration for

Tsongkhapa and her concerns about the views on tantric practices taken by some of his later followers.

f) The repeated mention of Thangtong Gyalpo's prophecy concerning her lifespan suggests that the biographer wrote in connection with her untimely death as a fulfillment of this prophecy and may have been involved in questions of succession.

g) The reference at the beginning of the narrative to the fact that the undertaking had been blessed by Vajrayoginī herself and the mention of Vajrayoginī's recollections concerning childhood experiences seem to indicate, albeit ambiguously, that the compilation of the biography may have been initiated by Chokyi Dronma herself as an incarnation of the deity (probably at the very end of her life). This is supported by the fact that the text plays, often and deliberately, with the identification between the deity and the princess as her human embodiment, creating a sense of fluidity between the two (see also chapter 4). This would indicate that the biographer must have been very closely associated with her and deeply involved in carrying out her vision.

h) Finally, the numerous direct quotations from the princess and from her attendant and friend Deleg Chodren suggest that the author must have had a close relationship with both of them, or at least with Deleg Chodren.

POSSIBLE SOLUTIONS

In other sources that mention people and events of the time, one figure stands out as the most likely potential author of the biography: Pal Chime Drupa. He was born in the first half of the fifteenth century and died sometime before 1496.[18] According to the sixteenth-century *History of Bodong* (*Bo dong chos 'byung*, folio 21a–22a), he was born in Ngari (i.e., Gungthang); became a scholar with the name Dharmapel at Sangphu,[19] the famous Kadampa monastery; and, following the Gelugpa tradition, reached the level of a master of the ten subjects (*bka' bcu pa*). He subsequently became a disciple of Bodong Chogle Namgyal and, together with Chokyi Dronma, received empowerments from him. He eventually followed Chokyi Dronma on her journey to Tsari; after her death and a period of three years of meditation he took care of her reincarnation, Kunga Sangmo. According to the *Bo dong chos 'byung*, he was seen as an incarnation of the deity Cakrasaṃvara, the male counterpart of Vajravārāhī.[20] Some of the information on him contained in the *Bo dong chos 'byung* is confirmed by other sources. He also is mentioned in the early seventeenth-century *History of Taglung* (*sTag lung chos 'byung* 449),[21] and appears several times in the sixteenth-century historical text *mKhas pa'i dga' ston* (1076, 1171, 1268) in the chapter on the Karma Kamtshang.[22]

On the basis of these sources, Pal Chime Drupa appears to have been part of the core group of disciples of Bodong Chogle Namgyal and Chokyi Dronma, among whom the biographer is most likely to be found. Pal Chime Drupa seems also to fit very well with the profile of the potential biographer:

a) He was born in Gungthang and followed her on her journey.

b) He was integrated in the Gungthang local community, where he resided for long periods.

c) He was a disciple of Bodong Chogle Namgyal[23] but not a member of the community of Porong Palmo Choding. He traveled through Yamdrog in 1454, just after Amoghasiddhi Jigme Bang, one of the rulers of Yamdrog, had completed his biography of Bodong Chogle Namgyal.

d) It is uncertain whether he had any allegiance to Thangtong Gyalpo. However, since he followed Chokyi Dronma on her journey, he also relied on Thangtong Gyalpo's network and was almost certainly in Tsari when she died. Their small community had recently moved to the area and almost certainly had to rely significantly on followers of Thangtong Gyalpo to meet their needs. Even though the compilation of the biography may have been facilitated by financial resources left by the deceased princess, the enterprise probably had to rely on their support as well. It is therefore not surprising that Thangtong Gyalpo's network, which had already been instrumental in assisting Chokyi Dronma's journey to Tsari, is explicitly mentioned and even requested, several times, to provide future support to her followers.

e) He was trained in the Kadampa and Gelugpa traditions. Therefore he was definitely aware and highly appreciative of Tsongkhapa, although not necessarily of all views expressed by the later members of his tradition.

f) Having followed Chokyi Dronma on her journey and presumably witnessed her death, Pal Chime Drupa was likely to be involved in issues of succession. He is mentioned in the *Bo dong chos 'byung* as having taken care of the next reincarnation, Kunga Sangmo. Gyurme Dechen's biography of Thangtong Gyalpo (309) refers to him as well, albeit briefly, as a certain Pal [Chime Drupa] who was ready to escort Kunga Sangmo on a momentous journey to

deal with the Mongols. Tsangnyon Heruka met him together with the young
Kunga Sangmo around 1472 in the Tsari region (see Biography of Tsangnyon
Heruka folio 32–33).

g) As he is identified in the *Bo dong chos 'byung* as an incarnation of Cakrasaṃvara,
complementary to Kunga Sangmo, it is very likely that he was deeply involved in her religious vision.

h) Having been part of the retinue of Chokyi Dronma, he was definitely well
acquainted with both her and Deleg Chodren.

However, there is one issue that seems at odds with this hypothesis: Pal Chime
Drupa is mentioned in the text three times in the third person. At first, this may
seem to rule him out. But on closer inspection, the nature of the references
undermines this assumption, since on all three occasions he is mentioned as part
of a list of people engaged in certain activities, i.e., as part of a group that was
listening to teaching (59b), as one of the scholars in charge of the edition of the
collected works of Bodong Chogle Namgyal (91a), and as a player of a musical
instrument during a ceremony of consecration (93b). Therefore, these three passages mentioning Pal Chime Drupa seem to provide further supporting evidence
since his name is mentioned with stark simplicity, devoid of any of the epithets
usually found in later sources, that indicate him as the incarnation of the deity
Cakrasaṃvara and the reincarnation of Phagmodrupa Dorje Gyalpo. This suggests that the text was written before Pal Chime Drupa was formally considered
part of the parallel reincarnation line on which the recognition of later Dorje
Phagmo incarnations would ultimately depend (see chapter 5).

On the basis of these observations, Pal Chime Drupa seems to me the most
plausible candidate. Perhaps he devoted the three years of retreat after Chokyi
Dronma's death, mentioned in the *Bo dong chos 'byung,* to the compilation of the
text. In writing the biography, he would have reenacted what Bodong Chogle
Namgyal's disciple Amoghasiddhi Jigme Bang had done for his spiritual master.
And by writing about Bodong Chogle Namgyal's female spiritual partner as an
incarnation of Vajravārāhī, he was providing the symbolic complement to the
biography of Bodong Chogle Namgyal, to whom Chokyi Dronma's biography
is dedicated in the initial passage.

Another, less likely, potential author is Taglung Ngawang Dragpa (1418–1496),
who is not mentioned in the third person in the biography and who was part of
the network of students of Bodong Chogle Namgyal. He became a prominent
scholar as the twelfth abbot of the Taglung monastery. He had some contact

with the princess, as a disciple of the same teacher. However, although he visited Gungthang and Kyirong, there is no mention in his short biography, reported in the *sTag lung chos 'byung* (421–445), that he was there over a lengthy period of time or that he had a particularly close relationship with the princess. Nevertheless, he was definitely part of the same group and he is mentioned, for example, together with Kunga Sangmo, the reincarnation of Chokyi Dronma, and Pal Chime Drupa in *mKhas pa'i dga' ston* (1171). He was crucially involved in recognizing the next reincarnation of Pal Chime Drupa in his spiritual son Chime Palsang, who, in his turn, would recognize the following Dorje Phagmo, Nyendra Sangmo (1503–1542)[24] (i.e., the reincarnation of Kunga Sangmo)—a decisive step in the establishment of the tradition (see chapter 5). Also, Taglung Ngawang Dragpa appears in a manuscript of the biography of Bodong Chogle Namgyal preserved at the Bodong E monastery, in a meaningful system of illuminations: Bodong Chogle Namgyal is located in the middle, Chokyi Dronma is in the right lower corner, and Taglung Ngawang Dragpa is in the left lower corner, in a symmetric position that may suggest a relation between the two of them. He may therefore have been the compiler of the biography, provided people like Deleg Chodren and Pal Chime Drupa had dictated the main narrative to him or had provided preliminary written notes.

Another, somewhat remote, possibility is that the author of the biography of Bodong Chogle Namgyal, Amoghasiddhi Jigme Bang, also wrote the biography of Chokyi Dronma. He was a disciple of Bodong Chogle Namgyal and the nephew of Namkha Sangpo, the ruler of the Yamdrog area who instigated the carving of xylographs of some of his master's works,[25] and was close to Chokyi Dronma's reincarnation, Kunga Sangmo. As in the case of Ngawang Dragpa, he would have needed significant input from people like Deleg Chodren and Pal Chime Drupa, which could have been available in the form of notes and oral information. However, the style of Bodong Chogle Namgyal's biography, erudite and rich in poetry, is very different from the rather linear narrative of Chokyi Dronma's biography. In addition, the passages on the Yamdrog area, the homeland of Amoghasiddhi Jigme Bang, are rather sketchy. According to the itinerary described in the biography, Chokyi Dronma and her retinue passed in the vicinity of Nakartse, where Amoghasiddhi Jigme Bang resided. Had he been the biographer, he would probably have given more details about the area he knew so well. Nevertheless, he cannot be ruled out, and it is also possible that he may have had some input, for example, as a donor and instigator, as he was a key patron in the development of the reincarnation lineage (see chapter 5).

Of course, I cannot exclude the possibility that the biographer may have been a less prominent and scholarly member of Chokyi Dronma's retinue. However, had he been a scribe writing for Deleg Chodren, it is not very likely that he would have put himself in the position of the authorial "I" at the beginning of the text. Works that were dictated to scribes usually appear as authored by the scholar who dictated them. The person who compiled the text must therefore have had some standing and a reasonable level of scholarly skills acknowledged by the community and by the potential patrons of the enterprise.

There is even the possibility that a woman may have written the biography using the male pronoun, *kho bo,* to acquire authoritativeness. However, this last option, which of course would open another range of alternatives, seems highly unlikely because the disguise could not have been easily hidden at the time and would have flawed the sense of authenticity of the text. Female authors from this period are rare but not unheard of.[26] A female author, however, would probably have acknowledged her own gender by using the female pronoun to preserve authenticity, which was paramount. Even so, the male-authored narrative shows a strong presence of female voices and an unusual visibility of female networks and actions. For example, there are several statements concerning the importance of supporting women and their religious practice; Chokyi Dronma's maternal kinship ties are strongly emphasized; the relationship between Chokyi Dronma and Deleg Chodren is unusually dominant, given the presumed relatively low status of the latter; the nuns who provided assistance with food and drink and other aspects of logistics are mentioned by name, whereas it is much more common in Tibetan sources to find nuns and nunneries mentioned generically, if at all; there are unusually frequent and detailed mentions of spinning, sewing, production of clothing, and particular types of food—all activities and items that tend to be part of female competence in the Tibetan context. Much of this can be explained by the gender of the protagonist. However, it also suggests rethinking the authorship of the biography in a more choral way—or even, in Bhaktin's words, a "dialogical" way—rather than following conventional assumptions about writing and subjectivity. Since the late 1960s the idea of multivocality, the notion that an author rarely writes alone, has emerged within debates concerning narratives and the self. Like many Tibetan texts, this biography appears to have received input from a range of sources and may have been compiled by a group of people under the guidance of one individual, and thus reflects the views of a whole community. I will, therefore, explore what is known and what can be inferred about the actual process of writing in this light.

83

*The Manuscript and Its Enigmas*

The group of adepts that gathered around Chokyi Dronma/Dorje Phagmo in her final years, among whom I have tried to identify the biographer, seem typical of what has been called "the extensive subculture of yogins who wandered freely across Tibet" (Gyatso 1998:121) and produced their own distinct schools of thought and accounts of their activities.

At the time of Chokyi Dronma, there was an extensive practice of taking notes of teachings, thoughts, and life events of the spiritual masters; for example, the secretary Konchog Gyaltshen did this for Bodong Chogle Namgyal, and the notes were later used in the compilation of his biographies. Bodong Chogle Namgyal's biography contains an impressive description of how he would dictate his teachings to a group of twenty scribes, seated in a circle around him.[27] Sometimes a master himself would take notes that would be subsequently edited and elaborated upon by his disciples; this was the case with Tsunpa Choleg (1437–1521), a contemporary of Chokyi Dronma from her region, whose biography was compiled by his disciples on the basis of his own autobiographical account (Everding 2000:223–226). Also, in Tibet oral biographical and autobiographical accounts were often dictated; Janet Gyatso gives the example of the biography of Guru Chowang, in which it is told that several disciples compiled the text, which the protagonist then edited (Gyatso 1998:283). More generally, she refers to the blurring boundary between biography and autobiography and underlines how some autobiographies were actually written by the disciples while "even biographies composed centuries later reproduce passages, from either oral or written sources, that originate with the subject" (Gyatso 1998:103).

As many male and female followers of Chokyi Dronma were literate to some extent,[28] it is extremely likely that some of them took notes during her life. For example, there is an explicit reference in her biography to the practice of taking notes during teachings and editing them afterward (folio 62b). She may have even taken notes herself, since it is known that she composed some works.[29]

Once the biographer had decided to embark on the project, I suggest that he drew upon whatever was available of such preexisting notes as well as the oral accounts of people who had shared experiences with Chokyi Dronma. For example, in the middle of the plain prose, a peculiar passage in rhyme (folio 63b), mentioning the secretary, seems to indicate that the biographer may have quoted directly from Bodong Chogle Namgyal's verse biography or other related material. This is also suggested by clusters of orthographic inconsistencies.[30] The heterogeneous materials were blended into or framed in the biographer's erudite narrative, producing a peculiar contrast between colloquial expressions and poetic images that echo classical Indian literature (*kāvyā, śāstra,* etc.). Given the sudden and untimely death of the princess, it is likely that the writing, possibly initially instigated by Chokyi Dronma herself, was done in a somewhat hurried way while trying to solve the issues relevant to the potential—and subsequently newfound—reincarnation, or shortly afterward to provide a rationale for what had already been done (see chapter 5).

I suggest that in creating the narrative, the biographer, who was fulfilling the mission of writing for the group, integrated or even merged his subjectivity with that of other members of the community. They were providing textual and oral accounts for the compilation of what can be called a "collective act of remembering" (Middleton and Edward 1990). This would explain the plural "our" used by the direct disciples of Bodong Chogle Namgyal to refer to the lama to whom the biography was dedicated.[31] The term "our" creates an intentional and neat contrast to the "I" of the biographer, writing as the agent of a shared vision. The collective process of drawing together the materials for the biography would account for its somewhat fragmentary character, the numerous reported speeches and thoughts, as well as the numerous inconsistencies in personal and place names.[32] In writing up all the diverse elements, the biographer was creating a unitary master narrative using his recollection of earlier biographical models (see below), in which he framed whatever was available from written and oral accounts and his own memory.

Chokyi Dronma's identity as the embodied deity appears crucial throughout the biography: it apparently informed the opening passage revealing that Chokyi Dronma was a human incarnation of the deity Vajravārāhī and that this was the "highest secret" (see introduction). It is difficult to know when and how the identification of Chokyi Dronma with the deity began toward the end of her life (see chapter 4). What is certain is that her life and the process of writing about it need to be seen against the background of Tibetan theories of human beings as possible worldly emanations of tantric deities (*tulku*) and of multiple levels of life, which are distinctive traits of Tibetan biographies (Gyatso 1998:103). I shall return to these themes in chapter 4 and in the third part of this book. Here I will just focus briefly on the link between biographical writing and empowerment through narratives of origin. Janet Gyatso sets this issue in the wider context:

*The Manuscript and Its Enigmas*

If we recall the relation that obtains between spirit possession and the recounting of origins in the Tibetan context, we can appreciate the significance of the fact that autobiography represents the voice of the very source, the subject, the experiencer of the meditative states and spiritual realisations that make the subject an appropriate recipient of devotion and support. (Gyatso 1998:120)

In a study on female oracles (Diemberger 2005:113ff.), I noticed that the narrative concerning the life of the oracle was an important empowering element that framed the actual divination. The oral biographical account of the oracle, in particular that of her becoming, appeared to be the very premise that enabled and positioned the dialogue between the deity (or sometimes the spirit of a deceased person) that possessed her and the consulting community, giving more or less validity to the process of divination. The life stories followed a model with clearly recognizable stages—a master narrative that made an oracle identifiable as such for the community. This master narrative, in the first place, was a sort of "script of life"[33] for the oracle herself, in which she had reframed her life experiences. It usually had emerged through a "dialogical" process that involved the oracle, her family, religious figures, and the entire community. At a later stage, a number of accounts concerning her life appeared, integrating the input of members of the community who had witnessed the events, and these accounts were often synthesized into the life story by the oracle's assistant—called "the translator" (*lo tsa ba*), i.e., the person who translated the divine speech for the human beings. This process—typical of grassroots oracles, i.e., those who were not institutionalized *a priori*—conferred the sense of authenticity and authoritativeness to the narrative that empowered the oracle for the community. This narrative was then recited again and again and framed the process of divination in a way comparable to Samten Karmay's description of narratives of origin that are recited to situate and empower a ritual (Karmay 1998:245).

It is possible to consider what happened around the compilation of the biography of Chokyi Dronma as a similar process, part of the construction of the story that had originated with accounts of her life experience and developed further after her death. The result was an empowering life narrative with an authorship that transcended both Chokyi Dronma and the biographer as individuals and had acquired authority and authenticity precisely through the multiple inputs. In addition, as an emanation of a deity, the persona at the center of this master narrative, like the oracle, was at the same time human and divine, individual and collective. The interesting parallels between oracles and incarnated lamas, noticed by several scholars and to which I shall return in chapter 5, cast a particular light on the process of narrative production, with its singularities and pluralities.

Brockmeier and Harré, discussing the complexities of authorship as part of the difficulties in defining narrative, draw attention to the fact that tales may be created jointly or cooperatively as part of "collective remembering" (Brockmeier and Harré 2001:46; Middleton and Edward 1990). More radically, they underline how "for Bakhtin every story is multivoiced and every world is 'multivoiced'; its meaning is determined by its countless previous contexts of use. Bakhtin called this the 'dialogical principle' of discourse, emphasizing its inherent interindividuality" (2001:46). Chokyi Droma's biography, like the narratives of oracles' life stories, seems to reflect, perhaps in an extreme way, the interindividuality of the process of authorship, involving herself, her disciples, and the biographer and embracing multiple temporalities—past, present and [prophetic] future, and multiple positions—human and divine, male and female.

Brockmayer and Harré also underline how "stories are told from 'positions,' that is, they 'happen' in local moral orders in which the rights and duties of persons as speakers influence the location of the prime authorial voice" (Brockmeier and Harré 2001:46). Accordingly, the voices of the members of Chokyi Dronma's retinue, whose input, I suggest, merged into the narrative, are heard not only in the reported speeches but also in the multiple positions that the main narrative voice seems to take. This gives a visibility to women's networks, women's kinship strategies, and female activities that is somewhat unusual for a male author and even highlights a woman's deliberate nongendered approach to a certain situation. Nevertheless, it is difficult to single out these other voices neatly and separate them from the voice of the biographer, since a unifying narrative inherently creates its own perspective. In fact, "narrative has a tendency to fuse diverse elements such as agents, goals, means, interactions, circumstances, unexpected results, and other factors into a structured but inherently biased 'whole'" (Brockmeier and Harré 2001:46).

It is thus necessary to look at the narrative in terms of the overall biographical project as well as of its different elements, and in relation to its aims within the context of the religion and politics of its time. The text aimed particularly at a readership of followers of the tradition who had a strong interest in the question of spiritual succession and in defending the fact that Chokyi Dronma, although a woman, was Bodong Chogle Namgyal's spiritual heir (see chapter 5). However, it aimed also at a more general readership of religious women and of male practitioners who supported the "soteriological inclusiveness" (Sponberg 1992:3ff.) of Buddhism against more gender-discriminatory views. Most importantly, it aimed at all those against whom these positions had to be defended.

Under this light, the methodology of the biography appears open to multiple approaches of investigation. It is useful to look at it as a historical source, analyzing the intersections between its narrative and other sources, as I did in chapters 1 and 2 in order to reconstruct the life of Chokyi Dronma in its historical context, and will do in chapters 5 and 6 in order to explore its later readings. At the same time it is important to recognize the difficulties inherent in the nature of Tibetan biographical writing that could be compared with the problems that led historians to be diffident of Western hagiographies. The biography of Chokyi Dronma, in fact, offers us a glimpse into the early stages of a process similar to that whereby the life of a saint appears as "the literary crystallization of the perception of a collective conscience" (de Certeau 1988:270). The narrative emerged through the actions and voices of the people who experienced Chokyi Dronma and eventually shared the vision that she had been revealed as the human embodiment of the deity Dorje Phagmo; from this point of view, the narrative shares similarities with other stories of revelation, like the Gospels.[34] Later chapters will show how the account of Chokyi Droma's life was re-read and reframed several times as the tradition developed over the centuries. At this stage, however, without aiming at a factual representation of the materials that the biographer wove into the text, I will just outline the most significant voices that a reader can perceive in the narrative.

Chokyi Dronma is clearly the protagonist, and the main narrative voice is deeply informed by her position. Even though at the outset of the text she is defined in relation to her main lama, a common feature in the life of Tibetan religious women, the complexity of her relationships and experiences makes her the center of the narrative in her own right. This is underlined by the numerous passages of her reported speech and thought. As outlined above, the quotations from Chokyi Dronma may have been based on notes she took herself, on earlier oral accounts she gave to the biographer, on oral and written accounts concerning her by Deleg Chodren, and even on the biographer's recollection and creative elaboration.

Deleg Chodren appears to have been a nun from an ordinary background (no family of origin is mentioned) and enters the narrative almost casually, as an attendant of Chokyi Dronma at the beginning of the princess's monastic life (folio 52). Her significance increases gradually as the narrative develops so that she becomes almost a second protagonist. Her name appears many times, and there are a few entire episodes that are centered on her alone. There are passages that deal with her spiritual development (e.g., folios 69 and 136), references to her relationship with Bodong Chogle Namgyal, and passages where the detail could only be known by her, for she was the only protagonist of these minor subplots (e.g., folio 102). As mentioned in the introduction, she represents a skillful narrative device for engaging the reader, embodying common sense and conventional thinking, strikingly human in contrast to the increasingly divine Chokyi Dronma. However, the numerous passages of her reported speech and thought suggest also that she actually provided a significant part of the information on which the biography was based. She almost certainly provided many oral accounts, and she may also have taken notes during Chokyi Dronma's life, as Konchog Gyaltshen did for Bodong Chogle Namgyal. Toward the end there is an enigmatic passage (folio 135a) in which Chokyi Dronma seems to empower her as the most worthy among the group in keeping the tradition of their master. Possibly she was the mastermind behind the biographical project, since she is reported as having been deeply involved in the events surrounding Chokyi Dronma's death and the search for her reincarnation (see Biography of Thangtong Gyalpo 308). The analogy with the oracle may shed further light on her role: in conveying the voice of Chokyi Dronma, both an extraordinary human being who had died and an embodied deity that transcended space and time, she may have been to the biographer like the "translator" mediating between the human and the divine.

In a more indirect way the narrative echoes the voices of Chokyi Dronma's spiritual masters (Bodong Chogle Namgyal, Thangtong Gyalpo, and, more briefly, Vanaratna), the people related to her, and other members of the community. Even though most of this material was filtered through the accounts of Chokyi Dronma and Deleg Chodren, some of the dialogues, rumors, and detailed descriptions suggest that the biographer had firsthand experience of the voices he recorded and the events he described. In addition, Thangtong Gyalpo's voice seems to be present in a direct way through his letters; indeed, the original of one of them—his letter of introduction that Chokyi Dronma took on her journey—is quoted in full (see chapter 4).

It is also possible to detect a number of different narrative layers that reflect a fundamental distinction between a biographer's metanarrative and the oral and textual materials he wove into it. The narrative shows variations in style that seem to reflect the nature of the different sources concerning different phases of Chokyi Dronma's life.

Childhood accounts seem to be rich in biographical tropes (especially related to the Buddha's life) and focus on the reading in hindsight that interprets the girl's miracles and extraordinary behaviors as early signs of her divine secret identity (even these are, however, interwoven with concrete and contingent detail). This part of the narrative seems to have been based on the many stories that usually start to circulate in a community when an extraordinary individual emerges, and perhaps on some recollections of Chokyi Dronma herself that the biographer heard from her or from Deleg Chodren. This section is only nine folios long, indicating the relative sparsity of detailed material available to the biographer (although the father, mother, sister, and brother were still alive, they were presumably not accessible as sources of information).

Accounts concerning Chokyi Dronma's secular life are highly dramatic and focus to a large extent on the scenes of her marriage, her renunciation of her royal life, and her liberating journey to the monastery; as in the previous case, the narrative seems to have been based on popular recollection of dramatic events, tropes based on the life of the Buddha and that of the female *mahāsiddha* Lakṣmīṅkarā (see below). These seem to be interwoven with direct accounts from Chokyi Dronma and Deleg Chodren; for instance, there are a significant number of passages of reported speech of the father-in-law and some of the mother-in-law and the husband. This section is more extensive than the previous one, at thirty-three folios, and covers approximately four years.

The description of monastic and yogic life is richer in ordinary detail and seems to reflect the fact that Deleg Chodren, presumably one of the main sources for the compilation of the narrative, had firsthand experience of the events. The (presumed) biographer starts to appear as a direct witness through the description of some episodes, for example, the extraordinarily detailed description of the production of books and statues after Bodong Chogle Namgyal's death. This section is longer, fifty-eight folios, and covers a period of approximately ten years.

The final journey is even richer in detail, some of which appears to be completely irrelevant to a conventional biographical project. The narrative is less expansive and florid and more descriptive in a dry, specific style. As the (presumed) biographer was part of the group that escorted the princess on her journey, the narrative concerning the final part of Chokyi Dronma's life seems to reflect both his eyewitness accounts and those of Deleg Chodren. This section is notable for the number of people who are named, ranging from significant donors (possibly because it is hoped that they will continue to be sponsors) to individual nuns carrying out relatively mundane tasks, presumably because they are still part of the religious community (folio 125). The biographer seems not to have had the time or the perspective to weave all the people and events he is mentioning in an overall framework that was functional to the narrative. The section, including the start of the journey to Tsari, is forty-three folios. Although this is less than the middle section, it covers a much shorter time span, some two years, an indication that more detail is being included about events that occurred during this period.

Although Chokyi Dronma's life can be subdivided into distinct phases (and I introduced subheadings in the translation), the narrative presents only one formal separation: between her worldly life and her religious life, which is a key temporal and narrative threshold. In addition, two other important transitions are highlighted by a particular emphasis given to geographical features: the crossing of the high pass between Chokyi Dronma's homeland and her country of destination as a new bride marks the transition between childhood and married life; on the same pass, a highly dramatic scene, bidding farewell to her mother and sister, marks her departure for her final journey. The crossing of the pass has thus spatial, temporal, and narrative dimensions. As a literary image it has particular poignancy, for such a crossing is usually a highly significant moment in a journey and is marked by a ritual act such as placing a stone on a cairn or hanging prayer flags. The pass may refer not only to a geographical and possibly political boundary but also to an important temporal boundary: stars "crossing the pass" are an important marker for the transition of time.

The narrative presents not only an overall teleological orientation toward the revelation of Chokyi Dronma's secret identity but also a number of different temporalities that reflect the different "narrative models" (Brockmeier 2000:59) of the sources on which the biography was based: vivid and timeless images of dramatic moments; cyclical representations of daily routines; the future of prophecy and utopian visions; Buddhist civilization and the Tibetan empire as a sort of classical antiquity that has to be revived; the ancestral past quoted in the present in a letter of introduction; flashbacks in which the biographer chooses to follow the temporality of communication rather than that of the actual events (for example, the announcement of the daughter's death arriving with a letter); the cyclical time of the seasons that mark the proper moment for begging trips or for traveling; the dates that mark birth and death in a stark, cosmic way.

The many voices and the different renderings of spaces and times are thus woven in a highly evocative narrative, distinctive for a complexity that exceeds any single predictable biographical project and transcends individual authorship in any sense.

## Genre, Purpose, and Style

In this section I shall look briefly at questions of genre, purpose, and style of the biography and try to explore the reasons behind these distinctive features. The biography of Chokyi Dronma can be considered an example of a genre popular among Buddhists of different traditions (see Tambiah 1984; Cook forthcoming). The narrative presents the distinctive soteriological and hagiographical features that are reflected in the Tibetan term defining this sort of biographical literature: *namthar* (*rnam thar*—i.e., "liberation from all [worldly phenomena and concerns]"). This is therefore an exemplary account of striving for enlightenment, written as a model for other followers of Tibetan Buddhism (Gyatso 1998:102ff.). In relation to the conventional Tibetan classification of biographies as "outer," "inner," and "secret," the text presents mainly—but not exclusively—the features of an "outer" biography, dealing with the concrete events of Chokyi Dronma's life rather than her doctrinal practices or her secret visions and mystical experiences. This is also reflected in the title that defines the text simply as a *namthar*, a biography, and not, for example, as a *sangnam* (*gsang rnam*), a secret biography.

The narrative is somewhat unusual in that it does not contain as many overblown and stereotypical elements as other contemporary biographies and includes a lot of apparently irrelevant detail. The structure is relatively loose, not trying to organize the narrative in "deeds" or categories of activities, as is often the case in this kind of work. Its linear style follows the events mostly in chronological order.

The introductory passage, however, immediately reveals one of the distinctive features of this work: the central aim of the narrative is not only to describe an exemplary life but also to establish the persona of Chokyi Dronma as an incarnation of the goddess Dorje Phagmo. The text has thereby a revelatory character that is explicitly expressed by the author's prayer asking for permission to be allowed to put into writing "the highest secret." This is further emphasized by the subsequent sentence that begins with "*de la*," i.e., "in relation to this [secret]," and continues by saying that the princess was born in a certain place with a certain ancestry. Even though it is mainly an "outer" biography, the text shows aspects of secrecy, revelation, and prophecy; these seem, however, to be related more to the nature of the deity Dorje Phagmo and the conditions under which the biography was written than to the genre.

A particular stylistic feature of this biography is its relative lack of homogeneity. It alternates between stretches of narrative that conform with conventional descriptions of deeds and passages that seem to be sketches taken straight from life, in all its concreteness and incongruity. There are episodes and details that are not very useful to the overall design and are occasionally at odds with the expected: singling out the names of the nuns who helped with organizing food and tea for celebrations; describing Chokyi Dronma's inability to read Thangtong Gyalpo's handwriting and her need for Deleg Chodren's assistance to decipher it; giving an account of her unsuccessful attempts at establishing a nunnery; revealing her inability to get the people of Palmo Choding to build water channels. This richness of extra and unexpected detail in the narrative underpins our assumption of closeness to the events. In this respect Chokyi Dronma's biography presents some parallels with that of Tsunpa Choleg (1437–1521), compiled on the basis of the lama's own autobiographical account (Everding 2000:223–226). This interpretation is also supported by other texts that report the deeds of great religious figures. Irrelevant detail and stories of failures that are not functional in a celebratory narrative are significant; for example, the *dBa' bzhed* (folio 11a–14a) reports the mission of Padmasambhava to Tibet as having had little success, and this is an indication that it was written closer to the events, before the rise of his major mythology, and can be seen as evidence to support his historicity (Pasang Wangdu and Diemberger 2000:14).

The numerous details may also suggest that the biographer had a specific commitment to accuracy due to the conditions under which the writing was being done: as part of a process of collective remembering that followed the untimely death of the princess, when most of the people who had experienced the events were still alive. Aiming to reveal and establish the secret identity of the princess, the text had to be seen as authentic and authoritative by the community of followers, at the cost of not always complying with expected literary models. The passage in Thangtong Gyalpo's biography (308–309) that reports Chokyi Dronma's death and the identification of Kunga Sangmo as her following reincarnation shows that the clear recollection of her previous life underpinned her authenticity. This was extremely important at a time when the line was not yet properly established and such claims had to be particularly well substantiated to be accepted. The stylistic features of the biography of Chokyi Dronma reflect the rationale of how it was compiled: the direct quotation of speeches, thoughts, and documents, such as Thangtong Gyalpo's letter, and the mention of direct witnesses to the events reinforce the feeling of authenticity and authoritativeness.[35] Yet these quoted passages are often set in stark contrast to the poetic descriptions of meaningful, emotion-filled moments—for instance, when Chokyi Dronma rides toward Po-rong Palmo Choding with the sunshine on her forehead (folio 45b), or when she heals a disciple of Bodong Chogle Namgyal who recovers like a withering flower after having been watered (folio 88a). A further remarkable feature of the text, which seems to be linked to the process of production, is its abundance of collo-quial expressions from the Tsang region and the numerous spelling and grammati-cal mistakes. Assuming that the biography was composed in a somewhat improvi-satory way, by gathering all possible sources and relying on unedited materials and oral accounts, it is not surprising that the text has the feel of an unpolished draft. However, the illuminations at the beginning, the opening verses, and the erudite and poetic style of the framing narrative testify to the fact that it was meant to be something much more authoritative than an informal compilation of notes.

## The Puzzling Title

The full title of the biography reads: "The Biography of the Venerable Chokyi Dronma, the Third Reincarnation of the Wisdom Ḍākinī Sonam Dren[ma]." This formulation raises some complex questions concerning our understanding of Chokyi Dronma's life and its relation to the establishment of a line of reincar-nations. Was she the first, the third, or an undefined number in a series? There are different schools of thought on this issue, which will be dealt with in chapter 5. Here I shall just address the specific questions raised by the title and its odd relationship to the narrative.

The biography definitely sets out to reveal that Chokyi Dronma was the ema-nation of the deity Dorje Phagmo; however, there is not even a hint in the text that she was the reincarnation of a historical figure. Sonam Drenma is not men-tioned at all, though it is possible that she appeared in the nonextant part of the text. In any case, it is certain that Chokyi Dronma was not recognized as her reincarnation until she was an adult. There is little doubt that she and her next reincarnation, Kunga Sangmo, were the ones who concretely established the tradition—as claimed by its current representatives (see Thubten Namgyal and Dorje Phagmo Dechen Chodron 1995:31–58).

The Sonam Drenma mentioned in the title was the tantric consort of Phag-modrupa Dorje Gyalpo (1110–1170). He was the founder of the Phagmodrupa monastery and of the subsect of the Kagyupa named after it, and was also one of the key figures in the opening of the Tsari shrine.[36] According to the *Bo dong Chos 'byung* (folio 20a) and the *'Brug pa chos 'byung* (406), Sonam Drenma was considered an emanation of the deity Dorje Phagmo and had some special links to the holy place of Tsari, particularly sacred to her. In a passage of the biography of Bodong Chogle Namgyal written in 1453 (391), there is a reference to her and to the fact that she was a predecessor of Chokyi Dronma. According to this reckoning, Chokyi Dronma was the third Tibetan incarnation of the deity. I shall return in detail to the construction of this lineage in chapter 5; for the moment, it can be observed that the title of the biography reflects an early attempt at constructing the lineage of the Dorje Phagmo's reincarnations, an effort that seems to have started toward the end of Chokyi Dronma's life. However, this is not reflected in the narrative and may, at most, have appeared in the final, nonextant part. Chokyi Dronma had apparently become her own divine persona before being recognized as the reincarnation of great women of the past.

## The Elusive End

One of the biggest challenges presented by the text is the lack of its final section. Fortunately, there is some information available concerning the last part of Chokyi Dronma's life, from two texts that presumably relied on her biography and other accounts for their compilation: one of the biographies of Thangtong Gyalpo and the *Bo dong Chos 'byung*.

Concerning the missing ending, two main hypotheses can be formulated: it has unintentionally been lost, or it was removed intentionally, possibly due to the problematic content of the text, which could have become unacceptable for continued circulation.

The first hypothesis is reasonably straightforward. For example, someone interested in the holy place of Tsari may have borrowed the final part of the text and used it as a guide; or perhaps the final part was made up of a few folios that were damaged and progressively destroyed by inappropriate storage. I have also heard about holy texts of which some pages went missing because they had become part of amulets and medicines.[37]

More intriguing is the second hypothesis, suggested by the fact that the whole portion describing the journey to Tsari is missing, which could indicate some intentionality. That part of the text included the travelogue of the journey, a description of her activities in Tsari, probably details of Chokyi Dronma's death, and a colophon describing time, place, and authorship of the biography. An additional part describing the identification of the next reincarnation of Chokyi Dronma, Kunga Sangmo, might have been included as well. It seems that Gyurme Dechen, while compiling his biography of Thangtong Gyalpo, relied on a source that detailed these events in continuity with the narrative of Chokyi Dronma, mentioning the same people and places and reaching up to the early years of Kunga Sangmo. The hypothesis of a deliberate removal of the final part of the text opens up a range of possibilities linked to the significance of Tsari, the death of the princess and the identification of her reincarnation, and even the conditions of production of the text.

Tsari has been a holy place in southeastern Tibet at least since the twelfth century. Different schools established their hermitages in the region, with a particularly strong presence of the Karmapa. A peculiarity of this place is that some of its holiest areas are not accessible to women, even religious women, and that it is surrounded by a recurring mythology of defeated transgression, i.e., a history of women who defied the ban and suffered the sometimes fatal consequences (Huber 1994:350ff.). This kind of narrative has reemerged in the contemporary Tibetan context. For example, in September 2005 in Kongpo, I was told that three nuns went on pilgrimage to Tsari and entered the forbidden area, claiming that in modern times this rule was no longer applicable; two of them died shortly afterward as a consequence of their transgression. The ban on women became particularly strict after the establishment of Gelugpa power in Tibet after 1642. If the text contained something problematic—such as Chokyi Dronma's access to prohibited places or highly secret information concerning her as the embodiment of the deity, awkward details of her death and reincarnation, or even controversial claims about the control of certain places or sacred items—it may have been withdrawn from circulation and kept in a guarded place or even destroyed. This may have happened because of the implementation of stricter rules concerning women in Buddhist hierarchies or a local clampdown on female religious practitioners or even claims on objects or places that had been taken over by Chokyi Dronma's followers. The text may also have contained controversial information concerning its compilation. The definitive answer must wait until the missing part turns up.

For the time being, it is possible to observe that both texts that give some information concerning Chokyi Dronma's final years refer to her death very concisely, without the miraculous events that usually accompany the description of a spiritual master's demise. Most sources that refer to Chokyi Dronma, however, mention a skull with extraordinary features connected to her, possibly a skull cup made from her own cranium. The biography of Thangtong Gyalpo by Gyurme Dechen refers to Chokyi Dronma's skull as related to the prophecy that he received from the deity Dorje Phagmo the first time he went to Kongpo in 1420: "Also, in the future the Dorje Phagmo will leave a skull with special features (*mtshan ldan thod pa*) in this place" (Biography of Thangtong Gyalpo 134). This prophecy was reiterated by Thangtong Gyalpo on several occasions when he announced at the monastery of Menmogang in Tsari Nesar, i.e., the "New Tsari" east of "old Tsari," that "a skull with special features" would come, together with a mountain dweller from Ngari.[38] This was considered to have come true when Chokyi Dronma, as the embodied Dorje Phagmo, came to Menmogang and died, leaving there the famous skull (see Biography of Thangtong Gyalpo 284; Stearns 1980:27; Stearns 2007). But was it hers, or an important preexisting relic to which she had gained access as incarnation of the deity? Cyrus Stearns (2007) follows what appears to be the most plausible hypothesis, suggested by Gyurme Dechen: dying there, Chokyi Dronma left her own "skull with special features" in the Menmogang monastery, a precious relic of her as the incarnation of the Dorje Phagmo deity. However, as Thangtong Gyalpo prophesied the arrival of the skull at Menmogang, the people are reported to have reacted with surprise and concern because they thought that another relic, the famous "skull with special features" located at old Tsari, would be transferred to Menmogang, leaving the main seat "vacant." This implies that the people were at first confused and concerned by the consequences of such a transfer, and also that the skull eventually enshrined at Menmogang was a different one, i.e., Chokyi Dronma's was one of many holy skulls . . . unless the main skull of Tsari ended up being transferred for a short period to Menmogang when she arrived there. This last hypothesis is less plausible than the one suggested by Stearns, but not impossible. The translator Sonam Gyatso, who visited Tsari in 1460, refers to the fact that "the skull with special features"[39] had just been brought back to its original seat, at Dongpokhar, after internal feuds at Tsari had prompted its transfer to Dakpo.[40] Before this, the skull had been seen at Dongpokhar by Go Lotsawa Shonnu Pal during his sojourn in Tsari in 1439 (before Chokyi Dronma's death) (see *Blue Annals* 824; Ehrhard 2002:57). The existence of a skull or skulls related to the Dorje Phagmo is supported by

Konchog Palsang and Monpa Dewa Sangpo's biography of Thangtong Gyalpo mentioning an enigmatic prophecy related to the skulls of Chokyi Dronma's past, present, and future lives.[41] Also, the sixteenth-century *'Brug pa chos 'byung* (406) mentions a similar prophecy according to which Dorje Phagmo's skull had come to Tsari in the twelfth century. The text refers to the girl "with special features," who was the consort of Phagmo Druba Dorje Gyalpo and an emanation of the deity Dorje Phagmo [i.e., Sonam Drenma]. It says that she died prematurely, and that her skull magically announced that it wanted to go to its shrine at Tsari and subsequently disappeared. However, there is no mention of Chokyi Dronma. There is only a clear reference to "Chokyi Dronma's skull with special features" being kept at Tsari in the brief text that goes with a small *thangka* of the white Cakrasaṃvara that was made under the auspices of Chokyi Dronma and is currently kept at the Samding monastery. The precious relic played a role in the reckoning of Bodong Chogle Namgyal's spiritual succession and the formation of the Dorje Phagmo reincarnation lineage. I therefore shall return to it in chapter 5. However, like the account of Chokyi Dronma's last days, the story of her skull remains elusive, perhaps hidden by the same ancient controversies[42] and confused by the shared identity between Chokyi Dronma and the deity of which she was an emanation and for which she was celebrated.

## Biographical Models That Informed the Writing

Several different biographical models are clearly identifiable in the narrative of Chokyi Dronma's biography. Buddha's life, as would be expected, is clearly a prime source of inspiration, a "paradigm" (Tambiah 1984). This is a default model in Tibetan biographical writing (Gyatso 1998:111). It is worth noting that Chokyi Dronma's life presented particular parallels with that of Prince Siddhartha, as they both renounced their royal background to devote themselves to their spiritual practice, and that biographical accounts of the historical Buddha, such as the *Lalitavistara,* are explicitly mentioned in the biography.

In the narrative the predictable hagiographic motives taken from the twelve deeds of the Buddha, adapted to the specific circumstances in which she lived, blend with the lively description of Chokyi Dronma's dramatic experiences. The Buddha's life was thus used as a literary model in a nongendered way. Accordingly, Chokyi Dronma follows the paradigm of the protagonist, Prince Siddhartha, rather than that of the female figures of the story. In spite of such nongendered or cross-gendered views, to which I shall return in chapter 4, a number of female templates are important. Chokyi Dronma's biography shares many similarities with the story of the eighth-century mad Indian princess Lakṣmīṅkarā, one of the eighty-four *mahāsiddhas*. As Chokyi Dronma became part of a lineage of Dorje Phagmo reincarnations, Lakṣmīṅkarā was considered the starting point; she is explicitly referred to in the biography of Bodong Chogle Namgyal (see chapter 5). Even though Lakṣmīṅkarā is not mentioned in Chokyi Dronma's biography, her history was clearly the source of some of the tropes that informed the writing, especially the episode of the marriage and the dramatic renunciation of royal life. She might also be indirectly evoked by a number of epithets used for Chokyi Dronma.[43]

Lakṣmīṅkarā's story is briefly narrated in Abhayadatta's *Stories of the Eighty-Four Mahāsiddhas* (Abhayadatta in Robinson 1979:250ff.; Shaw 1994:110ff.)[44] and is extensively referred to by Go Lotsawa in the *Blue Annals,* which indicates that at that time it must have been particularly popular.[45] Lakṣmīṅkarā is associated with Urgyen (Oḍḍiyāna), the land of the *ḍākinīs,* located to the west of Tibet, presumably in an area corresponding to current north Pakistan. She was the sister of the King of Oḍḍiyāna called Indrabhūti. As a royal princess, she had been promised to the king of a non-Buddhist country, whom she disliked. She married him but opposed the non-Buddhist practices that were meant to welcome her as a bride, and eventually escaped the unwanted marriage by pretending madness: she unbound her hair, rubbed ashes on her body, and behaved erratically. She took refuge in a cremation ground, where she dwelled clad only in her long hair, twigs, and dirt, and appeared light blue because of the ashes that covered her skin. After devoting herself to meditation in complete seclusion, she achieved ultimate spiritual realization and became the spiritual master of numerous disciples, including the man to whom she had been promised. Lakṣmīṅkarā is considered to be the author of a few texts that appear in the Tibetan Buddhist canon and is related to a distinctive practice of Avalokiteśvara that was particularly popular in the Mangyul-Gungthang area.[46] Chokyi Dronma's own experience of an unwanted and unhappy marriage and the conflation of the narrative of her life with that of the famous female *mahāsiddha* are probably why, over the centuries, she became the heroine of unhappy brides and lovers (see preface).

Chokyi Dronma's biography seems to have also been informed by the narrative model of the tantric consort, which is evoked right at the beginning. Whether this was meant only symbolically or referred to concrete forms of interaction with her spiritual masters is clouded in ambiguity (see chapter 4). Narratives of holy women who became consorts of their teachers were widespread at that time. There were extensive accounts concerning Maṇḍārava and Yeshe Tshogyal, consorts of the eighth-century tantric master Padmasambhava. They appeared conspicuously in the narratives concerning the life of this master that had flourished in Tibet since the fourteenth century (see chapter 1). The twelfth-century mystic Machig Labdron, who became one of the consorts of the Indian *yogin* Phadampa Sangye, was also famous. In addition, there was fragmentary information concerning less-known religious women from the princess's region (see Martin 2005:49ff.) such as Machig Shama, a contemporary of Machig Labdron, who was born in Phadrug in Southern Lato and became the consort of Ma Lotsawa and possibly of Phadampa Sangye. She was reckoned among the ancestors of Bodong Chogle Namgyal (Biography of Bodong Chogle Namgyal 16), and her story must have been fairly popular, for Go Lotsawa reported it in the *Blue Annals* (Roerich 1988:219ff.) in the chapter devoted to the *Lam 'bras* tradition.

Even though the lives of a number of Indian and Tibetan women may have informed the narrative as general templates, the biography does not seem to acknowledge any of them explicitly as an inspirational model. Intertextuality is generally reflected in the mention of evocative detail. The only specific mention of other famous holy women is two brief references to Machig Labdron: one in connection with her ritual cycle and the other in the reported letter of Thangtong Gyalpo, from which it appears that he considered Machig Labdron a sort of predecessor of Chokyi Dronma (see chapter 4).

A biographical model that applies conspicuously to the narrative of Chokyi Dronma's life is that of the crazy *yogin,* of which the twelfth-century *yogin* Milarepa can be seen as the Tibetan prototype. From this point of view Chokyi Dronma can be grouped with other fifteenth-century figures who challenged all sorts of conventions and the growing clerical orthodoxy, such as Tsangnyon Heruka and Drugpa Kuleg but also, to some extent, Thangtong Gyalpo (Samuel 1993:518), referred to in the biography by his full name and his well-known epithet, the "madman of the empty valley" (126). Under this light the mad princess Lakṣmīṅkarā and the *yoginī* Machig Labdron appear as female prototypes for Chokyi Dronma. Her unconventional behavior runs throughout the narrative, and I shall return to it in chapter 4. The theme of the transgression of social conventions also had a direct link with the deity she embodied: Dorje Phagmo was the Tibetan adaptation of Vajravārāhī. As already described in chapter 1, this female deity was at the center of an Indian cult of Śivaite origin that originally involved women, especially those of low caste, and aimed at transcending any duality and thereby liberating the mind. Spiritual awareness was achieved through practices that implied a ritual confrontation with what, according to convention, was feared and brought about defilement, such as charnel grounds, corpses, and menstrual blood (English 2002:35ff.; Tsuda 1978:167ff.).

A very significant and inspirational model for the biography of Chokyi Dronma was that of her master Bodong Chogle Namgyal, *Feast of Miracles* by Amoghasiddhi Jigme Bang, which is explicitly mentioned in the text. This biography is neatly organized in twelve deeds, like Buddha's biographical accounts. Chokyi Dronma's biographer, however, rather than emulating its rigorous structure and poetic language, seems to have used it more loosely: first as a motivation for writing, second as the basis for cross-referencing; third as a source of inspiration for common tropes.[47]

Finally, some of the distinctive imperial themes reflected in the biography were certainly informed by narratives concerning the dynastic period that were particularly popular in Gungthang at that time. They were part of the general revival of the imperial legacy (see chapter 1), and during the reign of Chokyi Dronma's brother and nephews the *Maṇi bka' 'bum,* the so-called testament of Songtsen Gampo, was printed in several editions,[48] as was Sangye Lingpa's *Padma bka' thang,*[49] a fourteenth-century hagiographical account of the life of Padmasmabhava.

*The Manuscript and Its Enigmas*

4

PRINCESS, NUN, *YOGINĪ*

*Porong, October 2004. We left Palmo Choding monastery at dawn, riding west toward* the village of Labuk and its ancient Bonpo temple. The first rays of the rising sun are touching the mountain peaks that frame the vast plain of the Palkhu Palthang as we climb toward a small pass overlooking the blue expanse of the Palkhu lake. Dawa, one of the best read and most knowledgeable Tibetan nomads I have ever met, is riding in front. He is young, energetic, and completely devoted to the history and the traditions of his region and his country, which he came to know from his family, from local documents, and from the recent reprintings of Tibetan classics.[1] These texts form an integral part of the paraphernalia and general clutter of his dark, smoky house and nomad tent, as he always takes some along on his travels. As we approach the summit of the pass, he stops and points to an indentation in the landscape, telling me that there Chokyi Dronma had started to build water channels, following the example of Bodong Chogle Namgyal. The water from the stream above should have been flowing in this direction to irrigate the area beyond the pass. There are still traces of ancient fields, channels, and a few ruins, although some might be more ancient than hers.

The microclimate of the Palkhu lake seems to have enabled agriculture in an area otherwise habitable exclusively by nomads. There are a few villages of farmers along the shore, cultivating some of the highest fields in the world, small pockets of land that can be irrigated by nearby springs. Chokyi Dronma, however, had grand plans. Like many former Buddhist masters, she wanted to transform arid slopes into cultivated land as the basis for a flourishing Buddhist civilization. That was five hundred years ago, but she still seems to be here—in Dawa's words, in the enthusiasm with which he narrates her deeds and those of her master, Bodong Chogle Namgyal. The plans of this extraordinary fifteenth-century woman seem ambitious indeed, and perhaps not exactly plausible—one can understand why they may have been controversial. Dawa's explanation, however, brings her story to life in this spectacular but harsh landscape at the interface between the agricultural and the nomadic worlds. Munificent princess and begging nun, idiosyncratic *yoginī* and divine incarnation, Chokyi Dronma seems to embody the conventional combination of outer, inner, and secret identities, which appears in her biography in a striking way.

Chokyi Dronma's biography vividly describes her experiences, the multiple ways she appeared in the eyes of her contemporaries, and the many transformations she underwent. In this chapter I explore some of the most interesting and distinctive themes raised by the narrative: personal traits, domestic details, existentialist crises, and how she was perceived in the religious and social context of her time. These are linked to wider issues such as gender, relatedness, and her symbolic representation as part of a reincarnation lineage.

## Agent of Innovation in a "Tibetan Renaissance"?

Tibet's unification under the Sakya-Yuan rule, seen both in continuity with and in contrast to the ancient empire, had substantially improved communication, long-distance commercial relations, and cultural exchange. The subsequent fragmentation into discrete polities made it possible for a number of local rulers to assert their own power. However, they were compelled to manage their defense, economy, and political prestige independently. Urban centers had grown up around their castles, especially those located at crucial intersections of long-distance trade routes. Political prestige and territorial control were achieved not only through military and economic might but also, more indirectly, through marriage alliances and religious patronage.

Chokyi Dronma's time was undoubtedly very turbulent, but also fertile and even seminal for many aspects of Tibetan culture, a fact that has been pointed out by numerous scholars of Tibetan art and religion (see for example Ricca and Lo Bue 1993:11–32). The general historical picture, however, which is often defined as the "Middle Ages" (Snellgrove and Richardson 1995 [1968]), "the rise of Ecclesiastic Power" (Stein 1972), is often characterized in negative terms, in contrast to Tibet's unification under the Dalai Lama. This kind of reading is sometimes reinforced by the evocation of medieval Europe, with its stereotypical images of feudalism, clerical power, rurality, and stagnation, as a parallel. But highlighting political unification as the central category of assessment neglects the important socioeconomic processes of this period, including the development of urban areas, trade and commercial relations, craftsmanship, and new technologies. This large-scale transformation had an extraordinary bearing on the cultural life of the time, which, as discussed in chapter 1, also benefited from the plurality of patronage and the lack of a hegemonic center (masterpieces such as the great *stūpa* of Gyantse emerged in this context). A variety of artistic styles and forms of cultural production developed in different areas of Tibet and in the different religious traditions, and these informed one another through continuous confrontation and borrowing.

The biography of Chokyi Dronma, especially if considered in relation to the histories of Gungthang, Southern Lato, and to a lesser extent Northern Lato, provides a unique insight into the great socioeconomic changes that made this innovative cultural production possible. Chokyi Dronma and the ruling family of Gungthang in particular were important agents in this process, which, somewhat provocatively, I call a "Tibetan Renaissance" (see introduction). In chapter 1 I suggested that, as in the city-states of the Italian Renaissance, political fragmentation followed increased urbanization, new commercial relations, the spread of literacy, the specialization of craftsmanship, and multiple forms of patronage that promoted artistic and technological innovations. These innovative visions were also informed by the creative revival of classical models through the rediscovery of ancient civilizations. My choice of the term "Renaissance" is thus set in contrast to static readings of Tibetan history that often fail to link individual achievements with the transforming socioeconomic and cultural context. In particular, it aims to evoke the dynamic aspect that has been read into the notion of "Renaissance" in the European context, which at an individual, narrative level was masterfully captured in the *Lives*[2] of its artists, as narrated by Giorgio Vasari.

The biography of Chokyi Dronma offers a glimpse into her world, and, remarkably, into her "city"[3] from her perspective as an elite woman devoted to the support of great deeds. After she completed the reproduction of the works of her master, his statue, and other items of religious art, she is reported to have paid the craftsmen and sold tools and materials to them:

[At the inauguration ceremony] the ocean of the monastic community, led by scholars and meditators, gathered there. There was Ponmo Sangring with the craftsmen who had made the statues, Lopon Ringyal with the painters, and the great secretary Konchog Gyaltshen with the carvers. There were also carpenters, statue makers, blacksmiths, and the ministers of the king, as well as all sorts of guests, ranging from officials to commoners, who had spontaneously gathered to watch. Everybody was offered food, as much as they wished, and a great deal of drink. Chokyi Dronma presented her father with a monastic robe and gave the others whatever they needed. Therefore, in this way, there was an excellent end to the celebration. The next day she paid all the workers. She also sold some items to them according to their request and for a price that was one fourth of the real price that would have been asked by good traders. In this way she kept all the workers happy. (94b–95a)

This passage shows clearly that there were groups of specialized craftsmen, they were paid, there was a market for tools and materials, and some of the craftsmen were well off enough to buy them. The relative prestige of the craftsmen is reflected in the prominence given them in the ceremony and in other passages that mention by name the leader of each group of specialists (folios 79b, 94a). In terms of technological skills, tools, and craftsmanship, Gungthang undoubtedly benefited from its position as gateway for trans-Himalayan trade and its proximity to Nepal, where artistic skills were highly developed, especially among the Newari population of the Kathmandu valley, and often exported. For example, Aniko, a Newari craftsman from Nepal, went to China during the Sakya-Yuan period and produced seminal artwork (Tucci 1999 [1949]:277). At the time of the Tibetan empire, craftsmen had been invited from Nepal for the production of religious monuments (for example, for the construction of Samye monastery; see *dBa' bzhed,* folios 11a, 12a), and Mangyul-Gungthang had been their main route of access. Nepali style is also reflected in several of Gungthang's monuments from the imperial period and from later centuries.[4] In the fourteenth and fifteenth centuries local rulers revived this tradition in a grand way. The lords of Southern Lato invited Nepali artists and craftsmen to create statues and other religious items.[5] Artists and craftsmen from Nepal apparently taught the people with whom they worked in Tibet, promoting the development of a local expertise that was inspired by Newari style but produced its own original syntheses. The names of the craftsmen recorded in Chokyi Dronma's biography are all Tibetan, which suggests the existence of established bodies of local specialized craftsmen and artists. Gungthang's thriving trade ensured that there was enough gold, silver, and other general equivalents to pay for tools, materials, and labor. It is curious that in the passage above Chokyi Dronma is described as having sold items under price, a hybrid act between a commercial transaction and a gift to those who participated in the enterprise. By asking for payment, she was able to give the tools to craftsmen who invested in and were likely to make good use of them. By keeping the price low, she pleased them and made it possible for those who were not particularly well off to afford the tools and materials. She thus preserved, at least in part, the morality of the donation while obtaining some income that she would reinvest in her subsequent deeds. The whole process seems to manifest Chokyi Dronma's entrepreneurial ability, the same skills that enabled her to support the numerous deeds of her masters. They benefited not only from her direct material support but also from what her kingdom offered as a thriving commercial center, a hub for specialized knowledge, and a melting pot of cultures. For example, Bodong Chogle Namgyal is the author of "one of the only surviving accounts of early Tibetan metallurgy" (Jackson 1996:96), which he undoubtedly produced by synthesizing and elaborating the technological knowledge available in the Gungthang kingdom and more generally in the region.

"The city" was Chokyi Dronma's model of civilization. Her innovative drive was informed by the revival of classical models in Buddhist India. The construction of irrigation channels and the expansion of cultivated areas was part of this ideal:

According to the idea of my omniscient great lama . . . the construction of the channels in the Palkhu area will benefit an area measuring one thousand *khal*. Everybody will benefit as long as no one raises a claim for a larger share. This will greatly help not only those who live on the Palthang plain next to the lake but also the many people from India and Nepal who come to Tibet regularly and face great hardship on the way. In ancient times people used to say that in order to establish a great monastery it was important to build it in an affluent big town to avoid problems with erratic irrigation systems; it was good to build it on the ruins of a former building so that completely new construction was not required. Also, the existing surrounding fields would produce large amounts of rice and numerous learned monks from many places would gather there. In the same way, scholars from Southern and Northern Lato and Ngari should gather here to study and practice his collected works (*dPal de kho na nyid 'dus pa*), spreading the doctrine of the Buddha. Also, thanks to these good deeds, this great land can remain peaceful. . . . [Despite her plan] the project did not go well after a while because what the local people said they would do was changeable. (folios 110a, b)

Bodong Chogle Namgyal had already tried to build water channels in the vicinity of Palmo Choding, but his attempt had failed because of a flood. Chokyi Dronma had tried to resume the plan on a grander scale, as part of her vision for the development of a Buddhist civilization that revived not only the ancient Indian model but also the early Buddhification of Tibet.

In imperial Tibet, Padmasambhava had a comparable plan to expand the cultivated areas,[6] which he tried to realize with the support of the Tibetan sovereign and the introduction of new technologies. His vision, however, was only partly endorsed by the Tibetans and met with serious resistance within the council of the ministers, which eventually forced him to leave the country. The *dBa' bzhed* and a number of other sources reveal his fundamental failure to fulfill his plan, although later, more legendary accounts tend to hide this detail. Both Padmasambhava and Chokyi Dronma faced opposition to their concept of radical transformation through the transplanting of technologies from other areas: presumably more sophisticated water engineering from Oḍḍiyāna[7] in the case of Padmasambhava; the irrigation system from agricultural centers such as Gungthang to nomad areas in the case of Chokyi Dronma. Padmasambhava had failed to win over the representatives of Tibetan indigenous culture and politics, who eventually imposed their view on the young Tibetan emperor; Chokyi Dronma never managed to find complete support for her enterprise in the nomadic communities of the high pasturelands of Porong.

Chokyi Dronma's grand plans were informed by the fact that Gungthang seemed to represent a distinctive form of urban agricultural civilization[8] and was in the vanguard in several domains. In chapter 1, I outlined Gungthang's important role in the development of printing in Tibet and how its carvers exported this expertise to other places. The passage describing the 1452 production of a new edition of the collected works of Bodong Chogle Namgyal, along with a statue of Bodong Chogle Namgyal and a wisdom *stūpa*, tells not only how she raised the funds, involving her father as well as a wide network of supporters, but also how she was directly involved in the work:

At the outset of the work, she had the contents list edited and proofread and ensured that the editors followed the same standards. She said, "If I do not act in this way, the deep meaning of this teaching will not be understood properly. This would damage myself and others." They proofread the work four times. The Queen of Knowledge herself carried out the first editorial process, together with Lama Kabchupa Pal Chime Drupa, Onpo Tingdzin, and the great *siddha* Changchubkyi Sung, as well as Loden and Osang, the two main attendants of the Omniscient. Then she involved forty-two skilled scribes[9] from Ngari under the guidance of Chogle Namgyal's great secretary, Konchog Gyaltshen. (folios 90b–91a)

Chokyi Dronma's crucial contribution to the reproduction of Bodong Chogle Namgyal's collected works seems to have disappeared in later accounts. The *Gung thang rgyal rab* states briefly that her father was the donor for

the White Residence of the omniscient Bodong Jigdrel [i.e., Bodong Chogle Namgyal] in the great monastery [i.e., Dzongkha Chode] and the statue reflecting the image (*sku brnyan*)[10] of this master. As far as his great writings are concerned, he made a printed edition of the *De nyid 'dus pa* [i.e., Bodong Chogle Namgyal's collected works] in the extensive, medium, and concise versions as well as of all his other works. (*Gung thang rgyal rabs* 123; see also Everding 2000:128, 129)

The remarkable role that Chokyi Dronma played in these events is visible because the biographer decided to highlight it on account of his own agenda—celebrating her as a divine woman. Her example may well have been more widespread than later historical records describe. The role of initiator and supporter, if not fulfilled by a particular throne holder, was easily neglected or just buried within bare lists of sponsors of great enterprises. The importance of Chokyi Dronma's own contribution and those of her kin and her network of nuns and noblewomen to multifarious enterprises may point to a pattern of behavior that was more than an exception.[11] It may reveal that women, especially from the political and economic elite, contributed to the great achievements of their times more significantly than it is formally recorded.

Chokyi Dronma's contribution to the reproduction of the collected works of Bodong Chogle Namgyal was crucial and seminal. Under her brother and his successors, printing flourished in Gungthang and enabled the circulation of some of the most important works of Tibetan literature (including the *Life and Songs of Milarepa* and the *Maṇi bka' 'bum;* see Ehrhard 2000:17). It was part of the process that later made the Trakar Taso monastery, located between Gungthang and Mangyul, an important printing house. A statue of its founder, Ngari Chogyal Lhatsun Rinchen Namgyal (1473–1557), is witness to the importance of the Gungthang royal family in this process.

Chokyi Dronma gave a great impetus to Gungthang's cultural development, as she was deeply committed to the spread of knowledge in the most comprehensive way, which included her wish to enhance access to religious education for women. She did not shy away from taking untrodden paths and challenging conventions. She even improvised herself, as a sort of choreographer and dance master at the request of Bodong Chogle Namgyal, creating the sacred dances for women that were performed by her nuns, despite their initial reluctance to dance in public (folios 80b–81b).

The description of Chokyi Dronma's enterprises, which includes references to individuals using their personal names and concrete details, vividly captures her ability to mobilize people and resources by relying on shared beliefs and networks of relations. At the interface between Tibet and Nepal, western and central Tibet, the agricultural and the nomadic worlds, the "traditional" and the "innovative," she seems to have been, in Frederik Barth's words, a "cultural entrepreneur" of her time.[12] She drew on her personal skills, which she had shown already as a young daughter-in-law in Southern Lato, as she started to take care of religious texts and buildings on her own initiative (folios 32–33). After she was ordained and became a begging nun, she was both a royal donor and a donee, which greatly enhanced the religious significance and the scope of her deeds. She channeled resources from a multitude of people of different standing toward the great achievements of her spiritual masters and became a spiritual master herself. She deeply understood the politics of patronage too. She readily accepted donations from members of local elites, who could not challenge her hierarchical superiority as a member of the monastic community and presumably also as a member of the Gungthang royal house, but was deliberately shy of interacting with the great rulers of her time who could have jeopardized her independence. Her approach was facilitated by the fact that there were several potential supporters, which gave her some leeway, but she could not avoid a visit to the Lord of Rinpung, Norbu Sangpo, as she passed through Shigatse. The hierarchical relationship between donor and royal or imperial donee was a delicate and controversial matter (see chapter 1).

Although it is uncertain to what extent she was a major artist or scholar herself, she definitely knew enough of the various skills to make things happen and inspire those who carried out her ideas or those of her masters. She often made a point of participating directly, not refraining from hard physical work and behavior unsuitable for her status. For example, when Bodong Chogle Namgyal visited her during the construction of a *stūpa,* he saw her carrying a stone and remarked, "'Why are you doing this? This might damage your reputation.'. . . She answered with a smile: 'If I don't do this kind of work myself, the nuns will not carry out this work well.' [He then commented]: 'This is extraordinary!'" (folio 75b).

Personal involvement and direct experience, beyond the established conventions, feature repeatedly in Chokyi Dronma's life and in the school of thought and art she participated in and promoted. The emotional intensity that had shaped her relationship with Bodong Chogle Namgyal while he was alive seems to have informed the artwork that faithfully reproduced his physical appearance in a life-size statue, with his human features given in great detail: "They made a statue of Chogle Namgyal that was one head higher than the previous one and had a face that was extremely similar to the real lama" (92b)—so similar that common people believed they beheld the deceased master himself (folios 93b, 94a).

Statues with realistic features have been produced in Tibet since imperial times and go back to a tradition attributed to the Buddha himself. He is said to have had his own image reproduced as it was reflected in water and to have had statues made to help with the diffusion of the doctrine after his death (Chayet 1994:113–114). Although the tradition of making realistic statues and portraits was not new, it must have had a particular momentum in fifteenth-century Gungthang. The statues belonging to the Bodongpa tradition show an exceptional resemblance to the actual features of the human models. This distinctive feature of Bodongpa art was highlighted by David Jackson and Gene Smith, who noted that the surviving bronzes are "strikingly realistic" (Smith 1970:48; Jackson 1996:101). This was probably due to both Bodong Chogle Namgyal's school of thought and local skills in metallurgy.

Bodong Chogle Namgyal, an eclectic spiritual master, was also highly innovative in the field of painting. He was deeply influenced by Newari art but promoted an original synthesis of different styles, reflecting Indian and Chinese traditions. He used materials, techniques, and proportions encompassing abstract theory and practical design. Following the Chinese tradition, he even gave a definition of the five fundamental colors (*rtsa ba'i dog*), which he described as luminous principles rather than as pigments, recalling Newton's view on the subject (Chayet 1994:192). He influenced the artistic production of his time and was instrumental in establishing the distinctive style of the region (Jackson 1996:95ff.). Like Bodong Chogle Namgyal's religious teachings, which passed into numerous different traditions, his views on art presumably affected a variety of later schools. The stunning and contradictory portrait of Chokyi Dronma at the Nyemo Chekar monastery, described at the beginning of chapter 1, seems to bear traces of Bodong Chogle Namgyal's style even though it was painted some 100 or 150 years later and is rich in the green and blue tones typical of the artistic school that emerged in the sixteenth century around the Karmapa (Chayet 1994:185).[13] Chokyi Dronma's simple but unequivocally worldly jewels, the long and loose hair, the tantric ritual items, and the monastic robe appear as an improbable combination of attributes that frame her person. She is seated on a throne, with her gaze, both affectionate and intimidating, turned toward an imaginary group of people outside the painting, and her face captured in a remarkable attempt at a three-quarter perspective. Even though she is made part of a larger composition centered on the Fourth Red Hat Karmapa, by then one of the most influential personalities in Tibet, she appears very much as her own person rather than as a mere element of the retinue or the spiritual lineage.

The realistic features expressed in the figurative art of Bodong Chogle Namgyal's tradition can be seen as related to the linear prose of the biography, with its wealth of concrete detail, the humanity of people and events captured through a suggestive, sometimes colloquial prose. Both seem to reflect a distinctive frame of mind, an innovative approach to artistic and religious expression. Chokyi Dronma's biography may represent a particular style of narrative that emerged in the context of fifteenth-century Gungthang or perhaps in the region more generally. The biography of Tsunpa Choleg (1437–1521), compiled a few decades later by people from the same tradition and area, shows a comparable attention to tangible, sometimes irrelevant details and suggests a similar preference for a plain, realistic style, highlighted by Karl-Heinz Everding:

The biography of bTsun pa chos legs can be reckoned among the most interesting and significant sources for the cultural development of Western Tibet in the first half of the second millennium. Considering the plain language and narrative style, the work seems to have been written without major literary ornaments, just as it was to told to his disciples by bTsun pa chos legs. (Everding 2000:224, my translation)

The new impulses in Tibetan literature that emerged during this period are also reflected in the fact that one of the greatest works of Tibetan biography, the *Life and Songs of Milarepa,* was compiled by Tsangnyong Heruka (1452–1507), one of the most renowned donees of Chokyi Dronma's brother, Thri Namgyal De. During the same period, in eastern Tibet, people began to compile an increasing number of texts reporting the Gesar epic (Karmay 1998:465), which seems to reflect an emerging Tibetan interest in putting into writing traditions that reflected the popular culture of lay communities. The biography of Chokyi Dronma itself presumably influenced popular works such as the biography of Thangtong Gyalpo (see chapter 3).

Chokyi Dronma can be seen as part of a larger movement that sought the new by reviving the lost roots of Buddhist civilization creatively. This approach was distinctive for its social and gender inclusiveness, eclecticism, cultural syntheses, exploratory drive, and innovation. It is therefore not surprising that after the death of her first spiritual master, Chokyi Dronma was attracted by Thangtong Gyalpo, one of the most striking and innovative personalities of her time—sometimes defined as a "Renaissance figure" and called the Leonardo of Tibet (Khalen 1993:138–149), due to the breadth of his interests and creativity. In many ways he embodied a vision comparable to Chokyi Dronma's own, not only through his religious practice but also through his extraordinary achievements in architecture and engineering. The construction of the great *stūpa* of Chung Riwoche and of his numerous iron-chain bridges must have appeared to the people of her time as true wonders. He was able to achieve these enterprises thanks to skills he had acquired on his extensive journeys. He had a particular competence in iron metallurgy, which enabled him to produce the iron rings for his chains from an arsenic-rich ore or by adding arsenic in the smithing process so that they would not rust (Stearns 1980:87, 132; Epprecht 1981; Kahlen 1993:138ff.). He also participated in the construction of grand *stūpas* such as Gyang Bummoche, built by Dakpo Sonma Tashi around the turn of the century, learning the skills that he would then develop and perfect in his own architectural masterpieces (see Stearns 2007). Thus he elaborated on whatever he had learned on his journeys and added it to the distinctive regional artistic and architectural production of his homeland. He is in fact considered another great representative of the so-called "La stod school of art" (Vitali 1990:133), even though he was active in many areas of Tibet and was thus a truly transregional figure. He was also profoundly aware of the politics of his religious and artistic deeds, and he appears as a staunch supporter of Tibetanness in all his biographies. The sense that his sheer presence was defending Tibet against the Mongols is said to have prompted him to request his disciple to hide his death for at least thirty years afterward (see Biography of Thangtong Gyalpo 341; Stearns 2007).

Thangtong Gyalpo, on his part, was definitely attracted by this extraordinary woman who was an offspring of the great Tibetan emperors and, despite her youth, had already proved herself a remarkable "cultural entrepreneur." Thangtong Gyalpo's deeds were grand not only in scope but also in the extent of resources and labor required for their realization. They needed a great deal of support, which he was able to secure from the local rulers and even the Neudong Gongma, the supreme rulers of Phagmodrupa. The scale of his enterprises allowed him to compete, with success, against the First Dalai Lama, Gendun Drupa, for craftsmen and labor (Jackson 1996:98). When Chokyi Dronma first met him around the end of 1452 or in 1453, he had already been building bridges for over two decades,[14] relying on the wide network of followers and donors established while traveling through Tibet. However, he still had very ambitious plans that included more bridges and the completion of the grand *stūpa* of Chung Riwoche. She had the wealth, coordination, organizational skills, and connections that could provide the further substantial support, resources, and mobilization of people required. In fact, she is described in her biography as having collected a great deal of donations in Northern Lato, eventually offered to Thangtong Gyalpo, and as having contributed to the construction of the *stūpa* of Chung Riwoche (folios 124–125). When she left for Tsari, he presented her with a piece of iron chain that he had kept with him on his journeys (folio 128a). This gift was not only a sacred object blessed by the master but also presumably a prototype for Chokyi Dronma's future activity at the shrine of the deity: the extraction of iron and the production of chains for the new bridges.

The sacred and the technical were not mutually exclusive for Chokyi Dronma or her masters, but complementary as part of the same vision—in Buddhist philosophy, especially in the Mahāyāna tradition, merit can be gained both from religious practice and from projects that benefit the community and the welfare of all living beings. Cyrus Stearns (2007) observes that

Thangtong Gyalpo repeatedly emphasized in his edicts that the Buddha had said that much merit was accumulated by constructing images, even more merit by writing scriptures, even more merit than that by creating representations of enlightened mind (such as *stūpa*), even more merit than that by building boats and bridges, and even more merit than that by saving the lives of sentient beings.

As pointed out in chapter 1, Situ Chokyi Rinchen, the father of Chokyi Dronma's father-in-law, was celebrated for his meritorious deeds that included not only the construction of temples and the establishment of religious activities but also the building of water channels and the improvement of pathways. Against this background the story of Chokyi Dronma and of the girl in whom she reincarnated was apparently not only a matter of esoteric religiosity but also a story of iron and gold (as will be further described in chapter 5).

In Tibet, various arts and skills were part of a comprehensive classification that encompassed all human knowledge, the "ten sciences," not discrete domains, as they are often considered in the West. Anne Chayet points out that "artistic creation as we conceive it in the West was not considered in Tibet" (Chayet 1994:98). Artistic, and sometimes even technical, creation was rather part of a larger process aiming at spiritual achievement; its aesthetic or functional value was just the worldly element, not its full scope. Ultimately the art object or the technical work was mere illusion, like everything else in the world, like the image of the Buddha reflected in the water. However, the worldly element was profoundly valued, as human beings are inevitably conditioned by the world of relative truth in which we live and in which we are subject to the law of cause and effect. This is the starting point for any spiritual striving.

In the world of relative truth, everything is conditioned; all phenomena are related and can be perceived differently by different subjects. The distinction between subject and object, person and thing can be blurred, as is perhaps generally true of art and sacred objects: the artistic masterpiece, the piece of blessed craftsmanship, the sacred relic, or the scripture may be endowed with its own "agency" (using Alfred Gell's terminology).[15] There are numerous Tibetan objects famous for their subjectivity and intentionality. For example, the Jobo, the famous statue of the Buddha in the Jokhang, which appears in the biography a couple of times, is said in earlier sources to have refused to be taken to China during the eighth-century anti-Buddhist persecution but to have accepted a temporary removal to Gungthang (*dBa' bzhed* folios 4a–5a), thus participating in the events of that time; the skull of Chokyi Dronma's previous incarnation, Sonam Drenma, is said to have spoken, as it wanted to be taken to the sanctuary of the Dorje Phagmo at Tsari ('*Brug pa chos 'byung* 406), thus contributing to its sacredness. Art objects and scriptures are produced through a process that endows them with divine agency (Kapstein 2001:271–276) and, especially after their consecration, acquire a sort of life of their own through rituals and narratives. The Mongols translated the Tibetan term for "consecration" (*rab gnas;* Skt. *pratiṣṭhā,* lit. "establish") with a word that literally means "bringing to life" (*amilah*). Like people, books are clothed in garments (*na bza'*) tied with sashes (*sku chings*) (see Phuntso forthcoming). The verb *chendren* (*spyan 'dran*), meaning "to invite" a person of high rank, is also used for statues and holy books. Accordingly, the biography tells that "At the beginning of the consecration ceremony the statue and the wisdom *stūpa* were 'invited' (*spyan 'dran*) in a carriage from Dongphub" (93a). The same treatment was given to the books embodying Bodong Chogle Namgyal's "speech" (*gsung*) and, on several occasions, to his multifarious relics.

For centuries these objects have embodied and extended the master's intentionality, with a sort of "personhood" distributed among the disciples of Bodong Chogle Namgyal and Chokyi Dronma, and more generally within the community through history. Apparently, not only did people act on objects, objects acted on people. For example, one of the realistic statues of Bodong Chogle Namgyal has become a symbol at the center of the exile community from the Porong area in Kathmandu, and also the model for new statues placed on Bodongpa altars in Tibet. Bodong Chogle Namgyal's collected works have a whole saga of their own that links the different Bodongpa centers in Tibet and in other parts of the world (see chapter 9). Thus artwork and scholarly production have blended with the cult of relics that has characterized the Buddhist world since its inception and has so often reflected, and driven, the vicissitudes of the religious community.

There is a sense of divinity in the production of great artwork and scholarship, often celebrated as "deeds," that permeates the whole process, the objects, the craftsmen, and especially the human instigator. These people were seen as highly realized, sometimes even as human emanations of *bodhisattvas,* who endowed all that they produced with their blessing. Some of these extraordinary masters had high aristocratic backgrounds or belonged to established religious families; others emerged mainly through the power of their actions, like Thangtong Gyalpo. There is no doubt that Chokyi Dronma was considered the incarnation of the Dorje Phagmo against the background of her imperial ancestry, but even more so for what she did. Her own extraordinary enterprises, in which the material and the spiritual blended completely, could not be achieved by conventional means. Epithets often used to refer to her, such as Magnificient Lady (dPal kyi dbang mo) or the Supreme Lady of Magnificence (dPal kyi dbang phyug ma), capture this greatness that encompassed political power, munificence, and spiritual stature. She lived at a time when innovation on all levels—by rigorous scholars, princely donors, or idiosyncratic *yogins*—was expressed in the idiom of sacredness and ultimate spiritual realization. Such an embodied divinity reflected in extraordinary deeds resonates, across cultures and across profoundly different religious systems, with that attributed to the greatest Renaissance geniuses and their patrons. Giorgio Vasari's *Lives* celebrated his homeland, Florence, and his patrons, Cosimo and the Medici family, who shone in the glory of the deeds of those they supported. In the first edition he described Leonardo (in a passage missing from the second edition) as human beyond human, a model of divinity:

> E veramente il cielo ci manda talora alcuni che non rappresentano la umanità sola, ma la divinità istessa, acciò da quella come da modello, imitandolo, possiamo accostarci con l'animo e con l'eccellenza dell'intelletto alle parti somme del cielo. (Vasari 1550:562)
>
> And really, heaven sometimes sends to us those who do not represent only humanity, but divinity itself, so that by taking this as a model, imitating it, we can get closer with our soul and with the best of our intelligence to the highest spheres of heaven. (my translation)

## Relatedness in Chokyi Dronma's Life

Chokyi Dronma's status as a member of an important ruling family inevitably shaped her life and her relationships to the people around her, even when she tried to transcend it as an ordinary member of the Buddhist monastic congregation, a regular begging nun. The peasants were surprised and confused when they encountered the princess on one of her begging trips and offered donations lavishly.

Chokyi Dronma was very aware of her worldly position, which she tried to transcend but also used strategically and linked with a distinctive sense of responsibility. For example, after having been seriously ill and close to death, she is reported to have addressed her parents-in-law and her husband in this way:

> Death comes to all, and even after death there is still suffering to endure. We are powerful people who have carried out important deeds, so we will also undergo greater suffering. If I were afraid of suffering, I would get a bad rebirth. If at this time I weren't thinking about a solution for my future, I would be very foolish. (27b–28a)

In her words, her status made her religious choice even more compelling.

Chokyi Dronma appears in the biography in three modes of being—worldly, monastic, and tantric divinity—concretely reflected in how she related to her family of origin, the family she married into, and the Buddhist congregation. I use the term "relatedness" (Carsten 2000) to map out these relationships because it includes what is conventionally defined as kinship but allows for a more flexible, culturally specific understanding. This term, which also translates a widely used Tibetan notion,[16] is particularly suitable for the analysis of cultural constructions that seem to cut across boundaries between kin and non-kin, which often exist in Tibet. I shall briefly outline the main figures as they appear in Chokyi Dronma's biography and how they were related to her.

Chokyi Dronma's father and father-in-law are benevolent and authoritative, both fathers and kings. They seem to epitomize the ideal Buddhist ruler, who integrates temporal with religious morality, the "golden yoke" of the worldly legal system with the "silken knot" of the discipline upon which the monastic community was based. They appear as remarkably similar personalities, powerful, respected, keen on justice, tolerant, affectionate, but also aware of their responsibility as guarantors and implementers of the moral order. They are the prime figures of authority with whom Chokyi Dronma negotiates when she takes crucial steps in her life.

Remarkably different from the men of the older ruling generation are the two young princes, heirs to the thrones of Southern Lato and Gungthang. Chokyi Dronma's husband is portrayed in many ways as the antihero: he is a Bonpo in a Buddhist family, unstable, prone to conflict; he even instigates a war for emotional reasons, discrediting himself in the eyes of his own people. He may have actually been a complex character with a disturbing medical condition related to his goiter[17] and may have been a practitioner of the local ancestral cults (which are still problematic from the Buddhist perspective). Undoubtedly, however, the biographer enhanced the negativity of this character in contrast to his father, the just Buddhist king, and Chokyi Dronma herself, a Buddhist hero. The narrative may also reflect the trope of the non-Buddhist husband that features in the story of Lakṣmīṅkarā, which undoubtedly had some bearing on the representation of these events (see chapter 3). Chokyi Dronma's husband seems to represent sheer "antirelatedness," for although he and Chokyi Dronma happened to marry, it is clear that the relationship does not work. The fruit of their union does not survive, supposedly on account of his religious beliefs and practices, and when

Chokyi Dronma takes her leave of him, requesting his permission (but merely formally, for everything has already been negotiated with the father-in-law), he states bitterly: "It seems that you are not to stay at my side for this life, and there is no hope that you will become my protector in a future life. Do what you wish, you do not need to ask me!" (folio 42b). However, she does give him gifts on her departure (folio 43b) and ensures that he has an appropriate Buddhist funeral, illustrating her compassionate side (folio 105a).

Chokyi Dronma's brother is almost a symmetric figure to her husband. Both are portrayed as embodying, in her eyes, the negativity of worldly involvement from which she wishes to escape. The young prince of Gungthang appears in the biography as a volatile character, involved in disputes with his father and generally impetuous in his decisions. He is depicted more positively in the later part of the narrative but is never celebrated as in later sources. This is presumably due both to the time of the compilation of Chokyi Dronma's biography and to his particular role in the Gungthang royal family from her point of view. He seals her destiny as a royal princess to be married out, puts her mother in a vulnerable position, and repeatedly creates family problems to which Chokyi Dronma responds by deploying her mediation skills. There appears to have been a complex political tension between competing factions in the ruling elite in Gungthang, which the biographer has described as a personal hostility between father and son. A careful look at the account of the dispute is revealing. It is not just the son who is "roaming around the plain" (folio 30b), upset and aimless. He has with him a group of ministers (*blon*). The elite seems therefore to have been split between the father and the son. This is reminiscent of the political structure of the Tibetan empire, so we can infer that the council of the ministers had significant power and was also likely to harbor factionalism.[18] Against this background the disputes within the royal family become more plausible and less personal. In addition, we understand more fully the emphasis with which Chokyi Dronma is repeatedly celebrated for her successful mediation. She was able to rally and unite the scattered and conflicting factions, and thus able to quell the malicious rumors that had surrounded her ever since her transgressive behavior had brought about the collapse of the marriage alliance with Southern Lato and possibly war.

The two main female figures in the narrative, who are kin to Chokyi Dronma, present remarkably contrasting features: her mother-in-law and her mother. Chokyi Dronma's mother-in-law seems somewhat narrow-minded and manipulative, caught up in both convention and common sense. She and Chokyi

Dronma appear involved, almost in a stereotypical way, in the common and predictable tension between mother-in-law and daughter-in-law. She seems to be repeatedly shocked by Chokyi Dronma's behavior (folios 21a, 41a). She is protective and concerned for the future of her son without Chokyi Dronma's stabilizing presence (folio 27b) and is disturbed by Chokyi Dronma's behavior toward their daughter (folio 29b). On the other hand, Chokyi Dronma's mother appears as the main reference in her relational life, from birth until their painful separation, which turns out to be crucial for the recognition of the reincarnation of the princess (see chapter 5). Chokyi Dronma's mother has the dream that prompts Lama Chopel Sangpo to acknowledge that the baby princess has given herself her name (folios 3b, 4a). She encourages her education, suffers deeply at their separation when Chokyi Dronma leaves to be married and when she leaves for the east, and supports her deeds extensively. Chokyi Dronma, in return, shows great affection and concern for her mother, who appears particularly vulnerable due to her position in the royal family.

Two other important, albeit more marginal, female figures appear in the narrative: Chokyi Dronma's grandmother and younger sister, who are both highly supportive of her and seem to be part of a wider network of female kinship relations on which Chokyi Dronma relied extensively. It is significant that in the biography, Chokyi Dronma's younger sister is supposed to replace her as a wife of the ruler of Southern Lato after the collapse of Chokyi Dronma's marriage. This swap never happened,[19] but apparently, sometime later Chokyi Dronma's niece was sent as a bride to Southern Lato to balance and continue the relationship between the two polities. Tsangnyon Heruka met this unfortunate princess who also had been married out. She had lost all her children, returned to Gungthang, fallen in unrequited love with him, and eventually died tragically (Biography of Tsangnyon Heruka 86–87). Tsangnyon Heruka later met another niece of Chokyi Dronma who had married out to the Neudong family (see chapter 5). Chokyi Dronma's network of female relatives, which appears both in the biography and in parallel sources, shows a wide transregional character, which reflected the kinship politics of the time.

When Chokyi Dronma abandoned her secular life and took her first monastic vows, "from being part of a family, she became without a family" (folio 46a) and formed a new set of relationships. Bodong Chogle Namgyal and Chokyi Dronma are often referred to as *yab-se* (*yab sras*), (spiritual) father and child, which indicates a spiritual relatedness that was a quasi-kinship relation. Without superseding the ties with her family, this teacher-disciple bond became dominant after she started her life as a Buddhist adept. During the last years of Bodong Chogle Namgyal's life, as she was recognized as a fully accomplished spiritual master in her own right, the two of them were also referred to as *yab yum,* i.e., father-mother of the Buddhist doctrine. This referred presumably to their role as spiritual parents to their disciples as well as their personal religious relationship (see below).

As the narrative develops, Deleg Chodren, the attendant and spiritual companion of Chokyi Dronma, seems to grow into the position of a junior spiritual relative, like a younger sister or a daughter. Chokyi Dronma is referred to as mother (*yum*) when supervising Deleg Chodren's spiritual practice (folio 57b). Gradually Deleg Chodren became empowered as her immediate spiritual heir, and she eventually took on a sort of parenting position in relation to Kunga Sangmo, the next reincarnation of Chokyi Dronma. However, she apparently did not have the status to enter into the lineage constructed in later sources (see chapter 5). The only record of her role is in the biography and the few brief mentions in the biography of Thangtong Gyalpo (308, 339).

Expressed in the idiom of kinship, these spiritual forms of relatedness were likewise seen as given, based on karmic links from previous lives; they seem to be simply revealed through encounter and interaction. Eventually, the disclosure of Chokyi Dronma's secret identity inscribed her in a further set of relationships, linking her to a number of sacred women of the past who were considered emanations of the same deity and to the women of the succeeding generations who would be recognized as her reincarnations (see chapter 5).

## Gender and Motherhood in Chokyi Dronma's Secular Life

The sociocultural milieu in which Chokyi Dronma was born, grew up, married, and became a mother had an important bearing not only on her worldly identity but also on her decision to devote herself to a religious life, for this was the setting in which she decided to renounce the world and "become without a family." Gender played a fundamental role.

Chokyi Dronma's status was given by the framework of relations into which she was born as a princess, a king's daughter. She had inherited the ancestral bones[20] from her father, which linked her with the Tibetan imperial legacy that the royal house of Gungthang had come to embody during this historical period. She had the royal bones, but she could not pass them on because she was a woman. She was firstborn, but not the awaited son, and this had a tremendous impact on her life from the beginning. However, the kinship system was not as rigid as it might seem; until a son was born, there was a remote chance that she could become the ruler of her kingdom by marrying a man who acted as an adopted son of the king and eventually succeeded him.[21] It is not clear whether she would have been in a position to formally inherit the throne, but that may have been the case if no other option existed.[22] Some of the royal symbolism used for Chokyi Dronma seems to indicate that her becoming a leader was considered a real possibility, at least by some. However, once a son was born (although to a junior queen), her destiny was that of an ordinary royal princess: she would become the important link in a marriage alliance, the representative of her kin and her kingdom in an unfamiliar, albeit allied, place.

Chokyi Dronma's concerns about women started with her own mother and herself. An important passage in the biography (see chapter 2) links the birth of a son to a junior queen to the anxiety of Chokyi Dronma's mother about having produced only daughters and to Chokyi Dronma's first wish to take the vows (folio 7b). This link is reiterated in later passages, so that the intricate questions of succession to the throne and family disputes seem often to epitomize worldly concerns (for example, folio 31a). The issue is also reflected in a peculiar inconsistency in historical sources.

Chokyi Dronma's biography states that she was born in the year of the tiger, i.e., 1422, as the first child of the King of Gungthang and his main queen, and that four or five years later a junior queen gave birth to the son who eventually took over the throne. In contrast, the eighteenth-century *Gung thang rgyal rabs* (125) states that her brother was born in the year of the tiger, to the same mother (who apparently was the senior queen). Chokyi Dronma is merely mentioned in this later source as being born to the same mother but without any date. The *Gung thang rgyal rabs* continues by saying that Thri Namgyal De, i.e., Chokyi Dronma's brother, was an incarnation of King Thrisong Detsen and was enthroned at the age of fifteen. If we accept the version given in Chokyi Dronma's biography as a more detailed and almost contemporary document, supported by the biography of Chopel Sangpo (folio 4b), it seems that the later genealogical account has confused dates between the siblings, highlighting the male heir to the throne as the first born.

The birth of a male heir to a junior queen altered not only Chokyi Dronma's position in the royal family but also her mother's, even though she retained the status of senior queen. More importantly, this event is likely to have changed the general political setting, bringing to the fore influential people linked to the junior queen, mother of the heir apparent, especially the ministers who were "roaming around the plain" with him. Tellingly, the biography contains a remarkable passage that follows the description of the formal, possibly second, enthronement of Chokyi Dronma's brother in the late 1440s. On that occasion Chokyi Dronma expressed an odd request to her spiritual master: "Folding her hands, the Lady of Prosperity said to the great teacher, 'Precious lama, if I die before my mother, please take care of her with love'" (folio 68b).

Since Chokyi Dronma's mother had not produced a son, she was dependent on the favor of her aging husband and the mercy of the young king, who was unrelated to her; furthermore, she was at the mercy of competing factions in the ruling elite. The formal enthronement of the heir was likely to entail a shift in Gungthang's internal politics, presumably not to the advantage of Chokyi Dronma and her mother (see above). Throughout her life Chokyi Dronma tried to provide material support; she built a house for her mother and provided her with a land tenure. She was very aware indeed of her mother's vulnerability against the background of kinship politics.

The biography provides a rich source of information about common views on gender and kinship at the time. Significantly, these were not necessarily consistent with each other. A remarkable statement about gender appears in the description of how Chokyi Dronma, after having given birth to a daughter, was told, "The most important thing is that your body is in good condition. There is no difference between boy and girl. Later you will give birth to one child after the other" (folio 26), evoking more the challenge that childbirth represented for women than the apparently popular gender discriminatory views. Also, when Chokyi Dronma discussed the education of her daughter with her husband, she seems to have referred to a bilineal system of kinship relations: "Later he suggested that Yungdrung Lingpa, a great Bonpo master, should become the child's teacher. The Magnificent Lady replied: 'Had this child been a boy, you would have had the power to decide. However, since the child is a girl, she will take refuge in the Jewel of Buddhism'" (27a). This is consistent with more general Tibetan ideas about kinship, according to which bones are passed on patrilineally while flesh and blood are passed on matrilineally. Even though the bones are usually highlighted, under some circumstances the flesh/blood line may be used to make claims and can become significant for the transmission of religious items and competences as well as ritual roles. The female line, represented symbolically by blood or flesh, can thus be used in two different ways: as a negative factor associated with impurity or as a positive factor that enabled women to negotiate certain rights on the ground of matrilineal relations, as in Chokyi Dronma's case.

However, other passages show that negative views about the value of women were probably prevalent. In describing an episode that was probably taken from the miraculous stories circulating at that time, the biographer links the prevention of female infanticide to the arrival of Chokyi Dronma:

> When the Female Buddha, Woman of Wisdom was about to arrive at Shekar as a daughter-in-law, the mother of a dumb boy gave birth to four daughters. The father of these daughters was very upset and tried to throw them into the water, but the dumb boy all of a sudden spoke: "They can't be thrown away! The four girls are four *ḍākinīs*. The head of the *ḍākinīs*, Konchog Gyalmo, is about to come here from Ngari!" (folios 33a, b)

We have to read this episode, of course, as the background against which the princess is depicted as a hero. It is possibly significant that the story refers to a dumb boy speaking. This can be interpreted as a need for a strong voice for female beings, and Chokyi Dronma is described later in the biography as fulfilling this role in a number of aspects.

Beyond the hint at female infanticide, another representation of female misery set contrastively against Chokyi Dronma's deeds is the story of an abandoned old woman whom she cares for irrespective of her repulsive aspect and the possibility that she is affected by a contagious disease (folios 99b–101a). On the whole, Chokyi Dronma had a profound sense of women's vulnerability and saw Buddhism as a way to address their plight, as she explicitly stated when she became ordained (see introduction and folio 46a).

When Chokyi Dronma became a mother herself, at first it seemed that she would act in a similar way to her own mother, as a strong supportive presence. In the first few months, this was the case; she is described as enjoying looking after her daughter, in princely conditions, and making a point of presiding over her education. It is therefore quite surprising to read that shortly afterward, when her daughter was still a baby, she declared that her role as a mother was completed. It is possible to detect here a reverberation of the episode in the life of the Buddha in which Prince Siddhartha leaves his wife and baby child to devote himself to his spiritual quest, apparently the model according to which the biographer framed Chokyi Dronma's experience of motherhood. Beyond the narrative model, however, there are several aspects of this event that seem peculiar and reveal the human complexity of Chokyi Dronma's experience.

The biography describes the following chain of events:

- a few months after the birth of her daughter, shortly after she has claimed her right to control the child's education, Chokyi Dronma travels to the hot springs, becomes ill, and almost dies;
- she recovers after the miraculous appearance of the Medicine Buddha;
- when she comes back, she does not take care of her daughter anymore; the mother-in-law criticizes this and Chokyi Dronma replies that a royal child has an innate, self-reliant character and that she has already fulfilled all that is necessary as a mother;
- she then travels to her homeland to mediate family disputes, leaving the child behind at Shekar;
- the child dies while she is away and the news reaches her by letter;
- Chokyi Dronma decides that the time to pursue a monastic life has come;
- Chokyi Dronma tells her parents-in-law that there is no reason to worry about the destiny of the child, as she will find her own way and will be soon reincarnated, but she also states that the death of the child was to be attributed to some anti-Buddhist activities that had been performed;
- her father-in-law seems delighted with this response; however, upon her return to Shekar there are rumors that she may feel some regret for how things went with her daughter, and it is hoped that she will produce other children in the future.

Although child mortality was certainly high at that time and the death of a baby was a common experience (as it still is in many rural areas), it is explicitly stated that the death of her daughter "gave her a lot to think about" (folio 31b). It is therefore probably significant that she finalized her religious life choice at precisely this time. The loss did not prompt it, for she had already expressed her wish to become ordained early in her life, but it certainly seems to have precipitated the final break with secular life.

There is, however, another layer of possible interpretation: the journey to the hot springs may have already been a response to a looming personal and family crisis. She traveled there on her own, with just her attendants, shortly after the confrontation with her husband over the education of their daughter. Illness often features in the life of young daughters-in-law who experience a breakdown in the new family setting and prompts the renegotiation of family relations.[23] The journey to the hot springs, the illness, and her subsequent avoidance of regular contact with her daughter may also have coincided with the weaning of the child. Returning to Shekar, Chokyi Dronma decided that she could not accept the situation in which she found herself. She ostensibly refused to continue to fulfill her role as a mother and, as the weaning or a milk nurse made her less indispensable, she may have tried to renegotiate her position, especially with her mother-in-law. Then another set of dramatic events caught up with Chokyi Dronma: she felt that she had to return home because of the conflicts that had exploded between her father and her brother. Her success as a mediator was displaced by the news of her daughter's death, to which she responded with the expected composure. It is not unlikely, however, that a link between the death and her mother's absence may have been read into the events by the people who witnessed them and perhaps even by Chokyi Dronma herself. It was a high price to pay, something that had to be explained and with which the people around Chokyi Dronma, and the biographer, seem to have struggled. Beyond the unemotional reply to her parents-in-law and the attribution of responsibility to practices promoted by the child's father, this was apparently what gave her "a lot to think about." Regret (*'gyod pa*) was a factor, and this term is explicitly mentioned in the biography, although through the voice of rumors. By highlighting the fact that people attributed this state of mind to the young princess, the biographer seems to betray Chokyi Dronma's own suffering, not only grief but also remorse at the inescapability of an event that could not be undone and for which she may have felt partly responsible.

Beyond the complexities of Chokyi Dronma's psychology and kinship relations, the narrative highlights some of the challenges raised by the transposition of Buddha's life as model for a fifteenth-century Tibetan woman. Prince Siddhartha's separation from his wife and child caused him great sorrow but was indispensable for his ultimate aim. However, his child was brought up by his wife, and after his enlightenment and the founding of the early monastic community, became one of his disciples. To what extent was this model of renunciation applicable to the life of a woman? The inclusiveness of some Buddhist approaches definitely allowed for this in principle, but how did the practicalities work out when a woman decided to renounce the world after having become a mother?

Other Tibetan religious women, such as the twelfth-century *yoginī* Machig Labdron, experienced motherhood with different outcomes and solutions. The dilemma of women torn between maternal commitments and religious aspirations is described in a striking way in the life of Ani Chola, a nun who lived in the same region some four centuries later and founded the female monastic community of Rongbuk (Rong phu). The story of her life is narrated by Dzatrul Ngawang Tendzin Norbu in his autobiography (folios 25–35), and I provide a brief outline here because it resonates in many ways with Chokyi Dronma's own experience.

Ani Chola, mother of three daughters, was originally the sister-in-law of the previous reincarnation of Dzatrul Ngawang Tendzin Norbu. They belonged to a reasonably well-off family of farmers in Kharta, an area directly south of Shekar. As her husband had decided to leave the household to devote himself to a spiritual life, she was asked to take another husband and take over its management. To everybody's surprise, however, she refused and said that she wanted to pursue enlightenment too: "She said, 'I had to come here as a daughter-in-law and suddenly I had three daughters. . . . I would also like to enter the door of the *Dharma*, but since I have little merit, my legs are surrounded by children. I cannot go, I cannot stay'" (Autobiography of Ngawang Tendzin Norbu folio 30a).

At that time a song was attributed to her:

> I came as a daughter-in-law without purpose;
> I closed the door of the *Dharma* and got stuck in the mud.
> You, children, rope of *saṃsāra*,
> As soon as you can get out of the house.
> I, the mother, will not stay and I will devote myself to the *Dharma*.
> Don't make obstacles to her practice.
> (AUTOBIOGRAPHY OF NGAWANG TENDZIN NORBU FOLIO 30B)

Eventually she was allowed to leave with her three daughters, who were brought up, juggling the difficult situation, between their father and mother, according to the spiritual master's suggestion:

"This summer leave the two elder daughters in Rongphu, and their father will teach them reading and writing. You should go back with the little one to Rabshi Phumar and start your preliminary practices there. After I have completed my retreat, we will be able to discuss your future." According to this decision, her husband stayed to practice meditation in Rongphu Lingme. Here he took care of the two elder daughters; they ate just a little roasted barley in the morning, in the evening, and at noon; they were crying all the time because they missed their mother. (folios 33b–34a)

The children are called the "rope of *saṃsāra*" in the vivid and emotive song; however, despite the challenge that they originally represented for their parents, they grew up and became the core community of the Rongbuk nuns. Motherhood epitomized the paradox of the human condition: entanglement in *saṃsāra* and opportunity of liberation through a human rebirth. In the lives of religious women who were also mothers, this dilemma can be highly dramatic and palpable.

It is impossible to know the exact impact of Chokyi Dronma's brief and tragic motherhood on her life and on her religious itinerary. Would she have left the palace to go to a monastery if her daughter had lived? Would she have been in a position to try an avenue similar to that of Ani Chola and involve her daughter in her radical choice? Or was it her daughter's death that precipitated the realization of her wish for a religious life, against the background of an already unstable situation?

When later, after becoming a nun, she defined herself as "the woman who was married and had children" (folio 54a), she identified that experience as epitomizing the secular world she had left behind. She had experienced *saṃsāra* in its depth through her own suffering and that of others, especially women. She thus announced at her ordination that she was dedicating herself in particular to the religious practice of women (see introduction).

Rather than lamenting the plight of women, a recurring theme in female biographies (Schaeffer 2004), Chokyi Dronma seems to have tackled the issue in a proactive way. This was undoubtedly facilitated by her privileged social position, her ability to raise funds, and the presence of spiritual masters who had very inclusive and non-gender discriminatory views. However, Chokyi Dronma's gender was not unanimously accepted in the religious environment. Bodong Chogle Namgyal often had to defend his attitude toward Chokyi Dronma, and women in general, to people who saw female presence as an element of corruption of the doctrine. Shortly after Chokyi Dronma's ordination as a novice, somebody had said to him:

"There is a girl who is like the apple of the eye of both Ngari and Southern Lato. Now she has cut her hair and entered the doctrine, corrupting it. How did you allow this?" The Lord answered, "She came according to links from previous ages.

127

*Princess, Nun,* Yoginī

You have no such links, how can you criticize me? She doesn't want to become the Lady of Ngari and Southern Lato, she wishes to become the protector of all living beings. The doctrine was not corrupted. In fact it is people like you, without virtue, who are corrupting the doctrine." (folios 47a, b)

He often went back to the Indian roots of Buddhism to suggest innovation, development, or reform concerning women's involvement in religion. He was thereby referring to the most inclusive approach that can be found in ancient Buddhist scriptures (see Sponberg 1992:8ff.). However, neither at the dawn of Buddhism nor in Chokyi Dronma's time nor in the current era have such positions been accepted without disputes.

## The Life of the Buddha as a Model of Renunciation

As mentioned in chapter 3, throughout Chokyi Dronma's life, the story of Prince Siddhartha is a constant theme, and probably as more than the literary model that informed the writing of her biography. She may have actually taken him as an exemplar in a context profoundly shaped by what Caroline Humphrey defined as a "morality of exemplars" (Humphrey 1997:25ff.). In Tibet and elsewhere, I have often come across religious men and women who reenact situations and interpret their lives according to narratives contained in exemplary biographies (see also Cook forthcoming, for comparable cases among Thai Buddhist nuns), a phenomenon that is also having a particular impact on the reconstruction of Buddhist traditions in contemporary Tibet (see chapter 8). Buddha's life as narrated in the *Lalitavistara,* quoted among Chokyi Dronma's readings and mentioned as a source of inspiration that informed some of her radical choices (folios 36b–37a), may have also provided a framework for her own reading of her life experiences in hindsight. The narrative model therefore appears to have influenced both the biographical writing and Chokyi Dronma's own life. Here are three interesting examples.

Chokyi Dronma, as a little girl, is depicted as having had a great awareness of worldly impermanence. This is described in a passage apparently inspired by the theme of the three sights—an old person, a sick person, and a corpse—that prompted Siddhartha's renunciation of royal status and the world:

She saw a very old woman holding a stick and leaning on it. She called the nanny, Tshebum, told her to come, and asked, "What is that?"

128

Tshebum replied, "That is a very old woman."

"Is this a human being?"

"Yes."

"Will I become like this?"

Tshebum, without thinking much, answered, "Yes, you will."

The girl got very scared and cried and cried and cried. Then Tshebum spoke some soothing words: "I was just joking! You will not become like this."

Later, she heard the sound of the drum (*ḍamaru*) from the charnel ground and asked, "What is that?"

"A corpse is being carried to the charnel ground."

"Will this happen to me?"

"No, it will not!"

"It will happen to me, I know. I'm afraid."

"If you are afraid, what will you do?"

"I'll do something that liberates me from the fear of death."

"How can you do this?"

The Venerable immediately went into deep meditation. (folios 8b–9a)

The narrative model is clear, but details such as the nanny who speaks without reflecting seem to add an unpredictable element taken from the living context.

A peculiar resonance with Buddha's life appears in the description of how a lama was invited and asked to convince her to give up her wish to take the vows and continue to lead a secular life. He said:

"You can practice meditation and you can learn all the deep instructions on how to reach enlightenment within one lifetime, while staying with your family. Rather than taking the vows and becoming ordained, it is much better if you stay with your family. In particular, if you do not keep the throne, conflicts may break out between these miryarchies and everybody will be extremely unhappy." Then the Great Woman resolutely countered, "I prefer to take the vows, focus on the Omniscient, and be liberated. Even if I were to bring about great prosperity, such a goal would be far removed from the taking of the vows. It would be like poison. Now nobody can change my commitment." (38a)

The lama was suggesting that, as a reasonable compromise, she could choose the pathway of the tantric practitioner without abandoning her secular obligations. This could be seen as a common-sense solution. However, she flatly refused it, explicitly stating that she wished to follow the example of Prince Siddhartha. This dramatic confrontation seems to evoke the final temptation of the Buddha before his enlightenment. David Snellgrove observed that on that occasion Māra spoke to Siddhartha "as a subtle tempter urging conventional good works as more profitable than the rigors of ascetic life: 'Live, good sir; life is better. Living thou shalt do good works. If thou livest the religious life, if thou sacrificest the fire-sacrifice, much good is stored upon you. What hast thou to do with striving?'" (Snellgrove 1987:18).

The passage describing Chokyi Dronma's refusal to listen to a lama who had been invited to give her sensible instructions on how to manage her situation highlights the radical conflicts that she faced, like Prince Siddhartha, when she had to choose between the conventional good of being an excellent ruler and what she felt to be the ultimate good, the striving for enlightenment irrespective of worldly commitments. The description of Chokyi Dronma's actual life events seems to be inspired by classic narrative models, yet invariably exceeds them, here and in many other more or less close resonances with further adventures of Prince Siddhartha and other Buddhist heroes: the seclusion in and escape from the royal palace, giving up a spouse and child for the pursuit of a higher spiritual aim, and life as a begging member of the monastic congregation.

The reference to the enactment of Buddhist narrative models is mostly implicit, but occasionally the Indian setting or the deeds of previous Buddhist masters are actually quoted. A very interesting example is the story of the disciple of the Buddha who, at Veluvana Park in Magadha, was led astray by heretics. This is quoted as a reference for Chokyi Dronma's confrontation with the Bonpo priests (folio 16b). The same theme returns in the description of Chokyi Dronma's life at Shekar, where she is said to have based her actions on the debate between Sakya Paṇḍita and the heretics when she had to refute Bonpo views (folio 19b). The biographer presumably was referring to the famous debate between Sakya Paṇḍita and Harinanada and other prominent Hindu masters, probably Śivaites, in Kyirong around the year 1238 (see Tucci 1999 [1949]:626; Everding 2000:353). In both passages of Chokyi Dronma's biography she reenacted preexisting models. These are remarkable examples of constructing "the others," the non-Buddhists, by merging the ancient Indian notion of heretics (Tib. *muthegpa*, Skt. *thirtikha*) with that of the followers of Shenrab, i.e., the Bonpo and/or the practitioners of local ancestral cults, and using it as a blanket term to refer to Tibetan pre-Buddhist religious practices. The opposition to local non-Buddhist cults is given such an emphasis in the biography that it cannot be explained merely by reference to standard narrative models. It has to be seen in the particular cultural setting of the region at that time: the biography of Chopel Sangpo (folio 4b), the court chaplain of Gungthang, mentions a conspicuous Bonpo presence in the area and the relevant Buddhist activity of containment. Even more significant is the fact that the rulers of Southern Lato performed ancestral cult rituals such as the worship of Pholha Lhatsen Gangmar (see *Shel dkar chos 'byung* folio 13a)[24] that may have included animal sacrifices, as these were widely practiced in the area until 1959 (Diemberger and Hazod 1997:261ff.). It is therefore likely that the local ancestral cults constituted the background for the life story of Chokyi Dronma as a hero in the Buddhification of Tibet, continuing the deeds of Padmasambhava and Milarepa. The distinctive use of the term "Bonpo," in particular, reflects a confrontational view and differs significantly from other, more conciliatory approaches. This view also seems to have informed the interpretation of the conflict between Chokyi Dronma and her husband, which is starkly depicted as the confrontation between a Buddhist and a non-Buddhist view of the world.

The ideal of the Buddhist scholar that is dominant in the biography of her master, Bodong Chogle Namgyal, is a further important theme that may have informed both Chokyi Dronma's biography and her life. Chokyi Dronma followed the Sakyapa school until she became a disciple of Bodong Chogle Namgyal (folio 19b). This affiliation is not surprising, given the importance of this tradition in Mangyul-Gungthang and the fact that her paternal grandmother was ordained as a nun in a Sakyapa monastic institution. After she met Bodong Chogle Namgyal, Chokyi Dronma's religious approach became more eclectic, and she followed the Bodongpa tradition. She studied, in depth, his monumental collected works dealing with all branches of knowledge. This had a great impact on her and helps explain the breadth of her interests, similar to those of her spiritual master. Later in life she received various teachings of the Nyingmapa and Kagyupa schools as well as a special initiation into the *Kanjur* and the *Tenjur* from Thangtong Gyalpo. Eventually she was given some further teachings by Vanaratna at the time of their encounter in Rinpung. The biography outlines her as a spiritual master in her own right, giving evidence according to the common standards of religious achievement: teaching, composing, debating, and meditation. According to this narrative, in her relatively short life she was definitely more oriented toward teaching and meditating than writing or debating, which is not surprising, as the latter activities often take place at a more mature stage in the life of a master. Many passages show the great respect that Bodong

Chogle Namgyal, Thangtong Gyalpo, and Vanaratna had for her, as she was often equated to buddhas and *bodhisattvas,* such as Mañjuśrī, Vajradhara, etc.

These masters seem to have viewed her according to the most inclusive approach to Buddhist practice, in contrast to more gender-discriminatory attitudes sometimes reflected in Buddhist scriptures and rituals. Thus Bodong Chogle Namgyal praises Chokyi Dronma's ultimate potential: "The Magnificent Lady replied, 'I wish to strive for enlightenment.' But the Lord remarked, 'You don't need to ask me for enlightenment. You have the ability to reach enlightenment yourself'" (folio 65b).[25]


## Fully Ordained Nun, *Yoginī,* and Tantric Consort?

The biography recounts that Chokyi Dronma was ordained first as a novice and eventually as a *bhikṣuṇī (dge slong ma),* a fully ordained member of the monastic community. This is very remarkable, as it has often been stated that the tradition of fully ordaining nuns never arrived in Tibet or was lost early (see introduction).

According to the Indian Buddhist tradition, the female congregation was established by the Buddha himself. After some initial reluctance, he is said to have accepted the request of his male disciple, Ānanda, on behalf of the Buddha's own maternal aunt and foster mother, to introduce monastic ordination for women. Thus Mahāprajāpathī became the first *bhikṣuṇī.*[26] According to the *Vinaya,* in both the Theravadin and the Mūlasarvastivadin traditions, the female congregation has to follow a larger number of rules that make it dependent upon the male congregation and ensure the protection of the ordained women (Karma Lekshe Tsomo 2004:45ff.). One of the requirements is that fully ordained *bhikṣuṇīs* must participate in the ordination of a female member of the monastic community.[27] The reestablishment of female full ordination is currently a very topical and controversial issue among both Mahāyāna and Theravada Buddhist congregations. Some traditions allow for dispensing with the required presence of *bhikṣuṇīs,* for there are texts such as the *Cullavagga Vinaya* in which the Buddha authorized this if no fully ordained nuns were available (de Silva 2004:125). This is also argued by saying that the presence of *bhikṣuṇīs* was originally meant to facilitate the candidate's addressing the more intimate questions, but if it could not be guaranteed, this would not invalidate the ordination (de Silva 2004:119).[28] The introduction of full ordination for women according to the Mūlasārvastivāda tradition of Nālandā, followed in Tibet, is currently intensively debated among Tibetan Vinaya authorities. For an outline of the various positions and a summary of the current state of affairs, see the introductory documents to a seminar organized May 22–24, 2006 by the Department of Religion and Culture of the Central Tibetan Administration at Dharamsala (http://www.thubtenchodron.org/BuddhistNunsMonasticLife). It is remarkable that in this debate a fifteenth-century movement that promoted women's full ordination, bypassing the lack of the *bhikṣuṇī* lineage by having the ceremony performed by fully ordained monks alone, is referred to as a potential precedent; this had involved famous spiritual masters such as the Sakya scholar Shakya Chogden (1432–1507), part of the teacher-student lineage of Bodong Chogle Namgyal, who had ordained his mother, and a female disciple (Biography of Shakya Chogden 164–165).

Chokyi Dronma's biography describes her full ordination according to standards that would apply to a male member of the monastic community. No other fully ordained woman was present (presumably because none was available). It is uncertain on which doctrinal basis Bodong Chogle Namgyal organized the ritual that took place at Porong Palmo Choding—whether he relied on the possibility of dispensing with the mandatory presence of *bhikṣuṇī*s, which he was able to identify in early Buddhist scriptures, or on a more flexible view of gender in the framework of the Tibetan society of his time, i.e., ordained her as if she were gender neutral (see Gyatso 2003:89ff). The fact that fully ordained women existed in ancient Buddhist India was well known in Chokyi Dronma's time. Early *bhikṣuṇī*s appeared in biographical accounts of the Buddha; Bhikṣuṇī Lakṣmī was a later example of an Indian fully ordained nun widely known in Tibet. A highly influential fourteenth-century Tibetan scholar, Buton, devoted a whole text to *bhikṣuṇī* monastic rules and their transgression, and similar texts are included in the collected works of Bodong Chogle Namgyal.[29] The *bhikṣuṇī* lineage, however, was apparently lost, so it was difficult to meet the requirements for a valid full ordination of women. Until more evidence emerges from a comprehensive study of Bodong Chogle Namgyal's work,[30] it is only possible to infer a plausible explanation for his decision. Bodong Chogle Namgyal may have tried to reestablish the practice of full ordination as part of his more general vision of a revival of lost Indian Buddhist traditions, like the sacred dances for women. Chokyi Dronma seems to have been in a particularly suitable position to spearhead this effort. She is said to have become the "spring of all fully ordained women of Tibet" (folios 51a, 60b), indicating that she was the initiator of a larger tradition and an example to be followed by other women. However, her example was not followed by any of the other women mentioned in the biography, not even Deleg Chodren, but may have had an influence on the ordination of other, later fifteenth-century women. Kurtis Schaeffer (2003) suggests that Chokyi Dronma's remarkable access to full ordination may be explained by her sociopolitical position, which gave her a unique privilege. There is perhaps an additional reason, in which Bodong Chogle Namgyal himself may have played a role, by rethinking some of his plans. Sometime after her full ordination, the biography reports, Chokyi Dronma set up a nunnery in the Palkhu area of Porong. Despite all her efforts, things did not work out exactly as she had hoped. Bodong Chogle Namgyal eventually thought it appropriate for her to reconsider her life choices. She then commented, "According to the great teacher's thoughts, if I wish to achieve my own liberation I can keep my hair without cutting it. In general I did everything I could for the doctrine and the living beings and in particular I wished to help all women (*skye dman*). It seems, however, that no great benefit has resulted" (72b). The detail that Chokyi Dronma was allowed to not cut her hair is highly significant. As an explicit symbol of the tantric approach, it seems to indicate that Bodong Chogle Namgyal suggested that, at this point in her life, she should follow the path of the wandering *yoginī,* which would allow her to practice meditation and engage in a nonmonastic life. The comment about the little benefit deriving from her enterprise seems to point to the challenges associated with the management of the nunnery and the apparent practical difficulties that she found in establishing monastic institutions for women. Later in the biography, difficulties in raising funds to support nuns are also explicitly addressed by Thangtong Gyalpo (118b–119a).

The problems faced by Bodong Chogle Namgyal and Chokyi Dronma in establishing the nunnery may have been as varied as the hazardous constraints of a remote and poor area; the complications of management that obstructed Chokyi Dronma's spiritual practice; and probably also the potential controversies concerning the application of the *Vinaya,* since he often had to defend his promotion of the religious path for women. All this may have ultimately prompted Bodong Chogle Namgyal to advise Chokyi Dronma to change course. She was to remain a unique case, not an example to be immediately followed by other female members of the Buddhist congregation. However, she may have been an important precedent for other fifteenth-century spiritual masters such as Shakya Chogden, who decided to ordain women relying on fully ordained monks alone (and who was criticized for this).

Subsequently, Chokyi Dronma spent a great deal of time in remote hermitages devoting herself to meditation and teaching. She had cut her hair to become a renunciate like the Buddha, and now she let it grow again as she embraced the path of the wandering *yoginī*.

Hairstyle signals explicitly the chosen approach to life and to religious practice. It also reflects the different approach to sexuality among Buddhist communities of numerous traditions and has interesting cross-cultural resonances. There are some striking similarities with the Hindu and Buddhist female ecstatics of Sri Lanka described in Gananath Obeyesekere's work (Obeyesekere 1984 [1981]). *Medusa's Hair* shows vividly how hair can be seen as one of the most significant "personal symbols," i.e., "cultural symbols operating on the level of personality and of culture at the same time" (Obeyesekere 1984 [1981]:2), that reflect different life approaches and sexual moralities: lay, renunciate, mystical. Women who came from traumatic family experiences used this symbol to reshape their subjectivity in religious terms and begin a new life as ecstatics. In an analogous way, Chokyi Dronma used her hair as a powerful personal symbol that signaled the way she fashioned her life and marked dramatic transitions: as she gave up family life, she cut her own hair in a violent way, harming herself and showing her determination to pursue her life choice. This was a prelude to the ritual haircut for her ordination, and in fact she had left a tuft of hair for the ceremony. When she shifted to the path of the wandering *yoginī* she let her hair grow wildly, assuming her distinctive terrifying aspect.

Sexuality is a delicate and controversial point in Chokyi Dronma's life, as the later tradition claims that she actually became a consort of her masters, implying a sexual partnership, even though she never gave up her monastic vows.[31] Tashi Tsering has explored this question without coming to a definitive conclusion, suggesting that more research should be done before anything certain can be said about it (Tashi Tsering 1993:42). Chokyi Dronma seems to be suggested as the tantric consort of Bodong Chogle Namgyal in the passage that opens the biography. This refers to Dorje Phagmo, who took an ordinary human appearance in order to complete the deeds of Bodong Chogle Namgyal and was thus incarnated in Chokyi Dronma. This, however, may have been a reference to a symbolic religious partnership without any statement about the actual interaction between them. Undoubtedly there was a very intense relationship between the young woman and her first spiritual master. When they first entered into a religious relationship, she was around twenty and Bodong Chogle Namgyal was around sixty-five. She had just experienced the loss of her daughter and was resolving her family disputes; he was a renowned scholar who had been invited as a religious teacher to Shekar. The encounter was already extremely charged. She was so entranced by him and his teachings that she felt completely at a loss when he left and decided that she wanted to follow him, which she eventually was able to do after a long struggle. After she joined him at Palmo Choding there was always great affection in the way she looked after his material needs and his physical condition. He was delighted with her and rejoiced at her spiritual achievements and grace, which the biographer symbolizes in beautiful poetic images: "When the Lord saw her, she was like ambrosia for his eyes, like a golden ear shaking in the wind" (61a).

As she assisted him during his last days, she offered him the "supreme achievement of relatedness" that had characterized their relationship by being together with him in meditation at the moment of his demise. This emotional involvement is also reflected in her subsequent grief, which is captured by the biographer in the bare description of the events with rare efficacy; her sense of loss is reflected in her wandering over the hills of her homeland in disarray, recalling her lama at any encounter.

Although Chokyi Dronma's relationship with Bodong Chogle Namgyal was undoubtedly profound, it is difficult to elicit from the biography the actual form of their interactions. Some passages refer to their tantric practices and even to the ultimate form of relatedness they enjoyed, like the following illustration of their spiritual deeds:

[They] had become the secret treasury of all Buddhas thanks to their extraordinary deeds of body, speech, mind, virtue, and action for all living beings. The Female Buddha (*de bzhin gshegs ma*), Lady of the Universe (*'khor lo bdag mo*), dancing the dance of illusion, with its many forms of ritual offering, satisfied the innate bliss of being beyond duality (*gnyis med pa*, i.e., not being two). This was a symbol of excellence (*mchog gi rten*) and a supreme achievement of relatedness (*'brel bar byung ba bla na med pa*). (79a)

Chokyi Dronma, operating at a divine level, may well have acted as a divine partner for her spiritual master, which is suggested by the terms "innate bliss," "dance," and "ultimate relatedness beyond duality." The biographer, however, chose a language that deliberately merged the metaphorical with possible bodily ritual practices, the philosophical with potential physical intimacy, without disclosing what actually occurred in an unequivocal way.

Chokyi Dronma's full ordination would suggest a purely metaphorical and spiritual interpretation of the ultimate bliss they experienced, as any actual sexual practice would entail the breach of celibacy vows. However, other great spiritual figures of this time seem to have been able to combine full ordination with tantric practices that involved sexual consorts. Thangtong Gyalpo, who would become the next important master in Chokyi Dronma's life, had himself achieved full ordination in his youth (Biography of Thangtong Gyalpo 47) but had consorts and a son (see Stearns 2007). The *Blue Annals* (818–819) describe an image of Vanaratna as a fully ordained monk (*bhikṣu*) engaging in secret tantric practices with a fully ordained nun (*bhikṣuṇī*), which suggests that at a certain level of spiritual attainment the conventional limitation attributed to *bhikṣus* and *bhikṣuṇī*s could be transcended.

Since the eleventh century there had been harsh debates about whether tantric initiations were acceptable and recommendable for ordained people, with Atiśa strongly advising against them.[32] However, it seems that during Chokyi Dronma's time certain practices were considered possible at the level of ultimate spiritual achievement, beyond duality, transcending conventional standards. The fact that different standards apply at different levels appears also in a passage referring to Deleg Chodren's training in *guruyoga* meditation: "They are not associated with each other as a human couple (*mi'i yab yum*); however, it is indeed wonderful that there is no fault (*skyon med*) in a divine couple (*lha'i yab yum*)" (57b).

The spiritual master alluded here to a divine level of interaction that transcended the human and allowed for what was unacceptable at a human level. On this occasion Deleg Chodren is said to have performed only the first of the outer, inner, and secret offerings of the Bodongpa tradition; it seems that she did not engage, at that stage, in the secret practices of the third initiation. Nevertheless, this was at least a possibility and may have entailed the offering of one's own body in sexual rituals.

The interpretation of descriptions of tantric practices is not straightforward. Tucci observed:

The processes of speculative thought are directed toward the erection of fine-spun philosophical and mystical structures which transform the erotic and sexual element into a symbol of stages of divine epiphany or into an object of meditation, sublimating it and purifying it to such an extent that it is not always easy to separate out the two interpretations and distinguish the real from the allegorical sense. (1969:44)

The biography does not provide full evidence of what actually occurred. It is very possible that the intense relationship between Chokyi Dronma and Bodong Chogle Namgyal was exclusively spiritual and symbolic, albeit extremely intimate. The biography discloses even less on the nature of the relationship between Chokyi Dronma and the other spiritual masters she encountered, Thangtong Gyalpo, Vanaratna, and Pal Chime Drupa. In all cases a sexual dimension remains a real but remote possibility. The biographer shuts the door, just as Vanaratna and Chokyi Dronma presumably did when "without letting the translator come along, they entered the narrow dwelling of *Samādhi* where he fulfilled all her spiritual wishes" (133b).

If sexual ritual practices had taken place, the metaphorical use of words was a skillful way to reveal what was otherwise bound by secrecy so that it could not be misused. Given the ongoing intense debates about the compatibility of Buddhist monasticism with tantric sexual ritual practices, the biographer made an undoubtedly farsighted step in avoiding any explicit disclosure that could lead to potential denigration of the tradition and of the people involved. Ultimately, at the level of divine interaction, there was no distinction between what was happening exclusively at the level of inner life and what involved the body. The readership of devotees would be able to understand the evocative passages in the correct way according to their respective backgrounds.

The long-lasting debates about the correct interpretation and application of the *Vinaya* were becoming increasingly significant not only religiously but also politically. Chokyi Dronma and the people around her were certainly aware of this, as we can gather from her own comments on Tsongkhapa and his greatness in emphasizing the *Vinaya* but warning against later spurious debates that might jeopardize the practice of *yogin*s and *yoginī*s (folio 139a).

## Illness, Religious Experience, and Healing

Reading Chokyi Dronma's biography, I perceived some remarkable resonances with the rich tradition of local oracles in Southern Lato that I had studied some years before (Diemberger 2005:113ff.). Oracles who did not belong to established lineages had a long history of illness, of physical and mental hardship often resulting from difficult family relations, unwanted pregnancies, and/or conflicts of various sorts. The illness was eventually recognized as divine (*lha nad*) and identified as a possession by a local god—in many ways comparable to a shamanic illness. In the case of oracles belonging to families where spirit possession had occurred before and was somewhat expected, the divine illness usually followed more predictable, ritualized patterns and was identified more easily. In all cases the illness was healed by the act of opening and cleansing the energy channels (*rtsa sgo*) through which the god would enter the medium on regular basis; this could be done by a lama, another oracle, or the god itself. The oracles who were recognized as "authentic" and objects of a "good possession" then became experts in dealing with illnesses and conflicts, individual and collective disturbances. The oracles I met during my fieldwork in Tibet and in the Himalayan valleys were often specialists in the many ailments of daughters-in-law who could not cope with the new situation and were harmed by all sorts of spirits. These oracles seemed to have transformed their experience of crisis into a particular religious competence that they used for the sake of the community.

Chokyi Dronma had transformed the challenges of her life into her own empowerment. In doing so she followed, almost paradigmatically, a Buddhist tantric approach, which seeks to change what is conventionally considered an obstacle into the very means to achieve spiritual liberation. The biography emphasizes several times Chokyi Dronma's healing abilities as part of her Buddhist spiritual competence. However, it seems also to evoke interesting parallels with popular healing practices and spirit possession. For example, Chokyi Dronma is depicted as sucking the thumb of somebody (*mi'i mthe po*) who had been stricken by a contagious disease, thereby eliminating the illness both individually and collectively. Sucking disease from the body of an ill person is a common healing practice of Tibetan oracles, called *jib* (*'jib*) (Diemberger 2005:138). In the lives of oracles and of tantric practitioners it seems that the very essence of the tantric approach may converge with the practices of territorial cults of pre-Buddhist origin, a theme that I will explore further in chapter 6.

Chokyi Dronma experienced illness (*nad*) repeatedly, and this seems to have marked the most critical moments in her life. She is reported as having suffered from an obscure disease called *tokhun* (*stod khun*) shortly after her birth. This illness may have been a reason Chokyi Dronma appears as a particularly sensitive child, who could not be easily touched—besides the imagery of royalty and sacredness that the biographer may be trying to evoke. Later, after the birth of her daughter, Chokyi Dronma became so ill that she almost died, which, as I have suggested above, may have been related to a more general crisis. She reflected profoundly about the meaning of life and eventually recovered after the Medicine Buddha appeared. This event seems to have precipitated her decision to renounce the world and take up a religious life. Chokyi Dronma's experience of closeness to death as a critical, empowering moment recalls that of sacred women belonging to various forms of popular religiosity, such as oracles and *delog*[33]—a theme that appears in the lives of other Buddhist female heroes such as Nangsa Obum (see Schaeffer 2004; see also Pommaret 1989).

She became ill again after the death of her master, when she is described as affected by what is called a lice disease (*shig nad*) and facing great hardship while wandering the hills of her homeland instead of going to some estates as she was expected to do. She seems to have been temporarily out of her mind, as she is described recalling her master at any encounter, whether the people she was talking to were able to understand what she was saying or not. She eventually recovered and initiated the reproduction of Bodong Chogle Namgyal's collected works. She was also able to help a fellow disciple who had suffered deeply the loss of the master (88a, b).

The biographer states in this passage that she was an expert in healing people with mental disturbances, which she had learned to do through her religious practice (folio 88b). A reference to her karmic relations with ignorant and crazy people seems to indicate that she had a specific healing competence deeply rooted in her own experience. Holy craziness, typical of the tantric transgressive approach, seems in her case to overlap with a deep and anguished aspect of her personality.

As a healer, and as a performer of miracles, Chokyi Dronma often had to deal not only with mental obscuration and individual ailments but also with contagious diseases. The nature of the epidemics mentioned in the biography is not described in the text, but it is well known that the plague and tuberculosis are still endemic in the region, and smallpox epidemics still occurred in the twentieth century. Chokyi Dronma often defied the common fear of disease, both in individual cases and in collective situations. The episode mentioned above, in which she took care of the dying old woman despite the reluctance of her mother, recalls the example set by Machig Labdron and the practitioners of *cho* (*gcod*). They specialized in charnel ground rituals as a means to achieve spiritual liberation and often took care of the dying and the corpses.

From the traumatic experiences of her life Chokyi Dronma gained great insight into human behavior, which became an asset for her in a variety of life contexts. Having dealt successfully with hardship, and perhaps with her own occasional mental instability, she could tackle other people's problems—sometimes as a diplomat, sometimes as a healer, sometimes as a religious teacher, operating on many levels.

## Many Names, Many Selves, Yet Intrinsically Selfless

Chokyi Dronma's life seems to have often combined what might appear irreconcilable ways of being. In the biography and elsewhere, she is defined through a rich variety of names and epithets, all of which are significant because they refer to her many different aspects. The princess's three main names seem to refer to three distinct modes of manifesting herself in different contexts: Konchog Gyalmo (Queen of the Jewel), her birth name; Chokyi Dronma (Lamp of the Dharma), the name she was given when she was ordained as a novice; and Dorje Phagmo (Vajravārāhī), the name attributed to her when she was revealed as an emanation of this deity. It is significant that all these names are used together in a letter, reported in the biography, written by Thangtong Gyalpo before Chokyi Dronma's departure from Northern Lato in 1454. She took it on her journey to introduce herself to the local rulers she would encounter. Somewhat comparable to a modern reference letter, it enabled Thangtong Gyalpo to give her credibility in an unfamiliar environment and activate his own wide network of support. The text of the letter is reproduced in the biography, apparently as a full quotation, and describes the princess concisely according to common views of her time. As it was produced through an immediate interaction between Thangtong Gyalpo and the princess, and she presumably understood and endorsed it, this passage provides a unique insight into not only how she was perceived by others but also how she saw herself through the eyes of this spiritual master, and in relation to her contemporaries.

According to the biography, this is the main text:

All former scholars and members of the monastic community acted for the benefit of other living beings, but now there is nobody who cares. Particularly since the death of Machig Labdron, there has not been a woman who was dedicated to the benefit of other living beings. Now there is a lady who stems from the royal lineage of the Gods of Clear Light ('Od gsal lha) who is devoted to spiritual liberation and to the benefit of all living beings. Her outer name is Lady Queen of the Jewel (bDag mo dKon mchog rgyal mo); her inner name is Female Teacher

Lamp of the Doctrine (sLob dpon ma Chos kyi sgron ma); her secret name is Vajravārāhī (rDo rje phag mo). Her residence is undefined. Her companions are undefined. And foremost, her lama is undefined (*nges med*). Since all elements are empty and have no essence (*bdag med*), she practices emptiness (*bdag med*). Now she is coming to your place, so please welcome her and give her adequate support at her departure. Follow the solemn commitment (*dam tshig*) of religion (*lha chos*). Refrain from shameful worldly customs. Wherever she stays, do not feel jealous about what is mine and what is yours. I, King of the Empty Plain, ask you, people living in the East, to keep showing the great kindness you have shown in the past to these followers of mine. In return for your kindness, the Female Teacher and her retinue are coming. Look after them well. (folios 127a, 127b)

The biography states that this letter was addressed to every local ruler, included a handwritten endorsement by Thangtong Gyalpo, and contained precious gifts. He was aiming to ensure that the rulers accepted her by accentuating her different attributes effectively. At the beginning he evoked Machig Labdron as a well-known sacred woman, almost as a role model, and as an "authorizing reference" (Gyatso and Havnevik 2005:22). Subsequently he emphasized the princess's royal descent. He then mentioned her three names. It is interesting that at this point the letter includes additional titles: lady (*bdag mo*) and female spiritual teacher (*slob dpon ma*). These highlight, respectively, her worldly status and her spiritual achievements.

This letter, however, also had a more profound meaning. By recalling her three names within the threefold classification of "outer," "inner," and "secret," a standard formula in tantric rituals and writings, Thangtong Gyalpo inscribed her ways of appearing in the Buddhist framework of multiple layers of relative existence and ritual practice. By then referring to her lack of attachments and her practice of emptiness, he also evoked the distinction between conventional and ultimate truth: conventional truth is susceptible to becoming manifest at different levels (epitomized by the threefold classification), while the ultimate truth is sheer emptiness, since all phenomena as we apprehend them are devoid of any essence (*bdag med*). This ultimate selflessness encompasses all worldly phenomena, including the illusory perception of oneself (*bdag*). This view informs what Janet Gyatso (1998) defined as the "apparitions of the self" reflected in Tibetan biographies (see chapter 3). The threefold classification is also used for biographies: an "outer biography" refers typically to concrete life events of all sorts; an "inner biography" to monastic life and religious training and experiences; a "secret biography" to intimate mystical experience and relation to the meditational deities. Thangtong Gyalpo knew, therefore, that by introducing the princess in this way he was referring to a system of notions that everyone would recognize and respond to. Thus he defined her as both threefold and one at the same time, combining her individuality with her multiple ways of acting in the world and her universality as a deity that transcended space and time. By mentioning her secret name, Thangtong Gyalpo was revealing to the recipient of the letter—as lama to his disciple—the ultimate secret: the traveling nun-princess was the incarnation of Dorje Phagmo herself. Finally, by highlighting that she was an accomplished practitioner of emptiness, he affirmed that ultimately she was selfless (*bdag med*), a buddha beyond all definitions and distinctions. He wanted to solicit the receiver's observance of their pledge to Buddhism and to Thangtong Gyalpo himself as lama, and to ensure that they behaved appropriately and provided support to her. Through the letter Thangtong Gyalpo would also be present at the encounter in one of his many forms, for which he was renowned—referring perhaps not only to his esoteric powers but also to his network kept together by a skillful system of communication.[34]

Thangtong Gyalpo's letter brings together the different forms in which this remarkable woman manifested herself in different contexts, acting "in the knowledge of . . . her own constitution as a person in the regard of others" (Strathern 1988:275). He referred to the names that she was given by others, which she had made her own in relation to others. They defined her within a Buddhist theory of the self as nonself, a radically antiessentialistic view that could account for the self's multiplicity, relationality, and irreducibility to a coherent whole. Building on the centuries-long preoccupations with the self that characterized Indo-Tibetan thought, Thangtong Gyalpo's views seem remarkably suggestive against the background of current endeavors to look at Buddhist philosophical reflection cross-culturally (Kapstein 2001) and anthropological debates on selfhood and the person (see, for example, Battaglia 1995), after Geertz's critique of the "Western conception of persons as a bounded unique, more or less integrated motivational and cognitive universe . . . organized into a distinctive whole and set contrastively both against other such wholes and against a social and natural background" (1979:229). Thangtong Gyalpo described Chokyi Dronma, practically and theoretically, according to a view of personal identity that contrasts with any notion of the individual as conventionally understood in Euro-American societies—and yet it seems profoundly evocative across times and cultures.

By choosing to quote the letter in this way, the biographer incorporated the lama's unifying act at a crucial point in the narrative: the moment when Chokyi Dronma set out for her final journey to the shrine of Dorje Phagmo, when she was about to abandon the familiar setting where she was known and respected. Now facing the unknown, her persona had to be redefined in relation to those she would encounter and would have to rely on. Her multiple appearances had thus to be condensed in the letter.

The use of Chokyi Dronma's names and epithets in the biography, as in the letter, is highly significant. There seems to be an underlying framework for when and how they are used. In fact, actual names are mentioned relatively infrequently; she is mainly identified through a wide variety of epithets, e.g., "Venerable Woman," "Magnificent Lady." The actual name Konchog Gyalmo and the abridged form, Gyalmo, always appear in reported speeches or in the presumably reported description of worldly events; this might well have been the name she most commonly used in day-to-day interactions over a long period of time, even after she became ordained. The name Chokyi Dronma appears for the first time in the passage mentioning her ordination as a novice (folio 46a), and it is used more rarely and exclusively in the monastic environment.[35] Finally, Dorje Phagmo, indicating that she was recognized as an emanation of the deity, appears for the first time in a statement by Bodong Chogle Namgyal while they were residing at Porong Palmo Choding (folios 63b–64a). In a dialogue, the spiritual master highlights that she is not only the Daughter of the Gods (*lha sras*), using the ancient (nongendered) imperial title, but also the embodied female tantric deity.

This was the first revelation of Chokyi Dronma's secret identity, which would be reiterated by Thangtong Gyalpo. It is significant that direct quotations with explicit statements about her secret divine nature appear relatively late in the biography, sometime after her full ordination. This may reflect the period of her life when she started to be publicly acknowledged as an incarnation of the deity. The biographer is likely to have reproduced the expressions used in the written and oral materials he wove together (see chapter 3). Throughout the biography, however, there are also frequent references to the princess as Vajrayoginī (Dorje Naljorma)—the female tantric deity of which Dorje Phagmo is a special form (see chapter 1). This indicates that the biographer decided to use this name to frame and orient the whole narrative. He was thereby promoting the reader to the level of the initiate to whom the ultimate secret was revealed, who was made aware, at the outset, of the secret identity of the princess. The biographer evokes the princess's divine identity especially whenever he describes her extraordinary behavior, in both social and religious terms. For example, she is the Dorje Naljorma who builds a wonderful wisdom *stūpa* for Bodong Chogle Namgyal and the Dorje Naljorma who is present at his death and conducts his funeral; and she is the Dorje Naljorma to whom her own mother prostrates as they part (the contrary would be appropriate for a regular daughter). Already in her childhood, she is described as an extraordinary girl who dances as if she were wearing bone ornaments of the deity and does not prostrate to her father or who beats up a local headman for not recognizing her as a divine being. These passages are part of the framing narrative that reads life events in light of her secret, esoteric nature that was later disclosed. Often, the events are described with such a wealth of realistic detail that both an ordinary and an esoteric reading of the same story are possible.

A remarkable example of narrative that allows for both a worldly and an esoteric reading is a passage about the marriage ceremony. When she arrived at Shekar as a new bride, some Bonpo priests celebrated customary marriage rituals; since the princess disliked this, she meditated on Dorje Naljorma and by appearing as the embodied deity, she scared them off. The passage plays skillfully with the ambiguity between the secret identity of the princess that could be revealed under extraordinary circumstances and the more ordinary fact that in order to realize a deity, practitioners in meditation actually visualize themselves as the deity. In merging the identity of the princess with that of the female tantric deity, this passage also recalls one of the earliest accounts of King Songtsen Gampo revealing himself as an embodied *bodhisattva*.[36] The merging of the identity of a temporal ruler with that of a deity through a system of multiple apparitions became a key feature of Tibetan political and spiritual leadership and was fully deployed by the Dalai Lamas. What makes Chokyi Dronma extraordinary is that she seems to have been a female counterpart to this. Blending the imperial legacy with the tantric sacredness of the deity would become crucial in the construction of the Dorje Phagmo as an institution, as we shall see in the second part of the book.

Chokyi Dronma's life embraces the worldy and the otherworldly in a dynamic way. It also epitomizes the union and the tension between the Mahāyānic idea of the accumulation of moral and intellectual merits and the tantric idea of the essential union of the individual existence with the ultimate reality, or the logic of yogic practice. The combination of the two approaches appears as "the sharp ridge of a mountain upon which one cannot find an inch of flat place upon which to balance oneself" (Tsuda 1978:167), producing the sense of crisis that can be perceived particularly in Saṃvara Tantrism. In this unresolved tension "both elements were indispensable for the dialectical development of tantric Buddhism itself. Tantric Buddhism was destined to keep walking along the sharp ridge" (Tsuda 1978:176).

The notion of "[transcendent] Union" (*zung 'jug*), the Tibetan translation of the Sanskrit term *Yuganaddha*, was particularly important to the Bodongpa and indicates the status of spiritual realization of the *yogin*. Nāgārjuna's *Pañcakrama* highlights it as a core notion of Buddhist practice; I shall quote here a few of the verses in the translation by Per Kvaerne:

(2) When, avoiding the two notions of *saṃsāra* and *nirvāṇa*, then it is called *yuganaddha*

(5) When there is no dual concept of "object" and "subject," but only nonseparation, then it is called *yuganaddha*

(24) Fully seeing through the net of *māyā*, having crossed over the sea of *saṃsāra*, having done what is to be done, the great *yogin* remains in the cessation of the two (modes of) truth. (Kvaerne 1975:132–133)

Chokyi Dronma crossed the sea of *saṃsāra* indeed. Her personality, as far as it can be glimpsed through the narrative, especially through "cracks" in the biographical models and predictable formulas, was definitely complex. How could she combine renunciation with keeping, at least to some extent, her role as a princess actively operating within secular networks? How could she combine full ordination with acting as a divine consort of great spiritual masters, as inferred by some Tibetan authors and ambiguously hinted at by the biography? There is little doubt that during her lifetime Chokyi Dronma operated consciously within multiple registers of discourse and different moralities. The biography provides evidence of this on several occasions. For example, it reports that, after having behaved as a perfect daughter-in-law, she politely expressed her wish to take the vows. When her request was not accepted, she decided to change her strategy: "So she thought that now she had to do something that appeared to be transgressive (*spyod lam 'khyog po*) to make the people of Southern Lato feel weary and lose their faith in her; internally she would devote herself to meditation and pray to the great Mother Tārā to fulfill her wish" (folio 38b). She eventually managed to free herself from her secular obligations by experiencing or feigning mental instability. Because of her ultimate aim, she felt that her behavior was morally acceptable,

FIGURE 4.1 Chokyi Dronma, after a mural painting at Samding monastery. *Yancen Diemberger*

at least temporarily, even though she consciously realized that "it diverged from what her spiritual master had taught" (folio 38a). The biography refers, several times, to the discrepancy between external appearance and interior attitude and between conventional good and ultimate aspiration. It often highlights Chokyi Dronma's awareness of the social order, which she sometimes complied with and sometimes deliberately transgressed to show the absolute priority of spiritual aims. The biography outlines how Chokyi Dronma, presenting herself in many different ways, was able to deal with multiple hierarchies and make difficult choices among conflicting moralities—the worldly, the monastic, and the mystical.

*Princess, Nun, Yoginī*

Chokyi Dronma in her own person embodied and unified the more general tensions of the Tibetan social and religious world: the contradiction between worldly involvement and religious renunciation as well as that between monastic discipline and mystical practices that implied the transcendence of rules. In this light Chokyi Dronma can be understood as equally multiple and one, deeply entwined with all the contexts of life in which she was engaged, yet ultimately selfless and free of worldly concerns. Like one of the readers of Thangtong Gyalpo's letter, presumably bewildered when confronted with this extraordinary woman, we are invited to approach her and the narrative of her life aware of her multiplicity and her ultimate spiritual aspirations.

To free all animated beings from the ocean of existence, cast a net of iron over the great rivers. In all living forms leave the seed of spiritual liberation.

—CHOKYI DRONMA[37]

# Part II

TRANSLATION OF
THE BIOGRAPHY OF THE
VENERABLE CHOKYI DRONMA,
THE THIRD REINCARNATION OF THE
*WISDOM ḌĀKINĪ* SONAM DREN

Chokyi Dronma. *Karen Diemberger*

Homage to Vajravārāhī!
Ultimate giver of pleasure to Heruka!
Head of innumerable *ḍākinīs,*
*Vajra* queen, mother of all buddhas,
Protector of the living beings of the auspicious age,
protect me!

Although she is still, in the peace of *dharmakāya,*
Her bodily emanations appear in many forms to suit
the minds of the followers.
I write the biography of the Vajra Beauty,[1]
who performs and enjoys the multiple magic dance.

(2a) In order to complete the deeds of our great lama, the omniscient Jigdrel,[2] Vajravārāhī, the female buddha, took a human body and enjoyed the magic dance of Mahāmudrā in this world. I am therefore writing a short biography of her. Through the blessings of His Eminence, the Delight of the Goddess of Divine Melody (dByangs can dga' ba) Chogle Namgyal, the embodiment of the wisdom of all buddhas, and of Vajrayoginī, the mother of all buddhas, may I be granted the permission to write the highest secret. As far as this secret is concerned, the Venerable was incarnated in the area of Gungthang in Ngari.[3] She descended from the unique parasol (*gdugs gcig pu*) that protected all the living beings of Tibet, the religious king Songtsen Gampo, who came forth from the Śākya lineage.[4] (2b) Her father was called Thri Lhawang Gyaltshen Palsangpo; her mother was called Dode Gyalmo. She was born in the year of the tiger [1422] in the capital of the Gungthang kingdom in the royal palace of Dzonkha, when the planets and the stars had auspiciously gathered.

## Birth

Two months before conception, her mother dreamed of a naked girl who wore only a bone ornament. This girl said, "Please let me come in!" Later the mother told this dream to her husband, the king, who decided that a lama should be consulted. (3a) The lama Chopel Sangpo[5] said that this was a prophetic dream announcing the birth of a precious reincarnation. When she was conceived, her mother dreamed of the sun and moon dissolving into her heart, felt intense meditative bliss, and was encompassed by a fragrant scent. The lama and the king looked after her very tenderly. The lama gave her a long life empowerment every day.

Two days before giving birth, the mother had a dream of a single white horseman who told her that a great guest would be coming two days later and that a great offering feast should be prepared. After saying this, he fixed his banner (*ru mtshon*) on the roof of the palace and left. Two days later, as the sun was rising, the mother gave birth to her without any pain. She did not cry, did not utter any sound, and there was no smell. She was beautiful to look at, like a polished shell, without any impure substances of the womb.

## Childhood

(3b) Two months afterward, the baby became ill from a disease called *tokhun* (*stod 'khun*). Vajrayoginī [i.e., Chokyi Dronma, many years later] at Tsari in Kongpo remembered: "Two months after my birth I became ill with *tokun*. The doctor Shakya Yeshe was consulted and called out, 'Your Highness, hold out your hand with raised finger!' and drew blood, wasn't this appropriate?"

When she was six months old she was able to play the bell and the hand drum (*ḍamaru*). When she was eight months old, her mother consulted a lama for the name-giving ceremony. The night before, the great female incarnation herself had said to her mother in a dream, "My name is Konchog Gyalmo. (4a) Since 'Konchog' means 'the Jewel' and I maintain the lineage of the Three Jewels of Buddhism, and since I'll be victorious in all directions, I'll be called 'Konchog

Gyalmo,' 'Queen of the Jewel.'" Later her mother told this story to the lama and he replied, "This is exactly the right name! Since the day of her conception, there were indications of her being an emanation. However, in order to avoid difficulties for her in later life, make it look as if I have formally given her her name. In fact, however, she has named herself."[6]

(4b) Even when she was a toddler, she had great compassion for all living beings; she picked lice that other people threw away and hosted them on her body. When the nanny mentioned that people were coming, she would straighten her body and act importantly. When her nanny touched her, the nanny would feel sharp pain, for her body was not to be touched by ordinary people. So the nanny had to use silk clothes to hold her. The little princess carried herself with elegance, spoke Sanskrit, and stayed in deep meditation. She did such extraordinary things.

When she was two years[7] old a great epidemic spread in the capital, and people were saying that everybody might die. (5a) As the little princess was sucking somebody's thumb,[8] her mother asked what she was doing. Her mother took it out of her mouth, pulled her along, and scolded her. However, the girl said, "Soon the disease will stop." Then the disease actually stopped and everybody recovered.

Once, when she was at the monastery called Gompa Shag, she went for a walk in the forest. At that time there was a great hailstorm. Suddenly she returned, completely naked, and started to cry. Her mother asked, "Where are your clothes?" Holding her mother's hand, she took her to a place where she had put her clothes to cover a mound crawling with insects. Then she said, "There will be liberation from *saṃsāra!*" (5b) Since she had great compassion, she would never have fresh butter and yogurt before the calves were fed. She would only eat old meat, she would never eat fresh.

Once, while she was with her mother in Kyirong at the fortress called Langpokhar,[9] they both fell down from the eighth floor but did not suffer any major injuries. The young princess[10] broke her foot, but she said that this would not matter as it would not have any long-term consequences.

At the age of three she started reading by looking at the alphabet. Without putting any effort into learning, she was able to read and write perfectly. (6a) Once while her mother held her by the hand and spanked her for the sake of her education, she wailed, "Lord! Death is coming to the people. Please help!" The mother asked, "Who is the lord?" She said, "Avalokiteśvara." When she was four, the ground shook with a great earthquake. The palace Deden Yangtse[11] cracked. The Magnificent Lady (*dpal gyi dbang mo*) performed a ritual gesture (*mudrā*) and recited: "Goddess Tenma,[12] please tame the earth!" The tremors stopped and the cracks mended on their own. Thus no damage actually happened.

Once in Longtse (Slong rtse), she saw a woman in rags; her dress had been stitched together out of patches. She got scared and ran up to the top of stairs and called to her mother for help. (6b) Her mother picked her up, put her on her lap, and asked what had scared her. She replied, "I'm scared of a woman like this who has not accumulated merit in the past and I'm scared of all those who are not accumulating merit now."

When the princess was five years old, during the day she used to fully participate in secular life. At night she used to read the *Bodhisattvacaryāvatāra*.[13] One day Gyaltshen, the headman (*dpon*) of Gangkar,[14] came to see her, the *ḍākinī*. He made prostrations to the Buddha statues (7a) but he did not bow in prostration to the venerable infant. The girl told her mother, "Gyaltshen neglected me today." The mother asked her, "How did this happen?" She smiled and said nothing. She just asked for a stick. The next day when Gyaltshen arrived, the girl beat him and said, "You, Master Gyaltshen, carried out prayers to deities made of stone and wood, but you did not make offerings to those that have a human body. Now you should prostrate to me first, and then you can do so to the statues!" (7b) When the headman, Gyaltshen, heard this, he was astonished and said, "This girl speaks like one of the highest deities; I'll pay her respect," and he prostrated before her.

While staying at the Gompa Shag[15] monastery, a junior wife of the king, one of the sisters from Bongdzog,[16] had given birth to a son.[17] Since Chokyi Dronma's mother had only two daughters,[18] she was anxious, and at one point she spoke bitterly to the Venerable and her sister, calling them "misfortune." The precious princess said, "Mother, please come here! Let's make a plan for all of us, mother and daughters." Her mother was surprised and asked, "Please, tell me what you think." She told her mother, "Although since I was a little girl I have wished to become a renunciate (8a), in the first part of my life I'll become a married woman because of the *karma* accumulated previously. For this marriage I would like to be sent to Guge[19] because we are part of the same lineage and it is a very wealthy kingdom. There I can eat good fruits rather than meat. However, I'm not likely to be that lucky. Anyway, in the first part of my life I'll follow your instructions and according to your words, as my mother, I'll lead a secular life. In the later part of my life I'll take the vows and fulfill my hope regarding my future. But please, don't call us 'misfortune,' I'm an excellent one!" The mother was impressed and pleased.

(8b) Once, when she was six years old, her sister fell over and hurt her head. She was unable to speak. The princess, the Excellent Inborn One (*dpal ldan lhan cig skye ma*), uttered the power of truth and her sister did not suffer any damage.

Once, when she was at Gompa Shag monastery, she saw a very old woman holding a stick and leaning on it. She called the nanny, Tshebum, told her to come, and asked, "What is that?"

Tshebum replied, "That is a very old woman."

"Is this a human being?"

"Yes."

"Will I become like this?"

Tshebum without thinking much, answered, "Yes, you will."

The girl got very scared and cried and cried and cried. Then Tshebum spoke some soothing words: "I was just joking! You will not become like this."

Later, she heard the sound of the drum (*ḍamaru*) from the charnel ground and asked, (9a) "What is that?"

"A corpse is being carried to the charnel ground."

"Will this happen to me?"

"No, it will not!"

"It will happen to me, I know. I'm afraid."

"If you are afraid, what will you do?"

"I'll do something that liberates me from the fear of death."

"How can you do this?"

The Venerable immediately went into deep meditation. When meditating she could not be distracted by any noise or any music around her. Once her brother shouted in her ear: "Sister!" but she did not react.

[folio 9b is missing]

(10a) The princess used to meditate taking Vajrayoginī (rDo rje rnal 'byor ma) as her meditational deity (*yi dam*). One day she went before her father, the King Son of the Gods (*lha sras*). Without performing any prostration and shaking her body, she said, "My whole body sounds as if I were wearing bone ornaments [like Vajrayoginī]." Her father thought, *She is too young to engage in such things, she must be joking!* and rebuked her: "How is it that you think that you are Vajrayoginī? Parents are not different from the Jewel of Buddhism; therefore, they should be honored by prostrating."

In Mangyul-Kyirong, many flowers and fruits[20] used to appear even in the winter. For this reason she liked to stay there. (10b) Once, when she was staying at

*Translation of the Biography of the Venerable Chokyi Dronma*

Kyirong, her father, the king, came to the area leading an army. When they arrived at a locality called Minkyu Drima Dzong,[21] a big flash flood occurred in the gorge and many stones were falling everywhere from the steep slopes. Everybody tried to escape but there was no way out, and when the flood was about to reach the army they seemed doomed. However, the young tantric queen (*rdo rje btsun mo*), by pointing her finger magically, made the water flow upward so that the army managed to proceed on its path without any damage.


## Marriage

A few years later Situ Lhatsen Kyab, the ruler of Southern Lato,[22] sent some envoys to ask the king of Gungthang for his daughter, so that she would become the wife of his son Tshewang Tashi. Her father accepted this request and, thinking that this would benefit everyone, ordered that she should go to Southern Lato as a bride. (11a) When she heard this, she said to her father, "I do not want to contradict my father's order this time. In order to benefit all living beings, I will go. However, I will take the monastic vows in the future, when the right time comes." Therefore she took an oath taking the deity Pañjaranāth (Gur kyi dgon po)[23] as witness.

When she was sixteen [around 1438], she became the wife of Tshewang Tashi, the son of the ruler of Southern Lato. More than a hundred officials and common people from Shekar, led by the official Jobo Kyab, came to Gungthang in order to escort the bride to Shekar. The whole of Gungthang was full of people and a great wedding was celebrated.

[According to tradition, when the bridegroom's party arrived at Gungthang, it was formally received:] the King Son of the Gods (*btsan po lha sras*) was seated on his throne; (11b) the brother, Thri Namgyal De, and other relatives were seated in the front row. Jobo Kyab, the mediator (*snye bo*), and four people were invited to enter the room and meet the king. The princess, the emanation body (*sprul ba'i sku can*), was seated in perfect stillness and according to worldly customs was weeping. When they saw this, her father, the king, and all the subjects were very upset, and cried as well. Her brother took his own precious earrings and offered them to her. Everyone was brokenhearted. Since all the people liked the Magnificent Lady[24] and respected her very much, some of them offered their earrings or necklaces to her; others offered precious rosaries. Everybody was thinking of this Great Lady (*bdag nyid chen mo*) with great affection. (12a) The official Ponne

Simadar (dPon ne Srid ma dar) said, "Homage to the most precious of all women (*bud med thams cad kyi mchog*) in Ngari. She is now gone from us. This is the custom, but the heart feels great sorrow," and saying so, he was shedding tears. For the ceremony the envoys took along a hat that had belonged to Shenrab, the founder of the Bonpo religion, and many items of clothing that had been offered to her by her future husband, Tshewang Tashi. The bride accepted the clothing and the jewels but threw away the Bonpo hat.

(12b) At that time there was a particularly wild horse, and in order to bring good fortune (*rten 'brel*)[25] the bride was asked to ride it for a moment. Meanwhile, another more tame horse was prepared for her journey. To the surprise of everybody, as soon as she mounted the animal, it started to tremble and sweat and eventually became very calm. Later she always liked to ride this horse. Everyone present was witness to these great deeds of body, speech, and mind and to the numerous extraordinary signs that appeared on that occasion: the sound of cymbals resounded in the valley; rainbows appeared in the sky and moved toward the east; all the birds of Ngari escorted the bride, flying toward the east; all the birds of Palmo Choding[26] came to welcome her [on the pathway that led toward Porong and Shekar]. (13a) All the living beings of Ngari felt as if they had lost their protector. It was as if the whole essence of the earth had been taken away (*bcud phrogs pa*) and the earth had turned bleak. Everybody felt very sad and was crying.

On the way, when she arrived at a pass from which she could see her father's palace, she prostrated toward it. She offered a white scarf (*kha thags*) with many flowers. Both the people escorting her and those welcoming her, when they saw this, wept. (13b) The people from Ngari felt as if they were being separated from their protector and asked the people from Shekar, "You are receiving the Ocean of Magnificence (*dpal gyi rgya mtsho*), why are you crying?" They replied, "Of course we are not crying because we came to welcome her; ours are tears of faith in the deeds of the Great Beauty (*dpal gyi sgeg mo*) [Chokyi Dronma]."

In order to avoid the threat of some bandits from Mustang (Glo ba),[27] they traveled over long stretches by night. Once they spent the night in tents at a locality called Koron. The people of the Shekar welcoming party thought, *It must be very hard to travel like this; she should have some proper sleep. (14a) However, she is not missing her daily meditation practice. We keep hearing the sound of bell and drum. It is wonderful that she is becoming our lady!*

On the way, the people who were closest to her were the people of the Ngari escorting party. Except for Jobo Kyab and four other people, nobody of the welcoming party was allowed to get close to her. Therefore, Jobo Kyab expressed a formal request on their behalf: "Everybody in the welcoming party is a close attendant of the ruler, so please allow us to get close to you!" Then she replied, "Tomorrow I'll satisfy your wishes." (14b) The next evening she opened the door of her tent and met everybody from Southern Lato. Jobo Kyab introduced every person individually, by name, descent, and place of origin. All the welcoming party from Shekar were very happy.

Eventually, the moment came when the people who were escorting her had to return to Ngari. The headman, Paldar Gyaltshen, said, "I don't have anything to say except that I ask you to think of us; please don't get too emotional!" (*thugs sna mi thung*). She answered, "When I left Ngari my father did not give me instructions, for I'm familiar with worldly customs. Please don't worry!" (15a) Then the people of Ngari, very upset, took leave of her. They prostrated and wept. The welcoming party was overjoyed. On the way [as she was crossing the Porong area], passing in the vicinity of Palmo Choding she sent some people to the monastery to ask the Revered Omniscient Chogle Namgyal whether she was allowed to visit him. He replied, "You cannot come here! I'll meet you on the way." (15b) They met at a place called Yau (gYa'u), a wide pastureland in the Palkhu area.[28] The princess said, "If there is water, this is a good place to camp." She took an iron stick, stuck it into the ground, and a power-ful spring appeared. They then proceeded to the Yeola (dBye 'o la) pass, where they met 500 soldiers who had been sent from Shekar to welcome her. On the way, wherever they arrived, people celebrated with songs and dances. Countless local headmen welcomed and escorted her. The lamas of all the local monasteries came, prostrated to her, and were inwardly driven to request her blessing.

(16a) The nuptial procession included more than 100 officials who assisted her. They were wearing elegant clothing and precious jewels. Smartly dressed horsemen proceeded in front while more than 1,000 soldiers surrounded the princess. The procession covered the whole area so that the birds had no place to land. When they arrived in the vicinity of Shekar, her future husband, who was a devotee of Shenrab, sent some 60 Bonpo priests, wearing woolen turbans and carrying drums and *shang*,[29] to perform some rituals of exorcism (*bgegs bskrod*). (16b) It was a depressing sight, like seeing Zangmo of Magadha leave the Buddha in the dwelling of the Anāthapindikavihāra and worship the heretical Jain teachers in the town of Buram shing phel. The princess said, "We can't stand this! Chase them away!" Her retinue responded by throwing stones and chased them away. The Bonpo escaped, leaving their ritual instruments at the cross-roads like stones and pebbles. Thinking of this episode, the great *yoginī* Chokyi Dronma invoked the victory of the Buddhist gods (*lha rgyal*).[30] This seems to be the first auspicious gesture by which she paid respect to the doctrine of the Buddha. (17a) By doing so, for the first time, she revealed to the watching people that she was an emanation body (*sprul ba'i sku 'dzin pa*). They did not dare to raise their eyes and said, "This daughter-in-law is extremely beautiful and has great power and majesty (*dbu 'phang mtho bo*)!" Later she heard this and thought, *This is a good omen* (rten 'brel)!

As Chokyi Dronma was to meet her future mother-in-law, the Lady Tsencham Gyalmo, for the first time,[31] she thought, *I was given by my father to this family, so according to worldly custom I must pay respect to them.* (17b) Accordingly she prostrated and offered flowers to her mother-in-law, who was very pleased with her. Later, while the Bonpo were performing some rituals in the royal palace, she said, "I am a Buddhist, I am not a worshipper of the Bonpo.[32] Please respect my beliefs!" Accordingly only one Bonpo teacher of her husband remained to celebrate some Bonpo rituals (*mnga' gsol*), assisted by four other priests. Then the Queen of the Buddhas (*rgyal ba'i dbang mo*), by meditating on her deity Dorje Naljorma [Vajrayoginī], revealed herself as the embodied deity, and the followers of Shenrab became extremely anxious and ran away, dropping their ritual instruments.

(18a) At Shekar a marvelous wedding was celebrated. All the ministers and all the subjects of the kingdom came. They performed dances and songs, and everybody enjoyed themselves. People feasted on endless food and drink and offered many gifts, from extremely precious items to ordinary goods. The festivities lasted over a month. The spirits of the place showed their respect as well: rainbows appeared in the sky; the earth was covered with flowers. (18b) The sound of cymbals resounded and many magnificent signs appeared. Then Chokyi Dronma, the spiritually accomplished woman, thought, *I came here with two tasks: one worldly and one beyond the world. For the sake of my ancestors I have avoided sins and accomplished virtuous deeds. In particular, I have paid respect and have provided service to the Buddha's doctrine. I have taken good care of our subjects and servants. However, I cannot stay long in this family. If I were to stay, I would be committed to showing respect to my parents-in-law* (gyos sgyug) *as if they were gods and providing them with good service forever.* (19a) *Therefore, when the appropriate moment comes I will enter the door of the precious doctrine and practice Buddha's teachings in the most appropriate way.*

## Life at Shekar

At Shekar she kept practicing her daily and nightly routine: after waking up, she would meditate on "The Stages of the Path to Enlightenment" (*lam rim*). She would then confess moral failings (*ltung bshags*), perform spiritual purification (*gso sbyong*), and wash her body. She also used to recite hymns to all the gods. She would then perform the "Stages of the White Torma [Offering]"(*dkar gtor gyi rim pa*); the praise of the Buddha, "The Twelve Deeds" (*mdzad pa bcu gnyis*); Sakya Paṇḍita's praise, "King of the Dharma" (*bstod pa chos kyi rgyal po*); and the ritual offering to Tārā (*rGrol mchod*). (19b) At that time, before receiving teachings from the Omniscient Chogle Namgyal, she used to rely mainly on the texts by the great Sakyapa, spiritual father and son [Śākya Paṇḍita and Phagpa]. Then she would eat. Sometimes she would write, according to her own inspiration. She and her husband used to debate, wagering garlands of jewels. Later she stopped doing this, but her husband insisted and she said that ordinary bets with jewels were not sufficient. Like Sakya Paṇḍita's debate with the heretics, she insisted on a debate between Buddhists and Bonpos with religion as the subject. (20a) But this did not happen. Afterward she would enjoy talking to some spiritual masters and some new people who had arrived to meet her. She would comment on what they were saying, and in doing so she used to impress and delight them. Before performing ritual offerings of *chang* and tea, she would read the songs (*gur*) and poems of former lamas to avert the demons. (20b) She also used to perform again the praises and offerings [mentioned above]. [sentence unclear] Common people were impressed by the way she behaved and lived. The Great Woman also used to behave very appropriately as a daughter-in-law in front of her parents-in-law, far beyond anyone's expectations.

(21a) Once, however, an official called Drungchen Kyabma came to meet her and she received him simply, without using any honorific language and proper protocol. When her mother-in-law, Tsencham, saw this, she was displeased and thought that she was behaving too arrogantly. Tshewang told the Magnificent Lady [Chokyi Dronma] about his mother's feelings. She answered, "It is a proper custom to show respect to one's own parents, but how your mother shows respect to others is her own business. She can show respect to the lords of Northern Lato if she so wishes, but my lineage is much higher than that. My relationship with Drungchen is like the relationship between lord and servant (*dpon yog*), and there is no custom prescribing that the lord has to show respect to the servant. (21b) The correct practice is that the lord takes affectionate care of the servants."

Later, she saw a simple monk of the Shekar monastery who was in charge of carrying water roaming around without finding a place to sit in the row [where people were sitting according to their rank]. Using her hand, she showed him a place and with great respect requested him to be seated there. Seeing this, everyone was very surprised. Her husband thought that this wasn't very appropriate, and as he met [Chokyi Dronma] the Queen of the Buddhas, he said, "You didn't show respect to Drungchen Kyabma, but you showed respect to a water carrier; this is very strange!" The divine compassionate princess said, "Even though the water carrier has very low rank, he is a monk. (22a) My ancestors who were *bod-hisattvas*[33] (*yab mes chos rgyal byang chub sems dpa'*)behaved with great kindness toward all living beings and showed great respect to those who were wearing the monastic robes. In the current bad times, this custom is not practiced anymore. The water carrier is a son of the Buddha and he should be respected." He replied, finding it difficult to accept her behavior, "This is hard to understand!"

At Shekar there was a *bsTan 'gyur*[34] written in gold that had been made by her ancestor Bumdegon Nagpo.[35] This had been taken from Gungthang by the Lord of Northern Lato and was later transferred (*spyan drangs*) to Southern Lato. One day she said that she wanted to see (*mjal*) it. When she arrived at the place where it was kept, at first she was unable to open the lock of the door. Then she said, "May the owner have power over her things!" and touched the lock, (22b) which opened immediately. She saw that the *bsTan 'gyur* was covered with dust. She cleaned it up and later added the parts that were missing. She provided for cloth (*nam bza'*)and strings (*sku rags*) to wrap it and appointed a custodian to take care of it. She also established the custom of celebrating offerings there.

She had great faith in the Shekar monastery even though she did not join the midsummer and winter celebrations.[36] On those occasions she used to come to the door of the garden (*kun dga' ra ba*) where these were performed. She would pray for the monastic community and prostrate to them. She would then be seated on a thin mat and have the *Yen lag bdun pa* prayers recited by the monks, and she would offer food and drink to the monastic community in great quantity. (23a) Thus she performed virtuous deeds, and the monks accepted them gratefully. When they completed the recitation of the prayer *bZang po'i spyod pa'i smon lam* [mentioning buddhas and *bodhisattvas*], they pronounced her name

*Translation of the Biography of the Venerable Chokyi Dronma*

as "The great Queen of the Dharma" (*chos kyi rgyal mo chen mo*) and thereby showed their great respect. When the ritual offering (*tshogs*) was completed, the monks came to her like insects on a lotus flower, prostrating to her and receiving her blessing. During the Saga month[37] many *tsha tsha*[38] had to be made. She made 100,000 of them in eight days and placed them inside a *stūpa*. When she completed this, a shower of flowers fell from the sky.

The princess always performed virtuous deeds. She always respected the doctrine, the great lamas, the monastic community, (23b) her parents-in-law, and her husband like the jewel of the crown. She never spoke anything that was untrue. She enjoyed repeating good sayings so listeners could enjoy her voice. She never spoke any rude words nor any words that would hurt other people. Her throat would not utter anything that could not be trusted. She greatly enjoyed giving donations. She would never indulge in wearing female ornaments such as bracelets. She would never loosen the golden belt represented by the awareness of what is shameful (*bag yod pa*) and what are the rules of proper behavior (*tshul khrims*). Her father-in-law, the Great Situ Lhatsen Kyab, was very satisfied with her. He used to speak all the time of her with great pride. (24a) He would let guests meet her for tea, and her conversation was eloquent and full of deep meaning. Everybody said, "Ah! We have got a wonderful lady to enhance the prosperity of Southern Lato. She fulfills the wishes of the whole of Southern Lato."

## Visit to the Parents

When she was seventeen, she went to visit her parents. She took along many presents and was escorted up to the Palkhu area by some trusted servants and also by numerous soldiers from Southern Lato. Her father sent many soldiers to meet her there and escort her to Ngari. As she reached the Jala (Bya la) pass, (24b) she was given a great reception by the monastic community of Gungthang Chode. Eventually she was escorted to the royal palace by many people playing music. Everybody said, "This Great Lady has now become a feast for two myriarchies!" Then, in the central palace called Utse (dBu rtse), she met her father. She prostrated and offered a white scarf. Her father took her hand and asked, "Gyalmo! Did you have a hard time?" They both started to weep and then had an emotional conversation. (25a) For a month she was busy meeting people and celebrating.

One time, a junior wife of the king requested her to be seated on the main throne. Chokyi Dronma said, "We are equivalent by birth, and I am also older than you; however, if I were seated on the main throne the ranking would look wrong because you are the queen, the wife of the king (*mnga' bdag rgyal po*), and I am only the daughter-in-law of the rulers of the Lato people. Therefore I will be seated on the lower throne." The people from Lato who witnessed this felt deeply humiliated.

(25b) During her stay at Gungthang her husband, Tshewang Tashi, sent a messenger from Shekar every three days requesting her to return soon. Therefore she only stayed three months and then returned with all her jewels, traveling back to Shekar in a similar fashion to her previous journey. Her mother-in-law, Tsencham Gyalmo, came to greet her a day's horse ride from Shekar. When they arrived at Shekar she was given a great reception and a great feast was celebrated.

## Motherhood

(26a) When she was eighteen [around 1440], she became pregnant. The Great Situ and her mother-in-law took very good care of her as if she were the apple of their eyes. They had religious services performed regularly for her. When the time for the delivery came, she gave birth, without any suffering, to a beautiful daughter. Her mother-in-law came and asked, "Did you have a good delivery? Did you suffer any pain?" She answered, "The birth was easy and I did not face any hardship; the baby is a girl." The mother-in-law said, "The most important thing is that your body is in good condition. (26b) There is no difference between boy and girl. Later you will give birth to one child after the other." Then her husband, Tshewang Tashi, came to see her. Her mother-in-law went into another room and left them alone. Her husband asked, "Did you face any hardship?" The princess, the emanation body, answered, "I didn't suffer. This time, even if there had been some suffering, I could have endured it easily. However, I can't stand the suffering of being caught in *saṃsāra*. The pleasure of emotional attachment is very short, it does not bring any long-term benefit. Permanent happiness should be aimed for." Her husband was speechless.

(27a) Later he suggested that Yungdrung Lingpa, a great Bonpo master, should become the child's teacher. The Magnificent Lady replied, "Had this child been a boy, you would have had the power to decide. However, since the child is a girl,

*Translation of the Biography of the Venerable Chokyi Dronma*

she will take refuge in the Jewel of Buddhism." The parents took affectionate care of their newborn child. They organized many nannies who provided food, milk, and play. Mother and child were staying in a beautiful room, had the religious service called *rGyal sde* performed by monks, and were constantly assisted by servants.

## Illness

Not long afterward the princess went, together with her attendants, to the hot springs.[39] There she became very ill and seemed about to die. The officials and the servants of Ngari and Southern Lato performed many religious services to assist her recovery. (27b) Everybody in both countries was very anxious. Her parents-in-law and her husband came to see her. Her mother-in-law seemed particularly worried; weeping and in despair, she asked her daughter-in-law, the spiritually realized woman, for advice. She replied, "It is not too bad. I won't die. If I wanted to die, I could do so easily, but this time it is not going to happen." Then her mother-in-law, trying to put emotional pressure on her, continued, "My husband and I are both already old. For us there is nothing in the world more precious than our son, Tshewang Tashi. He treasures you as the most precious thing in his life. If you were to die, how would we manage?" She replied, "Death comes to all, and even after death there is still suffering to endure. (28a) We are powerful people who have carried out important deeds, so we will also undergo greater suffering. If I were afraid of suffering, I would get a bad rebirth. If at this time I weren't thinking about a solution for my future, I would be very foolish. I am aware of what is sinful and what is virtuous. Please think about what I have said." Then she started weeping. Her parents-in-law wept as well. The Great Situ discussed the situation with his son and asked him, "What do you think?"

Her husband replied, "Perhaps what she said is right. I am now wondering what I would do if she did die. What do you, my parents, think?" (28b) The Great Situ said, "I feel extremely sad when I think that she might die. I feel as if I were dying myself. These thoughts have made me suffer very deeply."

At one point her husband sent Palchen, an attendant of the Great Woman, to her tent to see how she was doing. Palchen saw that on the bed where Vajrayoginī [Chokyi Dronma] was lying down, on the side of the pillow, there was the Medicine Buddha radiating light. In great astonishment, he fainted. When he regained consciousness, the Great Woman asked, "What happened to you? Please tell me!"

Palchen told her the vision. She commented, "This is not a hallucination. (29a) Consider this to be a dream and don't tell it to anybody. I won't die this time."

After that night, she started to recover. Then she said, "This is not my time to die. Since the people of Ngari and Southern Lato have performed rituals adequately, I will not suffer any longer. We should return to Shekar." The Great Situ suggested, "Let's go when you have fully recovered." She insisted: "Let's go now!" Therefore they returned to Shekar. Since she was still very weak, she traveled in a carriage. On the way they saw that every house had raised flags to celebrate her recovery.

When the princess arrived at Shekar she did not go to see her child, and she stopped taking care of her. Her mother-in-law was extremely upset about this and said to her husband, the Great Situ, (29b) "She hasn't been seeing her child! Even wolves or hawks take care of their offspring." When Vajrayoginī [Chokyi Dronma] heard what her mother-in-law had said, she commented, "Royal offspring have an innate, self-reliant character (*bzhin lhun gyis grub*). A good mother is also necessary, and up to now I have done all that I could do to look after this child. However, from now on it is not necessary for me to do so. I will not take care of her any longer, as it is all a source of suffering."

Her irritated mother-in-law said, "She might be a Buddhist. However, her behavior seems very worldly. If she is hurt by some words, she never forgives. (30a) It is very difficult to assess her." The Great Situ smiled and said, "Of course it is difficult to assess her. Currently nobody is superior to Konchog Gyalmo in central Tibet (dBu-gTsang). Mine is the best daughter-in-law!"

Not long afterward she received news that Ngari was going through a bad time, as major conflicts had started between her father and her brother. Therefore she went there, escorted by 100 horsemen as she didn't dare to go alone. When she arrived at Dzonkha, she realized that the situation had become very unstable; the gate of the palace was in a bad state and looked like the teeth of a horse's corpse; in the corners there were some monks; each room was occupied by an official on his own; her father had retired to the royal quarters and (30b) her brother, the prince, was roaming aimlessly around the plain with about 100 ministers. Then the Magnificent Lady spoke appropriately and the king and all the subjects listened and followed her instructions. The king and his son reached an agreement and came back together into the royal palace. The monks went back to their cells. The time became peaceful again. She visited her mother, deeply worried that she might have believed that she, her daughter, had died.

Before returning to Southern Lato, she went to see her father and said, "There is no meaning in worldly affairs. (31a) There was so much pain to endure when my brother was born, and after he was born everybody was delighted. And now this is the result. So I really have to follow Buddhism."

Her father replied, "You have just established the basis of your family. If you say this, it is as if the sun were setting immediately after dawn."

She countered, "Father! Do you forget that I swore I would become ordained, taking Pañjaranāth (Gur kyi dgon po) as a witness? For a woman, the age of twenty may well be the end of her life. We don't know what comes first, the next life or the next night. How do you know, Father, the limit of my life? Please send my sister, Dzamling Gyalmo, to replace me. However, I will carry out my duties until she becomes the proper age to replace me."

Then she started her second kind of deeds, giving up all thought of worldly life.


## Death of Chokyi Dronma's Daughter, Decision to Take the Vows, and Return to Shekar

(31b) While she was in Ngari the princess received the news that her daughter had died. This gave her a lot to think about. At first her mother-in-law did not have the courage to tell her. Eventually the Great Situ sent a letter: "You came here fruitfully, but we were not as fruitful as you were. As nothing else could be done, we tried to earn merit by conducting her funeral in the best possible way." The Great Yoginī thought that her daughter had died because her husband had requested some Bonpo priests to take care of her and wrote a reply saying, "It is the fate of any being that has been born to die. We cannot help it. However, the child should have lived longer, but because of the actions against Buddhism this did not happen. Now there is no point in worrying; this child will find its own way." (32a) The Great Situ was glad and relieved with this reply and showed it to everybody. The people of his court said, "Perhaps this time [Konchog] Gyalmo has some regret for how things have gone. Later she may be blessed by the birth of another child. The Magnificent Lady is still a source of good fortune for the ruler and his son."

Once, a certain Ponpo Lama (dPon po bla ma) from Sharkha Dripa (Shar kha dris pa) damaged many belongings of Palmo Choding monastery. The princess had great faith in the lama of that monastery [Chogle Namgyal] and was furious that this had happened. She felt she could not tolerate such an act and therefore took the aspect of a wrathful *ḍākinī* and punished him severely. The sinner gave up all his property and thought of leaving the region. At that point the Great Situ intervened, trying to mediate. (32b) However, the princess said angrily, "Chogle Namgyal has been a most precious lama for the whole of Tibet; since very early on he has also been the supreme object of devotion (*bla mchod*) for our own country of Lato. We should feel very ashamed about what has happened. This kind of person is an enemy of the Buddha's doctrine; he is against what is necessary for meditational practices, and we should get rid of him. Normally, we should reward good deeds and punish evil deeds. All officials should know this. How can we be indifferent? From now on I will take care of the people, wealth, and land of Choding." Following this incident, the Omniscient (Chogle Namgyal) was presented with many donations, including precious jewels. (33a) The Great Lama, delighted that she had dealt with evil deeds so skillfully and taken such good care of the doctrine, wrote a poem in her honor.

When Chogle Namgyal visited Shekar, he said, "You are the Queen of the Doctrine! You acted as a supporter of the Buddha's teachings. In particular, you took care of the people, wealth, and land of Palmo Choding. I am extremely grateful! Please continue your support in the future, establish monasteries, and have the *dPal de kho na nyid 'dus pa* [Bodong Chogle Namgyal's collected works] reproduced. (33b) The Kagyupa school has had until now an unbroken line of *siddhas* as lineage holders, starting from Vajradhara. I pray that you may become a holder of the doctrine in a similar way. This would be our great deed as spiritual father and daughter (*yab sras*)."

Much earlier, when the Female Buddha, Woman of Wisdom, was about to arrive at Shekar as a daughter-in-law, the mother of a dumb boy gave birth to four daughters. The father was very upset and in despair tried to throw them into the water. But the dumb boy all of a sudden spoke: "They can't be thrown away! The four girls are four *ḍākinīs*. The head of the *ḍākinīs*, Konchog Gyalmo, is about to come here from Ngari!" (34a) Later these girls became extraordinary beings, as had been predicted.

The princess, the spiritually realized woman, the one giving pleasure to Heruka, led this kind of life from the time she became the source of prosperity for Shekar until she became ordained. Holding the banner of spiritual liberation, she sometimes returned to her own home. She used to perform excellent offerings of body, speech, and mind, and therefore the king, the ministers, the subjects—in fact, everybody—praised her virtue. Under her influence, what had to be praised, like the precious doctrine of the Buddha, was praised, what had to be criticized, like the banner of Shenrab [the Bonpo religion], was criticized. (34b) An ocean of magnificence spontaneously gathered in the great myriarchy. The crops were plentiful, there was enough water to irrigate the arid soil, and the rains came on time. Everything became perfect. Her parents-in-law and her husband became very powerful and achieved great harmony. There was no fear of war from enemies. There were no epidemics or famine. It was a peaceful and prosperous time and everybody enjoyed it. The flag of the country's reputation waved in all ten directions.

## The Struggle to Take the Vows

Eventually, in order to show the path of the doctrine to those who were caught in a worldly life, (35a) she decided to take monastic vows. Therefore she asked the king, queen, and prince of Southern Lato for permission: "Now please satisfy my deep yearning to become ordained. I will thereby fulfill all the wishes of Ngari and Southern Lato."

Around that time she had invited the Omniscient Lamp of the World [Bodong Chogle Namgyal] to the palace and was listening to his teachings. Although she had put forward her request to priest and patrons [i.e., Chogle Namgyal and the royal family], neither agreed. When Chogle Namgyal returned to Palmo Choding, she presented him with many offerings and at the time of his departure she escorted him for a while. When she returned to her residence, she felt very sad, for she was missing the Great Body of Wisdom.

(35b) She then read the *dPal de kho na nyid 'dus pa* [the collected works of Chogle Namgyal] and understood it and memorized it perfectly. Spontanously she felt great faith toward the Revered Lama. She reflected, *I already had faith in this lama before, but never as much as now. I have never read a teaching like this. My life has become pointless. I must follow his teaching. Now is the time to pursue the great endeavor and take the vows from him.* Thinking of this, she started to cry. Then a shower of flowers fell for seven nights.

(36a) After reading the text, she acquired the ultimate faith and felt like following the deeds of the great lama. In order to ask their permission, she sent a letter to her father in Ngari and formally asked the Great Situ. However, they did not grant it to her. All the officials, having become aware of what she was trying to do, begged her to understand their situation, have compassion, and abandon her plan. In order to avoid opposing them, she decided to delay for a while. Meanwhile, Dzamling Gyalmo was invited to Shekar for a visit and was told about her sister's plans. (36b) The rulers of Southern Lato and their court thought that the situation had become more relaxed.

Around this time the princess read the *Lalitavistara*,[40] which describes the great deeds of Prince Siddhartha [who then became the Buddha]. He gave up his queen and all forms of worldly pleasure, and went to the forest and meditated under a tree. While reading this she developed great faith and regretted deeply that she was still involved in worldly matters. She said to herself, *The present situation is just like having received a blessing from the demons (*bdud*). It is like neglecting the great deeds of the Lord Buddha. Now I am meaningless, like a drop of water on the grass.* (37a) She felt great regret because she was caught in *saṃsāra*, and her mind became completely focused on the pursuit of enlightenment. She thought that even though she seemed to fulfill all the wishes of Southern Lato and Ngari, it was difficult for her to live a family life. Then she sent a messenger to her father with a letter saying that she would take the vows anyway, reminding him that she had taken an oath to this effect. She sent a similar letter to the ruler of Southern Lato. However, both of them strongly disagreed with her plan, and therefore she had to delay it yet again.

At that time her husband's mental condition declined. He was affected by some form of manic depression (*snying rlung*)[41] and could no longer control his behavior. (37b) Because of this, many people from Ngari and Southern Lato kept trying to persuade her to stay. In particular, the Great Master Sangye[42] was invited to give her teachings on how to lead a civil life, looking after her family while also supporting the doctrine. He asked her, "Are you disheartened because of his mind or because of his goiter? Concerning the first possible cause of unhappiness, if you were leading an affectionate life as a couple, the problem would disappear spontaneously. Concerning the goiter, this is just a minor physical problem and you should not be bothered. Why do you want to give up your family? If you keep carrying out your current role, it will be very good for the prosperity of the myriarchy and for the development of the Buddhist faith. You will be able to support the establishment of monasteries. (38a) You can practice meditation and you can learn all the deep instructions on how to reach enlightenment within one lifetime, while staying with your family. Rather than taking the vows and becoming ordained, it is much better if you stay with your family. In particular, if you do not keep the throne, conflicts may break out between these myriarchies and everybody will be extremely unhappy." Then the Great Woman resolutely countered, "I prefer to take the vows, focus on the Omniscient, and be liberated. Even if I were to bring about great prosperity, such a goal would be far removed from the taking of the vows. It would be like poison. Now nobody can change my commitment!" After this discussion, she was not prepared to listen to anybody's advice.

She decided that she would make the people of Ngari and Southern Lato angry with her. As she had not been able to achieve her aim so far, she changed her behavior, even though this diverged from what the Omniscient King of the Doctrine [Chogle Namgyal] was preaching. (38b) She decided that she had to do something that appeared to be transgressive (*spyod lam 'khyog po*) to make the people of Southern Lato feel weary and lose their faith in her; internally she would devote herself to meditation, praying to the Great Mother Tārā to fulfill her wish. Following her change in behavior, the monks of Shekar monastery kept watch over her by guarding the walls of the fortress and the monastery, and at each door a guard and a dog were set in order to prevent the Great Woman from abandoning her family.

(39a) Irrespective of how often she had been asked to stay, she would not listen. She promised that she would give up all attachment to the world and prayed to the Great Compassionate [Avalokiteśvara] that eventually she would be able to take the vows.

One night she heard a voice resounding in the sky saying, "All fruits have ripened over many ages; now you will succeed." Thinking that the right time had finally arrived, she stopped meditating. That night she gave up eating and drinking and spoke to the people around her very calmly: "Until yesterday we were all caught in suffering; now you can enjoy whatever you wish." (39b) Accordingly everybody started to drink *chang* and tea, enjoy dancing, and behave like crazy people on the charnel ground. They did so until they became unconscious. Then she said to the horse keeper Phurbagyal, "Please listen to my final words: at dusk, take my horse to the front gate. Please swear that you will do so." She gave him her earrings as a reward. Then when night was approaching she saw that every door was watched by a guard and a dog. As she could not escape from the palace in that way, she went to the roof of the building considering that she might jump, but then she thought, (40a) *If I cause any damage to my sense organs, then this could prevent my ordination.* She therefore went back. As she was walking back she heard many dogs barking along the narrow path. She said, "*tso tso,*" and they went quiet. She was able to open all the locks very easily by reciting a few words.

Meanwhile, according to his promise, the horse keeper Phurba [gyal] was waiting for her at the gate with a horse. Then there was a great thunderclap. The Great Situ, the monks, and the servants woke up and started to look for the princess. At this point the spiritually realized lady thought, *Now, by carrying out gentle actions, nothing meaningful has been achieved. I have to do something unheard of.* (40b) She undid her hair and started to chop it with a knife, leaving a tuft on the crown of her head.[43] In her haste she badly injured herself. At first nobody noticed her. However, as she became increasingly upset, people saw her terrible state. The Great Situ and his wife went immediately to where she had been seen and asked her why she had done this. She answered, "Even a king cannot close the door of the *dharma*. Since my wish was not accepted, this is the result," (41a) and threw her hair at the feet of her father-in-law. The scene was unbearable for all present. Everybody was startled; some collapsed; they were all frozen by the shock, like images in a painting, and eventually broke into tears. The lady's shaved head was an awful sight, wet like a skin container for churning butter full of buttermilk. Her mother-in-law, in tears, said, "If this is how you are going to behave, Tshewang Tashi has no other option but to die, and I would rather die first!" Since the great lord, her father-in-law, had a great spirit, he was not as shaken. (41b) In tears, feeling great compassion for the Great Woman [Chokyi Dronma], he calmed her down. Everybody in the court was puzzzled and did not know how to react. Then he said, "As long as you are here we cannot invite a new bride for my son. Please ask your family in Ngari to send your younger sister, Dzamling Gyalmo, to come here to replace you. But please, for the time being, don't let Tshewang Tashi see you in this state; just go to see him for a short moment. Keep my words in mind and eventually your wishes will be fulfilled." The princess was pleased with what he had said and decided to behave according to the old man's request. Eventually everybody left and went back to their own places.

(42a) She covered her head with a wig, sticking it to the tuft that was left. Dressed up in her best clothes and wearing all her jewels, she went to see her husband. Thanks to the skillful intervention of his father, he was not aware of what had happened. Later, however, he gradually realized that his wife's behavior had changed dramatically so that she was no longer a source of happiness and good fortune, and he was again affected by his illness. Meanwhile, in Ngari some difficulties caused the replacement of the princess by her sister to be postponed. Since it was impossible to wait for her any longer, one of the daughters of the

*Translation of the Biography of the Venerable Chokyi Dronma*

Headman[44] of Nyag, called Ponmo Chogyal, was invited as a new bride for Tshewang Tashi. When the Great Emanation Body [Chokyi Dronma] heard this news, she thought that at last all her wishes were being fulfilled. Feeling great faith in the Jewel, she was able to set her mind at rest.

(42b) Eventually, she went to see her husband with the formal request that she be allowed to enter the door of the doctrine. He replied bitterly, "It seems that you are not to stay at my side for this life, and there is no hope that you will become my protector in a future life. Do what you wish, you don't need to ask me!" She then gave back all the keys to the Great Situ and said, "I came here to take leave of you and show my respect to you, as I am going to become ordained." The Situ said, "The people of Ngari have done me wrong. There is nothing that Tshewang Tashi can do about it. Since you have made up your mind, I cannot stop you. Do whatever you wish!"

As she was about to leave for the upper regions [for the main seat of Chogle Namgyal], since nobody wanted to lose her, they said to her, "Please stay here in this area in a remote monastery or nunnery. Don't go to the upper regions. (43a) We will support you lavishly! If you follow our suggestion, we will rejoice and you will be pleased. If you do not accept our request, our wish will be frustrated and you will face hardship."

She replied, "I don't care, I don't need anything! This time I shall take the possessions I have been looking after from Majong (Ma ljongs) monastery to Palmo Choding, as I'm in charge of this property. As long as I'm in good health, I promise that you won't be harmed. Please, bear some hardship for the sake of the upper regions (stod phyogs)." Weeping, she continued, "It seems that I am not able to provide good service for you in this life. I pray that I will be able to meet you in heaven (mkha' spyod) in the next life." Then she prostrated.

(43b) Then the Great Situ spoke compassionately: "I will send a letter with you to the Omniscient with a formal request for your ordination. If I had a long life and death separated me from my wife, this would follow the natural course of things. Such a separation [between you and your husband] while you are still alive is a greater sadness." After saying this, he returned to his own residence.


Becoming a Nun at Palmo Choding

Chokyi Gyalmo felt that all her wishes were accomplished and left riding a horse. She said, "I prostrate to the gods who fulfilled my wishes!" and sent a letter of farewell with some presents to her husband. At last, she felt completely liberated from the chains of family life, which are the source of all suffering. She had entered the path of knowledge and liberation. (44a) Therefore she went to Palmo Choding, the residence of the Omniscient. The merit treasury of Southern Lato was suddenly left empty, and the town of Shekar resounded with the laments of the mourning people. The Great Situ said, "The people have a good reason to cry and be sad! They have been separated from my daughter-in-law, Konchog Gyalmo." While speaking this he felt extremely sad. When Tshewang Tashi heard the laments, he asked, "Who is this? This sound seems to pierce my heart." The servants replied, "It seems that the whole myriarchy is crying. Even the lord is crying." Tshewang Tashi asked, "What happened?" His father, the king of the *Dharma*, replied: "She left, but I am here. (44b) I do not have the option to leave [to devote myself to religion as old people do]. Wouldn't it have been better if I had gone?" After the departure of the Spring of All Things, the myriarchy lost all its magnificence; all that was there before, thanks to her blessing, was suddenly gone. The land and its people felt empty.

During her journey the Magnificent Lady walked by night and took rest in the morning. On the way, while sleeping, she dreamed of a *stūpa* of the Great Bodhisattva. The attendant who was looking after her horse also dreamed of a *stūpa* of the Great Bodhisattva so tall that it reached the sky. When they talked to each other about their dreams, she said, "This is a wonderful omen!"

Eventually they reached Palmo Choding (45a) and entered the monastery. As she set her foot on the stair that led to the door of the residence of the Omniscient Chogle Namgyal, the first ray of the morning sun was shining on her forehead. She said, "This is a good omen!" Then she met him, offered him the letter from the Great Situ, and asked for ordination. He replied, "There is nobody as precious as you in Ngari and Southern Lato. I cannot perform the rite of cutting your hair." She said, in tears, "It seems that I am not so fortunate as to be able to take the vows in this life. I pray that I will be able to do so in the next life and give up my life now."

Chogle Namgyal then sent messengers with letters to both Ngari and Southern Lato, requesting a formal authorization. From Ngari the king-father replied, "Since she is very strong-minded, please give her the ordination." (45b) From Southern Lato the Situ replied, "If she were to face great hardship, I would feel sorry for her. Please give her the ordination." While waiting for the return of the messengers, the spiritual master and the royal benefactress wandered around together on the grassland. Trying to console her, he said, "Don't be sad!" She

*Translation of the Biography of the Venerable Chokyi Dronma*

replied, "I have already been as sad as I could possibly be in the past. Now I don't feel sad anymore. Now my suffering is the suffering of *saṃsāra*."

Eventually, after they had received the approvals, a woman called Tsenkyong was asked to assist the princess in washing, making herself beautiful, and arranging her hair. The woman suggested, "Let's use my hair as a substitute for the hair of the Venerable." She was thus able to arrange the hair of the princess very beautifully. Dressed up magnificently, wearing all her jewels, she slowly walked toward the residence of the Omniscient, preceded by people offering incense and playing music. This image surprised and delighted all the monks. Some of them commented: (46a) "Compared to her extraordinary behavior and experience, we consider ourselves to be very simple." She went among the monks and offered some gifts such as canopies, clothes, and horses. She offered flowers that were worth 800 *sho*. Then she announced: "In general there is no significant difference between those who succeed in being born as male and those who fail and are born as female (*skye rgyal pham*). However, from now on, I will focus on supporting Buddhist practices for women (*bud med*), the source of trust for all women (*skye dman*)." Then she offered one silver *sho* to every male and female member of the monastic community (*dge 'dun skye rgyal pham*) and offered many donations to support the celebrations. Holding the banner of liberation, she took the vows as a novice (*dge tshul ma*). From being part of a family, she became without family. She received the name Adrol Chokyi Dronma.

(46b) Everybody from Palmo Choding came to meet her and show their respect. As soon as they saw her, they immediately felt great faith. They said, "She is like Sha rii bu."[45]

At one point the closest disciple of the Omniscient, called Konchog Gyaltshen,[46] said to her, "It is astonishing that you renounced all worldly pleasures and took the vows. Now the religion and political power of Ngari and Southern Lato will decline." She replied, "I do not have lesser aspirations now than I had before. I am not satisfied with the enjoyments of this life; I seek the enjoyment that lasts forever. I am not satisfied with being the queen ruling over Ngari and Southern Lato; I want to become a place of refuge (*skyabs gnas*) for all living beings." Hearing this, Konchog Gyaltshen felt embarrassed about what he had said.

(47a) Someone said, "The lady will need something suitable to drink." The attendant in charge of pouring tea[47] countered, "In Shekar she didn't drink alcohol or tea. Now she will drink the mountain water of Choding." When she heard of this discussion, she wrote a comment: "Alcoholic drinks and Chinese tea taste good, but these are enjoyments only for this life; the mountain water of Choding tastes much better. Stupid people should not get confused and misunderstand compassion." When people read this, they felt very embarrassed and acknowledged, "Our remarks were mistaken."

Once a person nicknamed "Goat-Bearded" because he had a beard like a Hor[48] came to meet Chogle Namgyal to get a blessing from him. On that occasion he commented, "There is a girl who is like the apple of the eye of both Ngari and Southern Lato. Now she has cut her hair and entered the doctrine, corrupting it. (47b) How did you allow this?" The Lord answered, "She came according to links from previous ages. You have no such links, how can you criticize me? She does not want to become the Lady of Ngari and Southern Lato; she prefers to become the protector of all living beings. The doctrine was not corrupted. In fact, it is people like you, without virtue, who are corrupting the doctrine. Get out!"

After losing Chokyi Dronma, the Ocean of Magnificence, the Great Situ couldn't bear to stay at Shekar and went into retreat in the holy mountains of Śrīri.[49]

Eventually the news that Chokyi Dronma had taken the vows came to the ears of Tshewang Tashi. He was furious. He ordered his officials to prepare an army to wage war. The officials replied critically: "There is a good dialogue between Ngari and Lato, and we are trying to maintain good relations. It is not right to behave like this!" (48a) Taking no heed of their advice, Tshewang Tashi retorted, "The discussion is already over. I have the nerve to do this. The moment of the lama and the disciple [i.e., Chogle Namgyal and Chokyi Dronma] has come! If this time I don't do anything to avenge myself, I may die very soon." Then he sent an army to the area above Śrīri [in the direction of Palmo Choding] and sent envoys to Ngari with a message: "Come to fight at Choding!" His soldiers were not in a position to refuse. Therefore they went, but among themselves they commented, "During this battle let's try to survive and let just the officials be killed." The local people, unable to prevent the war, expressed their feelings in rumors: "Tshewang Tashi with the goiter is responsible for all this!" Thus the army went toward the upper regions, causing great harm to the nomads of Ngari.

(48b) Eventually the army arrived at Gungthang, at the center of the Ngari kingdom. There the soldiers received a message from the Great Situ ordering them to cease the hostilities and return home. The subjects of the king of Ngari, distressed about what had happened, were very critical of the Great Woman. Later when she went home she heard many slanderous remarks and said, "Before, everybody liked me and had faith in me. From now on I'll have to live surrounded by slanderous rumors. However, this doesn't affect me. This is the result of having ripened bad *karma*. I shouldn't get angry nor pity myself."

Once her mother said, "Would it be good to offer turquoises to the king and the prince?" She replied, "Earlier in my life I was a royal patron of the monastic community. At that time I looked after the people of the court and my relatives as if they were my own children. I was respected like a mother by them. (49a) Now I have become the protector of all living beings. I don't need worldly goods and I don't need to cultivate relations with relatives in a worldly manner."

Later she went to Mangyul-Kyirong and celebrated a great offering of butter lamps to the Self-Generated Great Compassionate (*Phags pa wa ti*).[50] She offered butter lamps eight times, had a great prayer celebrated, and presented monasteries such as Dzonkha Chode with many donations. Subsequently she returned to Palmo Choding with her mother to listen to the essence of all the *tantra* as taught by the Omniscient. While she was still at Shekar she had asked the Omniscient to find a suitable teacher for her. (49b) Accordingly he had assigned her a teacher called Jamyang Dragpa,[51] for whom she had great respect. After taking the vows, she relied on this teacher as recommended by the Buddhist doctrine. She did not take into account differences of clan and lineage (*rigs rus*) and listened to everything diligently. Nevertheless, she was often shown respect and given offerings amid a great crowd of people. She thus absorbed the Omniscient's teachings in all their detail and profoundness.

While she was practicing *yoga*, meditating in solitude, the Omniscient became concerned, thinking that she was on her own without any attendants. He thus sent a trusted servant to make sure that she was getting enough food. (50a) When the attendant arrived, he saw that she was managing her food on her own perfectly well and reported this to the Lord, Chogle Namgyal. He was delighted with this news. He said, "This lady doesn't ignore anything! She will definitely become a protector of all living beings." He kept listening to reports about her. Once Kunsang, who was the attendant looking after the religious practitioners, came to the Lord of *Dharma* and reported: "The Great Lady is not practicing meditation, she is just studying texts." (50b) The Immortal said, "It is better that she studies texts rather than practicing meditation. She is already the best meditator among all those who have gathered here." Hearing this, Chokyi Dronma said, "If I am the best meditator, this is very good. Please continue to supervise my practice and grant me, step by step, all the teachings and empowerments that I have requested." After saying this, she returned to her meditation cell smiling.

Later a scholar asked the Precious Lord of the Dharma, Chogle Namgyal, "Is there currently any woman in Tibet who has greater wisdom than the Great Woman?" He replied emphatically, "She is beyond compare!"

On one occasion a senior practitioner, who was a perfect follower of the *Vinaya* and was participating in the evening assembly, was putting some effort into getting some food. (51a) Seeing this, the Lord commented, "The Great Lady is a follower of the vows of individual liberation (*so thar*); she is a Great Vehicle for the *bodhisattva* teachings; she is like Vajradhara for the tantric practice; she is like Mañjuśrī for knowledge. All these support one another. In order to follow one aspect of the doctrine, a practitioner should not neglect another. Although she is a novice, she is already behaving like a senior monk." Everybody felt embarrassed [comparing her behavior with their own]. When Chodzema, the Lady of Tagtse,[52] was studying there, she spoke to the Lord and remarked, "This venerable woman is extremely clever, she is able to learn everything just by studying a little." Thus Chokyi Dronma turned the Wheel of Dharma greatly and (51b) through her training reached the great perfection of *Samādhi*.

Once the Omniscient became very ill and seemed close to death. A doctor called Chagmen (Chag sman) was summoned to treat him while a great religious service (*sku rim*) was performed for the sake of his health. The Great Female *Siddha* looked after all the necessary arrangements excellently. Thanks to the accumulated merit, the Omniscient recovered.

Eventually Chokyi Dronma organized a great offering celebration (*tshogs*) and presented the Venerable Master with a turquoise. He accepted this joyfully and put it around his neck. He also dedicated an extraordinary prayer to her. The people who had gathered on that occasion said, "Such a teacher-disciple relationship is our great fortune! (52a) The deeds of this Great Lady benefit us all. The teacher is delighted; we rejoice. Such a Body of Virtue is very precious to us! Thanks to her, this year the teaching of the doctrine has taken place in an excellent manner, the monastic assembly was very good, and the Venerable was pleased. Let's pray that she will stay here forever!" Eventually the teachings came to an end and the autumn arrived.

## Begging Nun

The lady who would become the spring of all fully ordained women (*dge slong ma thams cad kyi dpyid du gyur pa*) planned to go begging for alms. Feeling that this was not very suitable for someone of royal stock, everybody asked her not to carry out her plan. However, she said, "Alms begging is the essence of monastic life as taught by the Buddha." (52b) So, taking her bowl, she left for a begging journey. On the way she went to a nomad encampment named for the lady Ponmo Chokyong. However, the people who invited her were feeling awkward and embarrassed. When she noticed this she said, "Do not misunderstand compassion!" Then the people provided excellent service and plenty of alms.

From then on the tantric queen (*rdo rje btsun mo*) was joined by the great woman (*skye mo chen mo*) Deleg Chodren, who had thrown herself at her lotus feet and had praised her more than once. She was her main companion ('*gran pa'i zla*), becoming very close to her, and always carried out her orders efficiently. She had taken the religious vows of a layperson (*dge snyen*) and on that occasion she was given her excellent name.

Together they went to Tagtse. Then Chogle Namgyal and Chokyi Dronma, the enlightened father and mother (*rgyal ba yab yum*),[53] with their retinue were welcomed by the lady of the place, Chodzema. She came with her standard bearer and offered a white scarf to everybody (*dar chan*). (53a) On this occasion the spiritual master took protection strings, made the ritual knot (*rdo rje mdud pa*), and after spitting on the amulets, gave them to the people. He gave a reading initiation (*lung*) on the *Bodhisattvacaryāvatāra*. Chogle Namgyal and Chokyi Dronma were received with great respect both at the castle and in the monastery, and they were provided with excellent service. They were offered full monastic robes and more than 1,000 heaps of harvested grain (*tshar cog*) as alms. They were even offered a horse, but they did not accept it. Then they arrived at Sharu and were welcomed by the headman, his son, and their court. He showed them great respect and provided them with very good service. There they were offered 500 heaps of harvested grain. When the common people saw this, they were startled and surprised and did not dare to offer their alms, as they felt embarrassed about what they were able to give. The Great Lady said, "As a receiver of alms, I'm the same as everyone else, any offering is appreciated." (53b) When the large number of people heard these words, they were very moved and immediately developed a deep faith. They offered whatever was in the fields, and she accepted their alms, taking into consideration their conditions.

On another begging trip she was welcomed by the monastic community of the Mutre (Mu prad) monastery with a procession of monks carrying sacred items. She was then invited to enter the monastery so that people could pay respect and prostrate to her. The monks, in tears of emotion, said, "You have endured great hardship!" She replied, "This is just an ordained person's duty." Then she went inside the monastery, planning to meet and prostrate to the Mutre Lama, who had just completed his retreat. However, as soon as he saw her, the lama prostrated to her instead. He then celebrated a grand ceremony and presented her with many donations. (54a) The Venerable Woman said, "Monks! You have too much faith in me!" The monks replied, "Don't say this! If we did not have faith in your great deeds, how would we be able to develop compassion?" She responded, "As a wife who was married and had children, I did not take the vows. Since being ordained, I have behaved like an ordinary member of the monastic community. Deeds can only be evaluated after death." The monks, embarrassed, showed her great deference.

Later she visited many places, one after the other, and was hosted by many local people. Everywhere she received excellent service and collected alms. Then she went to a nomadic area where the people, with deep faith, offered her a horse and invited her to ride it, but she refused.

(54b) Earlier, a headman called Geba (dGe ba) had a vision as clear as the moon shining in the darkness: he had arrived at a large market, where he saw a red woman with a red turban dwelling in the sky in the middle of rainbows. She was surrounded by many women, some playing music and some dancing and, at the same time, eating human brains. Then the image disappeared. Afterward, remembering his vision, he was so scared that he was covered in sweat, with a drop on the tip of every hair. Immediately he asked everybody around him, "I saw this image; is it good or bad?" Soon thereafter, when the sun was rising, the ears in the fields started to shake. Then Chokyi Dronma, the Śākya Bhikṣuṇī,[54] arrived with her retinue. (55a) Very excited, he said, "Last night I had a prophetic vision. This is it!" He summoned the nomads of the area and celebrated a great ritual offering (tshogs). Then he generously offered alms. He was pleased to be able to do this.

Then she visited many places, such as Shagru, where people offered her plenty of donations.

One night Chokyi Dronma, the Queen of the Buddhas, said, "Deleg Chodren! You took the vows as a novice (dge 'tshul ma), with the headman of Tagtse acting as your patron. This was not for us; this was for the benefit of the doctrine. Now it seems that the Tagtse family are finding it difficult to keep their current status." In fact, at that time the Tagtse family was in decline as the ruling local power, because they had no sons, only daughters. (55b) However, after the visit of the Bhikṣuṇī, the Lady of the Wheel of Dharma, on her begging trip, the ruler of

Tagtse regained control over his subjects, and some villages, such as Laru Dzong, came under his control. He acquired many new land tenures, achieved harmony among all the relatives, and was eventually blessed by the birth of excellent sons. Thus they enjoyed great prosperity. Similarily, all those who offered alms eventually enjoyed great prosperity.

During the begging trip, Chokyi Dronma found her path blocked by a great stretch of water. She ordered Deleg Chodren: "Please carry me across the water!" (56a) Deleg Chodren thought, *Since the Venerable is very heavy and I have a weak body, I won't be able to do this,* and replied, "I can't carry you." The Venerable said, "It doesn't matter. Carry me anyway!" Deleg Chodren did so, and while carrying her across the water, she didn't feel any weight on her shoulders. This event recalled something that had happened to Milarepa.[55] When he was staying at Marpa's place, before being able to receive his teachings, he had asked Marpa's wife, "Mother Dagme (bDag med)! Which kind of ability does Marpa, the spiritual father, have?" Dagme replied, "If one has a good meditational power and sleeps on straw, it doesn't matter how much one lies on it, the straw will not become compressed." (56b) This episode shows the extraordinary power of her practice of "wind" meditation (*rlung*).

Thus she spread prosperity in the area around the Brahmaputra River. Transportation gradually became difficult because she had received such a large amount of alms on her trip. Therefore she decided to stay for a while at a place called Gyalthang (rGyal thang). After a while the Omniscient sent his secretary, Rintson (Rin brtson), with a letter inviting her to return as soon as possible. However, she was enjoying staying where she was so much that Rintson, after repeating his request, felt that he had to seriously threaten her: "If you do not return I am going to die!" She bluntly replied, "I have just been doing deeds of merit; if you die this will be the limit of your own life. I definitely won't go now."

(57a) Eventually, feeling that she could not oppose her lama's order, she swiftly returned, with all the donations she had collected as alms, to the place where he was living at that time. She offered everything to the Omniscient and requested a prayer from him. The Lord, who was staying at a place called Kadrugma, said, "I will offer alms as well." He then asked Chokyi Dronma, the practitioner of wonders, and her retinue to sit down somewhere suitable. From the alms that had been gathered, three measures (*khal*) of barley and five measures of bamboo were offered to them. The Omniscient was delighted, and the Great Woman recited a prayer. She thus had become the Omniscient's field of merit, and the compelling evidence for her biography, the exemplary deeds for the universal liberation had become great. At that time some people said, "The magnificence of both Ngari and Southern Lato has waned, the sun has started to shine for the nuns." (57b) The Omniscient, hearing these rumors, said, "This is wrong. Whoever is related to her [and this includes all the living beings of Ngari and Southern Lato] is being led to the path of liberation."

During that time Deleg Chodren was given the first teachings of *guruyoga* meditation (*bla ma'i rnal 'byor*) that she had requested when she took the vows of a layperson (*dge snyen*) at Palmo Choding. The spiritual master said, "When one has requested *guruyoga* as the first among the teachings, everything shines. They are not associated with each other as a human couple (*mi'i yab yum*); however, it is indeed wonderful that there is no fault (*skyon med*) in a divine couple (*lha'i yab yum*)." As he closed his mouth, in silence, he gave her the initiation into *guruyoga*. The *dPal de kho na nyid 'dus pa,* the tradition of Chogle Namgyal, comprises outer, inner, and secret offerings. On that occasion she performed only the outer offering. Later she was asked about the meditation and she was very positive about it. She reported to the mother (*yum*) [i.e., Chokyi Dronma]: "Since I practiced meditation, everything has started to shine." (58a) Her training took place in a way that fitted her mind. She enjoyed her practice of deep meditation and thereby developed great kindness toward all the followers of the doctrine.

Later, Jigdrel [Chogle Namgyal] went to Ngamring. He instructed the Great Woman [Chokyi Dronma] that she should live at his seat with her attendants and followers. During this period she went to the entrance of a meditation cave with her retinue and taught them mental purification (*blo sbyong*). At the time of the first Tibetan month she completed a retreat and gave teachings to the common people in a way that fitted their minds. She then practiced religious fasting (*smyung gnas*) according to the *activity tantra* (*bya rgyud*) of the Mahāyāna tradition.

Once, together with the female *siddha* Chokyong Drencig (Chos skyong 'dren cig), she went secretly to various mountain summits. Chokyi Dronma, the Emanation Body, said, "I have not received any teachings on the practice of Machig;[56] please teach me!" (58b) Chokyong Drencig taught her all that she knew. After one night, Chokyi Dronma suggested, "After eating, we shall return to our residence!" Chokyi Drencig countered, "We should stay at least three nights." As Chokyi Dronma had learned some verses by Pang Lotsawa[57] from Jigdrel (Chogle Namgyal) that referred specifically to this practice, she recited

*Translation of the Biography of the Venerable Chokyi Dronma*

them: "A demon [of attachment] longing to perceive shape dwells at the [internal] spring of sight. [To conquer this powerful demon] practice *cho* (*gcod*) in that [internal] great site!" She then said, "These words indicate that now we have a special relation. Let's not stay here in the mountains aimlessly; let's return to the lama's residence, which is better." On the way they met a large group of hunters who started to pursue them, but since the women were extremely fast, the hunters couldn't catch them. (59a) This episode shows that Chokyi Dronma never opposed Machig's teachings and that she practiced her instructions and had achieved the meditation that enabled her to "dwell in the innate nature of phenomena" (*gnyug ma gnas pa*).[58] It also shows that she knew in advance that the hunters would come.

Later, on one occasion, a practitioner of meditation called Lama Chopel, who had faced major hindrances, placed an object (*be khri*?) in front of Lama Duldzin Ngawang ('Dul 'dzin Ngag dbang) and, trying to clear his obstacles, left in another direction. The Great Woman said, "If you behave like this, this is shameful for the community of meditators! Please bring it to me!" He followed her instructions and escaped from his hindrances. Then he returned to his meditation place in the mountains. Subsequently Chokyi Dronma made dough figures (*gtor ma*)[59] for the protectors' chapel and for her own cell. (59b) All the protectors were very pleased with this. Thus there was significant development in the spiritual deeds and realization of the people of Palmo Choding. This made everyone very happy.

Eventually Jigdrel, Chogle Namgyal, the Lamp of the World, returned to his main monastery and was pleased with the situation. At one point the lama said to Chokyi Dronma, "You should become the master of the tantric texts, but given my health, I can't teach you this. You should go to the spiritual master Shakyapa[60] to learn the *rGyud 'bum*[61] from him."

Accordingly she went to Ngari, where the spiritual master resided, and invited him to her father's palace. In the Gomang temple, she listened to the teachings on the tantric texts together with her father and mother, who had become treasurers of the faith, and numerous members of the monastic community such as the Kabchupa Pal Chime Drupa.[62] (60a) She then offered one silver skull cup (*kāpāla*) and one monastic robe to the spiritual master, as well as numerous presents. She celebrated a great ritual offering (*tshogs*), gave an unusually patterned large turquoise as a reward to the great monastery of Dzonkha, and recited a prayer in front of the Venerable Shakyapa. She did all this without encountering any hindrance.

# Full Ordination

Then she went to Palmo Choding, the great meditation center, to be fully ordained (*bsnyen rdzogs*). She took along numerous monks whom she had invited from the religious colleges of Gungthang. Jigdrel, Chogle Namgyal, who was particularly skilled in teaching the "Eighty-Four Thousand *Dharmaskanda*,"[63] performed the role of the *upadhyaya* (*mkhan po*). (60b) Seated on his throne, wearing his headgear (*cod pan*), the Venerable Chokyi Wangchug (Chos kyi dbang phyug), who was an expert in the *Tripiṭaka*, acted as the *karmacārya* (*las kyi slob dpon*). Surrounded by enough monks who were fully qualified, she became a real *bhikṣuṇī* (*dge slong ma'i dngos por bsgrub pa*). Further training in the monastic discipline had filled the vase of her mind, and she became an object of worship (*mchod gnas*) for all living beings.

The next day Jigdrel, Chogle Namgyal, summoned her at lunchtime. She, who had become the spring of all the *bhikṣuṇīs* of Tibet, visited the King of Dharma in his meditation house. She was wearing the Buddha's robe and had her alms bowl, which is the most precious of all things, in her hand. Her main assistant, Deleg Chodren, the novice (*dge mtshul ma*) who was able to dwell in the innate nature of phenomena, followed her. (61a) When the Lord saw Chokyi Dronma, she was like ambrosia for his eyes, like a golden ear shaking in the wind. He was delighted and said, "It is as if an *arhat* has descended onto the great plain, as if you were in heaven surrounded by a retinue of fifty *ḍākinīs* flying like birds." Then they had lunch together.

Afterward she returned to her meditation place and summoned Deleg Chodren. She asked her, "Are you happy?"

"I am."

"Everybody says that I'm a woman of wisdom (*ye shes ma*). This is not true. I just earn merit inspired by the *ḍākinīs*. (61b) Through this I met a great lama. I obtained the initiations and I learned how to practice the doctrine. This all made me very happy. Nevertheless, although the Great Lord is also your master in this life, eventually your relationship may decline. The fact that you have acquired a human birth, enabling you to seek enlightenment, met such a lama, and received part of the doctrine is already very satisfactory. You should be happy and strive hard."

The next day Chokyi Dronma visited the Great Lord and prostrated to him. Smiling, he presented her with a beautiful cover for her sacred items. The Venerable Lady accepted it with great delight. Later she commented happily, "My

*Translation of the Biography of the Venerable Chokyi Dronma*

lama has complete insight into past, present, and future. While thinking about the holy objects from my lama, (62a) I felt that I needed a cover for them. Knowing what was in my mind, he offered me precisely this." Wherever she went, she took this special cover with her. This was called the "blessed cover" (*byin rlabs rten khebs*).

After some time she went to Ngari, and over the summer she stayed at Mendong Sholphug (sMan gdong zhol phug), where she gave teachings regarding the spiritual practice of Vairocana (Kun rig). In the autumn she traveled around Ngari on a begging trip, and in the winter she went to Mangyul. Then she asked her brother to invite Jigdrel [Chogle Namgyal] and his monastic community for the summer session of religious practice (*dbyar gnas*). She provided one third of the necessary support, one third was offered by her brother, and one third was given by Gendun Sherpa.[64] (62b) They selected as the most appropriate venue the Utse temple, where Sakya Paṇḍita had held a debate against the heretics.[65] First they performed practices for the generation of the spirit of enlightenment (*byang chub sems bskyed*) and for mind purification (*blo sbyong*). Then they underwent religious fasting (*smyung gnas*) according to the tantric tradition. They then practiced each class of the *tantra,* fire rituals (*sbyin sreg*), and the *drug bcu pa* ritual as well as dancing, drawing, and chanting. They practiced *sahaja* yoga (*lhan cig skyes rnal 'byor*)[66] according to the Mahāmudrā tradition. They provided further insight into hidden meanings by teaching and listening. At the end the teachings were written up and edited.

(63a) The royal family tirelessly provided endless food and drink. During the sessions Chokyi Dronma was asked about worldly activities that are necessary but are usually delegated to servants because they are not considered to be appropriate for monastics. The Magnificent Lady said, "Since I was born until now, I have not taken the position of defining what are and what are not proper deeds of merit. I have never defined the worldly activities to be abandoned, nor have I defined those that have to be done. This human life is indeed to be transcended."

(63b) Later, since the royal family still needed to arrange some support for the spiritual master, the Great Woman said to the secretary Konchog Gyaltshen, "Tomorrow, early in the morning, go to the Lord to do some writing!"

The secretary, having spent most of the night drinking *chang* with people, at a late hour said, "As the constellation marking the lunar mansion[67] has appeared in the sky [i.e., it is getting late], the nectar I have been drinking has lost some of its taste. The orders of the beautiful Daughter of the Gods (*lha sras mdzas ma*) are heavier than a mountain.[68] As I'm old, it is time now to leave [to reach Chogle Namgyal's residence on time]."[69]

The next day, as they were having a conversation, the Great Lord said, "Do not call her just the beautiful Daughter of the Gods; she is also the Queen of All Knowledge (*Kun mkhyen dbang mo*)."

During this period someone called Chenpo Namrin, who wished to receive an initiation concerning all buddhas, came to see the Lord and expressed some doubts about her. (64a) The Lord said, "There is no contradiction! The Great Woman is the Phagmo Dorjecan [i.e., Vārāhī with the *vajra*],[70] the mother of all buddhas."

The evening before the Lord was due to give some teachings, Chokyi Dronma's brother changed his mind and left for a place called Sher. Suddenly, in his residence, strange things started to happen. Disappointed by this sudden change of plan, the Lord (Chogle Namgyal) said that he would leave. However, Chokyi Dronma said, "Don't worry." Her mind remained constant, and that evening the Magnificent Lady went to see her brother. The next morning, as the sun was rising, brother and sister arrived together and listened to the teachings of the Omniscient for the whole day.

(64b) The Omniscient gave many excellent instructions to the king, the prince, and their ministers. At the end he gave a stern order: "If you do not listen to my instructions, you will face serious consequences." The officials and the disciples were very intimidated by his words. Then Chokyi Dronma's father, the great King Son of the Gods, holding the Omniscient's object of devotion (*thugs dam*), pronounced an oath.[71] Suddenly, the earth trembled and the great town shook. Everybody felt great faith in the master.

(65a) Later when the king and the prince, the officials and the disciples were discussing this event, the Lord said, "When the prince[72] went to Sher, I lost my plan like a bird that had lost its nest. For a moment I even lost my trust in the Jewel, and everybody else was demoralized like me. However, the Great Woman was unshakable and said that there was nothing to worry about. It is clear that her mind is deep like the ocean where one can never reach the bottom. Compared to her, we are like the waters of small channels."

Chokyi Dronma presented the Great Lord with plenty of donations and he said, "The all-fulfilling jewel, Chokyi Dronma, seems to be in control of the treasury of heaven. With her body, speech, and mind she has always provided me with excellent support." He asked what she wished for. (65b) The Magnificent Lady replied, "I wish to strive for enlightenment." But the Lord remarked: "You don't need to ask me for enlightenment. You have the ability to reach enlightenment yourself." Then she asked, "Please pray that I may have a long life to serve the people." He then recited with delight many *vajra* songs (*rdo rje glu*) in her honor among the assembly.

During this period the Mangyul region [where the religious activities were taking place] was affected by several epidemics. One night a member of the retinue of the Venerable Chogle Namgyal called Lama Khampa, who came from eastern Tibet, had a dream: hail was falling everywhere; however, the roof of the house of the Magnificent Lady was protected by a sacred tent and many fires surrounded the house. Subsequently the people in the retinue avoided being infected by the epidemic.

At that time a *siddha* called the meditator of Mondron (sMon gron sgrub pa) came from Yarlung to visit the Omniscient. (66a) After he arrived, he had a dream in which he was told that all the people around Konchog Gyalmo, the Great Lady, had gathered in assembly, and he decided to join them. In his dream he arrived at Lhasa, where the holiest statue of the Buddha (*jo bo*) was located, and started to ask the people, "Which one is the Great Lady?" Someone pointed a finger in the direction of the statue and replied, "That is the Great Lady!" He then saw people praying and prostrating to the statue of the Buddha, and he did the same. The next morning the great *siddha* Changsungpa[73] came to summon the meditator of Mondron, saying, "Please get up! It is time to come and meet the Lord (Chogle Namgyal)! There is going to be a great ritual offering organized by the Great Lady, and many scholars from different areas have gathered to pray and receive blessings. You should go there to prostrate and receive her blessing." He countered, "I have already prostrated to her because I did so in my dream." The *siddha* Changsungpa, after having heard of the dream, said, "You certainly had a very good dream. She is a true *ḍākinī*." (66b) Then he met the great teacher and his disciples, and when he requested a blessing from Chokyi Dronma he felt deeply moved.

One day Chokyi Dronma, the Emanation Body (*sprul ba'i sku can*), touched one begging bowl among many and said, "Deleg Chodren! This is the begging bowl of Gyalse Thogme.[74] Would you like to get blessings from it?" As Deleg Chodren hastened to touch it, she said, "Aren't you happy to be able to be seated next to the great lama Chogle Namgyal? Compared to this, the blessing of Gyalse Thogme's alms bowl is very limited. You should show respect to the great lama in person day and night and follow his instructions. (67a) This is not failing to show respect to the precious Gyalse. It rather means recognizing our great teacher, who is a great sun among the scholars and the *siddhas* of the Buddha's doctrine. People, according to their relevant *karmic* links, should understand this." Afterward teachers and disciples engaged in religious dancing, tracing sand *maṇḍalas,* and chanting. Later they performed the rituals of the four classes of *tantras.* They also celebrated the fire offerings (*sbyin sreg*), according to the four kinds of *karma,* in the temple Tshondu Tonkhang. The great teacher himself performed the dance for the ritual taming of the earth. All the rituals were carried out magnificently.

(67b) Then the female *siddha* and her brother, the Son of the Gods, gathered a big assembly in front of the great teacher Chogle Namgyal, inviting his own retinue and all disciples from Gungthang Chode monastery to participate. On that occasion the precious Lord said, "This Lady is already a fulfilled *yoginī,* she does not need to ask me concerning enlightenment. In general the best *yogin* should be happy to die. The middle *yogin* should not be intimidated by death. The lesser *yogin* should not have any regret in the face of death. I am a *yogin* who is happy to die. The people who are gathered here today all have *karmic* links with each other and with me; it is thus enough that you do not lose your faith in me, the old monk." This was the highest deed of the teacher and his spiritual daughter.

(68a) Her brother and the royal retinue eventually returned to the capital. The people from the lower valleys offered assistance with transportation; the people from the capital came to welcome and escort him. Thanks to the great teacher and his disciples, the law of the country (*rgyal khrims*) had become like a golden yoke and the doctrine like a silken knot,[75] fulfilling everybody's wishes.

Chogle Namgyal and Chokyi Dronma went again to Mangyul-Kyirong and stayed at a place called Tashigang. One night, as the light of a butter lamp was hurting the eyes of the Omniscient, he tried to shade it. Promptly the Magnificent Lady intervened and said, "I'll do it!" The great teacher said, "You are taking too much care of me." The wisdom *ḍākinī* countered, "At least I'm able to prevent your eyes being hurt by the light of butter lamps." (68b) Then the great teacher said, "You have the ability to understand the *dPal de kho na nyid 'dus pa,* you don't need to pride yourself in being able to shade the light." They then continued to enjoy their conversation. Eventually, folding her hands, the Magnificent Lady asked the great teacher, "Precious lama, if I die before my mother, please take care of her with love." He replied, "People die gradually one after the other; perhaps I'll die first. However, if I have the chance to take care of your mother, I will certainly do so. (69a) Should I not be there, I will instruct some servants among my retinue to take care of your mother. Every nun will also take care of her. Please don't worry and remember what I have said!" Then Chogle Namgyal and Chokyi Dronma, the spiritual preceptor and the royal donor, returned to the capital.

The Son of the Gods, Chenneba,[76] her brother, now ascended the golden throne and to celebrate the event majestically, a magnificent feast was organized. All the subjects of the kingdom under the sky admired these events. Many commented that all this was happening thanks to the Precious Lady Konchog Gyalmo. Therefore the malicious rumors about her stopped.

Sometime afterward, while she was residing at Lingba Dragmar (Ling ba brag dmar), Deleg Chodren asked her, "Without the way of the secret *tantra,* no enlightment is possible. Please show me the tantric way to reach enlightenment."

(69b) The Magnificent Lady said, "First of all, you should awaken in yourself a strong feeling that there is no meaning in a worldly life and avoid any hindrance that would prevent liberation from the cycle of rebirths. Second, feeling like a parent toward all those who dwell in the six realms of existence, you should meditate on the realization of enlightenment for the sake of all living beings throughout your life. Third, you also need to take a qualified lama as a teacher. Following his instructions, you must keep the tantric vows (*samaya*), observe the rules, and offer everything you have, your body and wealth. Taking his teachings as a yardstick to distinguish between good and evil, you will be able to clarify all your doubts concerning listening to and learning the doctrine. These three aspects of religious practice should be practiced together, (70a) not privileging one while neglecting the other. If you believe malicious rumors, this will create obstacles to your practice. Therefore you need the weapon of diligence. Don't get attached to places that offer good conditions. At the right time you will understand everything that I'm saying now. This is a preliminary explanation. You need to be clear that I am not looking for a way without the secret *tantra.*"


## Life Between Porong and Mangyul-Gungthang

Later, following the Omniscient and his retinue, Chokyi Dronma and Deleg Chodren arrived at Palmo Choding, the Ocean of Magnificence. Here, as he had often done before, the lama gave instructions to Chokyi Dronma, speaking very earnestly: "Great Lady of Renunciation (*bdag mo kun spangs ma chen mo*)! As long as my body is in good condition, you should stay in the Palkhu area."

(70b) In order to follow his instructions, she left Sangngag Dechen Ling, one of the monastic buildings at Palmo Choding, and went to Migmang, a little settlement that seemed to be a suitable location for a nunnery. The Omniscient covered the expenses for the wood to build it and offered some nuns to become part of her retinue. The lama's letter of authority followed shortly afterward. When she arrived at Migmang, she organized the construction of her residence, the cells for the monastic community, and finally a surrounding wall with a big gate. She established the rule that no men were allowed inside the wall and defined monastic discipline according to the *Vinaya*.[77] As a result, many followers striving for enlightenment and (71a) practicing the *tantra* gathered around her. Giving teachings that fitted everyone's mind, she thus greatly turned the Wheel of the Dharma. The Omniscient with his retinue came to the nunnery to perform magnificent summer religious activities (*yar chos*), and the nuns listened and learned his teachings of the doctrine and practiced meditation. In order to accumulate merit, the great lama celebrated a great religious offering as well.

At one point Chokyi Dronma commented, "My retinue is composed exclusively of people who have given up worldly concerns; therefore, they are not able to sew the clothing that is required. I will do it with my own hands." Then she sewed all the robes for the nuns herself. (71b) Furthermore, in order to get food, the retinue spread the practice of the two wheels, and on this subject Chokyi Dronma said, "There is no teaching concerning the practice of 'extracting the essence' (*bcud len*)[78] that I haven't received, and this has to be practiced to endure hardship." She took care of the novices lovingly and she made sure that they would get proper food and earn merit by "extracting the essence."

Once the great teacher went to [Koron] Khabso, in the vicinity of the Palkhu Lake [and Migmang], and as he was on his return journey the Magnificent Lady went to meet him and pay respect. In a beautiful spot covered with flowers she prostrated. The great teacher dismounted from his horse and enjoyed chatting with his spiritual daughter.

(72a) During this period the life and deeds of the great teacher were flourishing beyond any imagination. He was able to understand past, present, and future at once and he was able to keep in his mind all issues, both in detail and comprehensively. At one point, fearing that some hindrances might appear and weaken her relationship with her tutelary deity, he said to her, "You were ordained to strive for the liberation of other living beings, not just for your own liberation. Earlier I thought that it would be better if I asked you to stay around here as long as my body was in good condition. However, since there is no togetherness

*Translation of the Biography of the Venerable Chokyi Dronma*

nor separation, I suggest that you stay where you wish. Please think whether it is really good for the sake of living beings for you to stay here or not. If you feel that it is better that you go somewhere else, please go. I won't prevent it." Deeply moved, she prostrated.

(72b) Then they returned respectively to Sangngag Dechen Ling and Thongmon,[79] the nunnery resonating with the sound of the conch shell. Commenting on his words, Chokyi Dronma said, "According to the great teacher's thoughts, if I wish to achieve my own liberation I can keep my hair without cutting it. In general I did everything I could for the doctrine and living beings and in particular I wished to help all women (*skye dman*). It seems, however, that no great benefit has resulted. As long as the Great Lord is in good physical condition, I do not want to go more than two days' distance from here. You, Deleg Chodren, stay at Thongmon to look after the nunnery now. I will be traveling without fixed direction for a while, but in the future I'll take care of the nunnery myself. Earlier the great teacher told me that you have earned great merit." She left the great woman Deleg Chodren in charge of the nunnery and left for Ngari.

(73a) Chokyi Dronma had a large retinue and gathered an increasing number of nuns around her. She established a good system for teaching the doctrine and the nuns developed good skills at reading the texts. She was delighted when the great teacher, Chogle Namgyal, pleased with their achievements, praised them: "These are my female practitioners!" he said. She kept traveling around, but she did not fail to visit the great teacher at least twice a year. She would request teachings and initiations, offering donations and presenting the retinue with gifts. She thus established the best conditions for bestowing initiations (*dbang*), so that the people, delighted, used to say, "Since the arrival of the Great Lady of Renunciation who recited prayers of request to the precious teacher, there has been a shower of initiations."

(73b) With her numerous disciples, she thus opened the gate of the treasury of the doctrine. Thanks to this, the followers of the doctrine who were at Palmo Choding did not experience hindrances while the Great Woman was there. Everyone who was part of the retinue of the great teacher felt that the Great Lady was taking care of him lovingly, fulfilling all his wishes.

Sometime afterward, Jigdrel, Chogle Namgyal, the King of the Doctrine, became very ill and seemed about to die. He requested that the venerable Chokyi Dronma[80] be summoned from Ngari. The excellent woman Deleg Chodren, swiftly and facing great hardship, set out to Ngari to ask her to come. At that time Chokyi Dronma had gone on a pilgrimage in the mountains and was staying at Longtse (Klong rtse) in Mangyul-Kyirong. As she arrived, Deleg Chodren prostrated and was asked:

(74a) "Why did you come?"

"The great teacher almost passed away."

"I was wondering whether you came here to bring bad news."

Hearing what Deleg Chodren had to say, she was completely shaken by unbearable suffering. Then she said, "I'll be able to see him, at least briefly," and organized a small retinue to escort her.

She left early in the morning, reaching Thongmon, where she stopped, in just one day, whereas usually four days were necessary for this journey. When she saw the Great Teacher he said, "Tonight have a good rest; tomorrow I invite you for a proper visit."

Then the Venerable Lady said, "Deleg Chodren! Tomorrow morning, please go and collect alms of wool in order to make white mattresses." Accordingly the nun went and returned with a lot of wool. (74b) Chokyi Dronma said, "It is an auspicious omen! It is very good indeed that you were able to collect all this." The members of Chokyi Dronma's retinue spun the wool and the Venerable Lady made thirteen white mattresses with her own hands. With golden thread, she then embroided the image of a *vajra* at the center and at the corners of each mattress. It took her half a day to do this. Afterward she visited the Omniscient Lamp of the World, Chogle Namgyal. She offered the mattresses and said, "Please sit on them!" Then the Venerable Lady recited a prayer requesting him not to pass to *nirvāṇa*. While she said the prayer, all the wonderful deeds of the great lama appeared in the holy shrine of Vajrayoginī's mind.[81] Immediately after the prayer, the great lama recovered from his illness.

(75a) Because her efforts to earn merit for the sake of all living beings achieved the greatest glory, she became the apple of the eye of the Omniscient (Chogle Namgyal) and his vast retinue. When she left the teacher and his disciples, he escorted her and saw her off very affectionately. The people of Porong Palmo Choding said that if the Great Lady of Renunciation were to live there permanently, all their wishes would be fulfilled.

Later she focused on earning merit for her teacher and decided to build a great *stūpa*. (75b) Together with her nuns, she took care of the work. They took the stones from ruins, they made the special woodwork (*spen ma*)[82] from the bushes of the hills, and they ground the colors that were necessary [for painting]. When the great teacher came to oversee the work, he saw Chokyi Dronma

*Translation of the Biography of the Venerable Chokyi Dronma*

herself carrying a stone. Pointing to her with a stern expression, he said, "Why are you doing this? This might damage your reputation." She answered with a smile: "If I don't do this kind of work myself, the nuns will not carry out the work well." "This is extraordinary!" he said with surprise and delight, and he gave three special stones (*bur rdo*) to the Magnificent Lady and one to each nun, and continued, (76a) "Currently, in their ability to accomplish deeds to gain merit, there is nobody as excellent as the female *siddha* and her retinue."

In this way the great wisdom *stūpa* was built by the hands of Vajravārāhī herself.[83] Afterward the enlightened being, with her spiritual children and all the other people, performed a great merit-making celebration for the great wisdom *stūpa*. Then numerous well-wishers performed another great merit-making ritual at Thongmon nunnery, where the great *ḍākinī* was residing. On that occasion the novice (*dge mtshul ma*) Deleg Chodren made, with her own hands, shapes for statues and ritual items (*'dzin tshug*) that were unimaginably wonderful. (76b) The Magnificent Lady said, "Nuns, under the leadship of Deleg Chodren you should look after the nunnery; learn and practice the doctrine in order to spread it and delight the lama. This is what I want you to do!"

One day, she ordered Deleg Chodren to take some good wool and said, "We both should spin wool yarn and offer it to the lama. I don't have many lamas, and when I visit one I never go empty-handed. Since I have been behaving in this auspicious way, I have never, in this life, been short of material things. It is difficult to imagine how *karma* works in the long term. If you wish to be happy you should offer to the lama all that you receive."

(77a) Taking with her a small retinue that included the lead nun, Chanchub Sangmo;[84] the attendant, Tharpa Sangmo;[85] the ritual assistant, Ponmo Lodro Gyalmo; and a few others, she then left for Ngari, where she established a hermitage near Dzonkha. After completing a period of meditation, she gave an auspicious speech. Meanwhile the Omniscient had announced: "I will go to the east for the rest of my life." All those who were escorting him as attendants reached Southern Lato, went to Shekar, and came back to Palmo Choding. Around that time Deleg Chodren therefore told the Magnificent Lady, (77b) "The Precious Lord has gone to Yamdrog,[86] there is no lama to prostrate to, what shall we do?" The female *siddha* said, "Don't be narrow-minded, the people of Palmo Choding can do everything. Even though the teacher is living in Yamdrog, according to the Buddhist method we are not tied to anything, whether we go or we don't go." [one apparently corrupted sentence]

Then the winter passed and the nuns heard rumors that the Precious Lord was returning to Palmo Choding. When he returned they went to welcome him, prostrating and presenting him with flowers on the way.

(78a) When the lama arrived, the Lady of the Doctrine was delighted and ordered her attendant to prepare tea. They wrote a formal statement (*bka' mchid*) about the prosperity of father and spiritual daughter. Its central meaning was that as the lama had returned to Sangngag Dechen Ling [i.e., Palmo Choding], this would become the center, the main place where all prosperity gathered. It also said that Chogle Namgyal hoped that he would be able to continue to be in charge. The female *siddha* thus kept providing the material conditions for initiations and teachings.

After a while the Magnificent Lady returned to Ngari. According to her instructions, in the autumn of the horse year [1450] the great woman Deleg Chodren took care of the consecration of the wisdom *stūpa* at Palmo Choding. (78b) She was authorized to do this by the Omniscient, who was also lavish in his praise for her.

Vajrayoginī [Chokyi Dronma] returned to Palmo Choding when the great religious feast, magnificent beyond any imagination, was celebrated. You can read the detailed description written in the great biography of the Omniscient called "Feast of Miracles."[87]

The female *siddha* and the Lama King of the Doctrine Chogle Namgyal, with their disciples, had become the secret treasury of all buddhas. Thanks to their extraordinary deeds of body, speech, mind, and virtue, and action for all living beings. (79a) The Female Buddha (*de bzhin gshegs ma*), Lady of the Universe (*'khor lo bdag mo*), dancing the dance of illusion with its many forms of ritual offering, satisfied the innate bliss of being beyond duality (*gnyis med pa*, i.e., not being two). This was a symbol of excellence (*mchog gi rten*) and a supreme achievement of relationship (*'brel bar byung ba bla na med pa*). Subsequently there were further celebrations with many different flowers, many different kinds of incense, many different ornaments, and it was said that this feast was an auspicious omen announcing the popularity of the *dPal de kho na nyid 'dus pa* [the collected works of Bodong Chogle Namgyal]. The people of Choding Breboche offered twenty-four measures of barley flour in support of the celebration.

(79b) The Hero Lamp of the World and Wisdom of All Buddhas, Chogle Namgyal, rejoiced and said, with a smile, "Like the lion, the king of the animals, shining with great majesty among all wild creatures, the patronage of Chokyi

*Translation of the Biography of the Venerable Chokyi Dronma*

Dronma, the Great Lady of Renunciation, shines over all of us practitioners of religion." Chenpo Dudul was leading the craftsmen, who had made many images. Samten led the painters. Chokyi Dronma, the Great Lady of Renunciation, led the donors.

The Great Woman had the reputation of being multiskilled and carrying out both great and small deeds perfectly. (80a) In the front row a seat was arranged for her, and she was offered milk as well as a cheese and butter dish (*thud*) blessed by Chogle Namgyal's saliva. His eyes were fixed upon her, unshakingly, and he offered her many other presents. Reciting the name of the female *siddha,* he performed a great celebration. At one point the Omniscient said to her, "If the *tantra* are practiced in a complete way, the *vajra* dance (*rdo rje gar*) is indispensable. However, this practice doesn't exist in Tibet. Nowadays people don't follow the original tradition completely and the teachings have been transformed from *tantra* into something else. Therefore the Buddhist rituals have been declining. Although, after listening to the doctrine of the Buddha, I wrote about his teachings and practiced them comprehensively, (80b) I never managed to establish a dance performed by women (*bud med*). If you, the Great Woman, cannot start this tradition, who else could do it in the future? It seems that there was such a tradition in India, but women have not been able to do the same thing in Tibet, so men usually perform female roles, wearing wigs and female masks. Now, Great Lady, you have attained the highest perfection; you should be the first practitioner to set up this tradition and let the nuns learn from you. Then during our next ritual meditation and offering (*sgrub mchod*) you will perform it for the sake of the Buddha."

According to the instructions of the great lama, she started to teach her retinue. However, some nuns said, "We don't know how to do it, (81a) and even if we knew how to practice it, we wouldn't be able to perform in public, in front of a crowd." Chokyi Dronma said, "There isn't anything else that would please our lama more than this; therefore we will do it. I'll try my best as well." Then she asked some craftsmen to make the masks, including those for the sixteen tantric consorts (*rig ma*). She earnestly told sixteen nuns, led by the great woman Deleg Chodren, that they should learn by heart the words of the rituals of the four classes of *tantra*. She then traveled all over the hills of Ngari, where she enjoyed the profound and clear ambrosia of the *tantra*.

At the end of winter, the nuns gathered at Dzonkha, (81b) and in front of Vajravārāhī herself [i.e., Chokyi Dronma as Vajravārāhī's emanation], they were trained to perform each ritual. At that time, during the day Chokyi Dronma was busy building a house for her mother as she had promised her, whereas during the evening she was practicing chanting (*dbyangs*). This was all done so that soon afterward the Magnificent Lady and her retinue could perform the whole dance (*gar*) at Palmo Choding.

## Illness and Death of Chogle Namgyal

At the beginning of spring in the sheep year [1451], while preparations were still being made in Dzonkha, a messenger arrived from Palmo Choding with a letter written by Loden, the attendant of Chogle Namgyal. The letter said, "The Precious Lord is very ill. The situation is critical. Please come immediately!" When she heard this news, Chokyi Dronma was brokenhearted and cried. She thought, *This might be the last time that I can see Chogle Namgyal.* She told her father, and he decided that they should visit the lama.

(82a) Therefore father and daughter, together with one member of the retinue, rode swiftly to Palmo Choding. On the way, when they arrived at a place called Kamgo (sKam mgo),[88] they came across someone who was leading a riderless horse. Immediately thinking that this was a bad omen, Chokyi Dronma stared with wide-open eyes at Deleg Chodren and said, "Let's hope that the great teacher is not yet lost to us." Then she continued, "But perhaps we are creating something in our minds from this ambiguous sign." Deleg Chodren replied, "This horse has no saddle, what do you think?" Then Chokyi Dronma said, "This is true. Perhaps this is the horse bringing future prosperity; who would dare to ride it now?" Eventually they arrived at Koron Khabso (sKo ron khab so). The Magnificent Lady was riding fast with snowflakes hitting her eyes, hurting like thorns.

At one point, feeling that she had to ride even faster to reach her lama as soon as possible, she said to Deleg Chodren, "If my father, the Dharma King, rides this fast, he may become overexhausted. (82b) However, if you and I, together with our strong attendant, don't ride as fast as possible, we might miss the chance to see the master alive. What shall we do?" After saying this she sent Deleg Chodren to her father, who was riding behind, with the following message: "We must leave tomorrow, at dawn, before the morning meditation. Precious father, you should travel at a speed that suits you. If I don't see the great lama I'll lose my heart. Therefore I must go that early." Her father sent the following reply: "*Bhikṣuṇī!* You should act as you think most appropriate!"

The next morning they left very early, as they had said. When the morning sun rose, the Lady of Propserity, exhausted, dismounted from her horse to have a short rest. Having offered incense and massaged her feet, she then continued. (83a) Two main attendants[89] of Chogle Namgyal and other people came to welcome her. Father, daughter, Deleg Chodren, and the servant Gyanam were able to arrive before the great lama died.[90]

Once there, she performed a magnificent religious service and begged him, "Please don't pass away!" However, this time he could not fulfill her wish, and she assisted him continuously in his illness as long as he was alive. Even during this time the lama gave many excellent instructions to her father, the King Son of the Gods. At one point the female *siddha,* praying, asked him, "In which *Dharma field* will you reside?" (83b) The lama answered, "I'll be residing in the heavenly palace of Akaniṣta where Buddha Vairocana was enlightened." In this way Chokyi Dronma[91] made notes[92] about his life and deeds (*rnam thar*). The lama continued, "I prophesy that I will be enlightened for the sake of my followers in the *maṇḍala* of Vairocana." Then the great king offered his last prostration to the master and returned to his palace, while Chokyi Dronma remained to assist the King of Dharma, the body of merit of the three realms.

Sometime later, since she was extremely exhausted, she told Deleg Chodren, "I need to rest for a while. Please lock the door and stay there to keep watch." (84a) As she was sleeping, she suddenly woke up and said, "We should go to the residence of the great lama." Precisely at the same time the attendant Loden came to call her. When she arrived at his residence, the Omniscient, in a sitting position, was pointing with his fingers in various directions. He was surrounded by the members of his retinue who, puzzled, were trying to understand what he meant. Having understood that the great lama wanted to practice *guruyoga* meditation, Chokyi Dronma offered him the practice of meditation and repentance. She took the vows of the Five Supreme Buddhas (*rigs lnga*) and then, while she was praying, the great king completed all his deeds in this world.[93] Showing clearly that he had gone to the Akaniṣta heavenly palace, he performed many miracles for the sake of his followers.

(84b) The deeds of the great master had been as if the great water of enlightenment could flow uphill, and his passing left his followers in deep distress. The next day they dressed the precious body with beautiful clothing and ornaments, so that this became pleasant to the eye like ambrosia. Chokyi Dronma herself was in charge of the funerary rituals until the construction of the *stūpa* as a reliquary for the precious remains was completed. She performed great ritual offerings to increase the merit of the great lama. The people from the different myriarchies and the disciples[94] had various views on how the body should be preserved. (85a) The Great Woman thought about this issue and thought that if the precious body was kept in Palmo Choding it would benefit that seat; if each headman tried to take it to their own place, the merit of the believers would decline. She then said, "In Tibet there isn't anyone who hasn't become a follower of the King of the Dharma (Chogle Namgyal). The precious body belongs to all, patrons and disciples. It is not sensible for somebody to try to keep it for themselves. It will make everybody unhappy. This precious body stands for the merit for all believers." Nobody opposed her view and everybody followed her instructions on the matter.

(85b) Vajrayoginī [i.e., Chokyi Dronma as Vajrayoginī's emanation] took care of the fire ritual, in person, and this was perfectly celebrated following the four classes of the *tantra*. As she opened the door of the reliquary, she thought that this was undoubtedly the body of the great Vajradhara, the wish-fulfilling gem. Later, in order to satisfy each and every headman and disciple, she announced: "I can satisfy everyone's wishes." First she collected the bone fragments; then she collected the ashes. She mixed the ashes with earth and made more than 10,000 *tsha tsha*,[95] which she then decorated with gold. At the end of the procedure she consecrated all the precious relics.

(86a) On the day of the great celebration, holding in her right hand a staff, she gave each monk and nun a fragment of the precious body. She then gave a *tsha tsha* to each of the laypeople. In this way she satisfied everybody's wish. At the Samtenling temple she celebrated a big ritual offering (*tshogs*) for the members of the closest retinue; first of all for the two personal attendants, Loden and Osang. She offered them turquoises, pearls, and robes and gave a good speech. In doing all this she was assisted by the *siddha* Changsumpa and Deleg Chodren. When she had finished, she said, "Now I'll go!" However, all the people gathered around her and begged her: "Now that the great lama is no longer here, Great Woman, please stay here forever, (86b) for the sake of the prosperity of Choding." She replied, "Previously I felt drawn here by the precious lama, but now I won't be attached to anything. Tomorrow I will leave." When she left, all the monks of Palmo Choding escorted the Magnificent Lady for the first stretch of her way. She was weeping.

After the death of the King of the Dharma and the completion of the magnificent deeds for his funeral, she never failed to perform the monthly rituals regularly. She was completely dedicated to him. Together with the whole retinue, she performed the rituals *rNam par snang mdzad mngon par byang chub, Je btsun kun rig dpal gsang ba 'dus pa, Mi bskyod rdo rje,* and *Bla ma mchod pa* (87a) and thus paid tribute to him in the best way. When she took leave of the people escorting her, she said, "I'll take care of your holy seat from a distance," and she exhorted them: "You must keep this meditation place properly, so that it won't become empty!" Amid a multitude of weeping and prostrating people, she then left, ascending the pass that led to Ngari. Afterward the religious practitioners of Choding discussed among themselves and said, "The Venerable Lady offered to the precious lama the enjoyment of the whole body; it would be more useful to offer her these robes rather than to keep them ourselves." So they sent his robes[96] to Ngari.

She returned to her remote hermitage near Dzonkha, and even though she stayed there over the summer, she was extremely upset at the loss of her lama. For this reason she did not go to the estates (*gzhi kha*) as she should have done and (87b) traveled all over the hills of Ngari, facing great hardship due to an illness called *ser ma* and suffering from a lice disease (*shig nad*). Affectionately she would say to the ignorant people she encountered: "Such a great lama is very difficult to find!" Feeling sorry for her, Deleg Chodren suggested, "I can take over all the lice from your body!" She answered, "Why shouldn't I bear such a small suffering? How much greater is the suffering in hell!" In this way she refused her offer.

After the Lady of Spiritual Accomplishment (*sgrub pa'i dbang mo*) had left for Ngari, the attendant Loden completed the construction of the wisdom *stūpa* by covering the reliquary with silver. In order to prevent leaks, he also built an additional room above the residence of Chogle Namgyal. In this way he accomplished everything he could do for the King of Dharma. (88a) Similarly, all the work of the retinue was carried out in the best way possible.

Earlier the attendant Loden had suffered from a disease caused by the wind element (*rlung*). Because he was so upset at the loss of the great lama, he was strongly affected by his old illness and became very depressed. Since he thought that the treasure of the teachings of the great master was now kept in the mind of the wisdom *ḍākinī* (Chokyi Dronma), he expressed his wish to become her attendant. Since she had been giving loving care to all the followers of the Omniscient, she readily accepted, as he had been the most respectful and devoted of all Chogle Namgyal's attendants. She then cleared all his inner and outer obstacles and he thrived again, like a withering flower that had been watered and had returned lush and colorful. (88b) The Venerable said, "In principle, nobody says that following the path of yoga it is possible to avoid all obstacles; however, I think that there are no obstacles in my own meditation practice." In fact, her way was certainly fully accomplished; and on that occasion she continued, "I have some particular karmic link with ignorant and crazy people. I think that there is no one better than me to clear your obstacles, because while practicing I accomplished everything that can benefit living beings with an obscured mind." In fact, exactly as she said, some ignorant people who were living isolated, secluded in their homes, at the touch of her saliva had become clever and learned.

(89a) Henceforth she took loving care of the seats of the Omniscient, including the small and remote hermitages. She would say, very emotionally, "People of Choding, orphaned without their father!" The people of the region, and the people of Palmo Choding in particular, enjoyed a tranquil life. Robbers didn't cause any damage, for if this happened they would be punished severely by her father, the king. All the religious practitioners said, "Since the Great Woman is taking loving care of the followers of the great lama, we can keep the religious places well."

As a general rule, the Great Woman showed great respect toward the lamas she decided to follow. (89b) This was particularly true in relation to the Omniscient, who was a great master of the *tantra* and the very essence of the Buddha. He was the best of all lamas. Commenting on this, she used to say, "My respect for the lama is a result of earlier times. When I decided to take the vows I knew that I had to rely on a lama for my practice. I first learned how to do this when I read the text of the *lNga pa* without misunderstanding a single word. Thanks to these auspicious circumstances, I am now able to do both great and small things well."

## The Editing and Reproduction of the Collected Works of Chogle Namgyal

Then she thought, *An excellent basis of the Buddha's doctrine is the set of collected works of Chogle Namgyal* (dPal de kho na nyid 'dus pa). *They should be reproduced as soon as possible in order to fulfill my great lama's wish.* (90a) Accordingly she ordered the scholar Lama Ringyal (Bla ma Rin rgyal) to perform a ritual service for the god of wealth, Vaiśravaṇa, and asked him to act as a messenger between her and the others. At first Ringyal, thinking that this order was to be carried out by someone else, asked, "Whom did you order?" She then explained: "In order to fulfill the wish of our precious lama, I want to initiate the reproduction of the collected works; since I am free of worldly concerns (*bya bral*), we will have to get the materials necessary for this from Vaiśravaṇa.[97] Until this work is completed, please perform rituals, offer dough figures (*gtor ma*), and recite prayers. When the work is finished I won't want anything else." (90b) He then carried out his tasks according to her instructions and dreamed of a horseman who gave him a bundle of keys and said, "Please offer this to Konchog Gyalmo" [i.e., Chokyi Dronma as referred to by her royal name].

Then some people were sent to Palmo Choding, the great seat of meditation, to get the original of the collected works. On the way they ran into robbers from Mustang. However, thanks to the great blessing of the Great Woman, they were able to return safely to the capital.

At the outset of the work, she had the contents list edited and proofread and ensured that the editors followed the same standards. She said, "If I do not act in this way, the deep meaning of this teaching will not be understood properly. This would damage myself and others." They proofread the work four times. (91a) The Queen of Knowledge herself carried out the first editorial process, together with Lama Kabchupa Pal Chime Drupa,[98] Onpo Tingdzin (dBon po Ting 'dzin), and the great *siddha* Changchubkyi Sung,[99] as well as Loden and Osang, the two main attendants of the Omniscient. Then she involved forty-two skilled scribes (*yi ke pa*)[100] from Ngari under the guidance of Chogle Namgyal's great secretary (*dpon yig chen po*), Konchog Gyaltshen.[101] She also established a suitable venue for the work in a locality called Dongphub (gDong phub).

The reproduction of the collected works was a symbol of speech (*gsung rten*). In addition, as a symbol of the body (*sku rten*), the Magnificent Lady had a statue of the Omniscient made, the same size as his seated body. As a symbol of the mind (*thugs rten*), she had a precious wisdom *stūpa* made that was one story high. She gathered all the craftsmen available to make the statues and all the carpenters to make the shelves.

(91b) It took four months to complete all the symbols of body, speech, and mind. Chokyi Dronma collected a great deal of food and drink as alms, and with these she took care of the workers' maintenance. Even though such a large undertaking could be seen as similar to the management of a big land tenure, she achieved everything as easily as if she were simply organizing a ritual offering at the Samten temple.

Ten days after the completion of the work, the whole community celebrated the event magnificently. In the morning they performed a ritual for the purification from grief (*skyo sangs*), and then they continued with ritual offerings and chanting. Seated at the head of the line of celebrating people, the female *siddha* (92a) offered everyone food and drink and, to the delight of everybody, recited a magnificent prayer.

While this merit-making activity was taking place, some demons felt upset and let a contagious disease spread throughout the area, so everybody became very anxious. Earlier, while the copy of the collected works was still being produced, a similar epidemic had spread. At that time, when someone had mentioned the damage caused by the illness, Chokyi Dronma, the Lady of Spiritual Accomplishment, reassured the people, saying, "You shouldn't be afraid!" She then built some big stone cairns (*mtho*) in the four cardinal directions and had some words written on each of them. Therefore the enclosed area in which they were working on the symbols of body, speech, and mind was not threatened by any illness. (92b) The epidemic then ceased in the areas that had been affected and the people relaxed.

On another occasion, rumors spread that the army of Northern Lato would come to Ngari, and everybody was afraid of the damage that this would cause. She spoke reassuring words and said, "The army will not come before the symbols of my great lama are completed." Accordingly no damage by the army came about.

At the same time they made a statue of Chogle Namgyal that was one head higher than the previous one and had a face that was extremely similar to the real lama. Into the ink with which the books were written, they had mixed blood from the nose of the Omniscient, and they provided suitable cloth, strings, and wooden covers for the books. Everybody said that this edition of the collected works was the most complete and was of the highest standard. All this was very marvelous.

(93a) They decided to place the symbols of body, speech, and mind in the white building that is the royal residence at the center of the monastery of Dzonkha Chode. They decorated the walls of the room where the Precious Lord used to spend the night when he was staying in Ngari with beautiful paintings and thus prepared it as a suitable shrine. At the begining of the consecration ceremony, the statue and the the wisdom *stūpa* arrived in a carriage from Dongphub. A procession of monks brought the precious books. Each monk carried a volume on his shoulders, placed on a suitable support. Members of the monastic community, wearing the three pieces of the religious robe and holding incense, arrived, preceding Chokyi Dronma, the great *bhikṣuṇī*, the spiritually accomplished female *siddha* (*dge slong ma chen mo byang sems grub pa' rdo rje ma*). (93b) Pal Chime Drupa and the other editors came carrying ritual instruments, playing wonderful music, and dancing. When the procession arrived at the monastery, the monks led by the great scholar and meditator of the Tripiṭaka, Palden Sangye,[102] performed the *vajra* dance (*rdo rje gar*). The monks led by Lama Gyalseng (Bla ma rGyal seng) performed the drum dance (*rnga 'cham*). All the other monks were standing in line to welcome the procession that had arrived carrying the sacred items. Meanwhile the Gungthang's King of the Dharma, the Great Son of the Gods (*lha sras chen po*), was watching from the top of the palace. The place was filled with a crowd of people who had come from all over to watch the event. At the sight of the statue, all the scholars were moved like ears in the wind by the deep faith they felt; (94a) the common people felt as if they were facing the real lama and uttered the sound "*A la la la*" in surprise. The crowd felt blissful and contented. They said, "These amazing deeds of merit have happened thanks to the grace of the Great Lady Konchog Gyalmo."

Eventually the sacred items were placed in the relevant chapel and a magnificent ritual offering was performed with abundant donations, resembling a cloud with butter lamps in its middle. When the actual celebration started, the King Son of the Gods came first in line. Then came the ocean of the monastic community, led by the scholars and meditators, who had gathered there. There was Ponmo Sangring (dPon mo Sang ring) with the craftsmen who had made the statues, Lopon Ringyal (sLob dpon rin rgyal) with the painters, and the great secretary, Konchog Gyaltshen, with the carvers. (94b) There were also carpenters, statue makers, blacksmiths, and the ministers of the king, as well as all sorts of guests, ranging from officials to commoners, who had spontaneously gathered to watch. Everybody was offered food, as much as they wished, and a great deal of drink. Chokyi Dronma presented her father with a monastic robe and gave the others whatever they needed. Therefore, in this way, there was an excellent end to the celebration. The next day she paid all the workers. She also sold some items to them (95a) according to their request and for a price that was one fourth of the real price that would have been asked by good traders. In this way she kept all the workers happy. Everybody felt that she was able to provide such great enjoyment because at the beginning she was offered the keys of Vaiśravaṇa's treasure. Her father, the King Son of the Gods, Grandmother Changsem,[103] the other relatives, and all her followers had also offered plenty of donations with great devotion. (95b) In addition, much was collected as alms. In this wonderful way the reproduction of Bodong Chogle Namgyal's collected works[104] (*dPal de kho na nyid 'dus pa*) and all the other great deeds could be completed. The Great Lady was able to achieve all this also thanks to her sister, Dzamling Gyalmo, and her mother, Dode Gyalmo, who had followed her instructions without hesitation or laziness. The Magnificent Lady, satisfied with the results and particularly grateful to them, said, "The sun of merit shone in my mind, but my mother and sister carried out the actual work."

(96a) The logistics of the enterprise, such as sending messages, roasting grain, and making *chang*, were managed by the lead nun, Changchub Sangmo, and the nuns who followed her instructions without hesitation or laziness. The novice Tharpa Sangmo, in particular, provided continuous and perfect assistance.[105] Since everything went so well, they celebrated a magnificent thanksgiving ritual. The ocean of protectors were very satisfied. The teacher Shakya Sangpo,[106] who was a very knowledgeable scholar of the *sūtra* and the *tantra* from Gungthang and who had been very close to the great lama's teaching, was then appointed as the caretaker of the collected works. Lama Tson O (Bla ma bTson 'od), who had an excellent character and great diligence and took the law of cause and effect into great consideration, was appointed as the caretaker of the temple. (96b) The ritual equipment that was necessary for regular religious practice was provided with unimaginable richness, and three places for offering butter lamps were set up. All these arrangements were made for the sake of the symbols of body, speech, and mind of the Precious Lord Chogle Namgyal, and the people said, in unison, "These great deeds were achieved by the Great Woman. First, she conceived the idea of renouncing her family life to stay in the forest in solitude; second, she managed to collect a great deal of wealth; third, she worked hard and became a model for others who then imitated her. Because of her attributes and activities, these deeds were achieved in a very short space of time."

After the completion of her work, a lot of wealth still remained and she said, "If I were to use what has been donated privately, it would not be appropriate." (97a) Therefore she performed marvelous celebrations at the great monastery of Dzonkha Chode and offered gifts to each lama. As she had not yet exhausted the collected wealth, she went to Palmo Choding and established a special ritual in honor of its great lama. She then sent whatever was left to her mother and offered some nice gifts to Gunglungma.

After a while there were some disturbances in Ngari. Paths and bridges were blocked. Nobody dared to travel between the southern regions [Nepal] and Tibet. Following Chokyi Dronma's suggestion, her father went with her to appease the son of Kansher so that the kingdom became very peaceful again. The Great Lady of Renunciation, born from her human mother, benefited all people like the sun.

(97b) The nuns of the retinue of the Magnificent Lady used to say, "Provided her health is good, everything is excellent." When the nuns were traveling on the road, the people used to step aside in respect. Whatever the Great Woman did, the people considered it to be excellent. Whatever the Great Woman said, the people considered it to be most reliable. Nobody could be compared to her since she was the jewel of the crown.

At that time there was a monk at Sholphug monastery (dGon Zhol phug) called Lama Palden Sangpo (Bla ma dPal ldan bzang po) who was very knowledgeable and diligent. When he read the *bsTod pa don gnyis lhun grub ma* ("The praise for the spontanous realization of both aims") in honor of Chogle Namgyal composed by the Magnificent Lady, he was so moved that he said, "The Great Woman seems to know everything about the *sūtra* and the *tantra.*" Later, having heard of this lama's comment, she said to her retinue, (98a) "When I was young I became the mistress of a household. At that time I didn't think about listening to the *Dharma,* thinking and meditating for the liberation of my body. I was assigned tasks by people who had very little knowledge and I had to obey them. Later I took a good lama as a spiritual guide and I understood the *sūtra* and the *tantra* without making any mistakes." Hearing this, her mother thought with great emotion, *She is beyond any possible evaluation!*

One night, while they were in the capital, Deleg Chodren said to her with great respect, "Lady of Knowledge, in Ngari you performed great deeds for both the secular and the monastic order (*lugs gnyis*). Now, Palmo Choding is the residence of the lama, but nobody is looking after the suffering that was caused by his passing. (98b) Nobody else is able to do this. Please, Great Woman, think of Palmo Choding." The female Buddha said, "Yours are respectful and honest words. Also the Lord of the Dharma spoke in a similar way. When the Lord of the Dharma was residing in Palmo Choding, even the birds of the sky rejoiced. However, if I reside at that monastery, I won't be able to look after all the issues that I need to tackle. I won't be able to go swiftly anywhere to solve problems. Consider the advantages and disadvantages of residing in Palmo Choding yourself. You could do everything by working hard with great patience and you would feel proud of doing this." Deleg Chodren rejoiced when she heard these words and promised that she would do her best. Following this conversation, the Great Woman decided to travel to Palmo Choding also because she needed to return the original of the collected·works to the monastery.

Dorje Phagmo incarnation in a sixteenth-century mural painting at Nyemo Chekar monastery, possibly Chokyi Dronma (according to local current identification). *Hildegard Diemberger*

(top) Recent mural paintings at Samding monastery showing the lineage of the Dorje Phagmo incarnations. In the middle is Bodong Chogle Namgyal.
*Bruce Huett*

(bottom left) The late Thubten Namgyal, designer of the mural paintings and former head monk of Samding monastery, showing one of Bodong Chogle Namgyal's shoes as a holy relic.
*Hildegard Diemberger*

(bottom right) Chokyi Dronma. Detail of the mural painting showing the Dorje Phagmo lineage.
*Bruce Huett*

(top) Late sixteenth-century murals at Nyemo Chekar monastery depicting the Fourth Red Hat Karmapa and several incarnations of the Dorje Phagmo.
*Hildegard Diemberger*

(bottom left) Tashi Ombar, protector of the Bodongpa tradition, depicted at Nyemo Chekar monastery.
*Hildegard Diemberger*

(bottom right) Chime Palsang, spiritual master of the Bodongpa tradition who looked after Nyendra Sangmo (the Third Dorje Phagmo). Together they established Nyemo Chekar monastery in the sixteenth century.
*Hildegard Diemberger*

(above) Dzongkha, the capital of the Gungthang kingdom, with the ruins of the royal palace.
*Carlo Meazza*

(left) Phagpa Lhakang, one of the main temples in the Kyirong valley, dates back to imperial times and has distinctive Nepalese features.
*Hildegard Diemberger*

(top, opposite page) The Palkhu Lake from the village of Labuk. Local farmers are winnowing barley.
*Bruce Huett*

(bottom, opposite page) Shekar. The ruins of the palace of the Southern Lato rulers and the Shekar monastery overlook the village at the foot of the mountain.
*Maria Antonia Sironi*

(top, opposite page) Porong landscape with Mount Shishapangma, seen from Palmo Choding monastery.
*Hildegard Diemberger*

(bottom, opposite page) Monks of Porong Palmo Choding monastery. The monk in the middle is holding an ancient statue of Bodong Chogle Namgyal.
*Carlo Meazza*

(above) Bodong Chogle Namgyal in a mural painting at Nyemo Chekar monastery.
*Hildegard Diemberger*

(right) Bodong Chogle Namgyal's statue, kept in Porong monastery in Kathmandu. This statue is renowned for its realistic features and for its sacredness.
*Carlo Meazza*

(above) The architectural masterpiece built by Thangtong Gyalpo at Chung Riwoche, on the northern bank of the Brahmaputra River. Chokyi Dronma contributed to its completion.
*Maria Antonia Sironi*

(left) Thangtong Gyalpo depicted on a stone at Lhasa.
*Bruce Huett*

(top, opposite page) The Phuntshogling bridge, one of the iron-chain bridges attributed to Thangtong Gyalpo, still in use in 1993. The bridge was recently destroyed by a flood.
*Maria Antonia Sironi*

(bottom, opposite page) Thangtong Gyalpo's bridge on the Brahamaputra River at Chagsam Chubori in the early twentieth century.
*Charles Bell. Pitt Rivers Museum, University of Oxford, 1998.286.116*

(top, opposite page) Yamdrog lake, from the Gampala pass. In the background is Nojin Gangsang, the mountain god protecting the Yamdrog area.
*Bruce Huett*

(bottom left, opposite page) Kunga Sangmo, the reincarnation of Chokyi Dronma. She carried on the tradition with the support of the lords of the Yamdrog area.
*Hildegard Diemberger*

(bottom right, opposite page) The cover of an ancient *thangka* belonging to Chokyi Dronma explains the history of the object and mentions Chokyi Dronma's skull.
*Hildegard Diemberger*

(above) Samding monastery in the early twentieth century.
*Charles Bell. Pitt Rivers Museum, University of Oxford, 1998.285.135.1*

(right) The Eleventh Dorje Phagmo, the "holiest woman of Tibet," according to Charles Bell.
*Charles Bell. Pitt Rivers Museum, University of Oxford, 1998.285.137.1*

Samding monastery with the "demoness lake."
*Bruce Huett*

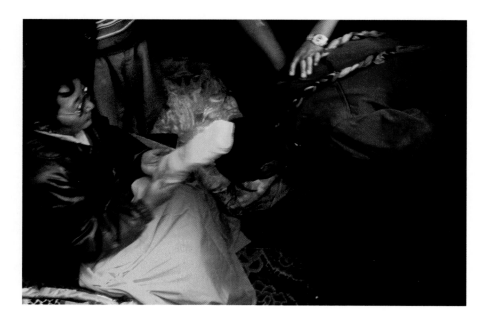

The Twelfth Dorje Phagmo blesses devotees.
*Hildegard Diemberger*

(top) Chokyi Dronma depicted on the cover of the biography of Bodong Chogle Namgyal.
*Hildegard Diemberger*

(bottom left) The Twelfth Dorje Phagmo on her throne at Samding monastery.
*Hildegard Diemberger*

(bottom right) Chokyi Dronma in a mural painting at Nyemo Chekar monastery.
*Hildegard Diemberger*

Festival at Samding monastery in July 1997.
*Hildegard Diemberger*

(above) The return of the collected works of Bodong Chogle Namgyal, reprinted in India, to Bodong E monastery.
*Maria Antonia Sironi*

(right) A senior nun from Lungmar nunnery.
*Bruce Huett*

Encounter with a young Dorje Phagmo.
*Bruce Huett*

The young Dorje Phagmo holding her mobile phone.
*Bruce Huett*

(99a) The evening before her departure, she told the attendant Osang, "You should go to central Nepal[107] in order to make the statue of Mañjuśrī, the tutelary deity of the Great Lord. You should do this work with great diligence and you should complete it in the most perfect way. If you can do this, I will be delighted." Then she offered him a piece of clothing and left.

As she arrived at [Koron] Khabso, most of the meditators of Palmo Choding were there to welcome her. She presented them with a nice copy of the collected works and some gifts. While talking with the people of Palmo Choding, she said, "If you wish that I reside at Choding, I will take care of everything. I will invite the expert in channel construction again, the *siddha* of Ganden[108] who has left. You, people who are still here, please remain constant. If the conditions are good, they will be appropriate for the great lama. If the conditions are not sufficient, whatever we try will not succeed; (99b) and if we are not able to achieve good conditions, it is not necessary for me to stay here. Earlier the lords of Ngari, of Northern and Southern Lato, behaved shamefully and sent armies to the monasteries to wage war. Now we are able to rely on the doctrine of Chogle Namgyal's collected works in all that we do. You should all look after it and spread it." Hearing these words, everybody rejoiced and promised that they would behave accondingly. Everybody was very satisfied with the good discussion.

After the Venerable Lady returned to Ngari, she stayed in a hermitage called Gunbe Phug (rGun be phug), where she gave teachings on *Mahāyāna* practices such as mind purification (*blo sbyong*). At that time she heard that an old homeless woman was wandering around and had fallen from a high bridge. She was badly hurt, her body was covered with injuries, and nobody was looking after her. (100a) The Great Woman felt great compassion and said to her mother, "If this old woman has not died yet, please send someone to bring her to me. If she has died, please send someone to take proper care of her body." Her mother voiced some doubts: "There are many monks traveling on that path; it is impossible that they didn't take care of her. If she was abandoned, perhaps this happened because she was affected by a contagious disease. Are you sure that it is necessary to bring her here?" Chokyi Dronma, in tears, said, "We used to pray to the *bodhisattvas* and promise that we would help all living beings. How can we not feel sorry for someone when we face a real situation, but only talk about it? Therefore I'll go to see her on my own." The mother was hurt by these comments and immediately sent someone with a carriage to fetch the old woman.

After a while the old woman arrived. (100b) She was in terrible condition and was a horrible and frightening sight. She was covered with pus and insects and

*Translation of the Biography of the Venerable Chokyi Dronma*

her body was giving off a terrible smell. The carriage was taken to a sheltered place that Chokyi Dronma's mother had prepared for her and the old woman was transferred to a nice bed. Even though Chokyi Dronma was actually in retreat, she took some clean water and cleaned the old woman with her own hands. She wiped away the pus from her eyes. She put her own saliva in the mouth of the old lady and with a smile she asked, "Poor old woman! What happened to you?" At the same time, she was removing, with her own hands, the lice from the woman's body. Then she blessed her. For nine days she fed her regularly. Every day she recited the [*Phyag*] *rGya chen mo*[109] seven times into the ear of the old woman. (101a) Assuming that the woman would be scared at the sight of the high mountains surrounding her dwelling, she placed a curtain that gave her the impression that her bed was located in a nice house.

When the old woman died, she administered the ritual of "the Great Transfer" (*'pho ba*), placed some ritual writing (*gdags yig*) on her body, and gave her the empowerment of Vairocana (*Kun rig*). The nuns participated in the celebration of the Vairocana ritual and the Great Woman said, "May the old mother enjoy a good life in the future."

## Thangtong Gyalpo: First Contacts

Sometime later, the Great Woman said to Deleg Chodren, "Our people of Palmo Choding don't behave properly. If they follow what I say we can achieve results, but they don't seem to do so. If they listen to me, there is nothing more precious than working together for the benefit of the monastery; otherwise I'll get tired of staying in the Ngari region. If this situation continues, I won't stay around here any longer and I'll go somewhere else (101b) in order to benefit the doctrine and the living beings. Since the Iron Bridge Lama, Thangtong Gyalpo, seems to have great magical abilities and extraordinary powers, now I will ask him for a prophecy about my dilemma. Previously I have not been allowed to develop a relationship,[110] so please visit him in order to establish an initial contact. Please ask him for clear instructions on the direction I ought to go in order to benefit the most living beings. Also ask him to send a guide who knows the area." Deleg Chodren was therefore sent as a messenger with a letter and a string of pearls.

At that time the great *siddha*, the Iron Bridge Lama, was staying in Northern Lato at a place called Pal Riboche[111] in the Chung area, where he was engaged in great achievements such as the construction of the marvelous *stūpa*.

(102a) He was practicing Mahāmudrā in tranquility. During the day he performed great deeds for the sake of gods and people in order to lead all living
beings to the path of spiritual liberation. At night he performed great deeds of
sight, hearing, and touch, for the sake of nonhuman beings.

Thangtong Gyalpo was an emanation of great wisdom and a shrine of the
virtue of all living beings. When Deleg Chodren arrived, he was in the middle of
a crowd, teaching. She prostrated to him and the lama *siddha* asked, "Where are
you from? Who sent you? On what business?"

"I'm from Ngari, and I was sent by the Lady Konchog Gyalmo to meet
you."

(102b) "Would you listen if I were to suggest that you, teacher and disciples
from central Tibet, should go to the east for the benefit of living beings?"

"We should go, if this benefits the teachings and the living beings."

"Do you have any letter and accompanying items?"

She promptly handed over the gift and the letter, which Thangtong Gyalpo
read amid the crowd of people surrounding him. As they discussed her plans, he
asked, "Are you going tomorrow or are you staying? Shall we plan that you stay
for three days?"

"I'll stay for three days."

"You will!" he confirmed.

In the evening before the day of her departure the nun was affected by a stomach illness due to a disturbance of the wind (*rlung*) element. She thought, *This
seems to be a wind illness* (gnas rlung). *If I eat fresh butter and fresh meat I should
be able to recover; I hope the great* siddha *can give me this. I'll ask for a token* (yig
rten) *to go with the reply that he is going to send. This is the Ngari custom, which is
somewhat different from that of other people.*

(103a) While she was thinking about her illness and her plans, a monk sent
by the great *siddha* arrived and said, "Nun from Ngari! The great *siddha* asks
you go to see him." Promptly she went to see him and prostrated to him as she
arrived. Thangtong Gyalpo presented her with one leg of meat, one container of
butter, and one cup of good barley flour. He said, "Have you had any stomach
problems? Please eat this! At Chagsam Khar[112] you were affected by an illness
caused by the wind element. There is no tradition here of sending a reply with
a token to go with it. However, you people from Ngari may say that the people
from Northern Lato let you go empty-handed. I, the bridge builder, would feel
very ashamed of this. Now please choose whether you prefer a token or a prayer."

"I prefer a prayer," she said. Accordingly, after recommending that she should

*Translation of the Biography of the Venerable Chokyi Dronma*

leave at night, he celebrated a magnificent prayer and recited some special verses for the departure of Deleg Chodren.

(103b) Thangtong Gyalpo sent a reply to Chokyi Dronma confirming that he had received her[113] letter, and gave some comments on doctrinal views, practice, and meditation. In his reply he also said, "I hope you are well! If you go to the east you will achieve great things, but there are doubts concerning the length of your life. If you do choose to go, the best option is to go to Kongpo, because throughout that area the people will provide you with good service. However, if you wish to live in one place, it is better that you stay in the upper areas [i.e., the Ngari region]."

Having returned safely to Ngari, Deleg Chodren went to see Chokyi Dronma. She was in the religious school giving some teachings concerning Padmasambhava to Pal Namkha Chogdrub (dPal nam mkha' mchog grub) and other disciples. Deleg Chodren prostrated to Chokyi Dronma, who asked, "Did you have a hard time? Did you accomplish the mission?"

"I did not encounter any problem and I was successful."

Delighted with Deleg Chodren's answer, she thanked her very nicely. (104a) The scholars who were gathered there asked, "Where did you go, nun? What did you do to make you so happy?" Chokyi Dronma, the Great Emanation, said, "She went on a great mission for us and for all living beings!"

In the evening before they went to sleep, Deleg Chodren gave a detailed report of her trip, to which Chokyi Dronma listened with delight. The next day Deleg Chodren handed over to her Thangtong Gyalpo's letter of reply. The letter had been written personally by the *siddha* and the Magnificent Lady was not able to read it. She then said, "I'm not able to read this handwriting." Deleg Chodren reassured her, "The *siddha* explained to me every single word of his reply," and outlined the content to her. With this help she was able to understand the meaning of the letter and lodge it in her memory. Chokyi Dronma was delighted with the words of the *siddha*. (104b) She briefly placed the letter on her head [showing respect and receiving blessing]. Then she said to herself: *Great man! Great man!* (*a pho khyo kha*).

Around that time Chokyi Dronma heard that her husband had died at Shekar. She felt great compassion for him, for she was a holy person, who had a great mind and great compassion toward all living beings. Together with a group of nuns she performed the ritual of "Buddha's Complete Liberation from Evil Rebirths" (*bCom ldan 'das ngan song yongs su sbyong ba*)[114] 100 times, gave teachings concerning the intermediate state (*bar do*) [between death and rebirth], (105a) and gave empowerments to the funerary wooden board with his name (*mtshan byang*). She said, "Most people would burn the wooden board, but that is not how I am going to behave!" She then placed the funerary wooden board in front of the reliquary of the Great Lord. When she did this, Onpo Tingdzin[115] said, "In general Tshewang Tashi had no respect for the doctrine and he did not perform any great deeds of merit. Venerable, why do you keep thinking about him so compassionately? This is making things difficult for everyone." She answered, "I am not thinking about his qualities, I just want him to reach enlightenment." In this way she continued to keep him in her memory compassionately.

After a while she gave an order to Deleg Chodren: "Now you should go to Palmo Choding to hold a memorial service for the great lama. (105b) What about the people of Palmo Choding building water channels? We need to think of this as well and do some preparatory work. Don't be narrow-minded." She gave her some gold to cover the expenses of the celebration. As soon as Deleg Chodren arrived at Palmo Choding, she had the service performed. She gave the instructions of the Magnificent Lady to the people, and they carried out everything very satisfactorily. However, the people of Palmo Choding said, regarding the water channels, "This year we can't make channels for the fields. However, if the Venerable were to live here we would follow all her instructions, including those concerning the construction of water-channels. This is what we hope for."

The Magnificent Lady did not want to stay in the Ngari region anymore and went to see her father. (106a) She presented him with the jewel box she had used when she was still living in Ngari as an unmarried girl and said to him, "I don't want to stay here anymore. I want to travel to other places. On my way I'll carry out some important deeds in Palmo Choding." Her father, deeply attached to her and aware of her great deeds, was very unhappy about what she wanted to do and disagreed with her plan. He spoke to her at great length. At that time the nephew of Chogle Namgyal,[116] who was a great scholar, had taken over as abbot at Palmo Choding, Bodong, Shekar, and Dzonkha. Even though she didn't have any previous religious link with him, considering the deeds that he would perform in his position, she decided to establish a good relationship and invited him to give a Long Life Empowerment (*tshe dbang*) at her hermitage near the capital. (106b) She offered him fifty *zhol* of gold and other precious items. She also made excellent offerings to the monastery of Dzonkha Chode, in Gungthang, and performed celebrations and offerings at a place called Tsaron (rTsa ron). With her mother and sister, she went to the Lord of the Dharma Shakyapa[117] to listen to the teachings on *Gra lnga* and she performed many offerings. Her mother and her sister helped her with everything.

At that time, Chokyi Dronma's father discussed with the great monastery where the great scholar, the nephew of Chogle Namgyal, was residing, as well as with lay officials, what they should do concerning the possibility that the Venerable Queen of the *Dharma* might not stay in Ngari. For two and half months everybody kept saying to her, "Stay here! There's no other option."

(107a) However, she didn't accept their request, as she felt that she had auspicious omens (*rten 'brel*) that led her to other places. She wanted to take her mother and sister as companions on the way. However, the patrons, officials, and subjects thought that Chokyi Dronma, the Treasury of Magnificence, was very attached to her mother and her father said to her, "*Bhikṣuṇi,* it is better if you stay in Ngari. If you don't feel like staying here, then please stay in Palmo Choding. I can promise that Ngari won't create any problems for Palmo Choding and I'll support you effectively. Later, as long as you stay in a place that can be reached easily, I'll send your mother to you. But this time you should leave her here." At first she did not accept the various requests. Then she said that she would consider Palmo Choding. Her father reiterated that he would send her mother as soon as she settled somewhere. (107b) The nephew of Chogle Namgyal also gave her a letter. When she eventually left, her father shed an ocean of tears. Her grandmother was very upset. Everybody lost heart. Her father promised to give her everything she needed. Then she said, "I'm free of worldly concerns (*bya bral ma*) and just want to practice the doctrine. I don't need any form of enjoyment." She refused to take anything from him except for some blessing pills from the Sakyapa masters and some ambrosia medicine. She accepted new waterproof clothing of good quality from her gandmother. Then the Great Woman, having achieved all that she had wanted, departed from the royal palace.

(108a) Before her departure she had given her mother very precious gifts so that in the future she wouldn't need to ask anyone for help. She gave her a very good land tenure where the master and his disciples used to reside. She gave her a field so that its revenue would pay for the cheese and butter dishes (*thud*) that she liked. She had a good storeroom for barley (*nas khang*) built in Kuthang [in Nubri]. All this was taken care of mainly by her sister, Dzamling Gyalmo. She had also given presents and instructions to her retinue. Eventually she left her homeland and went to the east in order to perform great deeds of merit.

(108b) Her mother and sister escorted her. On the pass it took them forever to say good-bye. Their body, speech, and mind were overcome by the pain of the separation. Her mother and sister prostrated at the feet of Vajravārāhī [Chokyi Dronma, as Vajravārāhī's emanation]. Her mother said, "I can't give you up, please let me follow you." She answered, "How can I give up my mother? Please keep your promise to join me later." She wiped her face and her eyes, which had become red, with her hand and continued toward the plain of Palthang without hesitating, followed by some members of her retinue who had also decided to leave. She first went to Ganden,[118] where new channels were being made, and gave many helpful instructions about the construction, on the basis of those that had been given previously by the Omniscient Great Lord Chogle Namgyal. (109a) She examined the place and chose the course of the channels toward Nyaphar, so that these were easy to build and would be reliable in the future. Then she arrived at Palmo Choding. At the same time the Lord of the Dharma, the nephew of Chogle Namgyal, had also arrived at the monastery and was welcomed by the meditation colleges. Many people of Palmo Choding joined Chokyi Dronma and her attendants in the construction work. She gave lengthy instructions on how to build channels and everybody said, "We're sure that our channels will be excellent!" She said, "It's difficult for you to carry out the work to my satisfaction, but making channels is important to benefit the doctrine and living beings." Then she performed a divination and requested advice by using dough balls (*zan ril*) in front of the statue of the Great Lama Chogle Namgyal. On this occasion, according to her instructions, (109b) all the monks and nuns gathered before the statue of the lama in deep devotion. After they prayed, the divination was performed.[119] Then she held the piece of paper, put it briefly to her forehead, and said, "It is a favorable prophecy!" She was delighted and the people of Palmo Choding were extremely pleased. The female *siddha* covered most of the expenses for the equipment and materials for the channel construction. The people of Palmo Choding provided most of the labor. She also asked the people from Phug Lango (Phug glang sgo) [in the vicinity of the Palkhu lake] to join in the work, and promised: "I will give you fields as well." The abbot also asked for special equipment to make noodles (*thug thal*) for the people. She sent a letter to her father asking for most of the items. (110a) The headman Onpo Tingdzin, who lived on the monastic estates of Palmo Choding, was also asked to support the work with some materials. Chokyi Dronma said to him, "There are favorable omens that if we work hard, the channels will be excellent." She thought, *According to the*

*Translation of the Biography of the Venerable Chokyi Dronma*

*idea of my omniscient great lama, wherever a religious seat is established in Tibet, it ought to be looked after by its own monks and patrons. There is no point in having additional people involved, as this would bring major difficulties and little benefit. The construction of the channels in the area of the Palkhu Lake will benefit an area measuring one thousand khal. Everybody will benefit as long as no one raises a claim for a larger share. This will greatly help not only those who live on the Palthang plain next to the lake but also the many people from India and Nepal who come to Tibet regularly and face great hardship on the way. (110b) In ancient times people used to say that in order to establish a great monastery, it was important to build it in an affluent big town to avoid problems with erratic irrigation systems; it was good to build it on the ruins of a former building so that completely new construction was not required. Also, the existing surrounding fields would produce large amounts of rice, and numerous learned monks from many places would gather there. In the same way, scholars from Southern and Northern Lato and Ngari should gather here to study and practice his collected works, spreading the doctrine of the Buddha. Also, thanks to these good deeds, this great land can remain peaceful for a while.* [Despite her plan,] the project did not go well because what the local people said they would do was changeable, (111a) like the tongue of a snake.

Eventually the Great Woman decided to go elsewhere. She said, "Even when I find a place that is suitable for building a channel, who can do it? I won't achieve what I want. It's hopeless! Now I'll go to the east."

The next day she set up new prayer flags (*dar lcog*) at the residence of the Omniscient. She offered a white scarf to the statue of Mañjuśrī. She raised a new banner next to the wisdom *stūpa*. She greeted each member of the monastic community of Palmo Choding, presenting him or her with gifts. She also recited prayers appropriate for everybody. When she had finished, she left for the east. All the *siddhas* escorted her until the pass called Labla.[120] (111b) The great *siddha* Changsungpa celebrated a *mendel* offering[121] and recited prayers asking her to have compassion for all living beings. She promised to do so. The attendants, Loden and Osang, went with her to Sogkha (Sogs kha)[122] to provide assistance.

The next day she performed a monthly ritual for the Omniscient. At Sogkha the people were very welcoming and looked after her well. During this period there was a drought that had significantly damaged the crops in the Brahmaputra region. After the Venerable Lady arrived, rain fell for seven days and all the crops recovered. Then she went to Sharu, where the local ruler saluted her with deference and presented her with offerings. Afterward she went to Laru. (112a) The noblewoman Onmo Palkar[123] and others offered her an unimaginable quantity of gifts, food, and drink. Then she crossed the gorge called Gyachu Drang (brGyad bcu 'phrang). Chodzema, the Lady of Tagtse, presented her with precious jewels such as turquoises and pearls, and performed a magnificent ritual offering. She spent one night in Semig. The day before she was due to meet the lama *siddha* (Thangtong Gyalpo), the Magnificent Lady said to Deleg Chodren, "Tomorrow, first I'll prostrate and ask him for teachings. However, I do not know what both attendants are going to do."

Deleg Chodren replied, "I'll go and ask them."

Then she went to ask Osang, who answered, "We cannot have two different ways of behaving. Please ask the other attendant what he is going to do, and I will do the same."

She asked Loden, the other attendant, who (112b) answered, "If the Great Woman prostrates herself first, I will do the same. However, I will not ask for teachings."

Deleg Chodren reported this to Chokyi Dronma, who said, "The people of Choding were satisfied with their own teacher. They shall do what they think best."

Leaving behind the nuns at a place called Gur (mGur), the Magnificent Lady, with the two attendants and Deleg Chodren, went to Chung Riwoche. When she and her retinue were approaching, they rested at the top of a hill to prepare for the meeting. She saw, from a distance, the *siddha* leaning out of his meditation hut and waving to them. She asked Deleg Chodren, "Who is that?"

"That is the *siddha*."

(113a) "He looks very cheerful!"

Then they walked toward him, offered white scarves, and prostrated. The *siddha* was wearing a new cloak and a new summer hat and kept his mouth covered with his cloak [in respect] while she was prostrating. She then offered him pearl earrings that had been given to her by Chodzema, the Lady of Tagtse. She also presented him with a brocade strap, a bowl of white sweets, and some medicines. Then she prostrated again and the *siddha* asked:

"Did you come here with everyone's agreement, or are you escaping?"

"I came here after getting my father and brother's approval."

"It is extraordinary that someone like you became liberated from all worldly concerns with the agreement of your father and everybody else. I am delighted! Now, please, sit close to me." (113b) Then he opened his eyes wide, looked at the two attendants, and asked, "Who are these two?"

*Translation of the Biography of the Venerable Chokyi Dronma*

"They are the attendants in charge of food and sleeping quarters of our Precious Lord."

"The attendants in charge of food and sleeping quarters usually welcome rather than escort someone."

Deleg Chodren interjected: "Why did you wave to us?"

"I waved because I was looking forward to meeting you as soon as possible."

Then, when the sun had set behind the pass, Deleg Chodren asked, "The sun is gone, where are we going to sleep?"

The *siddha* replied, "This is the first time that the people of Palmo Choding have come to meet Thangtong Gyalpo. It is said that guests who come from far away and people who are suffering from long illnesses need particular care. Therefore we are going to ensure that your stay tonight is very comfortable."

(114a) In the evening seven people were sent to make the relevant arrangements. Then he took some barley flour, enough for one person, and came to where they were staying. He ordered that a little food with some butter be given to everyone. He offered three lumps of molasses to the Venerable and gave one lump to each nun. Then he said, "I thought that you would be coming, so I had the place cleaned up." He ordered some water containers, made of bronze, to be taken there from his residence. Then she offered some donations, asking him for teachings. The two attendants had a discussion and decided that they would leave.

When they stood up and were about to go, the *siddha* said, "Please sit down, (114b) let's offer a praise for our friend, the female teacher." Therefore a praise for the female Buddha was celebrated. After this the *siddha* talked a lot and said, "I'll offer a praise to Buddha myself. Now, before this you must prostrate." He thus gave them no choice but to prostrate and perform a religious offering. Then he exhorted them: "You need to do what follows the ritual offerings. You perform a *mendel* offering and subsequently 100,000 *mendel* offerings and so on, isn't it so?" The two attendants who had tried to stand up felt embarrassed. Then, having changed their minds and acquired some faith, they felt that they had no other option but to ask the *siddha* for teachings. Chokyi Dronma was pleased by this and said to Deleg Chodren, "This will benefit them."

(115a) When the female *siddha* requested teachings from Thangtong Gyalpo, he asked her, "Which would you like to hear?"

"I would like to receive teachings on the generation of the spirit of enlightenment (*sems bskyed*)."

"In general, nobody received teachings from me in Northern Lato; in particular, nobody took teachings from me on this subject. It is marvelous that you wish to hear these."

Then he asked her to take off her shoes and gave her the teaching she had requested. He said, "You are different from the other people of Palmo Choding. I want to give you teachings about the list of contents (*dkar cag*) of the *bKa' 'gyur* and *bsTan 'gyur.*"[124] Then he read the list to her.

Later he said to the two attendants, "You both are in charge of the sacks of barley flour for the Lord of Dharma of Bodong and can act accordingly."

Loden, one of the two attendants, answered, "We can't do this."

The *siddha* said, "If this is the case, your master must have been very tired. I take care of my own sacks of barley flour, and if I don't receive the food on time from my estate, someone else will provide food for me. (115b) But really, attendants of the Lord of the Dharma of Bodong, I'm just joking!" Then he took some barley flour of poor quality from a very small sack and gave it to both of them.

Meanwhile he was looking at the Magnificent Lady and said, "Female teacher of Ngari! Vajrasattva resides in the east, Ratnasambhava resides in the south, Amithāba resides in the west, Amoghasiddhi resides in the north.[125] Wherever you go, you are like one of these deities. This time I feel that you came as the real Amithāba of the the west. However, please listen to my teachings and instructions. If you don't listen, there is no point in asking for them."

The female *siddha* said, (116a) "I decided to travel widely with the approval of my father, the king. Now I have decided that I'll go toward the east anyway. Please give me the relevant instructions."

"The best choice would be to keep traveling around in the upper areas above Palmo Choding [i.e., stay in western Tibet] in order to benefit the great seat. The middle choice would be to stay for one year in some holy places of your choice in Northern Yeru [i.e., in his region, Northern Lato] before leaving for the east. The worst choice is to leave before the summer rains have stopped.[126] You are equipped to travel, but the nuns are not. If you leave now, you will make it very arduous for the nuns of your retinue. You should think about them. If you like, if you stay here I can give you some teachings."

Then Chokyi Dronma promised that she would stay at least until the end of the rains. During this time she learned from the *siddha* some teachings of Padmasambhava (116b) and Machig.[127] She also asked for a teaching about *sahaja yoga* (*lhan gcig skyes rnal 'byor*) of the Mahāmudrā tradition, and therefore he gave it to her. The Great Woman learned all the doctrines very well and received all the ambrosia of the religious instructions from the Omniscient Thangtong Gyalpo, who was careful not to disappoint her. At that time he told her the following story:

Once, the scholar Kabshiba Namkha Oser,[128] who had heard of the fame of an extraordinary hermitess, the so-called Tshenden Rithroma, wished to receive some teachings from her. However, she was in retreat. On the path to the hermitage there was a cairn of stones with an inscription saying: NOBODY IS ALLOWED TO PROCEED BEYOND THIS POINT. Shortly after that was another similar cairn of stones.

(117a) At the door of the meditation hut, there was another cairn with the same writing. Ignoring the signs, the scholar arrived at her door. A nun who was part of the inner circle of the retinue of the *yoginī* came out and said:

"This is the place of our strict retreat, didn't you see the signs on the stone cairns? Why did you come here?"

"Since I heard of her fame, I came here to request some teachings. Please introduce me to her."

The nun went into the hut and reported this. The hermitess said, "Have you forgotten that I told you that if anyone arrived today they should not be stopped? Please let him come in and bring him to me."

The nun went out and invited him into the hut, where he saw the old hermitess. She had a frightening appearance with disheveled gray-blue hair standing up on her head.[129] He prostrated to her and asked for blessings. (117b) She didn't pay much attention to him and gave him her blessing with her hand that looked like the foot of a crow. Without any devotion, he thought, *Who brought me to this? Perhaps I was blessed by a demon.* And he completely lost his faith. Then she gave him some teachings and invited him to spend the night there at the hermitage. She said, "I'll give you some food such as soup."

He went out of the hut and, feeling uneasy, he stayed outside. Meanwhile the hermitess took some barley flour in a clay bowl and some soup in a container and went to him. She said:

"Scholar! There isn't any need to feel awkward; there is also no need to think that a demon brought you here. You can't know who has a deep knowledge of the doctrine just by appearance. Relax! Please drink some soup and eat something."

(118a) In this way she persuaded him. He thought, *She really knows everything! Even what is in my mind!* Therefore he really believed in her. The next day he was given a teaching on the Five Mahāmudrā. Thangtong Gyalpo continued:

"Now the jewel was really given to a true owner! This teaching was given to Chogden Legpe Lodro,[130] and I eventually received it."

Commenting on this story, the Great Venerable Lady said, "Since I was a disciple of Chogle Namgyal, how can you have doubts about my faith? He was a great *siddha*. The Omniscient gave me excellent teachings about the doctrine. Who else did this so perfectly?" Then she gave him an introduction to the nature of the mind (*sems sngo prod ba*).

The *siddha,* who was also a scholar, said, "I'm an excellent expert in this kind of teachings, but today I was conquered by the power of the female teacher and I gained a perfect insight."

(118b) At another time Deleg Chodren said to Thangtong Gyalpo, "Our Venerable is sheer spirit of enlightenment, but concerning everyday matters she is rough. You can't treat her like everybody else." He answered, "Of course! I have never deceived or lied to the followers of the doctrine, and I'm used to giving teachings to people who don't follow the doctrine. How can I treat her badly?" The next day he summoned Deleg Chodren and gave her a piece of good mutton meat and said:

"I do not dare to eat this, please give it to the female teacher. Tomorrow I'll go to a high area to perform funerary rituals for a headman who is a believer in the doctrine. I dare not invite the female teacher to go with me. However, I can't get any income for the nuns, so please come! (119a) You'll be given the same food as the monks. You'll go there and pitch your tent among the beggars."

When she reported this, the Magnificent Lady reflected, "How can I truly be completely free from worldly concerns? How can I stay back? Tomorrow I will go as well."

Deleg Chodren disagreed and said, "If you stay among the beggars you may catch a dangerous illness. Please don't go!"

"If you're concerned, you stay here and I'll go. At the crack of dawn most of the nuns will go there. They should set up a tent among the beggars and perform the Vairocana rituals. I'll arrive soon afterward."

All the nuns went and carried out her instructions.

Before leaving, the Great Woman stayed for a while with the two attendants, Loden and Osang, who were about to leave and gave them one roll of Indian cotton and (119b) many excellent teachings. Both were moved and took leave from her with great respect. They prostrated and received wonderful blessings. Then they returned to Palmo Choding.

Afterward, Chokyi Dronma, holding a stick and an alms bowl in her hands and carrying a sitting mat on her shoulder, went toward the place where the

*Translation of the Biography of the Venerable Chokyi Dronma*

beggars were staying without feeling anxious or fearful. All the beggars said, "This is incredible!" and all went to welcome her, prostrating and asking for blessings. She provided what everyone needed. Deleg Chodren was inside her tent among the beggars, feeling very sad, as she was missing her, the descendant of the Gods of Clear Light [i.e., the ancestral gods of the Tibetan emperors].

Soon after Chokyi Dronma had arrived at the nun's tent, the owner of the place came to see her, holding incense in his hands and (120a) followed by several great ladies. He invited her to proceed to his own house. There a lama, followed by some other people, came to welcome her and prostrated. When the prayer for the ritual offering started, Chokyi Dronma, who was in the middle of the group of monks, asked the lama to lead the celebration. However, he insisted that she do it instead. Eventually she agreed. Then she stayed there for three nights and was given excellent offerings. The rituals were performed perfectly.

After a while she went to meet the *siddha* [Thangtong Gyalpo]. One day, a girl who was from Chung arrived carrying a funerary ritual object (*byang bu*), with a paper with the name of her deceased father. The *siddha* recited some good prayers for him. He read the text of *Gyer chung* several times. Suddenly the ritual items (*bar lag?*) of both deceased people for whom the celebration was being held collapsed. The stones (*rtsig rdo*) supporting ritual objects both hosting the minds of the deceased (*rnam sems*) fell down. This provoked superstitious concerns.

(120b) Meanwhile the Great Venerable Lady, enjoying the sound of his voice, smiled. After the ritual was completed, the *siddha* asked:

"Female teacher! Did your Lord of the Dharma from Bodong know this?"

"He didn't!"

"If that is the case, I'm more expert than him."

Precisely at the moment he said this, the wind blew away the ritual paper with the name of the deceased and the girl started to cry. The *siddha*, looking at her with his eyes wide open, said:

"Girl! You don't need to cry, your father has gone to heaven." Then the girl stopped crying and the ritual paper was found at the foot of a hill.

The female *siddha* then said, "Please allow us to construct a *stūpa* for the achievement of merit."

"You and your disciples will find that this is very hard work and it might disturb your meditation practice. This should be done by laypeople."

(121a) When the work began, Chokyi Dronma was the first to be involved. Her retinue carried big stones and the work was completed successfully. Everybody was deeply impressed. Afterward she offered many gifts to the *siddha* such as silk, ten bundles of paper, ink, gold, turquoises, a good tent, and six good medicines. Then she said that she would go around in the Chung area to collect alms. The *siddha* said, "There is a bad epidemic in the area and there isn't much use going around. It's better for you to stay here."

She didn't listen to him and went around the Chung area to collect alms, and she was offered more donations than you could imagine. The epidemic stopped and she triumphed over the threat of poverty.

[Then she went to see the great *siddha*, Thangtong Gyalpo.] First they made offerings to him from the collected donations. He was delighted and said, "You collected more alms than I could imagine. (121b) People seem to love the new-comers! I'm not able to collect as many donations."

Once the *siddha* asked, "Could you help me, Spiritually Accomplished Woman?"

"Of course."

"I want to send an edict (*bka' chems*) to all monks and patrons of our region, including Kongpo and the areas west of it. Please write the relevant letters for me, as nowadays everybody respects the writing of the Queen of Ngari. Do you understand my point?"

She did this and wrote many letters. In addition, the *siddha* said:

"After I, the Bridge Builder, have passed away, my tradition may not continue. (122a) However, the tradition of the people of Palmo Choding will be there until the end of the world. I will die a nauseating (*sgyug bro ba*) death that has never happened to human beings before, and it will be said that it cannot happen to human beings!"

Deleg Chodren asked the Venerable Lady, "What kind of death is this?"

"Nothing is suitable except for disappearing, dying a death that has probably never happened before to ordinary beings."[131]

Later, the Magnificent Lady, who had a special affection for the seat of her lama, Chogle Namgyal, said to Deleg Chodren:

"You never let me down. Please go to Palmo Choding and ask the Lord of the Dharma[132] to mobilize the people of Palmo Choding to find a way to build the water channels. We, the people of Ngari, can do it, and the people of Northern Yeru can do it as well. However, if they don't listen to my instructions there is nothing that we can do. (122b) You should then go to Ngari."

Deleg Chodren went to Palmo Choding and told the Lord of the Dharma and others what the Great Woman had said. They replied, "If the Precious Lady

*Translation of the Biography of the Venerable Chokyi Dronma*

lived here, perhaps we could achieve it. Since this isn't the case, it seems that we cannot do it."

Therefore Deleg Chodren went on to Ngari.

(122b) Thangtong Gyalpo sent a letter with Deleg Chodren to Ngari saying, "Now the Female Teacher from Ngari is staying here, and she is about to go to the east. If she is allowed to go, this might not be good for the people of your region, the upper areas. What shall we do?"

Deleg Chodren arrived at Ngari with this letter and reported this to Chokyi Dronma's father, the Son of the Gods and Lord of the Dharma. He said, "Of course, I'll send some people to ask her to return home. However, it will be particularly difficult if I send tough people who put pressure on her." Then he sent Dron Nyerpon ('Gron gNyer dpon) and Lama Tson O (Bla ma bTson 'od) from the monastery of Gungthang. Chokyi Dronma's mother suggested that she might go to invite her to return as well, but the people of Ngari disagreed. (123a) Loden and Osang, the two attendants from Palmo Choding who had followed her previously, also went to invite her to come back.

Since Deleg Chodren took a long time getting there, Chokyi Dronma thought, *Perhaps something life-threatening has happened.*

When she heard that people were sent to invite her to return, she went to Mutre,[133] where she waited for them. Two nuns who had been sent to scout for information came to see her. They asked her to return to Ngari, but she refused. She let them stay for two nights and then sent them back. Then she returned to where she had been staying before. On the way the people of Tagtse invited her to stay at their castle. Earlier she had heard some rumors that the Lord of Tagtse had been ill and had already died. However, when she arrived there, he had recovered. She was delighted and said, "Your liberation from this illness is due to the white doctrine," and offered him a crystal rosary. She was looked after extremely well there (123b) and given precious donations such as gold. Every nun was also given a gift. She was delighted to give good instructions to the Lord of Tagtse and recited prayers for him. Then she spent one night with Chodzema, the Lady of Tagtse, who also treated her very well and even massaged her feet in the way she liked. However, someone saw this from the door, was very surprised, and said, with some hesitation, "A terrifying and powerful nun, different from any other, has arrived to visit our lady. Our lady is holding her feet on her lap and is massaging them with ointments."

Chokyi Dronma was then invited to visit by the people of Gur (mGur pa), and she was also looked after well there. Then she came back and went to see Thangtong Gyalpo. He was someone who was free from worldly concerns and usually he did not show special respect toward lamas (124a) and important people. However, he showed great respect toward the female *siddha.* He never indulged in chatting about ordinary things with her because he considered her to be a great scholar, a *siddha,* a holy being, and a protectress. She considered the Omniscient Chogle Namgyal her main lama; after him, this *siddha* was her most valuable spiritual guide. She followed all his instructions, and as long as she was there she used to spend most of her time with him, except for the night. She made unimaginable donations to him.

Once the *siddha* said:

"I had really wanted to receive teachings from your master, the Lord of the Dharma from Bodong, (124b) but I did not enjoy the auspicious circumstances to do so because people of the inner court [at Gungthang] made it impossible. If it had been possible, my status (*mgo 'phang*) would have been higher, but it didn't happen. If he had deliberately prevented our relationship, this would have damaged me. However, he did not do this. Instead, it was the lama Kunga Sangpo [Chopel Sangpo?][134] who prevented me from getting his teachings. Anyway, this didn't really harm me. Do you understand?"

On another day the *siddha* said, "Today we set up the main pole (*srog shing*) of the *stūpa.*[135] Female teacher and disciples, please join us."

As the Magnificent Lady and her retinue arrived at the construction site, the monks of the *siddha* had just tied ropes around a huge wooden pole.

(125a) With a loud voice the group of people raised the pole, and they managed to set it up within one teatime.[136] Even though to build this *stūpa* they had used slates that were big as the carcass of a sheep, there was no accident and nobody was harmed. The Magnificent Lady was very happy about this and said, "The lama and the monks don't seem to be ordinary people, as they are enjoying this work and doing it very quickly."

The *siddha* asked, "Please give some special blessing for the setting up of my *stūpa!*"

(125b) She then gave a special blessing and prepared some special materials for the *stūpa* such as the five precious items. The *siddha* then gave an order to two members of the retinue of the Venerable Lady, Palsang Dronme and Tharpa Sangmo: "You two! You shouldn't sleep before the space around the central pole is covered with earth and stones."

Therefore they followed his instructions, and during the night the space around the central pole was fully covered and thus the work was completed. The *siddha* said again:

*Translation of the Biography of the Venerable Chokyi Dronma*

"You, teacher and disciples, have no worldly attachment in either the upper or the lower regions of Tibet. You just practice the doctrine. I'm really happy with this. I just need to take care of any [such] hindrances that might be caused by demons."

(126a) First of all, he said that the story of the Magnificent Lady and her retinue was widely known; second, the *siddha* did not pride himself on his religious knowledge. His followers were very satisfied with him and [usually] didn't pay much attention to other lamas. However, Thangtong Gyalpo himself said:

"Followers of mine! Chokyi Gyaltshen and all the others, listen to the teachings from the female teacher from Ngari and respect her."

Therefore everybody took care of her as their great protectress. Then, shortly before she left, the *siddha* said:

"Today we shall gather in assembly under the auspices of the great seat (*bla brang*) of Thangtong Gyalpo, who is the madman of the empty valley and the headman of the beggars. Please, Lady Teacher and disciples, join the gathering."

(126b) The retinue of Chokyi Dronma thought that this would be like previous occasions. All the monks gathered. All the three kinds of craftsmen and the people who were doing the construction work gathered there as well. In the middle of the monks was the Venerable Lady, seated on a beautiful throne. A large amount of food and drink was offered throughout the gathering. At the end of this assembly, the treasurer exhorted the participants:

"Let's celebrate a religious service for the great Lama of Tsang [i.e., Thangtong Gyalpo] and all the gathered monks and recite a prayer for the deceased woman Dorje Hure from Kongpo so that she won't go to the lower realms of existence." Chokyi Dronma gave everyone a blessing pill made with the relics of the Omniscient. Everybody there was delighted. Then she went to see the *siddha* (127a) and offered him many items, ranging from gold to shoes, that she had collected while traveling in Northern Lato. Then, before she left for central Tibet, and Kongpo in particular, where she would continue to perform her great deeds, Thangtong Gyalpo sent a letter to all the areas of the country, including the Four Horns (*ru bzhi*) of central Tibet (dBu-gTsang), the three places called Chayul, Dagpo, and Kongpo,[137] and the three places called Lokhathra, Minyag, and Churug Mon Atsara (Glo kha khra, Mi nyag, Chu rug mon atsara).[138] In the letter, he said:

All former scholars and members of the monastic community acted for the benefit of other living beings, but now there is nobody who cares. Particularly since the death of Machig Labdron, there has not been a woman who was dedicated to the benefit of other living beings. Now there is a lady who stems from the royal lineage of the Gods of Clear Light ('Od gsal lha) who is devoted to spiritual liberation and to the benefit of all living beings. (127b) Her outer name is Lady Queen of the Jewel (bDag mo dKon mchog rgyal mo); her inner name is Female Teacher Lamp of the Doctrine (sLob dpon ma Chos kyi sgron ma); her secret name is Vajravārāhī (rDo rje phag mo). Her residence is undefined. Her companions are undefined. And foremost, her lama is undefined (*nges med*). Since all elements are empty and have no essence (*bdag med*), she practices emptiness (*bdag med*). Now she is coming to your place, so please welcome her and give her adequate support at her departure. Follow the solemn commitment (*dam tshig*) of religion (*lha chos*). Refrain from shameful worldly customs. Wherever she stays, do not feel jealous about what is mine and what is yours. I, King of the Empty Plain, ask you, people living in the East, to keep showing the great kindness you have shown in the past to these followers of mine. In return for your kindness, the Female Teacher and her retinue are coming. Look after them well.

This letter was sent to every local ruler (*sde pa*) in central Tibet. (128a) At the beginning of the letter Thangtong Gyalpo wrote two lines himself, and he added two lines at the end. Every letter was accompanied by a gift of gold, turquoise, and coral. Then each letter was wrapped in a cloth. The *siddha* told her solemnly:

"You should keep these letters yourself and just show them to the relevant person without handing them over."

Then he gave her one iron chain link and continued:

"I made this myself and I consecrated it. This traveled with me around Kongpo twice. Now I offer it to you as a present. I will send the headman of Sheldrong (Shel grong) as your assistant. Until you arrive at Bodong, don't show this to anybody. Please go to Mus [in Northern Lato] and stay there for a while. Before you go, you should leave here all the butter that was offered to you by the people of Tagtse (128b) and I'll give you an estate in the Lhasa region (dBus) in exchange. If you live around here it is uncertain how many followers you will have, but you will enjoy a long life. If you go to the east, the span of your life is uncertain, but you will accomplish great deeds for the benefit of other people. Anyway, please do what you think is best. Please, on your journey pay a visit to the Lhasa Jobo [the statue of the Buddha in the Jokhang]. The Chubori monastery[139] will then send some attendants to escort you when you travel to Kongpo. If you follow illusions, many living beings will be fooled. If you don't follow illusions, many living beings will avoid being fooled."

Eventually she offered a final prostration to the *siddha*. When she started on her journey she collected a lot of alms because she passed through the area just after harvest.[140] She didn't take the donations with her and sent a letter to Thangtong Gyalpo asking him to come and get them.

## Journey to Central Tibet

(129a) She then arrived at Ngamring, [the capital of Northern Lato], where she stayed two nights. She went on a begging trip. However, she didn't get much barley flour. She visited the great statue of Buddha Maitreya in the Ngamring monastery and offered butter lamps. She also offered a devotional object with vermilion writing. A local official gave her good assistance in all this. Having seen that the ruler Namgyal Dragpa Palsangpo[141] was residing in his palace, she thought, *It isn't necessary to meet the local ruler* (sde pa), and she did not go to see him. The people of Northern Lato looked after her well and wrote a letter of introduction for her to smooth her way. Then she reached Bodong, where she stayed for two nights. The tea servant (*gsol ja ba*) Phuntshog provided good hospitality. Then she went to the E monastery [the original seat of the Bodongpa tradition]. She said very devotedly, "This was the seat of the great lama!" Then she offered butter lamps and prostrated respectfully. None of the Bodong people recognized her. She asked one caretaker for water and was given water that wasn't clean. Nobody took care of her.

(129b) Then she reached Jago Jong (Bya rgod byong), where she met the monk Tengyurba (bsTan 'gyur ba), who was a follower of Thangtong Gyalpo. She said, "Please give me a drink," and accordingly she was given it. She continued: "Henceforth, if you meet my nuns who are traveling between Kongpo and Ngari, please give them hospitality even if you aren't able to feed them. Follower of the Iron Bridge Builder, you and I have a special relationship. When I arrived at Tashigang [where the Bodong E monastery is located] and visited the residence of my lama, nobody gave me anything, not even clean water when I was thirsty. It seems that my relationship with the people of Palmo Choding is just like this."

On the way east, two people who looked like Mongols (Hor) were sent by the ruler of Samdrubtse[142] as her assistants. While traveling toward Narthang,[143] she looked at Deleg Chodren and, pointing with her finger in the direction of the Ngor monastery, said:

"In that direction is the new Ngor monastery where Kunga Sangpo[144] resides."
(130a) Deleg Chodren asked, "Do you have any teaching links with him?"

"When I was a child I once listened to his teachings, but I didn't receive the empowerment (*dbang*). Should we go there sometime to establish a teaching relationship?"

She then arrived in the vicinity of the Samdrubtse palace and sent the two people to look for a place for the night, saying, "Please, tell the local people that some monks of the Iron-Bridge-Builder Lama are traveling to central Tibet (dBus). Don't mention me!"

However, they did not follow her instructions and said to the ruler, Drungchen Norsang[145] of Samdrubtse, "The Lady Konchog Gyalmo is arriving and we are scouting the way for her."

He then carefully had a dwelling prepared in the house called Tsherkhang Gongma ('Tsher khang gong ma) and sent a steward to take care of her. Then the next day he invited her to the castle.

(130b) She replied, "It is not necessary for me, a woman free of worldly concerns, to meet each local ruler. It is just a waste of time. Please give me a letter of introduction for the Rinpung area, which is under your rule, in order to make my journey easier."

However, she was told that having come here, it was impossible to avoid meeting the ruler and since Drungchen Norsang insisted that she come to see him, she finally agreed to go to the castle. She presented him with a relic[146] of the Omniscient Chogle Namgyal and she was looked after very well. They enjoyed a very good conversation. Later, when talking about Rinpung Norsang, she used to say, "He seems to be as powerful and charismatic (*yid 'dzin pa*) as a Mongolian ruler." Then she was invited to visit every area of the castle, which she did as a matter of courtesy, without much interest. (131a) When they arrived at the wing where the beautiful residence called garden of joy (*mngon dga'*) was, the Venerable Lady ran into her teacher Rabjampa Tenpe Nyima Jampal Dragpa (Rab 'jams bsTan pa'i nyi ma 'jam dpal grags pa). Since they hadn't met for a long time, both were extremely pleased. Subsequently a place for her to stay was arranged. The next day, this Lord of the Dharma went to her dwelling to see her and organize some teachings. Chokyi Dronma offered him a coral with the image of a two-faced Vajravārāhī and an object of devotion (*thugs dam*) made of crystal. She asked him to teach the nuns who had assembled there. Accordingly he gave them teachings concerning the four vows of the profound doctrine. He offered the Venerable Lady the cape of a monastic robe. The ruler, Drungchen

*Translation of the Biography of the Venerable Chokyi Dronma*

Norsang, sent a letter to Palrin at Rinpung asking them to provide assistance to the Venerable Lady on her journey. Subsequently, from the Nyugla (sNyug la) pass onward, support was to be provided by the Chubori monastery. (131b) In addition, Lhacho, the Lady of Dragkar,[147] was to provide support during her stay at Lhasa.

A reliable person was sent as her attendant to escort her for a while. As she proceeded on her journey, a few people who had some karmic links with her asked her to give them some teachings. She taught them in a way that suited their minds. Eventually she arrived in the vicinity of Rinpung.

At that time a great *yogin* called Pal Nagkyi Rinchen [i.e., Vanaratna], who was a great scholar from eastern India, was living in Rong at a holy place called The Five Goats (Rong Ranga). He was on his return journey from Neudong [i.e., the seat of the Phagmodrupa rulers] back to Nepal. The Venerable Lady had met him once before,[148] when she was still living at her father's palace in Ngari. At the time of their first encounter she had listened to many teachings from him. The holy man had invited the young girl to sit next to him. Feeling shy, she sat down on the corner of the seat. (132a) He had placed his hand on her head and was very pleased to give her some instruction. He then told her, "You should go to India!"

Now, as she arrived at the place called Rong Ranga, she went to meet [Vanaratna]. At that time he was in meditation and had said that during his retreat he couldn't see or speak to anyone. A member of his retinue called Lama Mangala had died recently, and he was practicing for the sake of him and his future rebirth. Chokyi Dronma, however, hadn't been told this.

On the way a local headman invited her to spend the night, but she refused and said:

"Tonight I'll just stay here and tomorrow I'll continue my journey to meet the lama."

"Please don't stay here, in a stable!"

"This is a good place!" she said and gave teachings to the horse herders. The next day she met the lama (132b) and offered him a *vajra* and a bell. He placed the bell close to his chest and let it resound. The lama said, smiling:

"I'm delighted to speak to you, Gyalmo!" Then he gradually asked about the health of her father and mother, her brother and Lama Dzoki.

"They are all fine."

"Since you gave up worldly concerns and became a nun, did your parents, your relatives, and all the subjects make it difficult for you?"

"I haven't done anything against my father except for devoting myself to the doctrine. Even though I had to go against my father to practice the doctrine, this is not sinful. Thinking about the suffering of *saṃsāra,* I'm not afraid of malicious worldly gossip. If one wants to become a follower of the Buddha, one can overcome all obstacles in this life. I don't have the right to stay with my parents if I can't strive for liberation; (133a) if I am able to accomplish great deeds, then I will be able to show my gratitude to my parents."

When the lama heard this, he was delighted and said, "If this is the case, this is very good. When you were a girl, I told you that you should visit India, did you forget it? Now that you have become free of worldly concerns, everything is easier. Would you like to go with me to India?"

The Magnificent Lady answered, "I'll do as you say."

The lama, smiling, said:

"I'm not going to India now. I'll stay for a while in central Nepal. Although developing a relationship with the King of the Nepal is not particularly useful, in order to practice the doctrine I need to be there. You gave up royal politics (*rgyal srid*) and were ordained. If you took the vows, this is a sign that you renounced worldly life. It is marvelous that you gave up the eight matters and became free of all worldly concerns. (133b) You did so even though the royal family usually lives comfortably. You should follow the verses that I offer to you."

He composed a poem for her in which the first stanza was a praise for Chokyi Dronma, the Magnificent Lady; the next three stanzas contained instructions for her. Then they continued a very enjoyable conversation. The lama put a gift in his alms bowl and, holding the bowl with both hands, he offered it to her, very respectfully. An attendant tried to take the offering out of the bowl, but the lama said:

"I am giving this to her together with the bowl, which is for collecting alms."

On that occasion she obtained some precepts (*lung*) from him that she hadn't received before from Chogle Namgyal. Without letting the translator come along, the lama and his disciple both entered the narrow dwelling of *samadhi* (*bsam gtan khang bu*) where he fulfilled all her spiritual wishes.

He also gave precepts (*lung*) about 'khor lo maṇi to Deleg Chodren and the other nuns. (134a) He gave the Venerable Lady a cloak that had been given to him by the female *siddha* of Yamdrog and a protection string. When the lama stood up from his seat to go elsewhere, his body emanated a very pleasant scent. The cloak emanated the same pleasant scent. This was the same scent that was

*Translation of the Biography of the Venerable Chokyi Dronma*

emanated by all objects that had been in contact with the Omniscient Chogle Namgyal. The same was true of all the objects that the Venerable Lady had been using, and everyone in her retinue would recognize it.

She continued her journey in the Rong area. Once, while talking with Deleg Chodren, she said:

"The Lama Great Paṇḍita has an excellent *samādhi* (*ting nge 'dzing*). (134b) From his behavior he seems to have acquired the power of reaching enlightenment."

"Between him and the Omniscient, who is superior?"

"Don't speak in such a silly way, only an absolute all-knowing person is in a position to assess their respective knowledge. Look after the gift given at Rong Ranga by the Lama Great Paṇḍita. Give it to me little by little until it is finished."

Then she gave a piece to each nun. Then she arrived at Ngumig (Ngu smig) and spent the night there. The nuns went to perform a purification ritual. While performing the ritual offering, the Venerable Lady was fasting and staying in *samādhi*. Gradually they traveled on and thought of stopping at Yarsib (Yar sribs).

(135a) Then she gave to the great woman Deleg Chodren a letter that had been given to her by the Omniscient Chogle Namgyal, together with some blessed items, and said:

"Originally, the belt that I am wearing belonged to the Lord of the Dharma. It is better that I do not keep it and that I offer it to the one among us who has received all his blessings in the best way. In fact, she received the blessings better than I did; therefore I untie my belt and leave it here."

She also offered to Deleg Chodren an object of devotion (*thugs dam*) made of red thread that was used by the Great Lord of the Dharma as well as a piece of cloth, six pills made with water of the sacred vase, bones, blood from the nose, and urine.

Having reiterated that many books were also necessary, she was about to continue on her journey. Some people, however, turned up. They were confused and hadn't so far been able to make contact with Dorje Phagmo [i.e., Chokyi Dronma as emanation of the deity] and hear the nectar of her voice. (135b) With their minds full of regret, they asked to become her followers in spite of their faults. They wished to receive the blessing of her body, speech, and mind immediately.

Afterward she proceeded on her own through a gorge and then crossed the Gampala pass.[149] When she arrived at a place called Gyale (rGya le), she knocked at a door with her staff. The owner of the house, hearing the noise and seeing her from the window, said to his wife with great delight:

"There is an exceptional person at the door of our house. Take some barley flour to meet her."

The wife opened the door. (136a) She was deeply impressed by her appearance and by the scent emanated by her body and asked, "Where are you from? Where are you going?"

Chokyi Dronma answered, "I have come from the Iron-Bridge-Builder Lama; I am going to Chubori."

Without offering her the flour, the woman returned to her husband and said that there was someone exceptional at their door and that they should invite her into the house. He agreed, and she invited her to come in. Chokyi Dronma accepted the invitation and climbed the stairs. She was then invited to take a comfortable seat, and as they were about to prepare tea, she said:

"Please give me what you usually drink, don't make anything special for me."

"You are a guest of Gyalepa (rGyal le pa). Please, have some proper tea."

"There is not a taste of tea that I don't know. (136b) Tea is very popular in central Tibet. However, I'm a person free of worldly concerns; if I were to start enjoying tea, I would keep roaming around without meaning, visiting all local headmen."

"What kind of person are you?"

"I'm from a lineage of Ngari."

When she was asked to stay the night, she refused and went on toward Chubori. She caught up with Deleg Chodren, who had already arrived there from Yamdrog. Deleg Chodren said to her:

"My thoughts on enlightenment are becoming clearer."

The Magnificent Lady said, "Without relying on means and wisdom together, no enlightment is possible, but if both means and wisdom come together, enlightment can be achieved."

She said that she wanted to continue the journey to Lhasa. A monk called Kabchupa, who was a follower of the Iron Bridge Lama, escorted her as her attendant. With her retinue she eventually reached Kyisho [at the confluence of the Kyichu River and the Brahmaputra River].

(137a) That night they stayed in Nyetang,[150] and she said, "This is a very precious place where the Great Lord Atiśa lived and passed away." She left the next day early in the morning. Remembering the words of the lama *siddha* Thangtong

Gyalpo, who said that she should stay one night in each of his estates in central Tibet, she spent a night at Chagpo Ri.[151] The next day, after breakfast, she also visited the famous statues of the Buddha in Lhasa. Surrounded by a multitude of butter lamps, she performed the rituals of *Yan lag bdun pa rigs lnga* and she recited *bZang spyod* prayers to the statue in the Tsuglagkhang. Then she visited Ramoche and did the same. With four well-fed nuns as her attendants, she went for lunch at the house of the headman of Lhasa. Then she visited the symbols of body, speech, and mind at [Tshal] Gungthang.[152] When she saw all that had been achieved by Lama Zhang, she recited many *mantras* with great devotion. She said to the nephew of Sheldrong who was escorting her, "The letter of the lama *siddha* should not be given to the Nepa[153] until I leave."

(137b) That night she traveled alone and saw that there was an estate of the *siddha* Thangtong Gyalpo next to the "nose" of the iron bridge in Drib (Grib) [on the opposite side of the river]. Meanwhile, the headman of Nepa questioned Deleg Chodren and the other nuns who had remained at Lhasa and asked them where the Venerable Lady had gone. Deleg Chodren told him her story in detail. He remarked, "Such behavior is incomparable!" Then the scholar of Chubori and the headman of Sheldrong were sent to ask her to return to Lhasa. However, she refused the invitation.

After having received lavish donations, she proceeded along the southern bank of the Kyichu River. Even though during the journey the nuns suffered great pain in their legs, she said, "We will visit the Ushangdo[154] temple, which was established by my ancestor, the King of the Dharma Ralpacan." Then they went swiftly toward it. Afterward she arrived at Sheldrong, (138a) where she was invited to stay for lunch. She agreed, but refused an invitation to stay overnight; nor did she stay for lunch on the next day. She gave teachings to local people, such as the Lady of Sheldrong. She was offered magnificent hospitality and lavish donations, and she gave many blessings and words of good fortune to the local people. Then she went to visit Cakrasaṃvara at the holy mountain Drangsong Sinpori (Drang srong srin po ri) and spent one night there. She performed the *Yan lag bdun pa* in the same way as she had performed it in front of the Buddha statues at Lhasa. She did this whenever she visited holy symbols. Thereby she introduced this marvelous practice, which included religious service (*sku rim*), spiritual commitment (*dam tshig*), and vows (*sdom pa*).

(138b) While traveling through Kyisho, she often used to speak to the monks she met. The name Precious Lord (*rje rin po che*) was mentioned many times. Deleg Chodren asked her:

"There seems to be a large number of followers of our Precious Lord, because many monks mention the name of the Lord (*rje*) again and again."

"This Precious Lord is not the same one that you are referring to. The name mentioned by these people is an epithet of Tsongkhapa Lobsang Dragpa from the east."

"If this is the case, comparing the deeds of both, our Precious Lord's deeds seem considerably less."

Chokyi Dronma explained further: "The doctrine is based on the *Vinaya,* and concerning the observation of the vows, the deeds of Tsongkhapa are unimaginable. However, some people, extolling their own merits, gossip about the difference beween the two masters. (139a) In doing so they are behaving like the fox occuping the lion's throne. Have doubts about those who might bring the practice of accomplished *yogins* and *yoginīs* to an end!"

In a locality called Doratshug, there was a man from the Lhopa and a woman from the Monpa who were jointly in charge of some possessions[155] of Thangtong Gyalpo. A conflict emerged between the two and when Chokyi Dronma heard about it, she said to Deleg Chodren, "We have the responsibility of mediating between them, and the signs are auspicious. You go first to take care of this matter and I'll follow later." Deleg Chodren went there to mediate. She thought, *Even though it may take a long time, I shall do everything according to her instructions.* After completing her task, Deleg Chodren returned to Chubori. When she arrived, Chokyi Dronma was performing some monthly rituals for the sake of the late Omniscient and was very pleased to see her.

(139b) A great assembly was gathered. Some people who had been sent by the headman of Sheldrong arrived with a donkey loaded with good barley flour and dry meat. This food was badly needed at Chubori. As Chokyi Dronma was pleased, she recited a prayer for them and gave them blessings. She gave most of the barley flour to the scholar of Chubori and to the followers of Thangtong Gyalpo.

After three days at Chubori, looking toward the northern bank of the river, she saw a monk with a red felt rug on his shoulder and with a red dog on a lead. When he arrived close to the water, he shouted, "I'm Rigsum Gonpo (Rigs gsum dgon po).[156] Please come and help me to cross the bridge!" The people living next to the iron bridge at Chubori said that the lama Rigsum Gonpo was coming, and went to help him cross the river. (140a) The lama arrived quickly in front of Chokyi Dronma, the fully ordained wisdom *ḍākinī.* He did not prostrate, but staying on his mat, took off his hat and looked at her wide-eyed and smiled. The scholar of Chubori asked:

*Translation of the Biography of the Venerable Chokyi Dronma*

"Why did you come here?"

"I had no other option but to come here," said he and continued: "There was a doctor called Lama Lhaje (Bla ma Lha rje) who was from Tsethang (rTsed thang) in Kongpo Thragyul (rKon po phrag yul). One day he went to Sumdrug (Sum 'brug) for some reason. On the way he stopped for his meal at a sandy place. When he was about to eat, he opened his leather bag to knead some barley flour. Precisely at that moment an old ascetic[157] with gray-bluish hair, a cotton garment (*thang g'yog*), and a scholar's hat, appeared in front of him. The doctor asked him:

'Where are you from? Where are you going?'

'I'm from eastern Tibet (Kham) and I'm going to central Tibet. What are you doing here?'

'I'm eating my meal.'

(140b) 'Can you give me some?'

'Let's eat together!'

'Can you act as my messenger? I have a letter from Thangtong Gyalpo that should be given to Lama Rigsum Gonpo and the other people at Tsari Tsagong and Thrag (Phrag).'

'Why didn't you give it to them on the way?'

'I've never traveled to Kongpo before, so I don't know the place.'

'How should I deliver this message to them?'

'Everybody, lay and monastic people, should gather at Drongsar Shuthri (Grong gsar bzhugs khri), and they should be told that Thangtong Gyalpo is now traveling in central Tibet in the Lhasa region (dBus). Please send a message saying that the senior monks should be summoned to go to welcome him.'

'Please show me the letter. You said you don't know the area, but you seem to know many place names.'

'I merely heard them.'

Then he handed over the letter, and the old man said, 'Please give me a piece of cloth!'

(141a) 'I haven't got any cloth.'

'You have a lot of cloth. I'll come to the Kongpo New Year. Please give me the cloth then.'

"The doctor promised to do so. While he was closing his leather bag, the ascetic suddenly disappeared. It seemed to have been an emanation of the lama *siddha* himself. The old man had vanished without leaving footprints, and wherever the doctor searched for him, he couldn't find him. The doctor was so shocked that he felt that he might pass out. Later the doctor read the letter to the people of Tsagong and Nepo (gNas po) at Drongsar Shugthri (Grong gsar bzhugs khri) and so on . . . as I was there, I was sent to welcome Thangtong Gyalpo. However, when I arrived at Chagpo Ri, he hadn't arrived. There was only a nun called the Queen of Ngari with a frightening appearance, the one that is now staying at Chubori. (141b) As I gave up all hope that the *siddha* would arrive, I cursed. In the evening, before returning to Kongpo, I fell asleep and had a dream. In my dream the sun was shining in the east, the moon was shining in the west. They were revolving in the sky. It was marvelous! After the dream I mentally apologized to the lama for my evil words and left for Chubori. This is why I came here."

After the explanation, Rigsum Gonpo handed the letter to the scholar of Chubori, who read it and said, "The style and the seal of the letter seem to be authentic." He continued, "You arrived here just at the right time. The Venerable Lady will leave for Kongpo the day after tomorrow."

(142a) Then the scholar of Chubori and Lama Rigsum Gonpo discussed the itinerary of Chokyi Dronma's journey. They suggested that the best option was to go via Drigung ('Bri khung) and avoid passing through the E valley [i.e., E lha rgya ri] because the people there were very rough. However, she said:

"We shouldn't go where there are relatives. The Queen of Drigung is our kinswoman; therefore I won't go there. In particular, the lama *siddha* said that during our journey from the Lhasa area (dBus) to Kongpo the people of Chubori will provide some assistance. Also, if we wanted to travel along the Nyangpo River, passing by Drigung, we should have gone with some of the monks from Baru Namtshal (Ba ru rnam tshal).[158] However, these monks have already left. Now, since the people of Tsari Tsagong came to welcome us, we will go through the gorges of Dagpo." Then she went to bed, accompanied by Deleg Chodren and Tharpa Sangmo. [Before falling asleep, she said to them,] "The lama Thangtong Gyalpo is extraordinary indeed! (142b) He thought that we might go via Drigung; therefore he sent the people of Baru Namtshal to receive us. Thinking that we may go via E, along the Brahmaputra River, he sent the people from Kongpo to receive us. This is truly miraculous."

Five days before her arrival at Chubori, twenty monks from Baru Namtshal had in fact turned up there; they were from one of Thangtong Gyalpo's estates in the border region between Nyangpo and Kongpo. Earlier, they had heard that the lama *siddha* would arrive and came to Chubori to receive him. As he had failed to turn up, they had left to return to their own place.

Two days later, Chokyi Dronma and her retinue started the journey. Originally she had thought that she might travel north of the river and take the opportunity to visit Samye.[159] However, considering that the nuns were likely to hurt their feet walking on the sand, she went directly toward Lhokha, traveling south of the river.

## Journey Toward Tsari

(143a) After leaving Chubori, she stayed the first night at Ling To (Gling stod). Then she arrived at Doratshug, where she met the Lhopa man and the Monpa woman, who had been reconciled, and gave each of them an item of clothing and a hat. Both apologized for their dispute. She also gave them some instructions on how to be friendly to each other and gave them the teachings on the generation of the spirit of enlightenment that they had requested. Then she continued her journey. When she arrived in sight of Samye monastery, she prostrated and recited a prayer. Then she went to Yarlung and spent a night in a threshing ground next to Tsethang. When the monks of the great assembly of the Nedong palace [i.e., the seat of the Phagmodrupa] heard that she had arrived, they sent a letter saying:

> Right now the Supreme Ruler is in retreat. Would it be possible for you to postpone the continuation of your journey for a few days? Wouldn't it be good for you to meet the Supreme Ruler? Also, the people of the E valley are very rough; you should think about how to ensure that you have a safe journey.

However, since she enjoyed being free from worldly concerns, she said, (143b) "I have no presents to offer to the Supreme Lord." Therefore, the next day, at the crack of dawn, she got up and continued her journey on the southern bank of the river. When from afar she saw Phagmodru, the glorious seat, on the other side of the river, she prostrated and recited a prayer. At that time the great treasurer of the lama *siddha*, Kunga Rinchen (Kun dga' rin chen) from Chagsamkha (lCags zam kha), joined her retinue as an attendant and sent messages to ease the journey as far as E. Chokyi Dronma eventually arrived in Dagpo. On her way she was given good hospitality everywhere and she was properly received and escorted even though the people of that area were having many disputes among themselves. The local people acquired great faith in her. In particular, when she arrived at Sekar (Zas dkar) in Dagpo, a local man visited her and said, "Great fe-male *siddha*! Today I invite you to my house and I'll offer you some food; please come with a member of the monastic community."

(144a) She accepted. She sent Deleg Chodren to get their alms bowls, and together they went to this person's house. There they were asked to be seated on a carpet on the floor. Smiling, she did so. Deleg Chodren said, "I'll go to prepare some food." Hearing this, Chokyi Dronma countered, "Henceforth I'll prepare food for you. I don't need you to prepare food for me."

Then the householder offered the teacher and the disciple rough flour of black beans with some butter and raw meat as well as a container of *chang*. Chokyi Dronma, realizing that Deleg Chodren was upset, said:

"Deleg Chodren! I really like to eat rough flour, the fine kind irritates my mouth."

Then, eating with her hands, she showed how much she appreciated the food that she had been offered. (144b)

"Are you really enjoying this food?" asked Deleg Chodren, and Chokyi Dronma, approving, said, "You should eat the fine flour that was offered by the headman of Sheldrong."

Then the householder said, "Everybody says that by facing hardship you achieve enlightenment. However, I wish to reach enlightenment without facing any hardship. Please, great female *siddha,* give me some essential instructions suitable for my mental abilities."

The Venerable Lady said, "Don't think that I have instructions about how to reach enlightenment without facing any hardship. Just go wherever I go and do whatever I say! I'll give you a letter that will be useful to you, for one month, on the way. Does this suit you?"

The landlord said, "Now, if this is the case, I'll go with you wherever you go." Then she gave him teachings and recited prayers. Later, Deleg Chodren thought, *Having received such poor quality food from this man, she gave him many instruc-tions that she hadn't ever given to anyone before. She's also never said a single word about these instructions before. He is a lazy person, and still. . . .*

[The biography stops here. The biography of Thangtong Gyalpo (283–284) tells, concisely, the episode of the mysterious ascetic with long, dreadlocked hair and conch shell earrings who had summoned Rigsum Gonpo in Kongpo and subse-quently disappeared. Following his instructions, Rigsum Gonpo met the vener

*Translation of the Biography of the Venerable Chokyi Dronma*

able lady, told her what had happened, and welcomed her. The text continues, "She then traveled to Tsagong Nesar, where she extended the meditation center of Menmogang. There was a heap of iron rings for the bridge that had been ordered by the great *siddha*. She gave great gifts to the Kongpo people because they had fulfilled the orders of the master, and escorted the loads of iron as far as Orsho. When the iron arrived at the Nyago ferry landing, the great *siddha* was delighted. Not long after that, the Venerable Lady passed away into the *ḍākinīs'* heaven (*khecara*), her true home. She left her skull with special features as the wish-fulfilling gem of the great meditation center of Tsagong. The great *siddha* had said earlier, 'A skull with special features will come to this sacred place, together with a mountain dweller from Ngari,' and thus the prophecy had come true, greatly enhancing the devotion of the Kongpo people."]

# Part III

## 5

# SUCCESSION AND SPIRITUAL LINEAGES
## *Meaning and Mysteries of Chokyi Dronma's Reincarnation*

## Identification as a Deity During Her Lifetime

*The biography reveals that Chokyi Dronma was an incarnation of the deity Dorje* Phagmo, and this theme is used as the narrative framework for her whole life. However, except for a hint that the baby princess was "a most excellent incarnation" (*mchog gi sprul ba'i sku cig*) because of her mother's dream, there is no statement that her formal recognition as the incarnation of Dorje Phagmo actually happened during her childhood, or that she was then seen as the reincarnation of a historical figure. The direct quotations reported in the biography suggest instead that she was recognized as an incarnation of the deity shortly after her full ordination by Bodong Chogle Namgyal, and this was later reiterated by Thangtong Gyalpo (see chapter 4). It is likely that only then did Chokyi Dronma's character and deeds make her appear as the embodied deity in the eyes of the people around her, and that this identification was presented as a secret that was eventually revealed.

Chokyi Dronma herself, in all likelihood, endorsed this view and acted accordingly. Like the deity, she was powerful, spiritual, and transgressive, and her deeds reflected her extraordinary nature as something beyond the human. As in the case of Avalokiteśvara and the religious hierarchs who embodied him over time (the Karmapas and most notably the Dalai Lamas), the individual human experience was interpreted as the manifestation of a divine being, who was thus able to act in the human world. This was one of the cultural features that made Avalokiteśvara a "real force within Tibetan history" (Samuel 1993:485), transcending time, space, and individual histories. In a parallel way, Chokyi Dronma's identity merged with that of the female deity Dorje Phagmo, who was thereby seen as acting in the world through her human manifestation. This structured the interpretation of all her experiences and was therefore reflected in her biography.

Initially Chokyi Dronma's identification with the deity did not entail reenacting the traits of any previous historical figure. This happened in a formal way only with her reincarnation in Kunga Sangmo. Although toward the end of her life Chokyi Dronma started to be identified with some other holy women of the past—as is hinted in the 1453 biography of Bodong Chogle Namgyal (see below)—it is unlikely that this had an impact on her earlier life; otherwise it would have been mentioned in the biography (see chapter 3). Chokyi Dronma's reincarnation, Kunga Sangmo, had a rather different experience: she was identified as the reincarnation of the princess in early childhood, and this became the central element in defining her as a holy person. She is said to have gone back to Chokyi Dronma's homeland, recognized her mother, and reenacted her role from the previous life (Biography of Thangtong Gyalpo 308–309).

Chokyi Dronma/Kunga Sangmo was not the first case of a female reincarnation in Tibetan history. There are records of at least one precedent: Drowa Sangmo, who was the consort of Gotshangpa Gonpo Dorje (1182–1258), was reincarnated in a certain Kunden Rema (1260–1339) (see van der Kuijp 2005:29). However, no further reincarnation followed, so this case never developed into a proper line. In contrast, Kunga Sangmo was followed by another reincarnation, Nyendra Sangmo, and then others, up to the current Samding Dorje Phagmo, who is the twelfth reincarnation of the deity, starting from Chokyi Dronma. This pattern became a line to which a number of predecessors were added retrospectively, in a series of reincarnations that was dated back to the Indian Mahāsiddha Lakṣmīṅkarā (see chapter 3).

Thus the transition from Chokyi Dronma to Kunga Sangmo and then to the establishment of a lineage raises a number of questions: How did it happen? Why was a successor reincarnation required? How was the "lineage" linked back to spiritual masters of Indian origin? Why did this become a formally recognized line of reincarnations?

To explore these issues, I use Chokyi Dronma's biography as the starting point, setting it in relation to the sources that provide information on the very final part of her life, her death, and the aftermath. As pointed out in chapter 3, the most important sources are the Amoghasiddhi Jigme Bang's biography of Bodong Chogle Namgyal, the *Bo dong chos 'byung,* and the biography of Thangtong Gyalpo by Gyurme Dechen. These all report the main events but show some significant discrepancies that reflect different viewpoints and political allegiances.

## Reincarnation Lineages in the Tibetan Context

Despite the reference to Indian roots, the reincarnation of religious hierarchs is a Tibetan phenomenon that cannot be traced directly back to a comparable practice in India. At the time of Chokyi Dronma, it had already been established within some schools of Tibetan Buddhism, most notably that of the Karmapa, but had not become as pervasive as it would be in later centuries. The line of the Dalai Lama was not yet established—the posthumously recognized First Dalai Lama, Gendun Drupa (1391–1474), was in fact a peer of Chokyi Dronma and was among the disciples of Bodong Chogle Namgyal.

There is an important difference between the incarnation of a *bodhisattva* or a tantric deity and the reincarnation of a historical figure. The former refers to the manifestation of a spiritual entity in a human being, whereas the latter implies the transmission of a principle of consciousness from one human being to another. The two are normally interlinked in the Tibetan context, as the reincarnating beings carry with them their divine attributes as emanations of the deity. Turrell Wylie, in his seminal article on the emergence of reincarnation lines in Tibet, points out: "The concept of incarnation, that is to say an emanation-body (*nirmāṇakāya* in Sanskrit; *sprul-sku* in Tibetan) dates from the early days of Mahāyāna Buddhism and is widely accepted in conjunction with the *bodhisattva* ideal. Reincarnation, however, is uniquely Tibetan in conceptualisation and late in origin, emerging for the first time in the fourteenth century. . . . [Terms for it include] Yang srid 'to exist again', yang sprul 'again emanated', also 'skye ba' 'birth, rebirth'" (1978:579).

*Succession and Spiritual Lineages: Meaning and Mysteries of Chokyi Dronma's Reincarnation*

Even though it has been proved that there were a few earlier, less famous examples (Van der Kuijp 2005:28–29), according to Tibetan tradition the Karmapa reincarnation lineage was the first prominent case. The Tibetan institution of the reincarnation lineage emerged in a specific historical context and was closely linked to the reenactment of political and religious relationships from one generation to the next. In particular, it has been amply demonstrated that Mongolian–Tibetan relations, and in particular the reenactment of the donor-donee relationship between Tibetan religious hierarchs and Mongolian rulers, was the background against which the Karmapa reincarnation line was established.

According to the Tibetan tradition, the First Karmapa, Dusum Khyenpa (1110–1193), was an incarnation of Avalokiteśvara, reincarnated in the Second Karmapa, Pakshi (1206–1283), and was thus the first to establish a lineage. Wylie suggests that in spite of statements that the first lama to be recognized as an incarnation was either the first or the second hierarch, the concept of reincarnation originated only in the lifetime of Rangjung Dorje (1284–1339), the third Karmapa hierarch (Wylie 1978:581). Wylie highlighted the important difference between incarnation and reincarnation and the fact that the actual recognition of a child as the reincarnation of a previous historical figure might date significantly later than the founding figure of the line. This provides an interesting parallel with the case of Chokyi Dronma, whose life seems to illustrate the shift from an individual incarnation of a deity to a system of reincarnations. This shift shows that incarnation and reincarnation are two different, albeit interlinked, aspects of the phenomenon as pointed out by Wylie. The notion of a *tulku* (*sprul sku*), a Tibetan word that literally means "the emanated body of the Buddha," with which most reincarnations are currently designated, encompasses both incarnation and reincarnation. In practice, *tulku* "refers to the person who is discovered through the distinctive practice of seeking out the young reincarnation of a recently deceased saint, in order that the child be 'reinstalled' in the religious community that the old master had left behind" (Germano and Gyatso 2000:242).

Tibetan reincarnation of important religious leaders is based on the ideal of the *bodhisattva*, which is central to Mahāyāna Buddhist theory, and on tantric ritual practices. *Bodhisattvas*, beings who have potentially reached enlightenment but remain in the world to strive for the enlightenment of all living beings, can choose to be reincarnated wherever they can best continue their mission. The doctrinal explanation of the procedure by which highly realized beings are able to reincarnate is often seen as related to the ritual practice called *phowa* (*'pho ba*), the "Great Transfer." This enables an achieved spiritual practitioner to control the detachment of his or her own principle of consciousness from the body and thus also control the process by which this is reincarnated after death. The *phowa* ritual is also used in funerary rites in a different but related way. All ordinary living beings are revolving in *saṃsāra,* from one life to the next, across different realms and different forms of existence without control over the process or memory of the previous state, except for some confused reverberations. Ordinary people therefore usually have the ritual of *phowa* performed by a lama at the time of death to assist their passage through the *bardo,* the intermediate space between life and rebirth, to their reincarnation in one of the six realms of existence.

Reincarnating *bodhisattvas* represent a powerful interface between ordinary temporally conditioned life as experienced by most human beings and the ultimate, almost messianic aim of the enlightenment of all living beings that transcends any temporality. This view is epitomized in Chokyi Dronma's statement in which she discards fleeting worldly joy for the ultimate joy that lasts forever (folio 46b) and in her numerous expressions of commitment to the enlightenment of all living beings. However, the worldly manifestations of *bodhisattvas* are caught, albeit in a relative way, in the impermanent existence they embody; thus they die, passing to heavenly spheres, before reincarnating. Deities and human beings at once, they are multiple and one at the same time: they have outer, inner, and secret identities and can be embodied in a number of different individuals. Accordingly, their life narratives often blend into and build on one another. In the Tibetan context, biography and genealogy are closely interlinked, as observed by Janet Gyatso (1998:116ff.), and Tibetan biographies and autobiographies often open with a description of the protagonist's previous lives over numerous generations, starting from a prominent and authoritative ancestor.

Reincarnation not only poses the question of a coherent explanation according to a Buddhist theory, a Buddhist "rebirth eschatology" (Obeysekere 2002), but also has to be seen in terms of contingent acceptable social practice. This was a particularly delicate issue when a reincarnation line was not yet established. The description of events reported in Thangtong Gyalpo's biography raises some interesting questions: how was it conceivable that the people who were searching for a reincarnation, possibly Deleg Chodren and other members of the group, were able to suggest to a local family that their baby daughter was the reincarnation of the deceased princess? There had to be such a strong narrative elucidating the extraordinary circumstances of the girl's birth in continuity with the death of the princess that it convinced the parents to entrust their daughter to Chokyi Dronma's disciples. Of course, if the family was already part of the inner circle of Tsari's religious practitioners and the girl already belonged to the group, then the process would have been quite straightforward. Even so, the transfer of little Kunga Sangmo would have implied a certain amount of negotiation and specific arrangements that had to be acceptable to all parties involved. The story reported in the biography of Thangtong Gyalpo implies that, for the contemporary audience, a girl could be formally transferred by her family of origin to a religious community that oversaw her education and took her to distant places to recognize people and locations from her former life. Whether a witness account of actual events or a later reconstruction by Gyurme Dechen, this episode provides a unique insight into the shared beliefs and practices within which the reincarnation line could be first established.

Several historians have pointed out that the notion of *tulku* might have some link with popular practices of mixed origin and possibly ancient non-Buddhist ideas of reincarnation. A passage in the *dBa' bzhed* mentions the reincarnation of two ordinary deceased children:

[A monk] said that the son was going to be reborn as a god and the daughter as a son. He placed a pearl half painted with red color in the mouth of the dead girl. One year later, a son was born to him. Everybody could see that in his teeth he had a pearl that was half red. Forty days after his birth, the boy recognized his aunt and other people. He addressed them just as [the girl] used to before dying. (*dBa' bzhed* folio 5a–b)

Anne Marie Blondeau, in her discussion of funerary rites, commented on a slightly later version of the same text, pointing out that this passage seems to refer to a different kind of reincarnation that can be made to fit Buddhist views only with considerable difficulty:

I sometimes underlined the striking contradiction between the concepts on which [the funerary ritual] is based and those of Buddhism. . . . How can this return of an identical individuality, born from the same parents, be reconciled with the rebirth conditioned by the law of *karma,* except by recourse to the sophism of scholasticism? In the face of such incompatibilities, it is common to see in them the survival of a hypothetical pre-Buddhist substratum; I even suggested this myself concerning the Tibetan *sprul-sku*. (Blondeau 1997:212–213, my translation from French)

The form of reincarnation described in the *dBa' bzhed*[1] seems indeed more similar to the rebirth theories that Obeyesekere observed among small-scale societies in which a "dead person will circle back to the same kin group; and [. . .] a neonate can be identified as a specific ancestor returned" (2002:xiii). Throughout Inner Asia, different notions of reincarnation are widespread; they do not always refer to a Buddhist background, nor are they necessarily "ethicized" like Buddhist notions of reincarnation (Obeysekere 2002). For example, Roberte Hamayon gives a very evocative description of theories of the "soul" and of reincarnation in the context of Siberian shamanism, which presents interesting reverberations with practices and beliefs that can be found among Tibetan populations (Blondeau 1997:213; Hamayon 1990:561–570). In particular, if a child died it was important to remember any distinguishing marks on the body in order to establish, once another child was born in the family, whether this was the same one come back. She also mentions divinatory practices used to establish whether a child was the reincarnation of a deceased member of the family.

Rebecca Empson (2007:58–82) refers to several similar cases of reincarnation, among common people in Mongolia, that seem to be tightly linked to ideas of ancestry and kinship, rather than to any Buddhist karmic "rebirth eschatology." She recorded the story of a child who had died in a fire and was subsequently considered to have reincarnated in a neighboring household. When a child with marks all over his body was born there, the marks were attributed to his experience in his previous life. The parents then gave the child to the other family, as he was seen to be the reincarnation of their deceased son. In this case it seems that ideas of reincarnation were also related to practices that could be called "adoption" in Western terminology, for they implied the actual transfer of parental rights and obligations. In this and other comparable cases, children's memories are believed to reflect experiences of their previous life and play a part in underpinning a particular form of relationship based on the idea of reincarnation. These forms of reincarnation, which seem to merge different rebirth eschatologies, accord with some popular Tibetan practices.[2] Trying to identify distinctive roots is, however, a challenge, for Buddhist and non-Buddhist notions were already blended in India, and the picture was further complicated by the process of cultural translation from India to Tibet when preexisting indigenous terminology was adapted and redefined. In any case, it might be worth considering the Mongolian in-fluence on the institution of reincarnation not only as the reenactment of the politico-religious relationship between Tibetan spiritual masters and Mongolian rulers, as suggested by Wylie, but also as a potential distinctive contribution to the merging of different rebirth eschatologies.

This merging adds to the historical and pragmatical aspects of Tibetan Bud-dhism that prompted some scholars to see a relation between reincarnated lamas and shamans, speaking even of a "Shamanic Buddhism" (Aziz 1976:343–360; Samuel 1993).[3] In contrast to other reincarnations, such as the Dalai Lama, the Panchen Lama, the Karmapa, and so on, the Samding Dorje Phagmo has been defined through the name of the deity and the location of its main seat instead of by a name or title of a previous incarnation. In this she is somewhat similar to oracles who are identified through the leading god that possesses them.[4] The Dorje Phagmo institution seems thus to reflect traces of Indian tantric spirit possession linked to the cult of Vajrayoginī (see chapter 1), ancient Tibetan terri-torial cults and healing practices (see chapters 4 and 8), and Buddhist soteriology against the background of a multiple rebirth eschatology.

## The Identification of Chokyi Dronma's Next Reincarnation: Kunga Sangmo

In Gyurme Dechen's biography of Thangtong Gyalpo, which was compiled in 1609 and draws considerably on the biography of Chokyi Dronma (see chapter 3), it is reported that Chokyi Dronma reached southeastern Tibet, where she stayed at Menmogang in New Tsari and worked on the production of chains at his iron mines. She died soon afterward, leaving behind a precious skull that was kept at the local temple. This biography also tells how he recognized the next reincarnation and gives a brief account of the life of the next Dorje Phagmo. As this passage is central for the discussion, I quote it in full:

> In order to report the fact that the venerable Chokyi Dronma had died in Kongpo, the chief nun, Deleg Chodren, arrived in front of the great *siddha* and asked, "Will a rebirth appear or not?" [He replied,] "Girl, let's keep quiet! She won't disappoint us! The new female reincarnation (*sku can ma*) will come soon." According to his prophecy, in the earth hare year [i.e., 1459] the venerable Kunga Sangmo was born in eastern Konpo. Deleg Chodren came to see the great *siddha*

again [with the girl] and asked, "Is this the true reincarnation or not? You must verify it!" Then he spoke the prophetic words that she was the authentic one and added: "In the snake year [i.e., 1461] she will reveal it herself." Then he offered her a mirror that, if wiped, would become clearer and clearer; a famous hand cymbal; and the flour of white barley that would bestow long life. Then when [the new incarnation] was five years old the great *siddha* took care of her and gave her a lot of teachings on the old and new secret *mantras*. Then he gave her the following instructions: "Go to the three domains of Ngari to tame the living beings." The servants[5] requested him not to let her go on the journey, as she was too young. [However,] he said, "In order to perform the *phowa* ('*pho ba*) funerary ritual[6] for Dode, the mother of your former life, you must go. We can gradually discuss everything else." She eventually arrived at Ngari Dzonkha and said [to Chokyi Dronma's mother], "When my mother escorted me as I was leaving for Kongpo, I said, 'I will surely come to the pillow of my mother when she dies.' Was this forgotten?" Then she recounted a lot of events from her former life, just as if she had woken up from a sleep, which caused great surprise. The great *siddha* had sent instructions in a letter: "Tame the living beings in the three domains of Ngari. Attendants! If you do not feel like going on such a journey you should ask her!" In fact, she said, "Even if I die, it wouldn't be possible for me to disobey the order of the lama!" Thus the young queen of the *ḍākinīs* decided to go. When they completed the collection of offerings in the three domains of Ngari, she received a letter from the great *siddha* that said, "You shall leave again to subdue the Mongols." All the people requested her not to go, as she might be killed by the Mongols. However, she said, "Even if nobody wants to go, Pal [Chime Drupa] and I will go." Eventually, around twenty followers who were ready to sacrifice their lives followed her and went to Maryul [Ladakh?].[7] Thanks to her wisdom and her magical powers, she was able to let the two kings of upper and lower Maryul negotiate. In some sixty towns in which the Upper Hor[8] had settled in Maryul she gave teachings on *maṇi* and on how to renounce sins and turn to virtue. In order to fulfill the wishes of the great *siddha,* she performed divinations to intimidate the Mongolian army. A scourge of mice destroyed all the barley, which caused a great famine and the spread of an epidemic among the Mongols. Therefore she did not give the army of the Western Mongols the opportunity to penetrate into the Land of Snows. Later she offered the Iron Bridge Builder all the donations that she had collected, such as gold, brass, coral, and amber, in order to support him in his virtuous deeds. The Iron Bridge Builder gave the head of the *ḍākinīs* excellent equipment for encampment, with many precious ornaments,

*Succession and Spiritual Lineages: Meaning and Mysteries of Chokyi Dronma's Reincarnation*

and she left for Kham [in eastern Tibet] to collect offerings for him. In U-Tsang she acquired innumerable followers who kept providing her with generous offerings. Eventually she settled down at Riwoche [in Lato].[9] Here she made a new pagoda roof of gold and brass for the residence of the great *siddha* and decorated the northern part of the *stūpa* with gold and brass. Furthermore, she worked her whole life without interruption in order to let the wings of the Iron Bridge Builder's great deeds fly. (Biography of Thangtong Gyalpo 308–309)

In this version of events, Thangtong Gyalpo seems to be in control of the process. He replies to Deleg Chodren's questions, gives her instructions, and eventually validates the reincarnation as authentic. That Deleg Chodren had asked whether there was going to be a reincarnation or not suggests that this was already considered a real possibility, which is not altogether surprising, as it was during the fourteenth and fifteenth centuries that reincarnation as the basis of spiritual lineages started to become widely accepted and many Tibetan lineages were established.

Whatever the circumstances in which Chokyi Dronma was reincarnated in Kunga Sangmo, memory seems to have played an important role: Kunga Sangmo recognized the mother of her previous life when she went back to Gungthang, like the child mentioned in the *dBa' bzhed* who recognized his aunt. In both cases the primary form of reenacted relationship is one of kin and is expressed in the recollection of an individual that seems to transcend death and the passage from one life to the next. The transfer of a spiritual principle seems to provide an idiom of relatedness that is an alternative to and might override that of the transmission of bodily substances from parents to children through the conventional notions of "bone" and "blood." Sometimes reincarnation lineages and kinship lineages coexisted without major problems; sometimes they were the ground for various conflicts. Tensions between the family and the religious community surrounding the care of a child reincarnation[10] as well as disputes concerning claims to titles and property between family and the reincarnation of a deceased lama[11] are not unheard of and bear witness to the very practical difficulties raised by the existence of competing idioms of relatedness. How reincarnation is connected to more general ideas of relatedness and notions of the person is a fascinating and far-reaching topic that needs further exploration, as does the question of the roots of reincarnation in Tibet. The evidence currently available indicates that the process of discovering Chokyi Dronma's reincarnation—before the formal establishment of a search committee, the formal process of identification, and the shared knowledge of the institution—could happen amid a blend of Buddhist and non-Buddhist popular practices of multiple origin.

Kunga Sangmo was taken care of as a child by the people who had been around the princess before her death; these included Deleg Chodren and Pal Chime Drupa as well as, presumably, the nuns, like Tharpa Sangmo, who had been close to Chokyi Dronma in various capacities. In this environment, the girl grew up seeing herself through the eyes of the people around her. The stories she was told formed the basis upon which she interpreted and organized her own experience and revealed herself as the embodiment of the deceased princess and as the incarnated deity. From her point of view, the narrative of Dorje Phagmo/Chokyi Dronma presumably blurred the boundary between what she was told and what she experienced, between her "semantic memory" and her "episodic memory" (Whitehouse and Laidlaw 2002:3ff.), transcending the sense of her own individuality. This is best reflected in the passage that describes how she told her story as Chokyi Dronma/Kunga Sangmo "as if she had woken up from a sleep" when visiting the homeland and encountering the mother of her previous life. The community of Chokyi Dronma's disciples was keen to recognize words and acts that recalled the princess they remembered and missed, and those provided a reassuring confirmation that she was still among them in a different form. Kunga Sangmo was thus becoming her own person through a dialogical process between herself and Chokyi Dronma's disciples around her. Mirroring herself in their eyes and in their spiritual aspirations, and thus revealing herself as the deceased princess and as the embodiment of the deity, she became part of the process whereby shared memories can be recalled by an individual and reproduced from one generation to the next. Spiritually and socially speaking, she was indeed Chokyi Dronma and Dorje Phagmo, for she reckoned herself within the same mental continuum. The community of the disciples defined itself through her while she defined herself through them. Thangtong Gyalpo is said to have presented the young girl with a magic mirror that would become clearer and clearer the more it was wiped. This ritual item seems to epitomize her experience of being and becoming. The mirror is indeed a ritual instrument important not only for tantric practice and funerary rituals, as a powerful symbol of the mind and means for divination, but also for oracles, to whom it reveals the deity possessing them (Diemberger 2005:133–136). In the narrative the mirror, along with the other gifts she received from Thangtong Gyalpo, seems an important metaphor that reflects the interaction among the girl, the master, and the community around them.

Taking a cross-cultural stance, it might be useful to think that we all embody words, narratives, expectations, and relationships that predate us and into which we are born. These are the background against which we construct our sense of individuality, what is defined in Buddhist terms as the illusory sense of the self. Rather than being an exotic, incomprehensible phenomenon, the reincarnation of Chokyi Dronma can thus be seen as a special case of a more general human experience, as a particular embodiment of a collective memory.

## Establishment of the Lineage: The Role of the Biography

As discussed in chapter 3, the biography was presumably compiled with the input of the other disciples' notes, letters, and oral accounts. It was a joint operation through which the individual recollections were blended into a shared and codified form of collective memory, the written text. Its compilation was an essential component in the establishment of Kunga Sangmo as the reincarnation of Chokyi Dronma. From this point of view, it shares certain features with a few other comparable biographies that were instrumental in the establishment of a reincarnation line, in particular the sense of revelation of a secret level of reality. For example, the so-called secret biography of the Sixth Dalai Lama narrates his escape from Chinese captivity in 1706 and his subsequent settlement in Alasha (Western Inner Mongolia), where he revealed himself as the Dalai Lama in disguise and recognized the reincarnation of the Tibetan regent who had found him, Desi Sangye Gyatsho (Aris 1989). The narrative provided the foundation and the guideline for the establishment of two parallel reincarnation lines at the Baruun Heid monastery, through which the Sixth Dalai Lama and the Tibetan regent, Desi Sangye Gyatsho, have been reincarnating up to the present day (Jalsan 2002:347–359). The biography was written in 1757, shortly after the death of the alleged Sixth Dalai Lama in disguise in 1746, and the identification of his reincarnation in a child who became the second Ondor Gegeen.[12] The biographer considered himself the spiritual son of the Sixth Dalai Lama and an incarnation of the Tibetan regent. Rich in detail from ordinary life and describing deeds that are not that extraordinary (Aris 1989), the work was mapping the events shortly after they had happened. It was part of the process of establishing the institution by legitimizing the past and presenting a master narrative for future generations.

The biography of Chokyi Dronma, like that of the Sixth Dalai Lama, was probably written by a disciple who was instrumental in establishing the reincarnation line, Pal Chime Drupa (see chapter 3 and below). It gave the authoritative revelation of Chokyi Dronma's secret identity as the deity Dorje Phagmo, the essential prerequisite for the legitimate recognition of a girl as the reincarnation of the princess. In all likelihood the biography informed and legitimized the search for and the education of Chokyi Dronma's reincarnation when no guidelines existed. It represented both a yardstick for the recollection of what she had been and a master narrative for the future. It provided the empowerment expressed in the language of Thangtong Gyalpo's prophecies and the basis for the ritualization of her persona through a set of clearly identifiable features. Chokyi Dronma's life narrative was also the background for the later accounts that would tell her story from different perspectives.

## Establishment of the Lineage: The Role of Thangtong Gyalpo

Compared to the previous biographers of Thangtong Gyalpo, Gyurme Dechen highlighted Chokyi Dronma more conspicuously, drawing on her biography. He may have decided to do so given the high profile achieved by the Dorje Phagmo reincarnations by the time he was writing, in the early seventeenth century. However, he was writing from the point of view of the master's tradition. According to his compilation, Thangtong Gyalpo played an important part in the early stages of the Dorje Phagmo tradition as embodied by the princess. He seems to have relied on Chokyi Dronma for support in his own enterprises, and he committed himself to protecting her and her followers when she left for Tsari, using his network. The death of Chokyi Dronma had therefore left a big vacuum also in the structure of patronage that held the community together and made many deeds possible. Both spiritually and materially, Thangtong Gyalpo must have considered the identification of her reincarnation as important for his followers as well as hers, and was presumably involved in making it possible. It is significant that one of Kunga Sangmo's first moves was to go back to Gungthang to be recognized there. She—or more likely those who were acting on her behalf—thus probably laid claims on what was originally under the control of the deceased princess and activated her personal network of relations. This would have included her possessions, ranging from ritual objects with great symbolical significance to precious materials and even estates, and donor-donee relations; accordingly the Gungthang kings appear among Kunga Sangmo's supporters. Despite Thangtong Gyalpo's backing, however, she might have been less

*Succession and Spiritual Lineages: Meaning and Mysteries of Chokyi Dronma's Reincarnation*

successful than he had hoped because she does not appear in the later chronicles of the Gungthang kingdom, nor in the life of Tsunpa Choleg, in which Chokyi Dronma's father, her brother, and some of her followers are mentioned several times.[13] Thangtong Gyalpo had a difficult relationship with Chopel Sangpo, the court chaplain of Gungthang, and perhaps other Bodongpa masters dominating the Gungthang scene. He might even have been the object of a poisoning attempt when he visited the area around 1435.[14] Whether this was real or an allegation, it is clear that Thangtong Gyalpo's relationship with Gungthang and the Bodongpa was complex and sometimes strained. Together with later sectarian differences and allegiances, this might be one of the reasons for a very peculiar silence concerning him in the *Bo dong chos 'byung*, in the passages that report the same events described in his biography.

Despite her difficulties in Chokyi Dronma's homeland, Kunga Sangmo embodied the legacy of the deceased princess with great success. Even though she spent the final part of her life in the territory of Thangtong Gyalpo, it seems that her main area of influence was farther east, in the U region and especially in Tsari and Jayul, where Tsangnyon Heruka met her in 1472, together with Pal Chime Drupa, and again a few years later when he visited Chokyi Dronma's niece, Dondrub Gyalmo, who had married into the Phagmodrupa ruling house in 1481 (Biography of Tsangnyon Heruka folios 32–33, 120–122).[15] Kunga Sangmo was able to gain support from numerous secular and religious rulers, including the Phagmodrupa, who were still the main power holders in the Lhasa region even though they had lost their position of supremacy, which had passed in 1434 to the Rinpungpa. In particular, she obtained substantial support from the lords of Yamdrog, who played a crucial role in getting her established.

## Establishment of the Lineage: The Spiritual Succession of Bodong Chogle Namgyal

Chokyi Dronma was a princess of Gungthang, a fully ordained nun, and an incarnated deity. She was the center of a group of Buddhist practitioners and managed a large and powerful network of political and religious relationships with links to Thangtong Gyalpo and the disciples of Bodong Chogle Namgyal. Furthermore, she was a candidate for the spiritual succession of Bodong Chogle Namgyal, for some of his disciples felt that she was the person who had been closest to their master and who had received most of his teachings (folio 88a).

Her sudden, untimely death had left a number of people not only bereft and grieving but also in a very insecure situation.

The lineage of Bodong Chogle Namgyal had so far been transmitted by kin, from uncle to nephew within a system that continued after his death. His nephew is reported as having taken over the abbot seats of Bodongpa monasteries (*Shel dkar chos 'byung* folio 46a), which is confirmed by Chokyi Dronma's biography (folio 106a). Chokyi Dronma, as an incarnated deity, a fully ordained nun, and a descendent of the Tibetan kings, had excellent credentials as a spiritual heir, but she was a woman, and making her into a successor was a daring choice, presumably not shared by the whole community. Anne Chayet (2002:66) points out that "Tibetan tradition reluctantly accepts female lineages," and underlines how in order to make any attempt to reach enlightenment, a woman had to first reincarnate as a male. She then mentions the most prominent examples of women, like Tsongkhapa's mother, who were incarnated as holy men before engaging in a religious career. Soteriological inclusiveness was Bodong Chogle Namgyal's approach, but not necessarily that of all his disciples and the local people. The divided opinions concerning Chokyi Dronma are indicated not only by the passages in which he had to defend his choice to admit her into the inner circle of his disciples when he was alive (see chapter 4) but also by a number of other factors: the difficult relationship between Chokyi Dronma and the people of Porong Palmo Choding; the personal distance between Chokyi Dronma and Bodong Chogle Namgyal's nephew, despite some belated efforts on the part of the princess to improve the relationship; and even Thangtong Gyalpo's prophecy that if she were to stay in her own region she would have "few disciples." All this seems to indicate controversies or even a rift among Bodong Chogle Namgyal's disciples following the death of the master. The move toward a transmission line based on reincarnation rather than kinship was at least an option.[16]

The ruler of Yamdrog, Namkha Sangpo, and his nephew Amoghasiddhi Jigme Bang, the author of the biography of Bodong Chogle Namgyal, played a crucial role in establishing Chokyi Dronma's reincarnation at Samding. They were disciples of both Bodong Chogle Namgyal and Thangtong Gyalpo, who visited Nakartse in 1433 (Biography of Thangtong Gyalpo 163). They were presumably involved from early on in the events surrounding Chokyi Dronma's reincarnation, since Kunga Sangmo was in their palace at Nakartse when the translator Lochen Sonam Gyatsho (1424–1482) visited around 1470.[17] The great translator described how he met Kunga Sangmo as an eleven-year-old girl and entertained her with songs (Ehrhard 2002:79) and later wrote her a letter that has been recently

*Succession and Spiritual Lineages: Meaning and Mysteries of Chokyi Dronma's Reincarnation*

FIGURE 5.1 The fortress of Nakartse, seat of the local rulers, after a photograph by Hugh Richardson and observation of the ruins. *Karen Diemberger*

reproduced as part of his correspondence (Ehrhard 2002:45–47).[18] The ruling house of Nakartse is also known to have later hosted, as a holy relic, the skull of Kunga Sangmo's reincarnation, Nyendra Sangmo.[19] The lords of Yamdrog are therefore likely to have had a seminal influence in establishing Chokyi Dronma as part of a lineage of reincarnations of holy women from preceding centuries. In fact, in the biography of Bodong Chogle Namgyal, Amoghasiddhi Jigme Bang reports some original verses either by Konchog Gyaltshen, the secretary of Bodong Chogle Namgyal, or by his nephew (see chapter 3): "Furthermore, there is the mother of all Buddhas, Dorje Phagmo, the holder of the secret treasury,[20] on the earth renowned as the fully ordained nun (*dge slong ma, bhikṣuṇī*) holding the secret of the emanations' dance" (Biography of Bodong Chogle Namgyal 259).

He then explains this passage and expands its scope:

As far as the most accomplished among all, the holder of the secret treasury, is concerned: In earlier times she became Palmo (dPal mo) [i.e., Lakṣmīṅkarā], the sister of Indrabhūti in the land of Urgyen (Oḍḍiyāna), then the divine princess Maṇḍāravā, the consort of the great teacher Padmasambhava. Now in honor of this Great Man [Bodong Chogle Namgyal], Dorje Phagmo herself, the chief of all *yoginīs,* incarnated in Chokyi Dronme. (Biography of Bodong Chogle Namgyal 268)

In Amoghasiddhi Jigme Bang's view, Chokyi Dronma was not only an incarnation of the deity but also a reincarnation of Lakṣmīṅkarā and Maṇḍāravā. While compiling his work a few years after the death of his spiritual master, he had decided not only to include the verses concerning Chokyi Dronma but also to emphasize them through his own exegesis. In doing so he ascribed her divine origin to Indian roots and mentioned some illustrious Indian predecessors, the "authorizing referents" (Gyatso and Havnevik 2005:22) that enabled him to craft her identity and position. He also recalled, in a later passage mentioning the people who took care of Bodong Chogle Namgyal's funeral, a brief reference to Chokyi Dronma's earlier Tibetan incarnations:

> In addition, there was the one who in earlier times was born in the locality called Phag for the accomplishment of the deeds of Phagmodrupa [Dorje Gyalpo], and now is rejoicing in the accomplishment of the deeds of the Omniscient, after having been born at the time of the [Gungthang] King Son of the Gods (*lha sras*), as the great Vajrayoginī Ache Droma Chokyi Dronme.[21] (Biography of Bodong Chogle Namgyal 391)

The references to Lakṣmīṅkarā and the consort of Phagmodrupa Dorje Gyalpo (1110–1170)[22] are not surprising. They were popular and were central to the mythology of the Phagmodrupa rulers, the Neudong Gongma, who dominated the political scene in fourteenth- to fifteenth-century Tibet (see chapter 1). He mentions Chokyi Dronma's predecessors almost as a quotation from a genealogy, undoubtedly a way of establishing her authority and legitimacy according to the ancient use of genealogies as a system of asserting power on the basis of origin (Stein 1972:195; Gyatso 1998:117–118).

A full system of Bodongpa reincarnations is described in the sixteenth-century *Bo dong chos 'byung,* which follows the literary model of the "genealogical" narrative more than that of the personal account. After outlining the life of Bodong Chogle Namgyal, the *Bo dong chos 'byung* has a passage that describes the appointment of his successors: his nephew occupied the seat of abbot in a number of

Bodongpa monasteries while Chokyi Dronma and Pal Chime Drupa established a twin reincarnation line embodying the deities Vajravārāhī and Cakrasaṃvara. Thus Bodong Chogle Namgyal's succession seems to have included both transmission by kin and a reincarnation line. I shall discuss here the relevant passage, from folios 18b to 26b.

Bodong Chogle Namgyal's nephew, who was expert in the *sūtra* and the *tantra* according to the three disciplines,[23] occupied the seat of abbot at Bodong and the other monasteries and spread the holy doctrine with philosophical teachings and through the practice of meditation. As far as the spiritual heirs (*chos kyi rgyal tshab*) are concerned: the venerable Chokyi Dronme, a fully ordained nun (*bhikṣuṇī*), emanation of Vajravārāhī, and Palden Chime Drupa, an emanation of Cakrasaṃvara, were empowered as representatives (*rgyal tshab*). According to the secret biography, the venerable Chodron [i.e., Chokyi Dronma] received the following instructions:
  "After having had three reincarnations,[24] take rebirth accordingly at Tsari! You shall perform great deeds for the living beings of the ten directions. You shall produce volumes made of gold, silver, and copper to be presented to the living beings of the ten directions. You shall go to the realm of the *ḍākinīs*."

Both the genealogical narrative and the prophecy reflect the issue of succession that the community of the disciples of Bodong Chogle Namgyal faced. Tellingly, two parallel principles are followed: kin and reincarnation. The account is consistent with the biography of Chokyi Dronma and that of Thangtong Gyalpo. However, it seems that in the *Bo dong chos 'byung* the role of Thangtong Gyalpo may have been intentionally omitted. Conversely, the role of Pal Chime Drupa, who was almost certainly a previous incarnation of the author of the *Bo dong chos 'byung*, was highlighted. He was definitely among the disciples of Chokyi Dronma (see chapter 3) but was apparently not important enough to be named among the closest disciples of Bodong Chogle Namgyal in the latter's biography. The probable reference to him, in passing, in the biography of Thangtong Gyalpo (309) suggests that he was there but in a less authoritative position than described in the *Bo dong chos 'byung*, which gives a full account of the genealogy of the two spiritual heirs as incarnations of Vajravārāhī and Cakrasaṃvara:

The genealogy (*khrung rabs*), i.e., rebirths (*skyes pa 'dzin pa*), of both Chokyi Dronme and Pal Chime Drupa, the heirs of the omniscient lord of religion, goes as follows:

256

In ancient times, Vajravārāhī was born as Lakṣmīṅkarā, sister of King Indrabhūti in Oḍḍiyāna. She was known as Bhikṣuṇī Lakṣmī, and her deeds were beyond human imagination. She led her own brother to the land of spiritual realization. Next she was born as Maṇḍāravā, daughter of King Indrabhūti "the Middle," also called Chenme Jorden, in Zahor.[25] She possessed the signs of accomplished spiritual realization. She became a *mudrā* of the great teacher Padmasambhava. In Tibet, she was incarnated as the *ḍākinī* Sonam Drenma and became a *mudrā* of Phagmodrupa at Phagmodru. Then she incarnated as the *ḍākinī* Sonam Paldren at Damsho in Kham and used to stay in retreat and perform deeds for the benefit of living beings. Then she was born as daughter of the King of Ngari Gungthang, Khri Lhawang Gyaltshen, and Dodelha Gyalmo. She was called Konchog Gyalmo, the chief of the *ḍākinīs*. Later she was ordained and became known as the venerable Chodron. Palden Chime Drupa lived as Indrabhūti, who was a brother of Lakṣmī; then as the father of Maṇḍāravā; then as Chenga Tshulthrimbar,[26] a disciple of Dromton;[27] then as Khampa Dorje Gyalbo [i.e., Phagmodrupa], who was one of the three Khampa disciples of Dagpo Lhaje;[28] then as Chogyal Nasathro of Sulphu;[29] then as the hero of Kham, Rinchenpal, who was together with Sonam Paldren.

The genealogy clearly refers here to the ancestry of the Phagmodrupa.[30] The actual link among Sonam Drenma, Sonam Paldren, and Chokyi Dronma remains an avenue for further investigation, and future studies concerning Sonam Drenma and Sonam Paldren may cast new light on this issue.[31] Like the biography of Bodong Chogle Namgyal, the *Bo dong chos 'byung* mentions Chokyi Dronma as an incarnation of the deity Dorje Phagmo with an ancestry of Indian and Tibetan predecessors, but in this source she appears as part of a proper lineage of reincarnations. It is interesting that the author found it necessary to specify with a note that the genealogy (*khrung rabs*) referred to a transmission "by taking rebirths" (*skyes pa 'dzin pa*). Relatedness by line of successive reincarnations was thus a distinctive mode of reckoning descent, parallel and analogous to transmission through patrilineal or matrinileal kinship ties.

The reference to an ancient spiritual bonding over centuries and generations propelled the tantric couple Chokyi Dronma and Pal Chime Drupa to continue the deeds of Bodong Chogle Namgyal:

They benefited the doctrine and performed deeds for the living beings as follows: After the venerable Omniscient (Bodong Chogle Namgyal) had passed away,

Chokyi Dronma took care of his funeral rites. Then she went to Tsagong, a holy place in Kongpo,³² and resided there. Following the example of her lama, she meditated deeply on the spirit of enlightenment of Mahāyāna. She passed away at the age of thirty-three in Bogong Menmogang where, for the benefit of all living beings, a *stūpa* was built in which her skull was placed as a sacred relic.

The locality of her death, the timing, and even the detail of the skull correspond with what is given in the biography of Thangtong Gyalpo, except for the conspicuous absence of Thangtong Gyalpo himself. After Chokyi Dronma's death, Pal Chime Drupa played a crucial role in the continuation of the tradition and in all likelihood compiled her biography (see chapter 3). The *Bo dong chos 'byung* devotes a brief biographical sketch to him, which proved very helpful in trying to identify him as the most likely potential author:

Palden Chime Drupa³³ was born in Ngari Gungthang. He was ordained during his youth and went to Sangphu in order to study philosophy. He debated on about ten volumes of the doctrine. He became famous as Kabchupa Dharmapal. He was also expert in the tantric tradition of Ribo Gandenpa (Gelugpa). Later, with the venerable Chodron [i.e., Chokyi Dronma] he became a follower of Jigdrel Bodongpa [i.e., Bodong Chole Namgyal]. He received all his teachings and instructions, and this tradition was entrusted to him. After the omniscient Jigdrel had passed away, he went with the venerable Chodron to Tsagong in Kongpo and offered his services to her. After Jetsun Chodron had passed away, he devoted himself to meditation for three years and showed signs of accomplished spiritual realization such as leaving footprints on rock.

According to this source, he took care of the next reincarnation of Chokyi Dronma:

The venerable Kunga Sangmo was a reincarnation of the venerable Chodron. She was born close to Srinmo Nyen in Kongpo as the daughter of Siddha Chogden Dorje and Jomo Dron. She was cared for by [Pal] Chime Drupa and together they went to Loro,³⁴ Lhodrag,³⁵ and Yamdrog,³⁶ where they organized a great gathering and established the holy doctrine. In the three districts of Ngari³⁷ and in the area of To-Hor,³⁸ she also performed great deeds that were beyond the grasp of the human mind. In particular, thanks to her instructions, the army of Hor did not come to Tibet.³⁹ The venerable Kunga Sangmo and Palden Chime Drupa went on to visit numerous places from To-Hor to Do-Kham (Eastern Tibet). The lords of central Tibet, such as the King of Ngari Me [i.e., Gungthang], the Ruler of Nedong, Tshenyi Rinpoche, and Garpa Donyo Dorje, all became patrons and followers of theirs, and they performed deeds limitless like the infinity of the sky. . . . Eventually he passed away at the age of fifty-eight at Kodrag kyar in Mar Kham.[40]

This account accords with that already described in Thangtong Gyalpo's biography. Pal Chime Drupa may have had a complementary role to that of Deleg Chodren and is presumably the "Pal" mentioned there. The network of patrons and the description of the deeds seem, however, to locate the focus of Kunga Sangmo's activity more in the U region of central Tibet, where she continued after the death of Pal Chime Drupa:

In Yamdrog she improved the Samding meditation monastery with the support of both Lhundrub Tashi, son of the Lord of Yamdrog, and the Lady Tshebum Gyalmo. She took care also of the Yasang[41] monastery with the support of Sonam Dorje, Lord of Yar To (upper Yarlung). The Desi Gongma[42] offered Yarlung Sheldrag[43] to her. In this way she founded new monasteries as well as taking care of the old ones. At that time in Tibet, the Land of Snows, there were no lamas greater than she and Karma Chodrag Gyatsho.[44] There was no difference between them. When they had the chance to meet, the Karmapa used to sit to the right and Kunga Sangmo to the left on identical thrones, and they each received equal attention. In brief, Kunga Sangmo contributed enormously to the prosperity of the doctrine of *dPal de kho na nyid 'dus ba*. At the age of forty-three she passed away in Lato Riwoche.

For the reincarnation system it was vital that the line of Pal Chime Drupa, complementing the other side of the tantric couple, continued as a source of authority for the recognition of the next Dorje Phagmo. Chime Palsang was thus recognized as the reincarnation of the deceased master:

The Omniscient Chime Palsang was an incarnation of Palden Chime Drupa. He was born as the son of Shonnu Gyaltshen, his father, and *ḍākinī* Tshogdag Karmo, his mother, at Ronggur, close to Taglung[45] in U. At the age of six, he was ordained and given the name Chime Palsangpo by Taglung Ngawang Dragpa.[46] He recognized some objects of Chime Drupa such as the vase for empowerment, and a painted scroll of Vajrabhairava.

Chime Palsang eventually recognized the reincarnation of Kunga Sangmo. Without this step, the reincarnation line would have stopped like the one of Drowa Sangmo, the consort of Gotshangpa, mentioned above. The *Bo dong chos 'byung* gives great emphasis to the fact that Nyendra Sangmo was vital for the continuity of the tradition. In particular, together with Chime Palsang, she established the Nyemo Chekar monastery:

> The venerable Nyendrag Sangmo was the reincarnation of the venerable Kunga Sangmo. She was born as daughter to Pawo Lhundrub, her father, and Tashi Pelbar, her mother, at Damsho in Kham. She was taken care of by Chime Palsang. She performed great deeds from Kongpo to Ngari. Both teacher and disciple [Chime Palsang and Nyendrag Sangmo] established a school of philosophy for the study of the *dPal de kho na nyid 'dus pa* at Nyemo Chekhar. Later, a monastery was founded under the patronage of the Lord of Nyemo. . . . It is said that without this, the doctrine of the *dPal de kho na nyid 'dus pa* would have survived in name only. . . . Eventually, she passed away, at the age of thirty-nine at Samding in Yamdrog.

Among the great deeds of this remarkable woman, the foundation of Nyemo Chekar was particularly prominent, as it became an important center for the Bodongpa. This was one of the main seats of Nyendra Sangmo and Chime Palsang and is the monastery where the mural paintings mentioned in chapters 1 and 4 are located. The author of the *Bo dong chos 'byung* described the line of reincarnation up to his own time and refers to the Dorje Phagmo that was still alive then, i.e., Urgyen Tshomo (born around 1543), and Chime Palsang, who had taken care of her and had died some time before:

> The incarnation of Jetsun Nyendrag Sangmo is the present Jetsun Urgyen Tshomo. Her father was Pawo Chuden, her mother Ḍākinī Thaggo, and she was born at Sobo Soshi in Kham. At the age of five, she was taken care of and served by the Omniscient Chime Palsang. . . . He attained the age of seventy. Thanks to his blessing, the doctrine of the Bodongpa spread, both in central Tibet and in the remote places. He passed away at Daki Samding. The venerable Urgyen Tshomo, despite her youth, took excellent care of the funeral arrangements and the construction of religious memorials.

At this point the author of the *Bo dong chos 'byung* himself enters the narrative in the first person, creating a sense of continuity with the previous deceased master:

At the age of twenty-three [i.e., in the 1560s][47] she went with me to southern Kongpo to benefit all living beings. Her activities spread as far as the horizon. Later, following the wish of Chime Palsang to build a tantric college, she was able, with the support of the religious lords of Nakartse, to found a college in Gya.

The author of the *Bo dong chos 'byung,* Chime Oser, was apparently the partner of Urgyen Tshomo. He does not mention whether he was formally recognized as the reincarnation of Chime Palsang, but his name would suggest that this was the case. Chime Drupa, Chime Palsang, and Chime Oser also appear within a reincarnation line located in the Rinpung region that was described in a nineteenth-century list compiled for the Qing Amban.[48] Chime Oser was active in many places over the whole of Tibet and had some success in establishing religious institutions. However, some passages betray the fact that he may have faced certain material difficulties, as he had "scanty ability in worldly affairs" and thus had "limited wealth." This description is supported by the *Shel dkar chos 'byung* (folio 54b), which mentions a period of little prosperity for the Bodongpa in the early seventeenth century, possibly linked to the more general unrest of the political and religious strife that involved Karmapa and Gelugpa, Tibetans and Mongols. The compilation of the *Bo dong chos 'byung* was in all likelihood an attempt to reinforce or even reestablish the legitimacy of the reincarnation line. It builds on the narrative model mentioned by Amoghasiddhi Jigme Bang, author of the biography of Bodong Chogle Namgyal, and develops it into a full genealogical account: a double reincarnation line of which Chime Oser was presumably part, as the reincarnation of Pal Chime Drupa and Chime Palsang. A prophecy announcing that the teachings of Bodong Chogle Namgyal would extend to the Eastern Sea (*Bo dong chos 'byung* folio 30a) reveals grand aspirations, possibly in relation to an imperial design inspired by the Sakya-Yuan example pursued by the competing powers of the time.

## The Dorje Phagmo and the Karmapa

The areas of Yamdrog and Rinpung were at that time a stronghold of the Bodongpa. By the beginning of the sixteenth century, a number of connected local rulers and spiritual masters, with the shared aim of continuing the spiritual legacy not only of Bodong Chogle Namgyal and Chokyi Dronma but also of Pal Chime Drupa and Kunga Sangmo, had brought to the fore a full system of reincarnations. After Kunga Sangmo's death in Thangtong Gyalpo's homeland around 1502, Chime Palsang recognized her reincarnation in the young girl Nyedra Sangmo. The parallel male/female reincarnation system was thus established. It was based on the reenactment of the tantric couple, just as other reincarnation lines are based on the reenactment of the spiritual father–spiritual son, i.e., teacher–disciple, relationship (e.g., Dalai Lama and Panchen Lama). This system of reincarnations was not located within the tradition of Thangtong Gyalpo but rather in that of the successors of the disciples of Bodong Chogle Namgyal, who developed close links to the Karmapa. The statement in the *Bo dong chos 'byung* that when Kunga Sangmo used to meet Karma Chodrag Gyatsho they would sit on equal thrones, one to the left and one to the right, indicated not only her high status but also the symbolic complementarity that she had achieved in relation to him. She embodied the feminine principle. Karma Chodrag Gyatsho points in this direction as well, as he is reported as saying that he has "outer, inner, and secret parents" and refers to the secret father (*gsang ba'i yab*) as the Lord of the Dharma Lokeśvara Camkrasaṃvara and the secret mother (*gsang ba'i yum*) as Vajrayoginī Adron (A sgron) (*mKhas pa'i dga' ston* 1207–1208).

Vajrayoginī Adron might be a reference not only to the deity but also to Chokyi Dronma, since Adron is the abridged form of Adrol Chokyi Dronme, the name that she was given when she was ordained (see folio 46a) and that is reported in the biography of Bodong Chogle Namgyal (391). Lokeśvara Camkrasaṃvara seems to refer to the deity as well as to one or more of the spiritual masters who embodied it. This esoteric passage has a broader scope than the reference to spiritual ancestry and is a remarkable prelude to the account of the birth of Karma Mikyio Dorje, the Eighth Karmapa, who indeed had a close relationship with the Samding Dorje Phagmo and the Bodongpa tradition: he was the author of a later biography of Bodong Chogle Namgyal (see chapter 3) and was offered a monastery by the Samding Dorje Phagmo (Karma Thinley 1980:92).

The distinctive black hat of the Samding Dorje Phagmo, which can be seen in both ancient and modern mural paintings and in photographs of the later reincarnations, is very similar to that of the Karmapa and is linked to the *ḍākinīs* and Khandro Yeshe Tshogyal in particular. The ancient paintings of Nyemo Chekar on the first floor of the monastery (see chapter 1) reveal a particularly close link between the Karmapa and the Bodongpa, or at least the Bodongpa branch that established Nyemo Chekar. The room shows large portraits of both Red Hat and Black Hat Karmapas as well as of the spiritual masters of the Bodongpa tradition. The reincarnations of the Dorje Phagmo, in particular, surround the portrait

FIGURE 5.2 The sixteenth-century mural at Nyemo Chekar. The central figures are the Fourth Karmapa (left), Chime Palsang (middle), and Bodong Chogle Namgyal (right). The Fourth Karmapa is surrounded by a sequence of Dorje Phagmo incarnations. *Karen Diemberger*

of the Fourth Karmapa, Chodrag Yeshe (1453–1524). Indeed, he is described· in *mKhas pa'i dga' ston* (1149) as the root lama of Nyendra Sangmo, the reincarnation of Kunga Sangmo: "He became the root lama of the fifth incarnation of the *ḍākinī* with the skull with marks . . . the venerable Nyendra Sangmo took her vows and listened to his teachings. Chime Palsang listened to the teachings by the great scholar Mañjuśrī."

The interaction between the Fourth Karmapa and Nyendra Sangmo must have been limited, as he died shortly afterward, while she was still a young woman. She was actually taken care of by Chime Palsang, but the profile of the Fourth Karmapa, by then a leading religious and political figure, must have made such a portrait compelling.

The "skull with special features," which appears in the passage mentioned above, is a recurring theme in narratives concerning Chokyi Dronma and her tradition and seems to reflect the complexity of genealogical readings (see chapter 3).[49] It is also worth noting that Nyendra Sangmo is described as the Fifth

*Succession and Spiritual Lineages: Meaning and Mysteries of Chokyi Dronma's Reincarnation*

Dorje Phagmo, which suggests that the reckoning system started in this case not from Chokyi Dronma but from Sonam Drenma, the consort of Phagmo Drupa Dorje Gyalpo (1110–1170).[50] This particular lineage, actually established with the transition from Chokyi Dronma to Kunga Sangmo, saw Chokyi Dronma as a foundational figure, presumably transplanted into the mythology of the Phagmodrupa tradition. This highlighted the merging of two sources of ancestral legitimacy: one rooted in Gungthang with its imperial legacy, the other rooted in Phagmodrupa's ancestral mythology.[51] Tashi Ombar, the "blue horseman," the special protector of the Bodongpa tradition depicted in the same room at Nyemo Chekar, has a somewhat parallel mythology of origin. It was explored by Guntram Hazod, who showed that Tashi Ombar was linked to the Phagmodrupa ancestry going back to the ancient dBa' clan but also to a separate Bodongpa mythology linked to Pang Lotsawa and his journeys to India[52] (Hazod 1998:68–72).

## Some Concluding Remarks on Reincarnation

While still a child, Kunga Sangmo reenacted the relationship toward the mother of her previous life, which conferred legitimacy upon her. She then reproduced a set of teacher-disciple and donor-donee relationships, expanding them. In the reenactment of kinship, political, religious, and economic relations, the underlying reason for the establishment of the reincarnation line and for the construction of the relevant genealogy can be identified.

The theory of the three bodies (*kāyas*) and the different levels of existence, as well as the general belief in reincarnation, can be seen as the religious preconditions for the establishment of the lineage. However, the reenactment of relationships appears in Chokyi Dronma/Kunga Sangmo's case, as in more prominent examples, as a determining factor; it created the conditions under which a complex interplay of religious, psychological, and social factors was not only possible but also highly desirable. This said, the recognition of a human being as the rebirth of a deceased one requires an understanding that goes beyond sheer instrumentality, which would imply a cynicism and a degree of manipulation by the parties involved that would be, at least in principle, incompatible with their own belief system. Credentials of genuine belief and adequate religious practice on the part of the validating authority are foundational and central to the claim of authenticity. This is one of the main points of contention in allegations of illegitimate and personally motivated authenticating procedures, as in current disputes concerning the selection of prominent reincarnations (see introduction).

The construction of lines of reincarnations that ultimately led back to India is directly related to the position of India in Tibet's spiritual landscape as the prime source of Buddhism. When the Tibetan Buddhist canon was first assembled in Narthang in 1310–20, the authoritativeness of a text was measured against the availability of Indian originals from which it was translated. Indian origin was thus an indicator of authenticity and authority. Indian tantric deities, with their rituals and narratives, were embodied in Tibet in many interrelated forms: landscapes, statues, paintings, melodies, gestures, and texts. A human reincarnation can thus be seen as similar to a sacred text that refers to an Indian spiritual ancestry. It is telling that the biography of Chokyi Dronma begins with an invocation to Vajravārāhī in which the name is not translated and is rendered in Sanskrit. This was not only an invocation but also a reference to the spiritual ancestry. Like a translation, the contingent manifestation of the deity in the local idiom had to be validated by someone with spiritual authority—in the case of Kunga Sangmo, either Thangtong Gyalpo or Chime Drupa or both. The question of authenticity, however, was a source of both legitimacy and potential competing claims.

Perhaps it is not a mere coincidence that the establishment of formal, institutionalized reincarnation lines acknowledged by the Tibetan tradition gained momentum roughly during the same period as the codification of the Tibetan canon as a standard body of scriptures, from the early fourteenth century. Sectarian divides had started to crystallize, often along the lines of politico-religious alliances, making the boundaries between inclusion and exclusion, authentic and spurious, acceptable and unacceptable increasingly important.

While the authors of the *Bo dong chos 'byung* and of Thangtong Gyalpo's most famous biography were writing, Tibet was ruled by the kings of Tsang, who seem to have supported the Bodongpa tradition—and notably the more prominent Karmapa. The kings of Tsang, who had seized power from the Rinpungpa in 1565, had become the open enemies of the rising Gelugpa. They also took over large areas in central and western Tibet, sealing, by 1620, the doom of the Kingdom of Gungthang in which Chokyi Dronma had been born almost 200 years earlier. The Tsang rulers seem to have controlled and supported the Samding Dorje Phagmo, for the *Shel dkar chos 'byung* (folio 54a) mentions that they appointed a woman called Yeshe Tshomo, an incarnation of Lakṣmīṅkarā, as abbess of Shekar and all Bodongpa monasteries.[53] She must have been short-lived as claimed by

*Succession and Spiritual Lineages: Meaning and Mysteries of Chokyi Dronma's Reincarnation*

the *Shel dkar chos 'byung,* for by 1654 the Fifth Dalai Lama was already interacting with her following reincarnation, Dechen Thrinley Tshomo.

It is not surprising that when the Fifth Dalai Lama rose to power after having defeated the King of Tsang, the Bodongpa tradition declined drastically, given its political and religious allegiances. The institution of the Samding Dorje Phagmo, however, did not fade under his authority but was reshaped and taken over by the new religious regime. Its profile was enhanced, like that of its main seat, Samding—the place where the tradition of the Dorje Phagmo was established and integrated within the ancient mythology of the Tibetan landscape that I shall discuss in the next chapter.

6

## "LADY OF THE LAKE"
### *The Dorje Phagmo at Samding*

*Urgyen Tshomo was the third incarnation of Chokyi Dronma, after Kunga Sangmo* and Nyendra Sangmo, and with her the term *tshomo* started to appear within the names of the Dorje Phagmo reincarnations: Urgyen Tshomo, Yeshe Tshomo, Dechen Thrinley Tshomo. *Tshomo* seems to be both part of the personal name and a sort of title; since *tsho* (*mtsho*) means lake and *mo* is a female nominalizing particle, the name or epithet can be glossed as "Lady of the Lake," which is reflected in some travel accounts (for example, Mageot 1974:179). The name was presumably related to the evolution of the Dorje Phagmo tradition that was gradually consolidating at its main seat, Samding monastery near the holy Yamdrog Lake in southern Tibet. It also evoked the more general association between the feminine and the lake that is pervasive in Tibetan landscape mythology and can still be found today, even in the name *gYu mtsho,* literally "Turquoise Lake," for the *Journal of Women's Studies* published in Dharamsala—the first issue of which, in 1993, featured an article on the Dorje Phagmo.

## Samding Monastery, the "Throne" Overlooking a Landscape of Lakes

Yamdrog Lake, one of the great lakes of Tibet, lies southwest of Lhasa. Known as Yamdrog Yumtsho or Palti, it has a complex and distinctive shape that resembles a scorpion. Between its "claws" lies another, smaller and darker lake, called the "demoness lake" by using the almost equivalent names Dumotsho (bDud mo mtsho), Dremotsho ('Dre mo mtsho), or Sinmotsho (Srin mo mtsho). Hills and marshland separate the demoness from the scorpion, and on one of the slopes overlooking the demoness lake and the narrow gorge of the stream flowing out of it lies the monastery of Samding.

The monastery dominates a vast plain, surrounded by hills and the snow-capped peaks of Nojin Gansang, the Karu La to the west, and the distant Kula Kangri to the south. The north-facing slopes of the hill where the monastery perches show what is left of an ancient holy juniper forest, one of the highest in the world. Across the plain is the village of Nakartse, where the ruins of the ancient fortress bear silent testimony to the grandeur of its former rulers and the monastery of Ngonga overlooks the old village and the new buildings and building sites that are quickly adding to it. Here, in 1453, the rulers of Nakartse completed the biography of Bodong Chogle Namgyal, defining the locality as:

> The excellent house of Nakartse, the site in which [Bodong] Chogle Namgyal accomplished his deeds of virtue, the palace of [the mountain god] Nojing Kangwa Sangpo (Nojing Gangsang), to the east of the great mountain Kailash, on the shore of the Yumtsho Chugmo (Lake Yamdrog), the abode of Tshomen Gyalmo [the Queen of the Spirits of the Lake], the protectress of the doctrine of the Great Teacher Padma-Akara (Padmasambhava). (Biography of Bodong Chogle Namgyal 415)

Samding has a prominent position in this landscape and is understandably called "the throne of Yamdrog Lake." A popular song goes:

> On the throne of Yamdrok lake
> Sits the Shabdrung[1] Dorjee Phagmo
> We delay not because we lack faith
> We are coming, after circumambulating the Yamdrok lake.
> (DHONDUP AND TASHI TSERING 1979:12)

The Yamdrog landscape has been a privileged site for Buddhist pilgrimage since Tibetan imperial and even pre-imperial times. The area that used to be known as Nub (sNubs) stretched westward from Yamdrog Lake, also called Nub Lake; it was reckoned as one of the petty kingdoms unified under the rule of the kings of Yarlung at the dawn of Tibetan history (see chapter 1). As was common practice all over Tibet, the local ruling house gave great emphasis to territorial cults, for the king's power was linked to the deities of the country he ruled. Samten Karmay observes that the ancestral deities called *kula* (*sku bla*) that played a major part in ancient Tibetan royal religion were widely venerated:

> They were propitiated by the kings as well as by their feudal chiefs residing in different territories under the dominion. Feudal chieftains propitiated their own particular mountain deities, often taken as their ancestral clan divinities, just as the kings themselves in Yarlung propitiated Yar-lha Sham-po. (Karmay 1996:66)

In this context, the relationships among territorial gods, frequently conceived in the idiom of kinship, often reflected hierarchical relationships among rulers. The ancient lords of Nub reportedly worshiped their territorial deities before being integrated in the wider politico-religious design of the Tibetan empire (see *dBa' bzhed* folio 30a). The Nub area was probably included in the emerging kingdom before the reign of Songtsen Gampo, for ministers belonging to the Nub clan appear already among his ancestors (Bacot 1940:100). Nub was the clan name of important ministers throughout the dynastic period (sixth–ninth centuries). In addition, the *Dunhuang Annals* and other dynastic texts mention some localities in this area as sites for the summer residence of the Tibetan sovereign, summer councils, and royal ancestral worship, whereas the *mKhas pa'i dga' ston,* written in the sixteenth century but notably based on earlier sources, tells of Songtsen Gampo's filling in one of the Yamdrog lakes (Petech 1988:261–269).

With the Buddhification of Tibet, the sacredness of the Yamdrog landscape was redefined in terms of Buddhist mythology. The Samding monastic community still tells the famous story reported in Sarat Chandra Das's travel account (Das 1988 [1902]), according to which the monastery keeps the demoness lake under control; if the monastery were destroyed, the whole of Tibet would be flooded and annihilated. This tale is part of both a general Tibetan and a more localized landscape mythology: Samding is located on the heart of a giant demoness lying on her back, covering the entire area up to the demoness lake.

Originally there was a small spring in that place, which was defiled when the demoness washed her hair in it. As a consequence, the spring swelled and became the lake. Guntram Hazod, reviewing this system of myths, observes that:

> The monastery and the cultic presence of rDo rje Phag mo serve to cast a lasting spell on the water, which otherwise would flood over Tibet if it was broken. Thus the foundation of the monastery stands in direct relation to the myth according to which Avalokiteśvara and Tārā, in the form of Ta mgrin (Hayagrīva) and rDo rje phag mo, overpowered the sea monster (*chu srin*, i.e., *makara*) of the Yar 'brog lake. (1998:67)

This Buddhist myth is reported by Sarat Chadra Das:

> In days of old, before the time when the Buddha Gautama appeared, there was a hideous monster called Matrankaru, who spread ruin and terror over the world. He was the chief of the legions of demons, goblins, and other evil spirits. . . . Finally the Buddha and gods held council to compass about Matrankaru's destruction, and it was decided that Shenrezig [*sic*] should take the form of Tamdrin ("Horse-neck") and his consort, Dolma, that of Dorje Phagmo ("the Diamond Sow") . . . both were lying prostrate at the feet of the two divinities. But their lives were spared and Mantrankaru became a devout follower of the Buddha, a defender of the faith. (1902:138–139)

This set of myths works on a number of interpretative levels, as it evokes many well-known themes: the subjugation of the demoness representing the Tibetan land through the construction of Buddhist temples that pin her down to the ground (Gyatso 1989:33ff.); the original lake and the related potential flood (Hazod 1998:67); the scorpion as a symbol averting evil; the Indian mythology of Buddhification through the defeat of evil monsters. The story's warning stands out in an examination of its modern history: the monastery—like many others—was almost completely destroyed during the Cultural Revolution. Now it has been rebuilt, thanks to the efforts of its monastic community led by the senior monk, Thubten Namgyal, and the Twelfth Samding Dorje Phagmo. Before turning to the complexities of the twentieth and twenty-first centuries, which I shall do in the next chapter, I will explore how the Dorje Phagmo in Samding monastery, on the "throne of Yamdrog Lake," has acquired, over the centuries, a distinctive symbolic character that links her to the sacred geography and the destiny of the whole of Tibet.

How did real human beings, like Chokyi Dronma, become inscribed in the landscape? This seems to have happened according to different paradigms: the transformation of deceased leaders and extraordinary human beings into ancestors inhabiting topographical features; Buddhist heroes subjugating pre-Buddhist deities; the integration of preexisting sacred sites in a "landscape *maṇḍala*" (Macdonald 1997; Huber 1999:26–29) with the interpretation of geographical features as the embodiment of tantric deities. I shall review those aspects that are most relevant to the establishment of the Samding Dorje Phagmo.

A number of scholars (Karmay 1996:59ff.; Huber 1999:21ff.) have noticed that, in general, two distinctive modes of understanding the sacredness of the landscape can be identified. When the landscape is perceived in terms of pre-Buddhist or Buddhified territorial deities, the entities that inhabit it are seen as endowed with their own subjectivity and agency. When the landscape is perceived as a place for pilgrimage, for the accumulation of merit according to a Mahāyānistic approach, it tends to be seen as the site, the *ne* (*gnas*), in which Buddhist personalities dwelled and a stage for the soteriological itinerary of the practitioner. These two contrasting readings inform, for example, the general distinction between *yullhas* (*yul lha*) and *neris* (*gnas ri*), i.e., mountain deities and mountains as pilgrimage sites. Both readings often coexist in the day-to-day practice of the lay and the monastic communities, albeit with different emphasis and purposes. They are two of the many possible ways of "being in the landscape" (Humphrey 1996:135ff.).

The tantric view of the landscape as a *maṇḍala* with embodied tantric deities offers a creative synthesis of these approaches and of Buddhist and non-Buddhist elements in general. After all, Buddhism is said to have been established in Tibet in the eighth century thanks to Padmasambhava, the tantric master and hero *par excellence*. Śāntarakṣita, the saintly monk who had been invited to propagate Buddhism in the Land of Snows, could not have made it alone and had invited him. The *dBa' bzhed*—one of the earliest sources on this subject—thus describes a salient moment of the taming:

> Padmasambhava performed a mirror divination . . . and pronounced the names of all the gods (*lha*) and water spirits (*klu*) that had caused the flood of Phang thang and the fire in the Lhasa castle, the epidemics among people and cattle, and the famines. Then, calling the names and the clans of all the wicked [gods and spirits], he summoned them to his presence. They descended into human beings[2] and were severely threatened by Padmasambhava. With the help of a translator,

Śāntarakṣita taught them the doctrine of cause and effect and made the truth evident. Afterward Padmasambhava told the Tibetan king: "Henceforth, practice the holy doctrine [i.e., Buddhism] as you like in the country of Tibet! Gods and spirits have been bound by oath." (*dBa' bzhed* folio 12a, b)

Invoking the names of local gods and spirits, he made them present, presumably like some priests of ancestral and territorial cults still do in remote corners of Tibet and the Himalayas.[3] More generally, this passage is a powerful metaphor for how Buddhification relied on the translation of ritual idioms and their adaptation to the preexisting religious setting.

Since the eighth century, from the foundation of the first Buddhist monastery at Samye and the deeds of Padmasambhava and Śāntarakṣita, a kaleidoscope of Buddhification myths has colored the Tibetan landscape. Toni Huber observed that the notions defining sacred places have no Buddhist characteristics per se, even if they can be integrated in Buddhist views (1999:23ff.). In Tibetan landscapes, therefore, we can see how pre-Buddhist beliefs and Buddhist representations merged in many places of memory and religious significance.

Rather than one coherent system or a fluid transformation, the process of interpretation and reinterpretation of the landscape can be seen as "dialogical," following Mumford's adaptation of Bakhtin's notion (Mumford 1989), for it blended different, mutually defining traditions and ways of "being in the landscape." Over the centuries various "landscapes" reflected the social agencies that produced them, lay and monastic, ancestral and tantric, local and pan-Tibetan, and more recently, sacred and secular. As observed by Caroline Humphrey in relation to Mongolian landscapes, "there is a connection between topographies, descriptive terminologies for landscapes and political structures, and . . . these 'place' different kinds of 'ego' in the world'" (1995:158).

At Samding, the head monk, the late Thubten Namgyal, used to say, "In former times Nojin Gangsang was the protector of Yamdrog; today it is Tashi Ombar" (Hazod 1998:65). The protector of the Bodongpa, Tashi Ombar, the "Radiant Light of Good Luck" riding his blue horse, has thus become integrated within a preexisting landscape mythology. Even though Tashi Ombar has become the central deity in the area, rituals and offerings of incense (*lha bsangs*) are celebrated for the ancient god Nojin Gangsang on a regular basis by both the lay community and the monastics. By custom, when a monastery is established, the monastic community takes over some of the local preexisting territorial cults, re-forming them. The words of Thubten Namgyal reflect the immediate relationship between lay religiosity and the Buddhist monastic institution, but on the basis of an ancient mythology that predates the tradition to which he belongs. The mountain god Nojin Gangsang is the territorial god (*yul lha*) protecting Yamdrog. Historically he was a particular protector of the Yamdrog ruling house and of the local rulers of the Rinpung and Gyantshe area (Hazod 1998:65). Oral traditions of upper Yarlung mention him as the brother of the ancestral mountain god of the Tibetan kings, Yarlha Shampo, making a direct link with the Tibetan imperial ancestry (Hazod 1998:66). Nojing Gangsang is also considered the male consort of the Yamdrog Lake (Karmay 1996:59), in a dyad that is invoked in the final verses of the biography of Bodong Chogle Namgyal and recalls other famous couples, such as the lake Namtsho and the mountain Nyanchen Thanglha, the lake Tangra Yumtsho and the mountain Chang Targo, and the lake Mapaham Yumtsho and Mount Kailash (Bellezza 1997).

Although specific rituals or myths are not necessarily ancient, they imply ritual idioms and metaphors that have been part of Tibetan imagery since imperial times. They are based on the ancient vertical tripartition of the cosmos: gods of the sky (*lha*), spirits of the intermediate space (*btsan*), and spirits of the underworld and the underground waters (*klu*). They also refer to forms of royal ancestral mythology and cults that are known from the oldest historical sources. Samten Karmay, on the basis of both textual sources and ethnographic evidence, states that "The idea of the local mountain deity as the ancestral origin of the local people goes back a long way into history. It bears a relation to the origin myth of the first Tibetan king, gNya'-khri btsan po" (1996:60). He also notices that in the context of territorial cults, "the prestige of the leader of the community is often thought to be due to the special favors they receive from the local mountain deity" (1996:59). Thus mountains had and have a central role in territorial cults. Lakes are important too, but often have a different connotation. They can be the abode of a sort of "soul" of the community, as *lamtsho* (*bla mtsho*), and are frequently associated with prophecy and oracles. They are also associated with very ancient categories of local spirits (*klu, klu mo, sman,* etc.). In the light of the mythology of the sacred landscape, the reference to the mountain god Nojin Gangsang and the lake goddess Tshomen Gyalmo, the "Queen of the Spirits of the Lake," at the end of the biography of Bodong Chogle Namgyal can be understood. The author, who was also the local ruler, invoked them as long-standing protectors of his territory and his ruling house, which undoubtedly reverberated with pre-Buddhist landscape mythologies beyond any Buddhist reframing of rituals and gods.

When the Dorje Phagmo tradition was established at Yamdrog with the support of the lords of Nakartse, the process followed the idiom and the views of tantric rituality. However, the Tibetan imperial legacy was evoked as well, and in a double way: through the imperial ancestry of Chokyi Dronma, the actual founding figure of the reincarnation line, and through the sacred landscape in which she became gradually inscribed. It is well known that both the Karmapa and the Dalai Lama, as competing spiritual and political heirs of Songtsen Gampo, the Tibetan sovereign and incarnation of Avalokiteśvara, harnessed imperial themes to shape their rule and assert their spiritual and temporal authority (Van der Kuijp 2005:24; Richardson 1998:339). The Samding Dorje Phagmo appeared as a symbolic counterpart in tantric terms as Vajrayoginī or Tārā (Dhondup and Tashi Tsering 1979). However, she also evoked older territorial cults in being associated with the lake, the prophetic, and the feminine. She might even have evoked the myth of the first Tibetan king, who descended from the sky on a mountain and married a female spirit of the underworld and the underground waters. This primal myth in many forms is widespread in Tibetan historical literature and very much alive in contemporary popular religion, as a part of the local symbolic exegesis of territorial cults (see Karmay 1996:60; Diemberger 2007). It seems to reflect a Tibetan "imperial metaphor," paralleling the definition that Stephan Feuchtwang has evocatively given to popular religion in China. Thus it shows a connection to imperial cults and refers "to the same cosmic time as the claims to legitimacy of the ruling dynasties," but is distinct from them (Feuchtwang 2001:vii).[4]

The sense of place and power of Tibetan territorial cults is equally imperial, yet distinctive. It is usually located primarily within the lay community rather than the monastic establishment (Karmay 1996:59–75), even though monasteries have, at times, taken over some aspects of popular religiosity. The relationship between the monastic and the lay communities is reflected and shaped in rituals in which both participate. Samding is a telling example: before the Cultural Revolution, a female oracle lived in the village below the monastery; she used to be possessed by a local mountain god, a certain Gangkar Gyalpo, King of the White Mountain—either equivalent or related to Nojin Gangsang.[5] Above the village, the Dorje Phagmo seated on her throne within the monastery represented the monastic institution in the eyes of its subjects in a way not very different from any other monastery. In the local context, the two holy women epitomized two different forms of sacredness, territorial and Buddhist monastic, with seasonal collective rituals (*yarsol* and *gunsol*) in which Tashi Ombar, the blue horseman protecting the Bodongpa tradition, played a central role (see also Tucci 1987:86), providing a tenuous but effective integration. In the broader Tibetan context, however, the Dorje Phagmo had a different, distinctive position not only as a tantric female deity but also as the lady of the Yamdrog Lake. She was the queen on the throne of Yamdrog, referring to a landscape mythology of holy mountains and lakes on a different spatial and temporal scale. The imperial metaphor could thus be experienced differently locally, regionally, or in a pan-Tibetan perspective. It could also be harnessed, but not fully appropriated, by a rising political and religious power. The Fifth Dalai Lama put great effort into reviving places of imperial memory and instigated significant reforms of other religious traditions and some aspects of lay religiosity. He integrated them selectively into his political and religious vision, which was built on that of famous precursors such as Thangtong Gyalpo and the Phagmodrupa rulers.[6] The Tibetan imperial metaphor, blending Buddhism with memories of ancient Tibet and territorial cults, was parallel to and potentially competitive with the imperial authority of China. A distinctive feature of Tibetan culture over the centuries, territorial cults were also an early and important part of Tibet's religious revival in the post-Mao era, and have been a powerful expression of regional and national identity up to the present day (Karmay 1994:112–120).

## From Princess to Symbol in the Tibetan Landscape

Local oral tradition claims that Chokyi Dronma erected the first buildings of what would become Samding monastery.[7] She came over from Tsari, following the Tsari protectors,[8] who showed her the way and who are still considered to inhabit two small shrines behind the northern wall of the monastery.

From a historical point of view, Chokyi Dronma's participation in the founding of the monastery is unlikely, albeit not impossible. There is no mention in her biography of her passing through Nakartse and Samding when she traveled through the Yamdrog area in 1454. Even though they were not far from the main route, a visit would have required a significant detour and is unlikely to have been omitted in her "travelogue." The *Bo dong chos 'byung* and the biography of Thangtong Gyalpo state that she reached Tsari a few months later and died there, aged thirty-three, in 1455/56. She would have had very little time to go to Samding and establish the monastery, while working on Thangtong Gyalpo's bridges. Also, none of the earlier sources mentions that she was actually involved

*"Lady of the Lake": The Dorje Phagmo at Samding*

in the founding of Samding monastery. It is thus more likely that Bodong Chogle Namgyal or another master first constructed a small meditation place at Samding, perhaps in a holy site that was already associated with preexisting territorial cults, and that Chokyi Dronma's reincarnation, Kunga Sangmo, built on that infrastructure. Kunga Sangmo is reported in the *Bo dong chos 'byung* as having restored Samding with the help of the Yamdrog rulers (see previous chapter).⁹ She came from southeastern Tibet, and it is quite possible that some of her deeds and those of Chokyi Dronma may have merged in the popular recollection. Such narratives blended individual lives and landscape mythology in innumerable ways that echoed and built on one another. Chokyi Dronma emerged as a foundational figure, embodying not only tantric sacredness but also the Tibetan imperial legacy associated with her persona. Kunga Sangmo reenacted and developed that imperial profile by taking an active part in the revival of ancient places of dynastic memory such as Yarlung Sheldrag (Sørensen and Hazod 2005:108). All this presumably informed the process of ritualization by which Chokyi Dronma, a living princess, became a spiritual entity, inhabiting Tibetan sacred landscapes and prophetic temporalities. She ultimately appears as the queen seated on the throne of Yamdrog, beyond the limitations of space, time, and human generations; and thus she still is, in the eyes of those who see her there.

Tibetan masters have long struggled with discrepancies in textual sources that were often clearly at odds with each other and with authoritative religious views. The case of Padmasambhava's journey to Tibet is perhaps the most famous example; contradictory findings concerning the length of his stay and extent of his deeds were often reconciled by referring to different levels of perception and of life, as in, for example, Dudjom Rinpoche's *History of Buddhism* (Gyurme Dorje and Kapstein 1991:518), following the example of many earlier Tibetan authors. This sort of solution, however, did not prove completely satisfactory for a "rationalist"¹⁰ such as the Tibetan historian Tāranātha (1575–1634), who stated:

> In the eyes of his disciple whose vision is pure, he is still alive now . . . whatever length of time is adopted [for his stay], it is appropriate since he is [capable] of simultaneously and permanently manifesting an apparition of his body in all paradises. This is true, but the juxtaposition of the early and the late periods is nevertheless not correct because what was the general opinion of men at that time has to be regarded as more correct than anything else. (Tāranātha in Blondeau 1980:48)

FIGURE 6.1 An incarnation of the Dorje Phagmo called Chokyi Dronme/a Kunga Sangmo, after a modern mural painting at Nyemo Chekar monastery. *Karen Diemberger*

In the spirit of both approaches, I have tried to elucidate Chokyi Dronma's undeniable link to Samding monastery despite its doubtful historicity. Chokyi Dronma and Kunga Sangmo were considered to be successive reincarnations of the same person and the embodiment of the same deity. That two successive reincarnations may, at times, be considered as one person is not unfamiliar in

277
*"Lady of the Lake": The Dorje Phagmo at Samding*

the Tibetan context, as shown by the case of the Karmapa (Wylie 1978:585). This perception also seems to underlie the visual representations of the Dorje Phagmo at Nyemo, where one of the women is called Chokyi Dronme Kunga Sangmo, merging the names of both reincarnations into one.

Samding monastery appears in several independent historical sources covering Kunga Sangmo's time,[11] so it must have already been functioning as a religious center. Kunga Sangmo, however, did not reside there permanently and spent a great deal of her life traveling around. Nyendra Sangmo, the next reincarnation, established a school of philosophy at Samding, which led to significant growth of the monastery. Around this time, Samding gradually became the main seat of the tradition, for it is where both Nyendra Sangmo and Chime Palsang died. At the time of Urgyen Tshomo (born around 1543), the Dorje Phagmo tradition seems to have been solidly established and had entered the landscape mythology of the Yamdrog region.

## The Time of the Fifth Dalai Lama and the Time of Manchu Overlordship

Eminent figures of the Gelugpa tradition such as Gendun Drupa (1391–1474), posthumously recognized as the First Dalai Lama, and Khedrub Geleg (1385–1438), posthumously recognized as the First Panchen Lama, had been disciples of Bodong Chogle Namgyal. At that time, teacher-disciple relations often cut across sectarian affiliations. However, that had changed dramatically in the intervening years, and the Fifth Dalai Lama seems to have been suspicious of the Bodongpa of his time, which is not surprising given their political and religious allegiances (see previous chapter). He first encountered the Samding Dorje Phagmo when he was three years old, around 1620. Reporting his sighting of the holy woman, at that time the elderly Urgyen Tshomo, the Dalai Lama mentions in his autobiography that he did not have any contact with her and comments on the fact that there was then no understanding of what was to be respected and what not in relation to doctrinal corruption (Autobiography of the Fifth Dalai Lama 50).

The fate of the Samding Dorje Phagmo might have been different if the mother of the Fifth Dalai Lama had not been from the ruling family of Nakartse. She was a remarkable figure and still an important historical figure when Giuseppe Tucci traveled through Nakartse in 1949, for he noticed a statue of her:

The daughter of the Nakartse prince gave birth to the Fifth Dalai Lama. A baked-earth statue of her is kept in the fortress temple, built above the ancient palace; a likeness with strong, marked features pointing to a bold nature, like that of her son, who was undoubtedly one of Tibet's outstanding personalities. (Tucci 1987:87)

For centuries the Yamdrog rulers had been supporters of Samding monastery, and the *Deb ther dmar po gsar ma* (58) states that the whole area followed the Bodongpa tradition. There must have been some regular interaction between the Samding Dorje Phagmo and the ruling family of Nakartse throughout the Fifth Dalai Lama's life. His autobiography tells that when he went to Shigatse in 1654 and stopped at Lungsang (in the vicinity of Nakartse), his maternal uncle, the Shabdrung of Nakartse, arrived there with Dechen Thrinley Tshomo, the reincarnation of Urgyen Tshomo (448). The relationship to the Samding Dorje Phagmo was by then much closer than it had been during his childhood. However, his attitude toward the Samding reincarnation probably reflected not only his maternal family ties and beliefs but also a wider political and religious design that bore the traces of Thangtong Gyalpo's vision (see page 275).

Having established the Tibetan government in 1642, thanks to the armed intervention of Guushi Khan and the Hoshuud Mongols, who defeated the King of Tsang and various rival Mongolian groups, the Fifth Dalai Lama instigated radical administrative and religious reforms of the country. He thereby reserved a particular position for the Dorje Phagmo, the incarnation of a female religious figure who had been close to Thangtong Gyalpo, a spiritual master who deeply inspired him. Within the new religious and political order, the Dorje Phagmo was enhanced, reformed, and redefined in relation to the Dalai Lama. Dechen Thrinley Tshomo, the successor of Urgyen Tshomo, and probably of a short-lived Yeshe Tshomo, became a new foundational figure, often more clearly remembered than Chokyi Dronma (Sarat Chadra Das 1988 [1902]:136; K. Dondhup and Tashi Tsering 1979:12). Her treatment is in striking contrast to that of another sacred woman of the time, the so-called Lhatse Ponmo, who was condemned for an unfavorable prophecy and escaped to eastern Tibet, where she became the founder of another, less prominent female reincarnation line, that of the Gunru Khandro (Chayet 2002:74ff.; Tashi Tsering 1994:27–47). The stories of the Samding Dorje Phagmo and the Gunru Khandro, together with those of female spirit possession and prophecy linked with the cult of Vajrayoginī (Germano and Gyatso 2000:246–247), seem to indicate that these female reincarnations, although exceptional, were probably related to a larger range of popular practices in which women played an important part. The destiny of these women and their traditions was inextricably intertwined with the politics of their day.

As the institution of the Dorje Phagmo was altered and enhanced, the tradition she actually belonged to waned. The decline of the Bodongpa under Gelugpa rule is clear from the accounts of how the new government of Tibet transformed some of their most important monasteries into centers of Gelugpa worship (*Vaiḍūrya ser po* 396–410; *Shel dkar chos 'byung* folio 61b). Remarkably, after a complex negotiation, some of these monasteries were allowed to retain Tashi Ombar, the blue horseman of the Bodongpa, as their protector, for he was able to defend monasteries and villages against weather catastrophes and famines (*Shel dkar chos byung* folio 65–66).

The late Thubten Namgyal, head monk of Samding until his death in July 2000, commented on how the weakening of the Bodongpa tradition paradoxically corresponded to the strengthening of Samding monastery itself. He reported that at the time of the Fifth Dalai Lama, the main seat at Bodong E became one of the tenures of Samding, which in turn became the most important monastery. In making this statement, he referred to land tenure documents, which unfortunately were destroyed in the Cultural Revolution, that reported Bodong E as one of the thirteen main tenures of Samding.

The new symbolic complementarity of the Dorje Phagmo to the Dalai Lama is reflected not only in the allocation of thrones inside Samding monastery but also in a series of mural paintings at Nenying monastery, near Gyantse. In a temple rebuilt after the destruction during the 1904 Younghusband military expedition are several mural paintings said to reproduce those that adorned the walls of the previous building. The portrait of the Fifth Dalai Lama with his two main disciples is located diametrically opposite to that of the Dorje Phagmo with two junior Dorje Phagmos. The numerous wrinkles on the face of the larger figure suggest that this was the Dorje Phagmo the Fifth Dalai Lama experienced first, the elderly Urgyen Tshomo. The smaller two, one with a red hat and one with a black hat, similar to that of the Karmapa, may refer to other reincarnations of that period.

According to the local monastic community, Nenying monastery was offered by Pholhane Sonam Tobgye (1689–1747) to the Dorje Phagmo as a reward for a favor in a crucial moment: she presented him with a horse when he was escaping from his enemies. Later, when he became the ruler of Tibet, he remembered this and expressed his gratitude generously. Like the more famous legend (see

FIGURE 6.2 The Fifth Dalai Lama and the Dorje Phagmo facing each other, after two mural paintings at Nenying monastery. *Karen Diemberger*

Preface) about how the Dorje Phagmo transformed herself into a sow to defend her monastery against the Dzungars, this story reveals the monastery's allegiance in the politics of the era.

Mongolian rule in Tibet, which in 1642 had allowed the Fifth Dalai Lama to unify the country and establish the new government within a loose alliance among Mongols, Manchus, and Tibetans, was characterized by a difficult relationship between Tibetan and Mongolian leadership. When Lhabsang Khan, a grandson of Guushi Khan, in 1697 reclaimed the title of King of Tibet and tried to restore the political authority his grandfather had wielded, these tensions exploded in a period of unrest and disputes that culminated in 1705 with the execution of the Tibetan regent, Desi Sangye Gyatso, and the deposition of the Sixth Dalai Lama. Many Tibetans were critical of the Mongolian ruler and welcomed the arrival of another Mongolian group, the Dzungar, who killed him in 1716. However, as the Dzungar started destroying monasteries and sacking villages, the attitude of the Tibetan population quickly changed. Amid internal strife and foreign invasion, Pholhane emerged as a powerful leader with the backing of the Qing emperors. In 1720 the Qing army intervened, pacified the situation, and established formal suzerainty over Tibet. Under their protection, Pholhane became the ruler and the Seventh Dalai Lama was enthroned. Samding seems to have been both supportive of Pholhane and hostile to the Dzungars. In gratitude, the Seventh Dalai Lama bestowed upon the Eighth Samding Dorje Phagmo the title of *Hu thug tu*. This indicated by the use of a Mongolian term a high reincarnated lama and ensured that the Dorje Phagmo was officially recognized by the Qing court, which she also visited during her lifetime (Dorje Phagmo and Thubten Namgyal 1995:40).

The eighteenth-century events were a further step in the institutionalization and ritualization of the Samding Dorje Phagmo, part of a larger process in which the Qing court incorporated Tibet in its imperial framework, instigating some reforms of Tibetan religious practices, especially those that had political implications such as the selection of reincarnations and the use of oracles. A decree in 1792 by Emperor Qianlong reveals the spirit of these reforms: "Improve their religion without changing their custom; straighten their policy without inconveniencing them" (Richardson 1974:78).

For example, the procedure for the selection of important reincarnations such as the Dalai Lama and the Panchen Lama, which had been redefined under the Fifth Dalai Lama in the new political setting, was increasingly formalized and brought under the control of the Qing empire through the introduction of practices such as the drawing of lots in the so-called "Golden Vase" ceremony.[12] The reforms benefited the Samding Dorje Phagmo, who enjoyed a rise in rank and recognition. This moment is illustrated in a mural painting at Samding monastery showing the Eighth Dorje Phagmo seated on her throne and being presented with her hat and numerous donations. She was indeed venerated, but appeared increasingly distant from common people's experience. Yet, every time a Dorje Phagmo died and was reborn, a human aspect once again came into play. A female child who showed spontaneous signs considered to be miraculous underwent the complex process of selection, which revealed her as the new reincarnation in the eyes of the search committee. Once the final decision was taken, the girl grew into her predefined identity. She adopted the distinctive ritualized behavior of the Dorje Phagmo and added further knowledge about what she had been in her previous life by learning preexisting narratives, just as Kunga Sangmo did after being recognized as the reincarnation of Chokyi Dronma.

Instead of the loose network of Chokyi Dronma's disciples, an institution called *labrang* (*bla brang*), which managed all the practicalities and the socioeconomic implications around a reincarnation, was in charge. The authority to declare the reincarnation as "authentic" now rested, formally, with the Dalai Lama or his regent, and was endorsed by the Qing emperor.

Commenting on reincarnation as a political innovation in Tibetan Buddhism, Wylie drew on Max Weber, suggesting that this change "would facilitate the transition from charisma of the person to a charisma of the office" (1978:584). "The office" was in this case identical with the deity/human embodiment as defined through a narrative template and a system of ritual behaviors. Dorje Phagmo's long hair, full monastic robe, and postures reflected the shared, often vague memory of the princess who had founded the line in the fifteenth century and the distinctive features of the deity. The Dorje Phagmo, through a ritualization that shaped every single moment of the life of the woman embodying her, had thus become incommensurably removed from the day-to-day experience of her worshippers. She was close to them in a different way as a religious icon. Her person itself had become the ritual—in her own behavior, in how people related to her, and in the way she was made present through ritual recitation. For example, a text dating from the second half of the nineteenth century, still in use at Samding, reports a set of prayers that invoke the esoteric manifestation of the deity and her human emanations. Its title is *The Prayer to the Genealogy of the Mother of the Buddhas Dorje Phagmo, Called the Steady Rain of Blessings.*[13] It consists of two parallel recitations; the first starts with an invocation to the deity Dorje Phagmo, followed by verses that mention the Indian and the Tibetan worldly emanations of the deity, recalling their salient features. The second ritual text, attached to this, is called *Prayer to the Biography of the Venerable Dorje Phagmo with the Sequence of Human Reincarnations, Which Brings the Rain of Blessing Nectar.*[14]

Reciting these prayers, the celebrating community creates continuity between the esoterical spiritual entity and its human manifestations, coming to the world as "a rain of blessings." The words evoke powerful images in the minds of those reciting and listening. They make the presence of the Dorje Phagmo immediately perceivable in her current embodiment and revive the memory of the women who have embodied her. They celebrate Chokyi Dronma as the first holder of the Bodongpa tradition and a foundational figure and recall all the great women of the past who have been authoritative referents for the followers of the tradition. Over the centuries, Chokyi Dronma's life became first a narrative, then part of a spiritual lineage, and eventually an evocative ritual recitation. Seated on the throne of Yamdrog, the Dorje Phagmo held an "office" that did not imply the rule of the country, as did that of the Dalai Lama, but a considerable symbolic and real power complementary to it.

### The "Holiest Woman of Tibet": The Dorje Phagmo in the Eyes of Foreign Travelers

As the Dorje Phagmo was among the highest ranking personalities of her time, some foreign travelers met her on religious and social occasions in Lhasa or Shigatse, while others visited Samding monastery, which was close to one of the main routes linking those two major cities of Tibet. In the late eighteenth century, the Samding Dorje Phagmo thus began to be mentioned in travel accounts and books on Tibet. In 1775 George Bogle and Alexander Hamilton, respectively an envoy and a doctor of the East India Company, had several interactions with the Dorje Phagmo, who was a relative of the Third (Sixth) Panchen Lama, and described her in the accounts to which I referred earlier (see Introduction). One century later Sarat Chadra Das, having fallen ill during his journey, took refuge at Samding and enjoyed a closer interaction with the Dorje Phagmo, which he described in his book, an invaluable source on the Dorje Phagmo and the Yamdrog mythology (Das 1988 [1902]).

The members of the Younghusband military expedition visited Samding in 1904 but did not meet the Dorje Phagmo, who was at that time a young girl and had taken refuge in Lhasa with her mother. Waddell, the doctor and archaeologist of the mission, was rather disappointed, as previous narratives of the sacred woman had undoubtedly captured his fantasy and titillated his sense of exploration of virgin territory:

> Taking advantage of our halt and that day's armistice, I rode over with a few others to see the sanctuary of the tutelary genius of this great sacred lake, the famous sorceress called the incarnated Pigfaced Goddess, a Tibetan Circe, who in holiness ranks almost next to the Grand Lama himself, and whose shrine does not appear to have been visited by Europeans before. ([1905] 1988:292)

In Waddell's eyes, the Dorje Phagmo represented a corrupted form of Buddhism, in contrast to what was perceived as more ancient and authentic, a classical Buddhist civilization gradually being rediscovered in the ancient sacred sites of India (Snellgrove 2002 [1987]:1–5) and capturing the imagination of Victorian scholars and travelers alike:

> This august, if youthful, lady is alleged by the Lamas to be the human reincarnation of one of those monstrous creations of later Indian Buddhists who followed the Brahmans in admitting female energies into their grotesque pantheon. ([1905] 1988:294)

To Waddell, the same "grotesque" Buddhism shrouded Lhasa, a sleeping beauty awaiting the kiss of Civilization:

> But now, in the fateful Tibetan Year of the Wooden-Dragon, the fairy Prince of "Civilisation" has roused her [Lhasa] from her slumbers, her closed doors are broken down, her dark veil of mystery is lifted up, and the long-sealed shrine, with its grotesque cults and its idolised grand lama, shorn of his sham nimbus, have yielded up their secrets, and lie disenchanted before our Western eyes. Thus, alas! Inevitably, do our cherished romances of the old pagan world crumble at the touch of our modern hands. ([1905] 1988:2)

Unfortunately, the fairy tale cost the lives of several thousand Tibetans and would have far-reaching consequences. It combined concrete imperial claims in the name of modernity and fascination with a world that was ultimately "other." It killed its people while "rescuing" the texts of its civilization,[15] almost like the paradoxical fascination of a rape: the fatal attraction that entails the damage or even the destruction of the object of desire. This attitude toward Tibet in many ways recalls the poetic metaphor of "Butterfly" used in Puccini's tragic opera that both denounces and reproduces the widespread orientalism of those times. From a historical point of view, this event triggered a series of chain reactions that would shape Sino-Tibetan relations throughout the twentieth century and set a powerful precedent for making claims on Tibet in the name of modernity. The military intervention represented Tibet's "violability" and the paradigm of its "violated specialness" (Barnett 2001:269ff.), which was reflected, kaleidoscopically, in innumerable later narratives both supporting and undermining the cause of Tibetan independence.

The Younghusband expedition opened the door to a more conspicuous presence of British officers in Tibet, who developed increasing interest in its

*"Lady of the Lake": The Dorje Phagmo at Samding*

civilization and had a determinant influence on the development of Tibetan Studies (McKay 2001:67ff.). These officers and members of their families, as in the case of Margaret Williamson, left telling accounts of their interaction with the Samding Dorje Phagmo and took the earliest photographic images.

Charles Bell met the eleventh reincarnation of the Dorje Phagmo in person in 1920; he could converse with her in Tibetan and even had photographs taken. He describes her with the following words:

> Twenty-four years of age, a pleasing face, bright rounded eyes, a low broad fore-head, high cheek-bones and a rather heavy mouth with small, regular teeth. Such was Dor-je Pa-mo, who, though of humble parentage, ranks above all the women, and nearly all the men, in Tibet. . . . I know not whether a jury of my country-men or countrywomen would find her fair of face. Perhaps not; but her sweet, though pensive, smile, her youth, her quiet dignity, invested the young abbess with a charm of her own. (Bell 1994 [1928]:166–167)

An increasing cohort of explorers and Tibetologists traveled to Tibet, including Alexandra David-Neel, an extraordinary woman herself, complimentarily defined by the Thirteenth Dalai Lama as an incarnation of Dorje Phagmo. In 1948, the Italian Tibetologist Giuseppe Tucci met the young Twelfth Samding Dorje Phagmo during a visit to the monastery and witnessed the celebration of one of the big rituals that involved both the monastic and the lay community:

> We stopped for two days at Nangkartse (sNang dkar rtse), a dilapidated fort watching over the unruffled mirror of the Yamdrog (Yar abrog) lake and the surrounding flooded meadows. We had to change horses there, and I could not leave the place without seeing the Samding monastery, built by Potopa Chogle Namgyal (P'yogs las rnam rgyal). That convent is famous on the account of the incarnation of the Dorjepamo (rDo rje p'ag mo), "the hog-headed One," sup-posed to dwell there uninterruptedly changing her mortal form. Never fear: the goddess's mortal mirror does not look that dreadful and was, at the time, a pretty girl of 13. The pilgrims were just gathering for the feast which was to take place within a few days (the 11th, 12th, and 13th day of the fifth month). Three garishly caparisoned horses stood patiently in the sun, listening to the monk's chant and smelling the incense being burnt in their honor, as they were supposed to imper-sonate the protecting spirits of the place (*gzhi bdag*) and had to be propitiated twice a year. They were known as "lungtangonpo" (*rLung rta sngon po*) [i.e., the

blue horse of good fortune] and their respective names were Phurburagpa (P'ur bu rags pa), better known as Trashi obar (bKra shis 'od 'bar), the most important of the three, Shinkyongbapa (Shing skyong lba pa), and Dritsangshagpa (Dri gtsang zags pa). The goddess to whom I was presently introduced received me very affably and, laying her hands on my head, bestowed her blessing upon me. We exchanged scarves and gifts. (1987:85–86)

That young girl shortly afterward saw the most radical transformation of her country. Through the multiple ways she has been interpreted at different times and by different people, I shall explore, in the next chapter, her life amid the dramatic and complex events that shaped the modern history of Tibet.

*"Lady of the Lake": The Dorje Phagmo at Samding*

# DORJE PHAGMO IN THE TWENTIETH CENTURY
*Embodied Divinity and Government Cadre*

*Lhasa airport, July 1997. Among the rucksacks and suitcases of incoming tourists, the* eight rectangular wooden crates seem incongruous. They are taken off the baggage carousel very carefully, placed on trolleys, and pushed toward the exit. There is no difficulty going through customs, as these items are accompanied by a letter of accreditation signed by the chairman of the Tibet Autonomous Region. Outside the entry gate, the Venerable Dorje Phagmo with her retinue welcomes the arrival, draping *khatag*s over the precious boxes as a welcome for the honored guests. The crates contain the collected works of Bodong Chogle Namgyal, a reprint of an original set that was taken to India in 1959, arriving in disarray but almost complete after a long and difficult journey from Porong Palmo Choding. The texts are to be taken to her monastery, where they will be ceremonially welcomed; other sets will follow soon, destined for other Bodongpa monasteries.

When one of these copies arrived at Bodong E, it was carried around the fields in a processional blessing ceremony by the community in full ceremonial regalia, the women in the traditional jeweled headdresses of Tsang and the men in their best *chupas*. Everywhere the books were welcomed as a blessing not only for the temples but also for the community and the land.

FIGURE 7.1 Procession of villagers carrying holy books to bless the fields (redrawn after a 1950 photograph by Peter Aufschnaiter). This ritual has been revived in many parts of Tibet since the 1980s and was performed when the collected works of Bodong Chogle Namgyal arrived at Bodong E in 1997. *Jana Diemberger*

The Dorje Phagmo and other members of the Bodongpa network were instrumental in making this repatriation of holy texts possible. This elderly lady, embodying a long line of holy women of the past, was playing her part in the reconstruction of her tradition in the complex political situation of post-Mao Tibet—icon and agent at the same time.

Over the centuries, the significance of the Dorje Phagmo has grown through a process of ritualization that increased the distance between the people who worshipped her and the women who embodied her. Every girl who was recognized as the reincarnation of the Samding Dorje Phagmo went through a complex process that merged her individual experience with the features of the deity and the memory of its previous historical incarnations. Some of these women came to embody the sacred persona in such a way that their individual identity almost disappeared as a simple name in the lineage, while others became significant personalities and scholars of their time over and above the sacredness attributed to them by their "office."[1] The Ninth Dorje Phagmo, for example, became a renowned spiritual master not only for Samding but also for the Nyingma tradition, discovered some *terma,* and died at Samye. Her skull is still preserved and worshipped as a holy relic in the Nyingmapa monastery on the island of

*Dorje Phagmo in the Twentieth Century: Embodied Divinity and Government Cadre*

FIGURE 7.2 Samding monastery as it used to be in the early twentieth century, after a photograph by Austin Waddell. *Jana Diemberger*

Yumbudo in Yamdrog Lake. The current Dorje Phagmo has survived and maintained the tradition in a socialist context, adapting to the varied ways political and social practices have transformed and shaped contemporary Tibet during her lifetime.

The Twelfth Samding Dorje Phagmo, who is currently the head of Samding monastery, underwent the same process of identification as her predecessors, but her life experience has been unusually eventful. Born in 1938[2] in Nyemo, she has lived through the most dramatic vicissitudes of modern Tibetan history, including the Chinese annexation of Tibet in 1951, the uprising in 1959, the Cultural Revolution, and the post-Mao era. As a religious leader she experienced both the extreme hardship of class struggle and the subtle ways prominent members of her class were co-opted as part of the modern political elite. She was included in the Chinese administration's effort to integrate preexisting political and religious leaders of minority nationalities, a strategy that is usually defined as the United Front policy and takes its name from the organ of the Communist Party that has the specific task of dealing with the noncommunist elements of society (see Dreyer 1972:416–450). The Samding Dorje Phagmo was appointed to various positions in the Chinese People's Political Consulting Conference (CPPCC) at both the regional and national levels in the 1950s and early 1960s, and again in the post-Mao era. In 1984 she became the vice president of the People's Congress of the Tibet Autonomous Region (TAR); she was reconfirmed in this position in January 2003. Praised as a heroine according to Chinese modernist propaganda that pleaded for gender equality and promoted women as revolutionary subjects, she received various appointments by virtue of her ethnicity and her religious role as well as her gender. She has been described in many official and semiofficial narratives and has even been made a heroine of Chinese novels and films. In sharp contrast to these images are the more critical narratives about her that have emerged from the Tibetan community, both in exile and inside Tibet. These highlight the controversies around her identification as Dorje Phagmo and the ambiguity of her political position, but they often reflect at least some of the respect customarily attributed to her sacred office. Yet, mocking her inactivity and powerlessness, Tibetans both outside and inside Tibet sometimes describe her—like other high-ranking female cadres, such as the female vice-party secretary of the TAR, Pasang—as one of the "ornaments" (*rgyan cha*) or "statues" (*sku*) of the political system (Barnett 2005a:296–297). However, to dismiss such political personalities simply as propaganda figures or collaborationists would not do justice to the complexity of their role (see Barnett 2005b:25ff).

So far, this book has explored the ways the Dorje Phagmo, as an institution, was transformed over the centuries to merge with the prevailing social and political climate, while retaining the spiritual tradition and the reincarnation lineage. The institution established with the death of the Gungthang princess was thus integrated in different political and religious frameworks: Bodongpa, Karmapa, Gelugpa, the Qing empire, and eventually the PRC. The last step was a huge leap and involved the transition from a Buddhist religious and political culture to a radically secular ideology: Chinese Communism. However, there are some surprising continuities with premodern political practices, for the United Front policy followed strategies that, in practice, had certain similarities with those of the Qing empire. Implemented by the Communist Party since its early days in order to secure control over Tibetan and Mongolian areas, the policy often required a process of negotiation with the local traditional leadership. This approach was important particularly in the 1950s and after Mao and tried to harness, strategically, the moral authority of the past within the modernist project of communist China; it was one of the many forms in which earlier social ranking and values were reflected in communist regimes (Humphrey 1999:375–389). It is therefore possible to detect some continuities between premodern and modern

*Dorje Phagmo in the Twentieth Century: Embodied Divinity and Government Cadre*

Tibet, across the conventional divide between "old society" (*spyi tshogs rnying pa*) and "new society" (*spyi tshogs gsar pa*).

When we first met in 1996, the Twelfth Samding Dorje Phagmo made clear to me that the contribution to her culture and her people that her position allowed her to make was very important to her. The revival of Tibetan Buddhism in contemporary Tibet had already gone a long way and the new policy of containment[3] had already started to have some effects, but was still in its infancy:

> After the destruction of the Cultural Revolution, the Samding monastery was partly restored, and now we are trying to improve the training of the monks by studying the scriptures of Chogle Namgyal and reintroducing some of the ancient ritual customs. This year, after many decades, we are again observing the great rituals of the fifth Tibetan month, which culminate in two days of sacred dances. These dances are peculiar to the Bodongpa tradition, and the great protector of this tradition, Tashi Ombar, is one of the main characters.

The Samding Dorje Phagmo's training followed the Bodongpa tradition, but she had not been able to practice for a number of years and found it difficult to perform her ritual duties. However, thanks to the head monk, Thubten Namgyal, who skillfully coached her, she had found a new spiritual life in the post-Mao era. The Samding Dorje Phagmo's combined religious and political role, along with Thubten Namgyal's scholarly knowledge, made it possible not only to reintroduce the Dorje Phagmo to religious practice but also to reconstruct part of the ancient building and to revive religious teachings, monastic debate, and Cham dances. The monastery has also benefited extensively from the support of the Samding Dorje Phagmo's elder sister, a member of the CPPCC in the TAR, who has proven very effective at generating support among the communities surrounding the monastery and even internationally, and at developing welfare projects for the lay population.

In her complex and often disputed position, the Dorje Phagmo can perhaps be considered in terms of the patterns of behavior and discourse we know from late socialist Russia, given the shared history and ideology between the two countries. Through the work of Alexei Yurchak it is possible to understand how cadres' multiple ways of speaking and behaving, their "heteroglossia," seems to have accommodated contradictory positions while keeping up the performance of communist practices and statements—yet the cadres adhere neither to the image of the collaborationist nor to that of the system's manipulator in disguise,

FIGURE 7.3 The Twelfth Dorje Phagmo on her throne at Samding in 1996. *Jana Diemberger*

for the paradox and multiplicity of living practices exceeds the binary model implied by notions such as "reading in reverse" or "hidden transcripts," which is often used to describe this kind of situation (see Yurchak 2003; Barnett 2005b). A "ritualization" of communist acts and words that partly detaches them from their immediate meaning and original intention seems to have opened new spaces for multiple interpretations, reconciling the irreconcilable. From this point of view, the Dorje Phagmo recalls many other religious figures in socialist and postsocialist contexts, such as Siberian shamans (Vitebsky 1995). In *The Archetypal Actions of Ritual* (1994; see also 2006; forthcoming), Laidlaw and Humphrey developed the theory that "ritual" is "a quality that action can come to have, rather than being . . . a definable category of distinctive kinds of events. Ritualization involves the modification—an attenuation but not elimination—of the normal intentionality of human action. Ritual is action in which intentionality is in a certain way displaced so that . . . participants both are and are not the authors of their ritual actions" (Laidlaw and Humphrey forthcoming). In this light, it might be useful to look at the Dorje Phagmo's shifting life arrangements and the pragmatic synthesis between heterogeneous forms of rituality, to which I shall return in the final part of this chapter.

## The Twelfth Samding Dorje Phagmo Through the Eyes of Her Sister: Life and Narrative Models

The life of the Twelfth Samding Dorje Phagmo illustrates, from a particular perspective, the general role of literary models in life fashioning and the specific complexities of the history she has experienced.[4] Her elder sister, Kesang Dronma, who was present at the most significant events of the Dorje Phagmo's life, gave me a detailed and contextualized recollection in an interview in July 1999. Putting aside the significance of this account as a source for an oral history, I primarily focus on it as a narrative. It is a remarkable example of an oral life story that frames events in tropes distinctive of Tibetan biographical writing, adapting them to new circumstances. This feature has been noted by Hanna Havnevik in the oral accounts of contemporary Tibetan nuns (1990; 1994:259–284), but is striking in this case for the profile of the protagonist. More generally, it is a clear example of how a distinctive literary form of cultural production such as Tibetan biographical writing has an important bearing on oral narrative, challenging the conventional divide between orality and literality and pointing to a creative interface between the two (Goody 1991; Ong 1982). The Dorje Phagmo's sister gave an oral account of the early life of the current reincarnation that appears to mirror, in certain details, the description of the life of Chokyi Dronma in the fifteenth-century biography, even though she had no access to the actual text. This ranges from the role of childhood illness to extravagant behaviors that in hindsight appeared as a sign of her divine secret identity. As in the case of Chokyi Dronma's biography, it is impossible to distinguish between literary models that informed the biographical account and those that informed how the protagonists enacted them in their own life. Literary models are not necessarily only applied *a posteriori* in the process of a biographical compilation. As illustrated in the first part of this book, Chokyi Dronma was presumably aware of a number of preexisting literary models, fashioned her own life accordingly, and interpreted her experiences against that background. Eventually her life became an inspirational narrative and sometimes an authorizing referent for later generations. Thus it became a powerful and lively part of an open-ended process in which written and oral stories of remembered lives are continually reenacted and interwoven.

Kesang Dronma gave an account of her sister's life that sometimes contrasts but is generally not incompatible with accounts of the same events written from other, more critical or controversial perspectives. It can be subdivided into five separate sections: a childhood recollection in which traditional biographical tropes are very evident; the more secular account of her sister's life in a gradually modernizing Tibet; the Tibetan revolt and the dramatic 1959 journey to India, which has almost an epic character rich in circumstantial detail; an interlude with brief flashes from the Cultural Revolution, intermingling common tropes with sketchy, random detail, typical of accounts that do not want to delve into the turmoil of that period; and finally the religious revival of the post-Mao era, in which biographical tropes of miraculous deeds partly reemerge. In presenting Kesang Dronma's account, I give a series of quotations in their original sequence and summarize the rest, to show as much as possible the structure and the temporality of her narrative.

Being older, Kesang Dronma recalled events earlier than those described by the Dorje Phagmo herself. She framed her childhood experiences in a narrative that placed them, with the benefits of hindsight, in light of the extraordinary events that led to the recognition of her sister as a reincarnation of the Dorje Phagmo and perhaps even of her reemergence as a prominent religious figure in the 1980s. The ordinary process of reading backward into a child's past had acquired a particular significance in her case: the actual recognition had been prefigured by her mysterious illness, the subsequent consultation of oracles, and eventually her encounter with a member of the entourage of the previous Dorje Phagmo. Kesang Dronma drew multiple figures into the story, members of the family and other people who were part of the events and of the collective process of decoding the child's behavior, in which Kesang Dronma had participated. It was the beginning of a continuous interpretation that has framed and reframed the Twelfth Dorje Phagmo's life up to now, as it did the lives of her predecessors. Kesang Dronma started her account by locating herself in relation to her sister:

I was two or three years older than her. When she was around three [i.e., two, about 1940] she became very ill. At that time there was no hospital. We used to

*Dorje Phagmo in the Twentieth Century: Embodied Divinity and Government Cadre*

ask for Tibetan medicine and to make ceremonies in a monastery and to ask the gods. The reply was that she was the rebirth of a religious practitioner, a monk, of someone with a high rebirth. If she were a boy it would have occurred to us that she could be the reincarnation of a lama, but since she was a girl we did not think any more about that. However, it was said that she should devote her life to religion and that she could not lead a secular life. If she were to do so, she would die. So, without knowing that she was the Samding Dorje Phagmo, it was decided that she should become a nun in the Tsangkhung nunnery [in Lhasa].

The gender of her sister was originally a reason not to consider her a potential candidate as a reincarnation. Indeed, almost all known reincarnations are male, which has definitely shaped the popular perception of the institution. Here we see a number of tropes drawn from traditional literature. There is the implicit disclaiming of any initial effort to promote the child, here explained by the fact that she was a girl. Then there is the highlighting of her mysterious illness, a common element in narratives referring to a spiritual calling, as we have seen in the case of oracles and Chokyi Dronma herself (see also chapters 3 and 4). The invocation of illness as a kind of liminal experience refers to a psychosomatic world in which body and mind display signs of prefiguration. Later Kesang Dronma told a series of stories that referred to signs that showed the natural world participating in the event. Almost all Tibetan accounts of rebirth feature a rainbow or a similar incident.

In Tsangkhung there is a resident local goddess. Some say that it is Palden Lhamo. Her birthplace was near Tsangkhung. In fact, our house was near Tsangkhung, so the goddess of Tsangkhung was her birth [protective] deity (*skye lha*). There were some extraordinary things that happened at the time of her birth. A rainbow appeared over our house. We did not see it, but people did and told of it. It is said that this was made by the goddess (*lha mo*) of Tsangkhung. When Mother was pregnant, a woman dressed as a lady from Kham came. At that time there was a cook in our house and this lady gave him some wool. "We do not need any wool! We are about to leave for the countryside," he said. "Keep it! The time will come when you will need it," said the Kham lady. So he took it and put in one of the empty spaces that are always there in our Tibetan houses. Then the time of birth came. The umbilical cord had to be cut. If the birth takes place in the hospital, the cord is cut and the remaining part is wrapped [in white cloth]. But at that time birth always took place at home. So when the cord was cut, this had to be wrapped in wool. The birth came all of a sudden and they were somewhat unprepared [as we usually were not staying in Lhasa]. So there was no wool. Then the cook suddenly remembered, "Here is some wool! It was given to me some time ago by a lady." But who was that lady? Nobody seemed to know or have any idea who she might have been . . . and then they started to think that this might have been the goddess of Tsangkhung. The goddess of Tsangkhung wears Khampa clothing. She looks as if she is originally from Kham.

Old marginal women, more rarely men, have a special role in Tibetan stories, appearing in some minor capacity and unrecognized at the time; they are always later identified as a visiting goddess or emanation of a high lama. This was the case with the carrier of Thangtong Gyalpo's letter in Chokyi Dronma's biography.

After recalling the extraordinary circumstances surrounding her sister's birth, Kesang Dronma went back to the episode of the first divination that was made because of the child's ill health:

Since the reply in the divination was that she had to become a nun at Tsangkhung, she became a novice. And she recovered from the illness. Two, three years after she recovered, we moved somewhere else. We went to a locality called Jorra. We had a manorial estate and Father was staying there. Our family stayed there for some two or three years. While we were there, she was always dressed as a nun and used to play with a girl from central Tibet. Together they used to play with earth and used to make little heaps, and she used to pick up a stick and act as if she were beating a drum. She looked like she was celebrating some kind of offering ritual. And she was mumbling, just like an *umtse* (a chant leader in a monastery) . . . though of course she did not know the words. We were very different in our ways of playing. I used to run around with other girls. At that time there was no school, was there? She was always looking for a quiet corner where she would sit and make her "offerings."

If illness reflects a spiritual calling, an adequate response brings about improvement or healing. This passage underlines the nature of the illness that had prefigured her religious life. This is further supported by the recollection of episodes showing that her sister had retained memories from her previous life. Many anecdotes pointed to her sister's extraordinary character. According to Kesang Dronma, when nobody had yet thought of the possibility of her being identified as a reincarnation, the family happened to visit an important state oracle; he behaved in a peculiar and unusual way in front of the child, but the family did not recognize the significance until later, in retrospect:

> One day we passed by Tolung. There is a god [i.e., a human being who gets possessed by a god] there called Gadong. He is the same as the Nechung Chokyong [the most important state oracle]. Gadong . . . was a state oracle. . . . At that time I was a little girl, and in front of this oracle I was scared, I shut my eyes, I did not dare to move, and I trembled in fear. . . . At that time my sister was very small and had to be carried. As soon as the god saw her, he suddenly stood up. Everybody was surprised. A god would stand up only if a lama were coming. We were quite confused. We also could not think of any reason the god would stand up. The god said, "Bring the offerings!"—I was young and my ability to remember is confused, but my father used to relate all these details—and gave them to the little Samding Dorje Phagmo. And the god gave her a red cord and a *khatag*. To laypeople he used to give white or green, but to the Samding Dorje Phagmo he gave a red one. The monks who assisted the oracle were surprised and wondered why he gave these offerings to this little girl. If it were a boy they would think that he was a reincarnated lama, but it being a girl, they just could not understand. A girl as a lama, this is never spoken of. They said, "Perhaps she is something special. Keep her pure." So we started to think that there was something special about her. Since she was quite sickly, many religious ceremonies were held for her.

This episode builds on and enhances the narrative of extraordinary indications prefiguring the revelation. Minor and almost ordinary signs give way to events that raise public surprise. The intervention of oracles in the revelation of reincarnations is not only a biographical trope but also an institutionalized practice. However, Kesang Dronma underlines that this was not a prearranged consultation but a fortunate coincidence that was not fully interpreted at the time, reinforcing the trope of a spontaneous revelation. According to Kesang Dronma, around 1941–42 the family came to know that the Samding monastery was searching for the reincarnation of the Eleventh Samding Dorje Phagmo in a casual, surprising way:

> At that time the monastery was looking for the reincarnation [of the previous Samding Dorje Phagmo], wasn't it? At that time we were living in Nyemo. The former Samding Dorje Phagmo had a very young assistant. Her name was

Nyipun. Nyipun arrived at our house together with a monk from the monastery. In order to find a reincarnation, they had to make many connections everywhere, didn't they? When Nyipun and the monk dismounted from their horses and came to our house, they directly bumped into my sister. The Samding Dorje Phagmo immediately said, "Nyipun has arrived, Nyipun has arrived." Nobody in our house knew them. But as soon as they heard her saying this, they started to cry. And she was very happy and behaved as if she were very familiar with them. Normally she would be shy in front of people she didn't know, like any child. But with them she started to play. And as they probably guessed something, they remained at our place for some days.

This passage follows the trope of highlighting the key role played by objects and people that were close to the deceased spiritual master in the process of selecting a reincarnation. However, it is also particularly evocative of the role played by Deleg Chodren in the identification of Chokyi Dronma's reincarnation. Given the popularity of Thangtong Gyalpo's biography, presumably this was, deliberately or unconsciously, a narrative inspiration. After this initial, rather private moment of disclosure of the girl's secret identity, a more public one followed, which was apparently controversial. The public recognition of the Dorje Phagmo also marks a change in the narrative, which becomes less emotional and more factual.

## The Twelfth Samding Dorje Phagmo Through the Eyes of Her Sister: Turmoil and Transformation

Kesang Dronma told a unique firsthand account of the process by which her sister became recognized as a reincarnation, and more generally the history of a woman of the Tibetan elite against the background of the radical sociopolitical shifts she experienced.

Kesang Dronma mentioned, just in passing, the controversies that surrounded the selection. These are generally ignored in the sources published in China, but are highlighted in the article by K. Dhondup and Tashi Tsering (1979:13–14), which attributes the identification to the close relationship between the father of the current Dorje Phagmo and the regent, Taktra. It reports the view that personal interests had flawed the process and refers to the problematic birth date of the selected Dorje Phagmo, who was allegedly born one year before the death of her predecessor, and the likelihood that one of the other candidates was more authentic (a girl said to have had hog bristles on her back).[5] They also emphasize the damage caused to the institution by the controversy and the loss of spiritual authority of the Dorje Phagmo. In contrast, Kesang Dronma highlights the final endorsement of the highest Tibetan authorities, evoking the common trope of multiple reincarnations and the fact that eventually all the candidates took a religious path, as an acceptable solution to the conundrum. Both readings are shaped by their authors' positions and by the time of writing/narrating. The 1979 article questions, from the perspective of the exile community, the authoritativeness of the current Dorje Phagmo in the light of not only the controversy concerning her identification but also her later political readiness to collaborate with the Chinese authorities. It is significant that this was written prior to the Buddhist revival in the Tibet Autonomous Region. Once acknowledged, the revival promoted a more differentiated interpretation of Tibetan cadres and religious personalities in general.[6] Kesang Dronma's narrative reflects the Tibet of the 1990s, in which the religious resurgence had already flourished for a number of years. It reveals her wish to endorse the status quo, arguing in terms meant to comply with Buddhist religious and moral premises. It is clear from both accounts that an identification was associated with such an elevation in rank and honors that having a child recognized as a reincarnation had become a very attractive opportunity and a frequent source of disputes. Both readings refer to the controversy around the discovery of the Dorje Phagmo against the background of the common privately motivated interference in spiritual/political matters, which made potentially flawed selections of reincarnations objects of popular jokes.

> When the time came to decide who the reincarnation was, there were naturally many other candidates. . . . There are always issues of there being many reincarnations, of body, speech, and mind, and so on [because a high lama can reincarnate in more than one body]. In any case, they [the other candidates] became nuns. There were people supporting one or the other. Then the Regent of Tibet, Taktra, was asked, and he replied that this was the one. Then Kundun [i.e., the Dalai Lama] was asked. If he gave approval, then the appointment would be definitive. And he confirmed it. The order was then passed on to the monastery, and the monastery could not oppose this decision. The process of identification was sorted out in this way.

In the recollection of Kesang Dronma, the transfer of her younger sister to the monastery went together with her full recovery. Kesang Dronma was also able to give details of the young Dorje Phagmo's training, which involved rigorous discipline and followed the Bodongpa tradition, relying on the network of monastic institutions in the region:

> She had a teacher, a monk from the monastery. His name was Dongag. He was very expert in the scriptures and followed the Bodongpa tradition. This teacher was not a lama in a strict sense. But he had an amazing spontaneous expertise in the texts. He was very learned and knew all the different aspects of religious theory and practice. He was also very good at writing, despite the fact that he never went to school. I learned some Tibetan writing from him. She stayed at the monastery until she was sixteen or seventeen. There was another teacher, Jiggyal Rinpoche, a lama. He was one of the Bodongpa followers. His seat was in Rong in the Rinpung area. Jorra Tulku also gave teachings and empowerments before he died. The Samding Dorje Phagmo received all the necessary empowerments, those of the Bodong tradition.

Except for short separations, the two sisters lived together in the monastery. There they witnessed the arrival of the Chinese PLA (People's Liberation Army), who had come to Tibet in 1951 to carry out its "peaceful liberation" after the controversial signing of the Seventeen-Point Agreement that conferred upon China full sovereignty over Tibet while recognizing Tibet's autonomy. This event marks another shift in the narrative, which becomes more secular according to the radical transformation of the background against which the events were taking place:

> At one point the PLA arrived. They constructed the road reaching straight to Nakartse. At that time we were still young. The soldiers were coming, loaded with their packs on their backs. Nakartse county was founded. One of the army leaders came to the monastery. They showed some movies they had brought with them. We were invited to a banquet in Nakartse county. The soldiers brought a lot of gifts.

As a member of the traditional elite, the Dorje Phagmo was given great attention by the Chinese officials (see, for example, Mangeot 1979:108ff.). This was part of the United Front policy of making strategic alliances with members of the local elite in areas where the Communist Party was not otherwise able to assert its control. In 1956 the young Dorje Phagmo, at that time a teenager, was appointed as a vice president of the Buddhist Association, with the Dalai Lama as president and the Panchen Lama also a vice president. This organization had been established by the Chinese administration in order to manage the relationship with the Buddhist religious elite. As a high-ranking religious dignitary, she was invited to Beijing twice. Kesang Dronma did not go along on these trips, in which her sister had the chance to meet Mao and other top-ranking Chinese officials:

> Around 1955 the Samding Dorje Phagmo went to Beijing to pay a visit. Many aristocrats went there to see the place before she went. Many lamas and aristocrats went. It was not the first time [that people were sent to see mainland China]. The Samding Dorje Phagmo and Mother went together. At that time the road was not good. They went by car. It seems that they went by car until Xi'an and then from there went on by rail. When she came back from her trip she became the vice director [president] of the Buddhist Association.

Soon afterward she left again for Beijing, this time with her father. It was an eventful journey, both personally and politically, described through the eyes of the Manchurian secretary of the Buddhist Association in an account published by Silvain Mangeot (1979:112ff.). Kesang Dronma did not refer to any personal relationship between her sister and this adventurous Manchurian. She focused, rather, on the fact that the prolonged absence of the Dorje Phagmo created some discontent in the monastery. In fact, the management and the whole system of lay support of the monastic institution would function only if the sacred donee was present:

> In 1957, they were sent again to visit China. That time Father went as well. When they came back, the monks expressed their concern about the fact that there was no lama in the monastery. And they said that if no lama was staying in the monastery, they could not really practice religion. They conveyed their request for their lama to the government. If no lama is staying in the monastery, then the patrons also become fewer and fewer and the monastery falls into decay. The monastery had big land holdings, yaks and sheep, and if the lama was not there all this was not properly managed. . . . The request was forwarded to the Religious

Affairs Bureau. So after coming back from China they went back to living in the monastery.

Having obtained permission, the Dorje Phagmo resumed her residence at Samding, engaging in religious training and practice. Meanwhile, the general political situation was becoming more and more tense, for a Tibetan uprising that had started in the east had been crushed and the unrest was spreading to central Tibet:

> In 1958 the Samding Dorje Phagmo was living in the monastery. At that time she went to Lhasa, met the Dalai Lama, and received the empowerment on Yamāntaka. She received the empowerment on Vajrayoginī from Trijiang Rinpoche [the Dalai Lama's tutor]. After the empowerment she went back to the monastery.

While there, the Samding Dorje Phagmo saw the onset of the big 1959 uprising during which the Yamdrog area became a stronghold of Tibetan guerrillas. They were Khampas coming from the east, and their organization went under the name Four Rivers Six Ranges (Chushi Gangdrug).[7] The description of this event marks a radical shift in the narrative and a change in its temporality. This is the prelude to the epic journey that would take both sisters to India:

> The whole of the Yamdrog area was controlled by the Chushi Gangdrug (*chu bzhi sgang drug*). In the countryside there were guerrillas. The road was blocked. Father and Mother were in Nyemo. We could not move back and forth. We were isolated. I was already married at that time and my husband had become one of the four treasurers of the monastery. The monastery had started to do quite well just as the [1959] uprising broke out. While the Chushi Gangdrug were here, they used to come to the monastery to get butter and other kinds of food.

In the middle of the turmoil, the Dalai Lama escaped from Tibet to India. The two young women were quite uncertain about what to do, but eventually they decided to follow the example of their leader and flee:

> At that time we escaped. At that time in Nakartse there was one Chushi Gangdrug leader; he was called Amdo Legshe; he seems to have been a monk before. He sent us a note saying that the Gyalwa Rinpoche [i.e., the Dalai Lama] had already

*Dorje Phagmo in the Twentieth Century: Embodied Divinity and Government Cadre*

gone to India and that all the major lamas were supposed to leave, and that it was better if we went as well. The Chushi Gangdrug sent a group of ten soldiers to protect us. We knew nothing about where to escape. We were very young. We went to the lake and then continued. It was 1959, the third or fourth month. Since the Dalai Lama had already left, there were many people leaving with their yaks and donkeys and their belongings. . . . We took the ritual instruments and the famous hat. This was the hat of Khandro Yeshe Tsogyal.[8] The hat had inside it some real hair from Khandro Yeshe Tsogyal. This hat does not exist anymore; it was destroyed in the Cultural Revolution.

Her account is a travelogue that highlights how everything was happening in a rushed and confused way and also how everybody was expecting this journey to be a short-term expedient:

On the way my husband went to visit his own place at Lhodrag Bodong, and then we continued to Bhutan. My father-in-law came along. They were a rich family; they had gold and silver, but he just came with his pack. He had taken along a new pair of shoes. As he said, "On the way, if the shoes get torn it is a big problem, unless you have shoes to change into." He did not think at all about taking along silver or gold or any precious things. He had one small bag of *tsampa* and just went with that. They had taken along the three children . . . or were they four? . . . no, one was already with us. They had the one bag of *tsampa* flour and just went. The mother had her Lhokha hat. This hat is absolutely useless if it is cold or hot or whatever, it is just a useless thing. It just looks nice.

They arrived at the border with Bhutan (on the route leading via Monla Karchung pass to Bumthang), immediately to the south, which was a natural port of call both for its geographical proximity and for its ancient religious ties. The account published by Sylvain Mangeot hints at the fact that Dorje Phagmo's journey may have been motivated by personal reasons—her involvement with the Manchurian secretary of the Buddhist Association and her attempt to trace him after he had left for Bhutan. However, this is not mentioned in Kesang Dronma's account, nor is the story that her father-in-law had tried to leave Tibet with a caravan loaded with valuables and belongings and was beaten to death either by guerrillas or by Bhutanese, as reported by some sources in various, discrepant versions (Mangeot 1974:201; K. Dhondup and Tashi Tsering 1979:16). Kesang Dronma concentrated on the events she had seen unfolding before her eyes:

At that time there were many people coming from Tibet. . . . The journey lasted some fifteen or sixteen days. The path was quite tough and many got foot injuries. But all the way, since people were very religious, we found a lot of help. Many of them invited us to their houses; they often came offering *khatags* and provided food. We arrived at Tsampa, the Tibetan-Bhutanese border, and there were many aristocrats from the Dewashung [the Tibetan government]. The area there is densely forested; people stayed in tents. We made an improvised shelter from some cloth and stayed there. . . . Gradually the food ran out. We started to go into the forest to look for berries and whatever was there that was edible. Some people got poisoned because of eating the wrong things. Lots of people died.

At that time the Indian Premier Nehru spoke on the radio and announced that the Tibetans could come to India. So the authorities of Bhutan were told to allow the Tibetans to pass through their country. . . . The Bhutanese let the lamas and the aristocrats proceed along the main route. The others, soldiers and ordinary people, were sent by an alternative path which went through the area of Lo. This path was considered to be quite bad. It is said that those who went by this other route had a hard time on the journey. When we arrived in the area where the Bhutanese government was, we were guests of Ashi (Princess) Pema Chodron.

In Bhutan the two sisters were particularly welcomed by people who followed the same religious tradition and were devoted to the Dorje Phagmo:

Truly speaking, Bhutan is very pleasant. It is a very nice land. In Bhutan there is a big monastery on the top of a hill that follows the Bodong tradition or something similar. It is said that one of the former Samding Dorje Phagmos had resided there. . . . The Samding Dorje Phagmo was riding a horse, and the people were offering bushels of green rice to her horse. Everybody was very happy. In this way the Samding Dorje Phagmo went to perform an offering in this monastery. Many people came to see the famous hat of Khandro Yeshe Tsogyal.

From Bhutan, the two sisters moved to Assam. While they were fighting their way through the refugee camps in India, their parents were still in Tibet, but as soon as the situation had stabilized they started to look for their daughters:

At that time Father and Mother were in Nyemo. The road was blocked by the fighting around the iron bridge at Chushul [over the Brahmaputra River]. Since Father and Mother had received some sort of salary from the Chinese government,

*Dorje Phagmo in the Twentieth Century: Embodied Divinity and Government Cadre*

the Chushi Gangdrug were very suspicious. They took away all that they could from the family. Mother was badly beaten while Father managed to escape to Lhasa. However, we had also helped the Chushi Gangdrug in Yamdrog, and later we had to face quite a few difficulties for this. In fact, all the treasurers were put in jail for this. We ended up in the middle of the war; we were between the two fronts and were "beaten" by all sides. Since we were in the middle, both fronts considered us as belonging to the other side. In the Yamdrog area most families had stories of this kind.

Histories from this period of successful and failed attempts to steer a middle course between opposing fronts, of equivocal behavior, and of shifting alignments across fragmented families are common. Personal and political issues appear inextricably intertwined in a multitude of survival strategies. The Dorje Phagmo and her family were in this sense a high-profile case of a widespread phenomenon (Mangeot 1979:182). In order to track their daughters, the parents of the Dorje Phagmo relied on PLA support:

Mother and Father came accompanied by the PLA to look for us and got as far as Bhutan. However, they did not find us and went back. . . . They sent some people from Phari [near the border with Bhutan, where the monastery of Samding had an estate] to look for us. From them we heard that we should come back and that the monastery did not suffer any damage. They confirmed that during the uprising many people had died, but said that if we were to return to Tibet now, nothing untoward would happen. In that difficult situation the idea of returning home became the simplest one. Once we had taken this decision, we established some contacts with the Chinese embassy in Delhi and stayed there for a few days.

According to K. Dondup and Tashi Tsering (1979:16), the Chinese trade agent at Kalimpong, whose duties included trying to convince China-friendly members of the religious and political elite to return to Tibet, had a major part in reestablishing contact between parents and daughters and in organizing their return. It is unclear at what stage this became an important political matter. Certainly, at some point it became a most public affair, for the return of the Dorje Phagmo and her sister was managed with the involvement of the highest authorities in Beijing:

From Delhi we were sent by plane to Afghanistan and Pakistan. Then we went to the Soviet Union. We arrived in Moscow. Then we went also to Outer Mongolia. We stayed two or three days in Afghanistan. We stayed three days in the Soviet Union. At that time the Soviet Union was very famous, and there were such big houses there. Food, however, was not that good, and for a little food one had to pay high prices. We visited some exhibitions and museums. We saw some military displays concerning space exploration, etc. We tried to visit the mausoleums of Lenin and Stalin, but that day they were closed.

Kesang Dronma told about this adventurous journey, showing a few photographs that were taken during their visits. Eventually, the two young women arrived in Beijing. It was just before the celebration of the tenth anniversary of the founding of the PRC, on October 1, 1959 (see also Wangdu 1999:119), and they were given a special welcome as patriotic heroines:

We arrived at Beijing exactly for the *shi-yi* [Chinese: the first of October, China's national day since 1949]. It was 1959. How quick we were! In that same year in the fourth month we had left, and by the ninth we had come back. We went by plane. As we arrived, there were so many people showing happiness and welcoming us.

In Tiananmen Square, Mao Trushi (Chairman) was above [in the rostrum]. We were there with He Long. He was so big, majestic with his short beard, even intimidating. Besides him there were many generals. The honorable lady (*lhacham*), the wife of Ngabo [the former Tibetan cabinet minister and general], was with us. That evening they gave a banquet at the Great Hall of the People. At that time Zhou Enlai gave a speech and said that it was very good that the female lama had come back from abroad. He said something like, "She chose to follow the luminous path." I cannot say much about that. When the speech was finished, we toasted. All stood up, toasted. There was so much food at one time. . . . One evening, just at sunset, suddenly an invitation came to go to Zhongnanhai [the central headquarters of the Communist party and the government of China]. At that time we did not go. The Samding Dorje Phagmo met Zhou Enlai and later Chairman Mao. He praised her all the time as a female living Buddha. At that time Chairman Mao spoke about freedom of belief. Chairman Mao said that the policy of freedom of belief and the nationalities policy (*mi rigs srid jus*) would remain unchanged. This is also what he said to Lhalu [another Tibetan former cabinet minister]. Lhalu repeated this in some meetings of the CPPCC.

The return to China had given the Dorje Phagmo a particular position in Chinese propaganda narratives and imagery, which was used not only by displaying her at the grand celebration of the anniversary of the PRC but also in broadcasting her later statements on the radio inviting Tibetans to return (K. Dhondub and Tashi Tsering 1979:17). In the 1980s, the epic journey was narrated in a novel and a film, called *Female Living Buddha* (Ch. *Niu Huofu*), that celebrated her loyalty to the motherland and reiterated the invitation to Tibetans abroad.[9] The increased symbolic value of the Dorje Phagmo was also reflected in the positions to which she was appointed after her return to Tibet in 1960. These were briefly mentioned by Kesang Dronma in a flat, factual account leading to her recollection of episodes from the Cultural Revolution: "After returning to Tibet she received various appointments in the Buddhist Association, as a representative in the People's Congress in Lhokha, as the vice-party secretary of the Political Consultative Conference of Tibet, as a vice director of the People's Congress of the Tibet Autonomous Region, as a member of the committee of the Political Consultative Conference of China [at national level]."

The fortunes of the Samding Dorje Phagmo and her sister would change radically a few years later. In 1962 the Panchen Lama denounced what was actually happening in the Tibetan areas in his famous 70,000 Character Petition[10] to Zhou Enlai, in the hope that he could enter into a dialogue with the Chinese leadership according to the terms agreed upon in the 1950s and convince the highest authorities to change their course of action. Li Weihan, the head of the United Front, at first took the Panchen Lama's suggestions into consideration. However, in 1964 Mao declared the petition "a poisoned arrow aimed at the Party by reactionary and feudal overlords" (Barnett 1997:iv, xx), and subsequently the Panchen Lama underwent struggle sessions and spent almost ten years in prison. Around the same time, Li Weihan, the mastermind of the United Front policy, lost his position and numerous members of the traditional elite who had worked together with the Chinese authorities as part of this policy fell into disgrace. Kesang Dronma briefly commented on this, saying, "In 1964 Panchen Rinpoche [i.e., the Panchen Lama] got in trouble, and as a result of this problem other people got into trouble as well. So in 1965 our father was put into prison."

This was a prelude to the Cultural Revolution, which began in 1966. Like many lamas and aristocrats, the two sisters went through a period of hardship, yet they were luckier than others: during this period a great number of representatives of traditional political and religious institutions, as well as many ethnic cadres, were killed. The monastery of Samding, like many others, was destroyed:

The monastery was destroyed in 1966. Before that it was quite well preserved. A few things were missing, but on the whole all the religious symbols were there. Since she was considered a lama who had come back and was friendly to China, the monastery had so far been specially protected. The treasurers, however, had been put in jail for the support that the monastery had given to the guerrillas. Then during the Cultural Revolution the monastery was completely destroyed. They tried to take her [the Dorje Phagmo] around—like many other lamas— wearing that hat [to be ridiculed in public struggle sessions], but they were prevented by some leaders. So she was spared from this, but the famous hat was lost in Lhasa. I was sent to a road construction unit. At that time the children of poor families were assigned more comfortable situations, while the children of big families were sent to remote places and assigned very hard work. During the Cultural Revolution Dorje Phagmo was under some sort of house arrest or in a labor camp (sa 'khul). The government gave her the money to live, but she was constantly under control. If one was assigned to such a situation one had to carry out all kind of tasks that were assigned, from farming work to emptying toilets.

The sisters faced some hardship but survived. Their father suffered significantly and died shortly after being rehabilitated in 1978. Like many other religious dignitaries, the Dorje Phagmo was rehabilitated after Deng Xiaoping had inaugurated his new political course in 1978. His government relaunched the United Front policy in minority nationalities areas and restored many arrangements that had been first set in place in the 1950s. Premier Hu Yaobang visited Tibet in May 1980; he expressed a formal apology for what had happened there during the Cultural Revolution, invited the Tibetans to take advantage of their autonomy, and explicitly revived the memory of the Seventeen-Point Agreement (Wang Yao 1994:285–295). He inaugurated the new political course that promoted the revival of religious practices and of "minority nationality traditional customs" (Ch. *minzu xiguan*) as well as the establishment of new education and research institutions. From a new position of relative power, the Samding Dorje Phagmo intervened on behalf of her destroyed monastery:

From 1977 or 1978 she was appointed as a vice chairman of the Political Consultative Conference of the TAR. She immediately asked for a rehabilitation of the monastery. . . . The Samding Dorje Phagmo and I, together with an official of the Religious Affairs Office and an official from the United Front, went to the monastery. It was completely destroyed, and we had to work out a plan. We all felt very sad on seeing the condition of the monastery. We went to look for the former monks. They were dispersed. Once we had gathered them together, we could start organizing the work. Thubten-la [Thubten Namgyal] organized the monks who had responded to the call.

Thubten Namgyal thus became the leading force in the monastic community that had gradually started to gather again at Samding. They were taking care of the restoration work on a day-to-day basis:

At that time the Samding Dorje Phagmo and I were both staying at the Political Consultative Conference [office]. Thubten-la, together with the late Tsondru, was taking care of the actual organization of the work. He purchased everything that was necessary in Lhasa, and then with great hardship started the reconstruction and the restoration. They did the hardest part of the work.

Official permits and government support made it possible for the monastery to be revived on a solid basis, attracting further local and international support:

In 1987 it was possible to establish the monastery properly with the support of the Religious Affairs Bureau and the United Front. . . . Among other things, it was possible to solve the problem of water. Thubten-la remembered the site of an ancient spring, and by digging the ground there we were able to find the water. He performed a ritual for the spring and made a *lukhang* [a temple to the water spirits (*klu*)]. The water gradually increased and then became a good spring with good water.

Thubten Namgyal was a driving force as an excellent scholar who mastered both traditional and modern forms of scholarship, but he also had special knowledge concerning the spirits of the place and embodied the memory of what Samding used to be. Thus the restoration of the monastery acquired an epic character in Kesang Dronma's narrative, similar to the establishment or restoration of monasteries and shrines in traditional Tibetan biographies. Reconstructing the monastery meant reviving what Caroline Humphrey has defined as the "moral authority of the past" (Humphrey 1992:375–389) in a late socialist or postsocialist setting. Samding Dorje Phagmo and Thubten Namgyal in their article refer to the ancient glorious past of the Tibetan empire and to the relevant prophecies, to the history of the Dorje Phagmo tradition, and to how, with the help of the old monks, it was possible to restore the monastery "without fault compared to how it used to be" so that it was "alive and prosperous for the practice of the doctrine" (Dorje Phagmo Dechen Chodron and Thubten Namgyal 1995:46). This feeling is also expressed in many ordinary acts, like using ancient monastery seals along with new ones in correspondence. Thubten Namgyal was typical of the many monks and laymen who reconstructed the fabric of Tibetan cultural and social life within the new political spaces that Deng Xiaoping and Hu Yaobang had opened. Kesang Dronma concluded her account by describing the impact that Hu Yaobang's visit had on the Tibetan way of life, even in small everyday things:

> Before Hu Yaobang came to Tibet there was no Tibetan clothing to be seen in the shops. When he came he gave instructions that Tibetan clothes should be made and sold on the market. In one meeting that I also attended, he said, "Your traditional Tibetan nationality clothes are so beautiful, why do you not wear them? Why do you wear these Chinese clothes instead? The multicolored *pangden* (apron) is so beautiful, how come you do not wear it?" . . . After Hu Yaobang's visit, the people wearing Tibetan clothing became more and more numerous. Hu Yaobang visited monasteries everywhere. After this, when Wu Jinghua was appointed Party Secretary of the TAR [in 1985], the attention given to Tibetan culture increased a lot, the support to the monasteries increased, and the custom of wearing Tibetan traditional clothing became more and more widespread. He used to visit the Samding Dorje Phagmo often, and they discussed many issues. At that time also, people like Ren Rong [the previous Party Secretary in the TAR] and Tian Bao [a leading official] used to visit her. For example, they used to come to visit her at New Year. . . . Wu Jinghua used often to wear Tibetan clothing. His *chuba* had been offered to him by the Panchen Rinpoche. Things have changed now!

Kesang Dronma's final comment was presumably hinting at the new political climate in the TAR and the general change of policy that followed the Third Forum. Since 1994, in fact, Tibetan cultural and political life has been increasingly restricted. Anything related to claims of ethnic difference, autonomy, the practice of traditional customs, and, to varying extents, religion had become an increasingly risky matter, in principle legally tolerated but liable to be seen as akin to "splittist" attitudes and thus the object of sanctions. Most notably, monasteries underwent a series of campaigns examining the political allegiance of monks and nuns, many local festivals were reduced in scope or eliminated, and Tibetan cadres were carefully examined to make sure that they had the correct thinking in relation to culture, ethnicity, religion, and motherland. The list of special measures did not stop there. Chen Kuiyuan, the Party Secretary appointed in 1992, had become a local icon of the hard-line policy, with moments that peaked into what sometimes was labeled as "the second Cultural Revolution." The tension appears to have eased since his transfer in September 2000.

## The Power of Silence, the Agency of the Statue

The Dorje Phagmo is one of the longest-serving Tibetan cadres in the administration. She has managed to sustain both her political and her religious position over a long period of time and many changes of policy. Throughout her career she has been rather silent, limiting her public words to the minimum necessary to fulfill what was requested. This is undoubtedly a feature of her personality, but in being silent she seems to have deployed a common survival strategy of minority nationality cadres. Her image allowed for multifarious interpretations: a modernist heroine standing for the new society and women's emancipation in earlier slogans; the orientalized beauty and sacredness of the Tibetan nationality; an expression of loyalty to the motherland in Chinese novels and films; an icon of Buddhism in the communist setting when she was described as the inhabitant of "the only house with a prayer-flag" in a compound of high-ranking cadres (Wangdu 1999:109).

It is also clear that there have been many activities (political, charitable, and religious) taking place in her name, linked to very different networks of people and institutions operating on her behalf. It might be useful to see the Dorje Phagmo as a representative of what Robert Barnett has called "constructionist politics"—the strategic pursuit of practical achievements, such as building schools or encouraging rural development, in lieu of suspended or inadmissible larger objectives (Barnett 2005:319). Through her efforts in monastery restoration and initiatives in favor of rural communities she is, like Pasang, "rescued in the popular imagination from the apparent subservience of her public position" (Barnett 2005:320).

This point is also supported by an example from a different perspective. During the same period, a Tibetan communist cadre became famous for his involvement in the regeneration of Tibetan culture and attacking poverty in the rural areas. He has become a hero in popular narratives and has started to be labeled, in popular hearsay, as an incarnation of Avalokiteśvara. He was eventually transferred, but when he later visited Lhasa Tibetans spontaneously lined up to pay respect to him, offering the traditional white scarf as if he were a lama. The rumors that went around are witness to the unique sense of sacredness associated with him in the popular imagination. The respectful act of offering the white scarf was similar and yet radically different from the thousands of times in which the same gesture has been a simple display of "traditional Tibetan customs" in the modern setting. It reflected a intentionality and a reverence that transcended any formal, ritualized repetitions of gestures.

Looking at these minority nationality cadres merely in relation to how they participate in what Yurchak calls "hegemony of form" focuses on only one aspect of their political practice, and probably not the most significant one. To analyze the act of raising the hand in a meeting "only for its truth conditions—as 'real' support or 'dissimulation' of support—is to miss the point" (Yurchak 2003:486). An official once told me, "In our situation we have to be like those tantric deities that have many faces and many names." As in the case of Chokyi Dronma, it has been a long-standing practice for Tibetans, especially for religious personalities, to have several identities and names, often defined as "outer," "inner," and "secret," that allow them to operate according to different "selves" in different spheres (see chapter 4). A multilayered understanding of the political and the religious can thus be rooted in both ancient cultural notions and political practices of the modern communist state. These arrangements recall and parallel those of the Siberian shamans in their communist context (see, for example, Vitebsky 1995). In the modern Tibetan world, ancient spirits and communist bureaucracy may appear strangely similar, capricious, mysterious, and manageable only, if at all, through the use of the appropriate ritual language and a creative translation of political and ritual idioms.

When the grand seasonal celebrations take place, local people gather at the monastery to receive a blessing, monks and nuns from branch monasteries come to pay their respects and join in the religious activities, officials come from the county seat and from Lhasa, and even a few tourists might turn up. Everyone makes a different sense of the Buddhist and communist rituality blending in a continuum that seems much less paradoxical than it sounds when described. Is the event genuine or staged? Is it a strategic use of religion for political purposes or a strategic use of politics for religious purposes? The answer lies with each of the participants, mirrored in their personal view of the occasion and in

*Dorje Phagmo in the Twentieth Century: Embodied Divinity and Government Cadre*

the different "interpretative communities" that they create. As in contemporary Christian movements in China, such "interpretative communities" include those groups of people "defining the meaning of symbols and practices . . . which are not identical to the interpretation of official media and education" (Feuchtwang 2000:170) and may include representatives of the state in a private capacity (Diemberger 2007). This multiplicity of interpretations allows for different, sometimes contradictory positions to coexist in a milieu that continuously generates readings and re-readings, transcending any binary opposition between the authentic and the disguised, the genuine and the staged, the common people and the state. It is a metaphorical space that enables, in practice, many creative arrangements, whose potential and fragility I shall refer to below and in the next chapter.

## The "Meeting Monastery" and the Network of the Blue Horseman

After arriving in Lhasa in August 2000, I was told that Samding's head monk, Thubten Namgyal, was in the hospital, terminally ill with liver cancer. Together with the Samding Dorje Phagmo's sister, I was able to pay him a last visit. He asked us to support the doctrine in his monastery, and asked about the whereabouts of the text *dPal de kho na nyid 'dus pa snying po, The Essence* of the tradition.[11] He also said, in a sad and enigmatic way, "I have been excessively caught up in the new work. I became sick for this." He died the next day. I did not think much about his last words until we visited the monastery a few days later. The place was more splendid than ever, a huge restoration having been just completed. The famous stairs, which had been rebuilt in the 1980s according to the original shape, had been replaced by new larger ones of polished and glittering stone. But there was a strange contrast between the luxury of the building and the monastic community that looked more exhausted and lost than ever. They seemed to feel something deeper than the demise of the man who had been their spiritual guide. Gradually the story behind the restoration became clear: after the Karmapa's escape from Tibet in January 2000, the government gave more attention to the high reincarnated lamas in Tibet and had allocated huge funding to the monastery, while increasing its control on the Dorje Phagmo herself. The money, however, had to be used exclusively for construction, and the monks had been largely preoccupied with managing the restoration work. So the monastery appeared as a wonderful shell, emptied of its spiritual content with the loss of the monk who had achieved a successful compromise between the genuine pursuit of the doctrine and the demands of the administration. In 1996, when we had first met, he had told me, "It is not so important to make a beautiful monastery; what really matters is a solid spiritual training and practice."

The nickname that some local people had promptly invented, the Tsondu Gompa (Tshogs 'dus dgon pa), the "monastery of the [political] assembly," mocked the propaganda use of the monastery. The Samding Dorje Phagmo in her secluded life in Lhasa did not seem to be in a position to restore the spirituality of the place, at least for the moment. The "statue" was scarred by the loss of one of its important faces. It seemed that along with Thubten Namgyal, the delicate balance achieved in the 1980s, thanks to the political space granted by the so-called United Front policy, had passed away. The policy that had enabled Tibetans to do a great deal of reconstruction after the Cultural Revolution seemed to have met its end in the Chen Kuiyuan[12] era.

Some time later, a story started to circulate among the Bodongpa communities: someone had knocked at the door of the Dorje Phagmo's residence, but when it was opened, no one was there. Then they saw an ancient rosary that they had believed lost on the threshold. It was said that the blue horseman, Tashi Ombar, had been calling on her. As time has passed, some of the monks seem to have resumed the legacy of solid religious commitment of Thubten Namgyal, who has become a revered spiritual ancestor of the Samding community.

Meanwhile, the world around the monastery has been rapidly changing. Since 2005 Nakartse has become reachable by a new paved road that replaced the old dirt road, and Samding now seems much closer to Lhasa than it used to be. Grand infrastructural projects are changing not only the geographical but also the political and cultural landscape of Tibet, and while I am completing this book, the new railway from China is being inaugurated. All this is going to transform the landscape radically, with a vastly increased number of people gaining access to the area, representing an unprecedented challenge to the social and natural environment. Nakartse is already expanding at the speed of light, with new hotels, restaurants, discos, and shops. Will this just mean increasing urbanization, secularization, and tourist consumption of the land? Samding recently obtained some support from a Chinese donor from Shenzhen, a wealthy Buddhist trader. Things are changing yet again, in unpredictable directions.

*Dorje Phagmo in the Twentieth Century: Embodied Divinity and Government Cadre*

8

# THE LIVING TRADITION AND THE
# LEGACY OF THE PRINCESS

*The legacy of the fifteenth-century princess lives on in the most ritualized form, her* current reincarnation as the Twelfth Samding Dorje Phagmo, and also very much in the minds and deeds of all who revere her as an emanation of the deity, beyond the controversial issues that concern her current embodiment.

Furthermore, Chokyi Dronma's legacy is reflected in the deeds of the less conspicuous monks and nuns of the Bodongpa monastic community who have reconstructed and revived monasteries, nunneries, and shrines all over Tibet since the 1980s. They are part of the wider process of revival of Tibetan Buddhism in the post-Mao era (see Goldstein and Kapstein 1998) that sometimes goes under the name *yangdar*, i.e., the "further spread" of the doctrine, following the "earlier spread" in imperial Tibet and the "later spread" after the tenth century (see chapter 1).

The Bodongpa nuns perhaps epitomize this living legacy best, in all the hardships and difficulties that they have faced over the last few decades—like those of their male counterparts, but with an additional gendered dimension (see Karma Lekshe Tshomo 2004). Except for Samding, which has direct patronage from the Twelfth Dorje Phagmo and, through her, links to government resources,

FIGURE 8.1 Hands with prayer beads.
*Karen Diemberger*

the Bodongpa monasteries are small and not particularly wealthy. They often struggle to survive under the new economic regime. However, quite a few remain and seem to have managed their situation more or less successfully.[1] Surviving Bodongpa nunneries are much more rare, and fewer of those that existed before 1959 have been revived.

On the way from Samding to Gyantse, beyond the Karu La pass, there is a small farming village. It is overlooked by a modest square building, a newly rebuilt nunnery that hosts a small community of eight Bodongpa nuns. A steep climb leads to the simple entry gate that gives access to the courtyard. Inside the enclosure is the main temple, a new and naked cement building, the walls adorned only by a couple of modern prints of deities. On the simple altar are new statues of Avalokiteśvara in the four-armed form and one in the thousand-armed form, Tārā, and of course a statue of Bodong Chogle Namgyal, the founder of the tradition. An energetic-looking nun in her forties is currently the abbess; she wears her hair short like a regular nun. I had first seen her when she had come to Samding in June 1997 for the celebration of the Cham dances; then she wore her hair long, as did the other nuns who were with her. I am told that a few years ago it was strongly recommended[2] that they wear their hair in the "proper" fashion

*The Living Tradition and the Legacy of the Princess*

for nuns—even though long hair used to be a distinctive feature of nuns here before 1959, and of Bodongpa nuns more generally. Eventually, they decided to conform.

However, the senior nun, who masterminded the reconstruction, still wears her hair long. She is seventy-four and lives most of the time with her family. She told her story and that of her nunnery:[3]

Lungmar nunnery was originally established in a tenure of a local ruler from Bonpo Tengchen. He had a daughter, a princess who wished to become a nun.

I became a nun when I was seventeen. I was born in a family of farmers and as one nun had left the nunnery, I became a nun in her stead. At that time, we used to participate in family life and go to the nunnery for ceremonies.

When I was 28/29 [around 1960], the nunnery was closed down and was eventually destroyed. At that time I did not have two avenues to choose from. I had only one. So I married and had seven children.

When I was about 50 [around 1982], a small group of friends came together and decided to rebuild the nunnery. We started to collect funds as begging nuns, wandering all over the region. Part of that original group was a nun who had stayed at Chagsam Chubori, the residence of Thangtong Gyalpo. She died some seven years ago.

At first we asked permission to build a small place, the size of two pillars, for the practice of ritual fasting (*smyung gnas*). It was very difficult. We applied to one officer, who then referred us to another officer, and so on. We were allowed to practice, for the local authorities were good to us, but it was difficult to get a formal permit. Eventually we managed to receive it. It was 1993. I then became the formal leader of the nunnery and some nuns joined in. For the construction we received some donations from Samding, including some wood. The local people provided labor and we kept collecting funds as begging nuns. Recently because of my health I moved away, but I still go back when there are ceremonies.

The legacy of Chokyi Dronma seems to live on in her resilience, her fund-raising activity as a begging nun, her religious tradition, and her memory of another princess, who had a similar wish to renounce the world and first established the Lungmar nunnery:

In general we go to Samding for training and for major ceremonies. We practice the Bodongpa tradition, but we also practice the *dKon mchog spyi 'dus* ritual cycle of the Nyingmapa tradition and ritual fasting according to the Gelugpa tradition.

We have tried our best to arrange the altar with the symbols of body, speech, and mind, but I was not able to find a model of the statue of the thousand-armed and thousand-eyed King of the Sky (Namkha Gyalpo).[4] He used to be the central image on the altar and the main focus of our practice; I have looked for a model, but to no avail. What we have now is a regular Avalokiteśvara, but it is different. I would love to have that image on the altar again, if we were so lucky as to find a model and have it reproduced.

Chokyi Dronma's legacy is also reflected in the life of the many nuns who dwell in lay homes, keeping their vows and practicing, where they have been unable to restore their ancient monastic buildings. In the vicinity of Yamdrog Lake, not far from Samding monastery, lies what is left of a nunnery called Shugseb, the "juniper grove"—the same name of the more famous nunnery where the venerable Lochen[5] used to reside. A photograph by Charles Bell (1994 [1928]:169) shows its original appearance; now only ruins remain beside a small stream, with a few juniper bushes and the deep blue of the lake in the distance. The nunnery was allegedly destroyed in 1959.[6] It is said that the nuns had repeatedly tried to restore it but could not obtain a permit. By now they have all died except one, at that time a novice, who practices while living at home and who often performs ritual services for the village communities around the lake. Dorje Phagmo's husband also mentioned a nunnery that was successfully established in 1984 in the Rinpung area, hosted fourteen nuns,[7] and was recently dissolved for lack of the proper permits.

The experience of these Bodongpa nuns reveals the fragility of the informal enterprises that are protected only by the good will of grassroots cadres; without legal recognition, they lack formal protection when policies and cadres change. Looking at the current number and the condition of monasteries and nunneries, it seems that the administration has not managed to live up to its claims of more gender equality. While celebrating femaleness in Buddhist or communist terms in the person of the Dorje Phagmo, the administration seems to have reproduced the female subordination that Chokyi Dronma had experienced and tried to address and that is part of the lives of nuns generally. Charlene Mackley observed how contemporary nunhood retains "a cultural logic of gender hierarchy that grants primacy to maleness" while offering some possibility of resistance and autonomy, "representing a far more ambiguous gender identity than monkhood . . . tethered on the boundary between monastic and lay worlds" (2005:276).

FIGURE 8.2 People in Lhasa. *Karen Diemberger*

Chokyi Dronma's story resonates with that of the nuns who went to Tsari on pilgrimage claiming that modernity gave them a new access. When they encountered some misfortunes, rumors blamed their transgression (see chapters 1 and 3). Nuns who try to take innovative routes do not always achieve success.

Chokyi Dronma lives on, perhaps, in her skull, still preserved and worshipped somewhere in Tibet, and in what she represents for the transnational network of the followers of Bodong Chogle Namgyal's tradition (Diemberger 2002:33–58), on which the forthcoming work by Jill Sudbury will provide further insight. The name of the blue horseman, Tashi Ombar, the special protector that appears in any monastery and nunnery of the Bodongpa, old or new, has become an e-mail address for the Research Centre of the Bodongpa in Dharamsala.

The biography tells us that Chokyi Dronma was aware of the need to ensure an unbiased distribution of the relics of Bodong Chogle Namgyal, independent of rank and monastic status, to prevent conflict. She therefore distributed the bone splinters among the members of the monastic community, converted the ashes into innumerable *tsha tsha,* and distributed them among the lay community. The blood of his nose, mixed with ink, presumably blessed the first printed edition of his collected works and is still preserved in some of his effigies. Thus her master has lived on in the relics and his written works and in the hearts of his innumerable followers of varying rank, gender, and religious affiliation. His scholarship and his blessing are reflected in disciples who became leading scholars within the different schools of Tibetan Buddhism.

Chokyi Dronma's endeavor to reproduce the texts of her master also continues, in the ongoing attempt to reassemble the collected works of Bodong Chogle Namgyal, a search for missing volumes and effort to identify the organizing principles that allow for a better understanding of the extant collection. The endeavor involves numerous small networks of scholars and adepts both inside and outside Tibet. It is a collective effort made of infinite individual acts and aspirations—like Thubten Namgyal's deathbed request that a copy of the ancient block print of the tradition's *Essence* (the *dPal de kho na nyid 'dus pa snying po),* produced in the fifteenth century at Nakartse and preserved in the British Library, be returned to Samding monastery. This text was among those transported out of Tibet by Waddell during the Younghusband military expedition (see chapter 7); in June 2007 copies were delivered to Samding and Nyemo Chekar.

Chokyi Dronma's legacy is also reflected in the modern copies of the biography that have returned to her twenty-first-century followers in Tibet: in what it may represent not only for exceptional women, for whom she can be one of their "authorizing referents" (Gyatso 2005:22), but also for ordinary women and men, lay and monastic, in their challenges and life choices in contemporary Tibet and elsewhere.

# EPILOGUE

*September 2005, Kongpo. A web of multicolored prayer flags festoons the way up* to the main temple that takes the name Copper-Colored Glorious Mountain (Sangdog Palri) from the heaven to which Padmasabhava has retired after his worldly adventures. It is a fine building, with a distinctive pagoda shape, that owes its construction to the daughter of the late Dudjom Rinpoche (the leader of the Nyingmapa tradition, who died in 1987) and her husband, a renowned spiritual master and artist.

While we are climbing up the narrow dirt lane, all of a sudden a woman comes down the slope, hopping among the stones and ruts in the ground. As she comes closer, she slows down and takes a more majestic posture. She looks remarkable: a jolly face with a bright smile, round features, long wild black hair hanging loosely over her shoulders, two big white conch-shell earrings adorning her fleshy earlobes, a maroon monastic robe, and a cell phone in her hand! A few steps behind, two nuns follow, more withdrawn but similarly curious. They wear monastic robes as well, but their hair is short in the typical monastic haircut. As she approaches, we smile and introduce ourselves. To my question about her name she replies: "Dorje Phagmo." I am taken aback. She is in her late twenties and is from a remote place in Chamdo prefecture, where she has been a nun for ten years. She is here with two nuns of her retinue to receive religious teachings. Her master, her root lama, has sent her here with a recommendation letter, so she will stay for two months. I tell her about my research and then dare to ask, "Are you an emanation of the deity Dorje Phagmo?" She smiles, is silent for a moment—and then replies, "Ask the lama."

Later, intrigued, I brought up this question in a conversation with the lama. With some hesitation, he said, "People say that she is a Dorje Phagmo emanation. This is what people say. She is here to receive teachings on Throma, the wrathful *ḍākinī;* for the Nyingmapa it is equivalent to Dorje Phagmo." He added a few details about her place of origin and the fact that she was sent by her lama; then the conversation moved on to different themes. I had no definitive answer or clarification to my question, for apparently it was not to be given. It was uncertain or had to remain her secret, at least for the time being. Perhaps it will be written down one day; perhaps it will just remain unrecorded, like many of the appearances that Dorje Phagmo has undoubtedly taken over the centuries.

Much later I came to know, through a lama from her area, that there is indeed someone considered to be an incarnation of Dorje Phagmo, living in a small nunnery. Others said, "Yes, she is, but she is just one of the many new incarnations and oracles that are emerging these days." Is she authentic? Perhaps.

# TWIN REINCARNATION LINE AND TENTATIVE CHRONOLOGY

Vajravārāhī

Lakṣmīṅkarā (seventh/eighth century?)

Maṇḍāravā (eighth century)

Sonam Drenma (twelfth century)

Sonam Paldren (fourteenth century)

CHOKYI DRONMA (1422–1455)

Kunga Sangmo (1459–1502)
Nyendra Sangmo (1503–1542/3)
Urgyen Tshomo (born 1543)

Yeshe Tshomo?
[reform under the Fifth Dalai Lama]
Dechen Thrinley Tsomo
   (seventeenth century)
Chodron Wangmo (died 1746)
Kesang Chogden Wangmo
   (1746/7–1774/5)
Choying Dechen Tshomo (died 1843)
Ngawang Kunsang Dechen Wangmo
   (born around 1857)
Thubten Choying Palmo
   (born around 1896)
Dechen Chokyi Dronme (born 1938?)

Cakrasaṃvara

Indrabūthi

Indrabūthi "the middle"

Chengnga Tsultrim Bar (1038–1103)

Phagmodrupa Dorje Gyalpo
   (1110–1170)

Kham Rinchenpal
   (fourteenth century)

Pal Chime Drupa (1420s–1480s)
Compiler of the biography
   of Chokyi Dronma?

Chime Palsang (1480s–1550s)

Chime Oser (sixteenth to early
   seventeenth century)
Compiler of the Bo dong chos 'byung

This tentative dating is based on the *Bo dong Chos 'byung* and the biography of Chokyi Dronma. It roughly corresponds to Tashi Tsering's dating based on a set of independent sources. Tashi Tsering's chronology is followed in the later part of the genealogy except for the last Dorje Phagmo (see Tashi Tsering 1993:39–40).

# THE FAMILIES OF CHOKYI DRONMA

**Gungthang**　　　　　　　　　　　　　　　　　　　**Southern Lato**

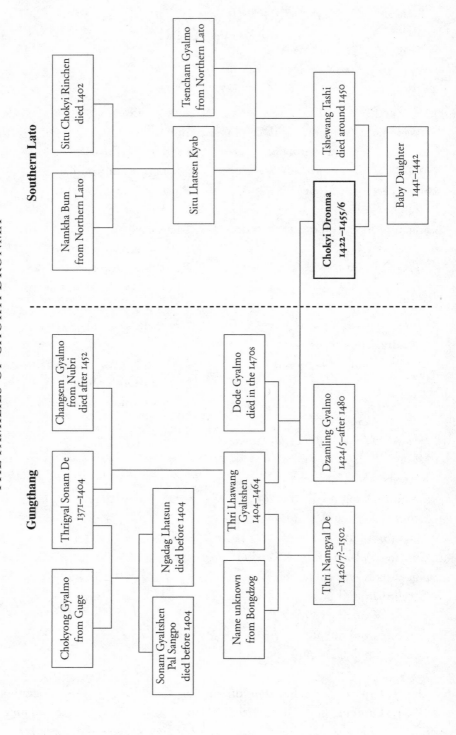

# NOTES

## Preface

1. Quote from my interview with her in July 1999 (see also chapter 7).
2. The tradition established by Bodong Chogle Namgyal to which the Dorje Phagmo belongs (see chapter 1).

## Introduction

1. The Oxford English Dictionary defines a dynasty as "a succession of rulers of the same line or family." Seyfort Ruegg noticed this distinctive feature of Tibetan religious leadership and commented that "Religious heads, abbots and spiritual masters . . . are regularly invested with temporalities that are frequently considerable and sometimes truly princely; very often therefore, they are in effect abbot-princes in hierocratic lines" (Seyfort Ruegg 1988:1249).
2. As pointed out by Steinkellner (2006:194) and Seyfort Ruegg (2004:329,223) in relation to Tibetan texts: "innovative creativity in the Tibetan tradition does not occur in the garb of originality, which is only pejoratively attributed to results of 'personal invention (*rang bzo*)' but occurs in all efforts to restore the final intentions of the Buddha's

teaching with an awareness of the various Indian systematic and exegetic traditions." This applies more generally to cultural production aiming at the restoration of Buddhist traditions. There was, however, a significant degree of creative innovation that was possible within this framework and this varied significantly according to historical period, religious school, and individual.

3. Heruka is a male tantric deity of the *Anuttarayogatantra,* often seen as a partner of Vajravārāhī (Dorje Phagmo).

4. *Sanchen lana mepa* (*gsang chen bla na med pa*).

5. From the *Mahāparinibbanasutta* (60), translated by Henry Clarke Warren in *Buddhism in Translations* (1984:107).

6. I am using the term "Renaissance" as a metaphor applicable to Chokyi Dronma's time in a different, although not unrelated way from Davidson's usage of the term to define Tibet's revival of Buddhism between the tenth and the thirteenth centuries (Davidson 2005). Some of the dynamics that characterized that period reemerged in the post-Sakya era in a new cultural and political context of regional powers competing for control over Tibet. It is to this that I am referring. The term "Renaissance," a trope that refers to the interpretation of a number of movements of cultural innovation in European history, in any case precludes "any facile comparison" with the Tibetan context (Davidson 2005:19).

7. Looking at examples of translation practices between other languages, I operated according to what Lawrence Venuti (2000) defines as the "relative autonomy" of translation, i.e., translation as a literary work in its own right, trying to go beyond the blunt question of faithfulness/unfaithfulness to the original. I aimed at a compromise that rendered the Tibetan in an accessible prose that respects the distinctive features of Tibetan narrative without "colonizing the text" for the sake of ease of reading (Ferme 2002:16). I also tried to provide a certain amount of technical detail when this was significant. More comprehensive information can be obtained by consulting the Tibetan original that will be available in a separate publication (Diemberger and Pasang Wangdu forthcoming).

8. For a general overview on the literature about these exemplary women see Shaeffer 2004.

9. This was remarkable given that her mother called her and her sister "misfortunes!" since she had given birth only to daughters. Chokyi Dronma rebuked her for this, saying, "Don't call us misfortunes (*byur mo*), I am an excellent one" (*dpal chig*), and announced that she wished to take the vows (folio 8a).

10. Alan Sponberg (1992:3–36) describes different, sometimes contradictory views concerning gender in early Buddhist sources. Soteriological inclusiveness is the only one that is egalitarian and includes women as full religious subjects.

11. In transliteration: *Bud med dus chen.*

12. In transliteration: *Bud med mnyam 'brel lhan tshogs.*

13. In transliteration: *g.Yu mtsho.*

14. In transliteration: *Bod kyi bud med rig pa'i dus deb.*

15. See Bulag 2002 for an analysis of the wider implications of this political notion conspicuously used in policies concerning minority nationalities of China.

16. On political practices of Tibetan cadres, which transcend the conventional dichotomy martyr/collaborator, see Barnett 2006:25ff.

17. See Schein and Strasser 1997:7ff.; Yanagisako 1997:33ff. for a more general discussion on "intersexions" between gender and other issues.

18. Female full ordination is currently being reintroduced in Tibetan Buddhism, and the modalities were discussed, for example, at the Third Seminar of Vinaya Scholars About the Bhikṣuṇī Lineage, organized by the Department of Religion and Culture (DRC), in Dharamsala, India, May 22–24, 2006 with the participation of His Holiness the Dalai Lama. This process parallels what is currently happening in other Buddhist traditions where the practice of female full ordination was lost (Karma Lekshe Tsomo 2004:8–9; de Silva 2004:119).

19. The earliest block prints in central Tibet presumably followed the technology of the "Mongolian prints" (*Hor par ma*) of Tibetan works made under the Yuan emperors in the late thirteenth and fourteenth century (see Ehrhard 2000:11; see also van der Kuijp 1993:279–98).

20. It is probably not a coincidence that the earliest known prints made in Tibet were those of the Collected Works of Tsongkhapa (see Ehrhard 2000:11), the founder of the Gelugpa tradition that would become dominant in later centuries.

21. Caroline Humphrey, studying the notion of "regret" in the Mongolian context, outlines it as a reflective state in which "the subject separates itself into two, seeing itself doing something at another time, and this vision of 'me doing' is the object of reflection and evaluation. . . . Regret can be self-oriented, and unspoken painful reflection addressed dialogically to oneself alone." But it can also be expressed publicly and have political importance (Humphrey 2005:4).

22. Biographies and autobiographies of Tibetan women are rare compared to those of male Buddhist personalities, and most famous biographies were compiled long after the demise of the protagonist. The fifteenth-century biography of Chokyi Dronma is one of the earliest examples of a biography written by a contemporary of the female protagonist. The autobiography of Urgyen Chokyi is the first female autobiography known so far and goes back to the seventeenth century (see Schaeffer 2004:49ff.).

23. Dan Martin (2005:49ff.) and a number of Tibetan scholars (http://www.thubten chodron.org/BuddhistNunsMonasticLife) have recently demonstrated that there were a few holy women in Tibet who were defined as *gelongma* (Skt. *bhikṣuṇī*) at different times in Tibetan history. On this issue see chapter 4.

24. Many archives and libraries (e.g., Drepung, Sera, Potala, Sakya) are currently revealing a wealth of unknown sources that have survived the Cultural Revolution. Many books that were withdrawn from circulation at the time of the Fifth Dalai Lama are

now becoming accessible, and this is going to transform Tibetan studies (see Kapstein 2006:24; Steinkellner 2006:193ff).

25. For example, *Xinhua* (*New China News Agency*) on January 16, 2000 reported a remarkable description of the search for the reincarnation of Reting Rinpoche: "Following the passing away of the Sixth Reting on 23 February 1997 the Tibet Autonomous Regional Government and Lhasa City Government formed a leading group to search for a reincarnated boy soul, aided by a leading search advisory group composed of senior Tibetan monks, and began the search according to religious rites and to the traditions of searching for a boy soul. . . . [The boy was discovered and had features that were] in accord with the indications of divinations and the observations of the lake. The discovery was later reported to the state Bureau of Religious Affairs under the state Council for approval."

# Part I
## 1. The World of Chokyi Dronma

1. *Feast of Miracles: The Life and the Tradition of Bodong Chogle Namgyal (1375/6–1451 A.D.) According to the Tibetan Texts "Feast of Miracles" and "The Lamp Illuminating the History of Bodong"* (Diemberger, Pasang Wangdu, Kornfeld, and Jahoda 1997).

2. I discovered later that Chokyi Dronma had left her own one-year-old daughter with the child's grandparents when she left for a momentous journey.

3. The PT 1287, one of the most significant documents among those found in the caves of Dunhuang, which goes back to the ninth/tenth centuries (see Bacot, Thomas, and Tuissant 1940). See also OTDO (Old Tibetan Documents Online), http://otdo .aa.tufs.ac.jp/archives.

4. In ancient Tibetan political systems, *uphang* (*dbu 'phang*) and *ngathang* (*mnga' thang*) were key notions linking political power and prosperity to religious cults (e.g., Sagant 1990:151ff but also *dBa' bzhed* folio 27–28).

5. For example, in the "*Songs of Victory*" (*rGyal gzhes*), a cycle of epic songs and dances typical of the Porong area (see Ramble 2002:59–84).

6. This radical change can also be perceived in a profound, albeit gradual, alteration in the way people were named. It is not certain how extensive the use of clan names was in imperial Tibet—whether it was only among the political elite or included the rest of the population (see Sneath forthcoming). In any case, from the twelfth century onward the ancient clan names seem to have almost disappeared from records except for reported passages from earlier sources (Uray forthcoming). Birthplace and residence, administrative units, and religious affiliation became the dominant defining principles of the society, superseding clans in many areas of Tibet.

7. In his analysis to this effect Tucci quotes a telling example from the *Blon po bka' thang*: "By an embodied fiend the Hor [i.e., Mongols] will be invited (to come); the royal race's descendants will be brought into subjection; due to their coming, people will take

vows and become initiated, monks will wear the Chinese cap and following the Hors' customs, evil will be accumulated" (Tucci 1999 [1949]:253).

8. The Phagmodrupa rulers, the Neudong Gongma, i.e., "sovereigns of Neudong," still claimed supremacy over Tibet at the time of Chokyi Dronma's birth in 1422. However, in 1434, taking advantage of a succession dispute in the ruling family of Neudong, the lords of Rinpung were able to seize power. They moved their main seat from their place of origin in the Rinpung area to Shigatse, where in 1454, on her way to Lhasa, Chokyi Dronma paid a short visit to the ruler of her time, Norbu Sangpo.

9. This term is derived from the Italian word for bell tower (*campanile*) and indicates an extreme form of identification with local interests. In English it can be glossed as parochialism.

10. Arts seem to have flourished not only thanks to but also in spite of the patrons, as Peter Burke points out on the basis of the contrasting comments by Filarete, praising the patrons, and Michelangelo, denouncing the constraints imposed by them (see Burke 1999:89–124).

11. I have seen and photographed this inscription. It is also reproduced in a publication by Pasang Wangdu (1996:56–63).

12. It used to be called Lower Shangsung (Zhang zhung smad) and later became known as Lower Ngari (mNga' ris smad).

13. The *Gung thang rgyal rabs* was compiled by the Tibetan historian Rindzin Tshewang Norbu (1698–1755) on the basis of historical documents he had collected. This text has been translated into German and published with a detailed set of notes and an extensive study of the history of Gungthang by Karl Heinz Everding (2000).

14. The local houses recall those of other Himalayan valleys and are different from the houses on the Tibetan plateau. In Kyirong I have also seen several temples with Nepalese features, like the typical pagoda roof, dating from different periods of Tibetan history. Most famous are the Chamdrin Lhakang and the Phagpa Lhakang that go back to imperial times, but there are later examples as well (see also Martin Brauen's edition of *Peter Aufschnaiter's Eight Years in Tibet,* 2002).

15. Tea had already come to Tibet during imperial times, but it was the object of renewed attention in the fourteenth and fifteenth centuries, as is witnessed by the account of the introduction of tea and porcelain mentioned in the fifteenth-century source *rGya bod yig tshang chen mo* (172–176).

16. This relationship (*thugs grogs*) that produced Thri Lhawang Gyaltshen is also mentioned in a fifteenth-century source, the biography of the court chaplain Chopel Sangpo (folio 4b), which indicates that the lover was from a local ruling family (*dpon chen*). The name Jamyang is given in this source, but it is not completely clear whether it refers to the woman or her father.

17. This is reflected, for example, in the imperial titles lhase (*lha sras*), ngadag (*mnga' bdag*), and tsenpo (*btsan po*), used in both Chokyi Dronma's biography and the *Gung thang rgyal rabs* to refer to her father and brother.

18. She is called Dode Gyalmo (mDo sde rgyal mo) in her daughter's biography (folio 2b), Dodelha Gyalmo (mDo sde lha rgyal mo) in the *Bo dong Chos 'byung* (folio 20a), and Lha Gyalmo (Lha rgyal mo) in *Gung thang rgyal rabs* (124). There is an important discrepancy between the *Gung thang rgyal rabs* and the biography of Chokyi Dronma in this respect (see chapter 4).

19. *Shel dkar chos 'byung* folios 4a–34b.

20. He took over the throne in 1402 after the death of his father. On his genealogy see *Shel dkar chos 'byung* folio 7a, 31, 130.

21. This principality kept its semi-autonomous status until 1959, thanks to the support provided to the Tibetan government for the Tshewang Rabten military mission to Ladakh in the seventeenth century and to its privileged relationship to Pholhane in the eighteenth century (according to documents owned by the Porong community in Nepal).

22. Dreyfus, following Hobsbawm, identified these feelings, which had already appeared in the eleventh century, as proto-nationalism. During the fourteenth and fifteenth centuries, the sentiment gained particular momentum.

23. One of his texts giving an apocalyptic vision stated: "The line of Gungthang will be cut by the demon. The end of Tibet begins in Gungthang" (*sNying tig kyi man ngag don bdun* in *rGod ldem gter chos,* quoted by Everding 2000:488).

24. For example, the text indicating the way to the Hidden Valley of Khenbalung says that the proper time for opening the door will come when "the monastery of Samye will be completely ruined . . . the lineage of the Kings of Mangyul Gungthang will be contracted by the sword" (Diemberger 1997:324).

25. A large portion of it would become part of the popular ritual text *gSol 'debs le'u bdun ma.*

26. Thangtong Gyalpo reckoned among his teachers Kunpang Donyo Gyaltshen and Lhadongpa Sonam Chokpa, who were both disciples of Rindzin Godem (see Stearns 2007).

27. "Gods of Clear Light" was a title that referred to Sakya rulers as well as the ancient Tibetan emperors (Everding 2000:493).

28. Red is very often associated with blood, *ḍākinīs,* and female tantric symbolism in general.

29. Dynastic and early postdynastic sources often refer to the notion of "majesty" and describe how in the early days of the Tibetan kingdom political rule was intrinsically linked with territorial cults. In an account concerning an eighth-century debate between Buddhists and anti-Buddhists, an anti-Buddhist minister is reported to have pleaded for keeping the ancestral custom as follows: "The lords of the petty kingdoms were conquered and the kingdom obtained great majesty and became endowed with the sacred law. The view and the practice of the priests acting as *kushen* (*sku gshen*) was good and the funerals celebrated by them were great and auspicious. . . . If we were to reverse this, political authority based on the relationship between the lord and the subjects would certainly decline" (*dBa' bzhed* folio 28a).

30. In Tibetan terms, however, this is reckoned as a nephew line (*dbon rgyud*), i.e., the focus is on the male representative of the lineage, which is not defined in terms of female transmission (e.g., *zha rgyud* = flesh line, or *khrag rgyud* = blood line).

31. In fourteenth-century Tibet, references to Vajrayoginī are found in the teachings of Lonchen Rabjampa (Germano and Gyatso 2000:239ff.).

32. Vanaratna together with the great translator Sonam Gyatso translated a Vajravārāhī sādhana centered on the realization of Vajravilāsinī, the "*dpal rdo rje phag mo'i sgrub thabs rdo rje rnam par sgeg ma*" (TTP 4681; Derge vol. phu folio 43–45; see also Erhard 2002:117; Roerich 1988:824).

33. Toni Huber observes that "by equating the Tsari area with the Indian Tantric charnel ground of Cāritra (or Tsaritra in Tibetan) the Tibetan accounts link it into a complex cosmic and terrestrial network of sites" (1999:43).

34. See Huber 1990:125ff. for a detailed discussion of this dispute.


# 2. The Life of Chokyi Dronma

1. This date is based on that given in the biography and is used as a starting point for the periodization given there. On chronological discrepancies, see chapter 4.

2. The biography gives Chokyi Dronma's age according to Tibetan convention, which means that she was in her sixth year of life, corresponding to the age of five according to Western count.

3. The *Maṇi bKa' 'bum* is a popular text considered to be the testament of Songtsen Gampo. During the reign of Chokyi Dronma's brother, Thri Namgyal De, this text was first printed in Gungthang (see Ehrhard 2000:15). The *rGyal rabs gsal ba'i me long* is an important history of Tibet compiled in the fourteenth century by Lama Dampa Sonam Gyaltshen, belonging to the Sakya tradition but with particularly close links to Bondong E (see Sørensen 1994).

4. The river called Arun in Nepal.

5. Also called Śrīri, this is a rugged mountain chain that became famous as a retreat for great masters such as Phadampa Sangye and Gotshangpa and as a site for pilgrimage.

6. Alias Chokyi Dronme (Chos kyi sgron me), as she appears in other sources.

7. According to the biography of Chogle Namgyal (385–390), this took place on the 29th sliver of moon of the third month, that is, April 30, 1451. He was then cremated on the first day of the fourth month, May 2, 1451.

8. After the date of the death of Bodong Chogle Namgyal (1451), no dates are mentioned in the biography. It is possible to reconstruct an approximate time frame following the seasons and the events. Since she left Southern Lato during harvest time (i.e., autumn) and met Vanaratna on the way, their encounter can be tentatively dated: the biography mentions that the Indian *paṇḍita* was on his way back from Phagmodrupa,

and it is known from Thrimkhang Lotsawa's account that he was returning toward Nepal via Rinpung in autumn 1454 (Ehrhard 2004:245–265).

9. The fact that she died at age thirty-four is mentioned in the *Bo dong chos 'byung* and is consistent with the chronology of the events given in the biography of Thangtong Gyalpo (see chapter 5).

10. Thangtong Gyalpo was by then ninety-five years old (see Gyurme Dechen, biography of Thangtong Gyalpo, 283; Stearns 2007). The prayer is reported at the end of the biography composed by Konchog Palsang and Monpa Dewa Sangpo (586–588).

## 3. The Manuscript and Its Enigmas

1. Amoghasiddhi Jigme Bang belonged to the ruling family of the Yamdrog area, which had a seminal influence in the establishment of the Dorje Phagmo reincarnation line (see chapter 5). He is also mentioned in the *Blue Annals* together with other disciples of Bodong Chogle Namgyal as the recipients of teachings by Sonam Gyatsho (1424–1482), the spiritual son and translator of Vanaratna (*Blue Annals,* Roerich 1988:829).

2. The Eighth Karmapa.

3. According to Gene Smith, a copy of this text was seen by some scholars in Nepal but is currently not available. It was compiled by Ngawang Gyaltshen, the nephew of Bodong Chogle Namgyal, when his uncle was still alive (see Biography of Bodong Chogle Namgyal 414–415; *Shel dkar chos 'byung* 46b). The author of the *Feast of Miracles* quotes and comments on verses from this biography extensively.

4. See Konchok Palsang and Monpa Dewa Sangpo, 464–466. They also quote verses by her, interspersed in the biography. In the biography by Konchok Palsang and Monpa Dewa Sangpo (466) there is a reference to the Dorje Phagmo reincarnation in the Tsari area and then in Bhutan, which might be related to the Dorje Phagmo tradition related to Thangtong Gyalpo that flourished there (Bell 1992 [1928]:165). Currently there is a Dorje Phagmo Tulku in Bhutan who was recognized by the Sakya Lama Rikey Jatrel, considered an incarnation of Thangtong Gyalpo. In 1976 this lama established the Thangtong Dewachen nunnery at Zilungkha in Thimphu, which follows the Nyingma and the Shangpa Kagyu traditions. His current incarnation, Thangtong Tulku Ngawang Thrinley Lhundrup, is eighteen years old. The Dorje Phagmo is currently a member of the monastic community of this nunnery.

5. For example, the biography of Thangtong Gyalpo by Gyurme Dechen describes events that appear in the biography of Chokyi Dronma, such as the construction of the *stūpa* of Chung Riwoche (281–282), Thangtong Gyalpo's prophecies concerning her life and her mission in southeastern Tibet (282), Lama Rigsum Gonpo's prophetic statements concerning Chokyi Dronma's journey to Tsari (283), and an explicit reference to a dialogue between Chokyi Dronma and Deleg Chodren concerning Thangtong Gyalpo's announcement that he would die in an extraordinary way (338–339).

6. This has been suggested also by Kurtis Schaeffer in a paper presented at the American Academy of Religion conference, November 20, 2003, and by Cyrus Stearns (2007).

7. The most striking case is the passage concerning the completion of the *stūpa* at Chung Riwoche, where Gyurme Dechen inserted the description of the episode taken from Chokyi Dronma's biography within the narrative copied from Sherab Palden (see Gyurme Dechen 281–282; Sherab Palden 485–486).

8. This passage is a discrete narrative that follows an unrelated quote of an edict by Thangtong Gyalpo and precedes an unrelated section taken from Konchok Palsang and Dewa Sangpo's biography (see also Stearns 2007). It mentions Deleg Chodren and Chokyi Dronma's mother using the same orthographic features found in Chokyi Dronma's biography.

9. The author of the *Blue Annals* explicitly states that although the Bodongpa school was important, he did not have adequate sources to write about its history accurately (*Blue Annals,* Roerich 1988:346).

10. A few examples: marginal people who are reported in Chokyi Dronma's biography appear also in the biography of a contemporary of hers from the same area, Tsunpa Choleg (1432–1521), compiled on the basis of the lama's own autobiographical account (Everding 2000:223–226). In addition, Chokyi Dronma's two encounters with the Indian scholar Vanaratna are perfectly consistent with the dates of his journeys (Ehrhard 2004:245–265). Also, the meeting with the lord of Rinpung in 1454 is consistent with the fact that he was ruling at the time and was also known as a patron of Bodong Chogle Namgyal.

11. See folios 102b, 103b, 128b.

12. In the account given in the biography, Chokyi Dronma seems as reluctant as Bodong Chogle Namgyal to meet the Neudong Gongma, whereas Thangtong Gyalpo, who played an important role in establishing the second reincarnation, had a solid relationship with him. Among other things, the Neudong Gongma offered to Kunga Sangmo the monastery of Yarlung Sheldrag (see chapter 5).

13. See folios 131b–134b.

14. Some passages in the biography of Thangtong Gyalpo by Sherab Palden seem also to indicate his familiarity with the narrative of Chokyi Dronma's life as reported in her biography (even though Sherab Palden did not draw as extensively from it as Gyurme Dechen did). This would also suggest a compilation date before 1485.

15. Kurtis Schaeffer in his 2003 paper given at the American Academy of Religion conference comes to the same conclusion.

16. Forty-three folios cover the period when she related to Thangtong Gyalpo, whereas 58 folios are devoted to the 9 years when Chokyi Dronma was mainly relating to Bodong Chogle Namgyal.

17. The theme appears repeatedly but is explicitly stated in the most poignant way when Chokyi Dronma, not recognized, is offered dirty water at Bodong E and states that this is a sign of her relationship with the Chodingpa (folio 129b).

18. The year 1496 corresponds to the death of Taglung Ngawang Dragpa, who recognized Pal Chime Drupa's reincarnation.

19. Sangphu was one of the great centers of philosophy before the rise of the Gelugpa. It belonged to the Kadampa tradition.

20. The *Bo dong chos 'byung* described a parallel line of reincarnations of Cakrasaṃvara and Vajravārāhī (see chapter 5).

21. In this source it is mentioned that Taglung Ngawang Dragpa, the disciple of Bodong Chogle Namgyal who became the twelfth abbot of Taglung monastery, recognized his spiritual son, Chime Palsang, as the reincarnation of Pal Chime Drupa, who was in his turn a reincarnation of Phagmodrupa. Chime Palsang passed on the Bodongpa teachings to Pawo Tsuglag, author of *mKha's pa'i dga' ston* (see Tibetan Buddhist Resource Center, http://www.tbrc.org).

22. "Karma Kamtshang" is the chapter devoted to the Karma Kagyupa school in this important historical work. Pal Chime Drupa is mentioned as the previous incarnation of Taglung Ngawang Dragpa's disciple Chime Palsang, who had a particular relation to the Queen of Ngari, i.e., Chokyi Dronma. He also appears as a member of a group of important teachers that included Taglung Ngawang Dragpa and Kunga Sangmo.

23. He is mentioned by name in the *Bo dong chos 'byung* but not in the biography of Bodong Chogle Namgyal. So he was probably one of the disciples who were more loosely connected to the master.

24. For a reconstruction of the dates of Dorje Phagmo reincarnations, see "Twin Reincarnation Line and Tentative Chronology" and chapter 5.

25. The blocks of the *dpal de kho na nyid 'dus pa snying po* preserved at the British Library were produced by him (Ehrhard 2000:13), possibly as part of a larger Bodongpa collection (the collected works according to Samding monks) that survived until the 1960s (see also Demo 1970:212).

26. Slightly later than Chokyi Dronma, the *yoginī* Kuntu Sangmo compiled the biography of her master and consort, Dawa Gyaltshen (1418–1506), a master of the Baraba transmission of the Drugpa Kagyu sect (see Tibetan Buddhist Resource Center, http://www.tbrc.org).

27. Diemberger, Pasang Wangdu, Kornfeld and Jahoda 1996:73.

28. From the biography we learn that she spent considerable effort in teaching the nuns of her retinue how to read and write, and that she and her retinue were involved in the extensive work of editing the collected works of Bodong Chogle Namgyal.

29. A text is mentioned in her biography; others are referred to and quoted in works by Thangtong Gyalpo's disciples (see chapters 1 and 4).

30. For example, the name Chokyi Dronma is consistently given in the form Chokyi Dronme in the whole passage related to Bodong Chogle Namgyal's death.

31. If Pal Chime Drupa was the biographer, we may see here a clue to his choice of being present in the first person at the beginning of the text, in contrast to mentioning himself in the third person, as part of the context, in the narrative proper.

*3. The Manuscript and Its Enigmas*

32. For example, the princess herself appears as Chokyi Dronma (Chos kyi sgron ma), Chokyi Dronme (Chos kyi sgron me), and Chokyi Droma (Chos kyi sgrol ma).

33. I am borrowing this term from Weintraub (1978) and Gyatso (1998:111), who used it in the context of biographical writing.

34. See the synoptic Gospels and the relevant discussion about authorship, dating, and genre (for example, Sanders and Davies 1989).

35. A further factor that is likely to have informed the enumeration of people's names is that most of them were presumably still alive at the time of writing. It was therefore particularly important that help was credited, loyalties were expressed, and patrons were duly praised so as to properly recognize the members of the group who had been particularly supportive and the social networks in which the group was embedded.

36. Phagmodrupa Dorje Gyalpo (1110–1170) was the chief disciple of Dagpo Lhaje, who founded the Phagmodrupa Kagyupa tradition. In fifteenth-century sources, he was considered to be an incarnation of Indrabhūti (see *Blue Annals* 1988:553). He was instrumental in the opening of major Tibetan holy places identified with the Indian *pīṭha*s of Cāritra, Devikoṭa, and Himavat, i.e., Tsari, Lapchi, and Kailash (Petech 1988:357; Huber 1990:121ff.).

37. Personal communication from Professor Klimburg Salter at Vienna University.

38. See both Sherab Palden's biography of Thangtong Gyalpo (411, 488–489) and Gyurme Dechen's biography of Thangtong Gyalpo (139; 283–284). The prophecy is reported in a slightly different way by these two authors.

39. There is no specification in the original Tibetan text of the *Blue Annals* whose skull that was, and George Roerich suggests in the English translation that it was Milarepa's. This is, however, not certain (see Ehrhard 2002:57).

40. This is likely to be the object preserved at the Bodongpa monastery called Drog Gangding, in the vicinity of Samding, where Situ Chokyi Gyatsho (1880–1925) passed by and observed that there was a Nepalese-style painting that had belonged to a Chokyi Dronma, consort of Thangtong Gyalpo (Stearns 1980:27). According to the description attached to the *thangka*, it was given to Phagchog Rinpoche when he went to Tsari to see Chokyi Dronma's skull. Phagchog Sonam Dar was a specialist in Lakṣmīṅkarā's teachings on Avalokiteśvara and a disciple of Khenchen Sonam Sangpo (1341–1433), a disciple of Bodong Chogle Namgyal and Vanaratna (Roerich 1988:1017; Ehrhard 2002:39). He was also the teacher of Gyaltshen Oser, one of the teachers of the author of the *Blue Annals*, Go Lotsawa Shonnu Pal. The fact that a text explaining how the *thangka* was handed over was attached to it "to avoid misinterpretation" and that the skull was transferred several times "due to local feuds" emphasizes that holy places and relics were likely to be at the center of conflicting claims.

41. In particular, a skull cup revealed by Terton Kunkyong Lingpa (1396–1477) in 1416 from Padmasambhava's white *stūpa* at Samye (see Stearns 2007).

42. The "skull endowed with special features" (*mtshan ldan thod pa*) was used as a ritual item by Lochen Sonam Gyatsho when he went on pilgrimage to Tsari in 1460,

*3. The Manuscript and Its Enigmas*

which is mentioned in his biography and in the *Blue Annals,* albeit without reference to Chokyi Dronma (see Ehrhard 2002:57). It is also said that at the time, this skull was taken to Dagpo because of Tsari's internal feuds, which had caused the monastery where it was preserved to fall in ruins (Roerich 1988:824).

43. Many epithets for Chokyi Dronma contain the common word *palmo,* meaning "glory, magnificence, prosperity," which is also used to translate the name Lakṣmī.

44. In the eleventh to twelfth century Abhayadatta compiled a text with short biographies of the eighty-four *mahāsiddhas.* It is available in English in the translation by James Robinson (1979). The earliest known image of her shows her with Indrabhūti in a thirteenth-century *thangka* of the Drigung Khagyu tradition; see Klimburg-Salter 2004:48–53; Lucanitz 2006:82–83.

45. Go Lotsawa (*Blue Annals,* Roerich 1988:552–554) outlines the ancestral mythology of the Phagmodrupa, suggesting that Phagmodrupa Dorje Gyalpo was an incarnation of Indrabhūti and implying that Phagmodrupa's consort was an incarnation of Lakṣmīṅkarā. This theme was picked up more explicitly by later sources such as the *Bo dong chos 'byung* (see chapter 5).

46. Shaw 1994:110–113, 231; Dowman 1998:179–183; Ehrhard 2004:294.

47. For example, the story of the protagonist who, as a child, uses his or her own clothing to shelter insects and is eventually found naked is applied almost identically to the account of the childhood of both Bodong Chogle Namgyal and Chokyi Dronma.

48. Copies of these early print editions are preserved both in the National Archives of Nepal (see Ehrhard 2000:15) and at the Cambridge University Library.

49. There is record of a block print produced in Mangyul dated 1535 (see Ehrhard 2000:16).

# 4. Princess, Nun, *Yoginī*

1. Despite the fact that Dawa is largely self-taught, with one year of formal schooling, he took full advantage of the reprints of classical texts that became more accessible beginning in the 1980s.

2. *The Lives of the Most Excellent Painters, Sculptors and Architects,* first published in 1550 in Florence, and revised and extended for a second edition in 1568.

3. Although the term "city" might be somewhat of an overstatement in reference to Gungthang, it captures its particular feel of a bustling trading center. This feature is also reflected in the distinctive urbanistic structure of what remains of the ancient citadel and the royal palace.

4. The most famous go back to imperial times, like the Phagpa Lhakang and the Chamdrin Lhakhang, but there are later buildings in this style as well (see chapter 1).

5. *Shel dkar chos 'byung* folio 29a, b.

6. "Padmasambhava made a number of suggestions: the sand of upper and lower Ngamsho should be transformed into meadows; many springs should appear in upper and lower Dra, Dol, Shung and up to Tagla; thanks to the fields the people should have intensive farming activity for their livelihood; the rivers and lakes should be trained with gabions and [made such that they can be] crossed; the barren Tibetan land, becoming fertile, would enjoy happiness" (*dBa' bzhed* folio 13a). This sort of account appears not only in the dBa' bzhed but also in later sources such as the fourteenth-century *rGyal rab gsal ba'i me long* (Sørensen 1994:369).

7. Oḍḍiyāna, the homeland of Padmasambhava, is considered to correspond roughly to the Swat area of northern Pakistan. That region, like other areas in Central Asia, seems to have had access to very advanced irrigation technologies particularly suitable for arid climates, which made it possible to transfer water over long stretches of desert (see, for example, al-Hassan and Hill 1986). Nepal had advanced irrigation technologies as well, but more geared toward humid environment agriculture.

8. The polity encompassed both nomads and farmers, part of a large network of trans-Himalayan trade, but the core of Gungthang was definitely a predominantly agricultural community. Some of the recurrent internal fights within Gungthang can be understood against the background of the complex interface between nomadic and agricultural groups (see, for example, Everding 2000; Vitali 1996:1023–1036).

9. *Yikeba* means scribes, and may refer to both the people copying texts of a manuscript edition or the people involved in copying texts in the production of a printed edition. Chokyi Dronma's biography does not refer explicitly to carvers and uses a generic verb such as "produce" (*bzheng*), which leaves all hypotheses open. The *Gung thang rgyal rabs* speaks explicitly of a printed edition. However, until extant block prints become available, it is difficult to make any definitive statement about the production of a print edition of this massive collection of texts at Chokyi Dronma/Thri Lhawang Gyaltshen's time. The biography mentions that after completing the work Chokyi Dronma offered a copy to Palmo Choding (folio 99a), which implies the production of more copies and possibly a printed edition. The amount of carving work, however, would have been extraordinary for that time, comparable only to much later canonical productions. The technology was definitely available, since it is well attested that it became increasingly important during the reign of Chokyi Dronma's brother, Thri Namgyal De (see Ehrhard 2000:12–13) and was also used by the Yamdrog rulers for Bodongpa prints (see page 82).

10. The term *kunyen* (*sku brnyan*) indicates a realistic reproduction of the image of a master. Originally it referred to the silhouette of Buddha reflected in the water as his portrait was first painted (Chayet 1994:114).

11. Women, especially noblewomen and nuns, are conspicuous in the lists of donors of multifarious deeds (see, for example, Biography of Tsunpa Choleg folio 147). Sometimes they are important instigators, such as the nun Changchub Sangmo, who requested Tsunpa Choleg to give an account of his life and was thus instrumental for

the compilation of his biography (Biography of Tsunpa Choleg folio 2b). Encounters between masters such as Thangtong Gyalpo or Tsangnyon Heruka and women who were involved in their deeds are too numerous to single out.

12. I am referring, loosely, to the notion that Frederik Barth used in the very different context of the Lop Swami, where certain individuals played a crucial role in recombining elements of different cultures and instigating cultural change (Barth 1963).

13. Cross-fertilization between Bodongpa and Karmapa is evident in the case of Nyemo Chekar, established by the Bodongpa master Chime Palsang together with the Third Dorje Phagmo. He was also a teacher of Pawo Tsuglag (see chapters 3 and 5).

14. The first one was built in 1430 (see Stearns 2007).

15. See Alfred Gell's *Art and Agency* (1998).

16. The Tibetan term *drelba* (*'brel ba*) has many connotations, some of which are covered by Carsten's term "relatedness."

17. Goiter is due to an abnormal growth of the thyroid gland because of iodine deficiency. It is very widespread in the Himalayan regions and is at times linked with mental conditions.

18. During Tibetan imperial times ministers were so powerful that they could occasionally put serious pressure on the sovereign; they repeatedly split into competing groups of interest that supported or opposed Buddhism and eventually caused the collapse of the empire. Some of these ministers, known as *zhang blon*, i.e., uncle-minister, belonged to clans that provided queens to the sovereign and enjoyed a high status as "bride givers." There is sparse evidence of the identities of ministers in fifteenth-century Gungthang. Maternal uncles of kings and their kin were also called "uncle-ministers" (*zhang blon*) and were important both inside and outside the kingdom: as ruling elite of allied polities, as ministers, or as religious personalities. For example, the court chaplain, Chopel Sangpo (see chapter 1), was related by kin to Sakya and was the maternal uncle of Chokyi Dronma's paternal great-uncle, Thri Chodrub De, the king who was murdered before Chokyi Dronma's grandfather ascended the throne. In Rindzin Godem's prophecies there are telling references to dangerous evil-intentioned ministers (*nang blon nag po*) as well as to uncle-ministers (*zhang blon*) who fail to be trustworthy (see Everding 2000:619–627).

19. The biography says that it was indefinitely postponed and that Chokyi Dronma's husband eventually married a local girl. The sister of Chokyi Dronma was still residing in Gungthang in the late 1470s, as "Dzamling Gyalmo, the sister of the king" is mentioned as arriving at Tsangnyon Heruka's retreat together with the king's daughter, i.e., one of her nieces (Biography of Tsangnyon Heruka 88).

20. As commonly in Inner Asia, Tibetan kinship is conceptualized here as referring to substances that make up the human body, bones and blood in particular, and are transmitted by the parents to their children (see chapter 5).

21. In Tibet there are a few areas where matrilocality seems to be dominant, but Gungthang does not seem to be one of them (see Diemberger and Ramble forthcoming). Even where patrilocality is the rule, cases of men marrying into their wife's family

formally taking over as head of the household are common even now. An example is also provided by Thangtong Gyalpo's father, who married into the house of Thangtong Gyalpo's mother (see Biography of Thangtong Gyalpo 12).

22. There are numerous cases of powerful female regents, although I know of only one case of a princess who formally inherited the throne from her father: Qingwang Tashi Tsering, who, in 1940, ascended the throne of Henan in the Tibetan-Mongolian borderlands. See Dhondup and Diemberger 2002:197; Diemberger 2007. The powerful Tibetan regent Thrimalo (d. 713) may have been an interesting precedent, for she ruled powerfully and for a long time bypassing the rules of the patrilineal Tibetan dynasty (Uebach 2005:37). She was close to, and perhaps inspired by, a remarkable and controversial female political figure of her time: the empress Wu, Tang emperor Gaozong's consort, who was recognized as an incarnation of the bodhisattva Maitreya and ruled in her own name, establishing her own dynasty. Although Thrimalo's reign is conspicuously absent from later historical works, she is mentioned as Thrichen (Khri chen), "great throne," in a thirteenth-century Sakya work reporting the Tibetan imperial genealogy (Uebach 2005:38). It is not impossible that Lama Choepel Sangpo, closely related to Sakya, used this precedent to support his political design. He may have also tried to use the concept of Buddhist emanation to contrast female exclusion from formal political rule.

23. During my fieldwork in the Himalaya I often heard of such incidents, and daughters-in-law in crisis were often healed by an oracle (Diemberger 2005:141ff.).

24. The *Gung thang rgyal rabs* (130) mentions the fact that Thrigyal Samdrub De, a nephew of Chokyi Dronma, being born at Dingri Gangar, "is said to have worshipped Dingri Gangmar as his birth god" and makes a direct link between this deity and the protectors of the Tibetan emperor Thrisong Detsen. This passage and the relevant link between territorial and personal deities and ancient royal cults has been analyzed extensively by Ariane Macdonald (1971:300). The Buddhification of Gangmar, however, was probably not as complete as assumed on the basis of textual sources.

25. Women's ability to reach enlightenment is stated here very explicitly; this is remarkable, as it has often been a controversial point (see Paul 1985 [1979]).

26. This famous account, written down sometime after the Buddha's demise, seems to express a number of discrepant positions concerning gender that were present in the early monastic community and to reflect a compromise among them (Sponberg 1992:14–18).

27. Ten or twelve fully ordained nuns who complement ten fully ordained monks, see Karma Lekshe Tsomo 2004:54; Havnevik 1990:24ff.

28. Currently this is being discussed in relation to the introduction of full ordination in Tibetan Buddhism; see, for example, Bhikṣuṇī Jampa Tsedroen 2006 ("Conference of Gelongma Ordination Creates Awareness," http://www.thubtenchodrron.org/BuddhistNunsMonasticLife).

29. See volume 23 of the collected works of Buton, Lhasa Zhol gsar edition; see also volumes 20 and 21 of the collected works of Bodong Chogle Namgyal (*Encyclopedia Tibetica*).

30. Geshe Pema Dorje and other scholars in India are currently involved in a systematic study of the extant work of this master, while other scholars in Tibet are trying to find the missing parts of his collected works.

31. Cyrus Stearns (1980:49–50; 2007), following the views of contemporary Buddhist masters and Situ Chokyi Gyatsho (1880–1925) and the editors of the biography of Bodong Chogle Namgyal (1991), mentions Chokyi Dronma as the consort of either Bodong Chogle Namgyal or Thangtong Gyalpo or both.

32. This issue has been raised again and again since Atiśa's time; see Karmay 1980; Snellgrove 1987:475; Onians 2002.

33. *Delog* (*'das log*) are human beings, usually women, who have experienced death and have returned. They are considered to have acquired extraordinary powers through this experience; see Pommaret 1989.

34. The biography of Thangtong Gyalpo (270) describes how his many bodies (*sku*) are engaged at the same time in grand deeds in different areas of Tibet.

35. Nevertheless, the biographer chose it for the title (see chapter 3), according to the standard practice of using ordination names after one has joined the monastic community.

36. For example, the *dBa' bzhed* (folio 3a–4a) tells the story of two monks of Khotan who had come to Tibet after hearing that the Tibetan ruler was the incarnation of Avalokiteśvara, the god of compassion. As they arrived and saw the effects of draconian Tibetan laws, they doubted their original beliefs. Songtsen Gampo, however, took them to a secluded place and countered their skepticism by revealing himself as the deity; he showed his body as being the body of Avalokiteśvara. The two monks were delighted and prostrated to the king *bodhisattva*. This episode became part of many later narratives around Songtsen Gampo as the incarnation of Avalokiteśvara that inspired a number of leading Tibetan political and religious figures.

37. Verses by Chokyi Dronma reported in the biography of Thangtong Gyalpo by Monpa Dewa Sangpo (167–168).


# Part II
## Translation of the Biography of the Venerable Chokyi Dronma

1. Rdo rje rnam par sgeg mo (Vajravilāsinī).

2. Jigdrel ('Jigs bral) is a frequently used name for Bodong Chogle Namgyal.

3. The term "Ngari" (mNga' ris), spelled in various ways in the text, refers in this context to the region of Mangyul-Gungthang, also known as Ngari Me (see chapter 1). Gungthang is the name of the central part of the kingdom. Currently this area is part of Kyirong County in Shigatse Prefecture.

4. The ancient kings of Tibet are considered to have descended not only from the gods of heaven, as usually described in older sources, but also from the Indian dynasty

*4. Princess, Nun, Yoginī*

into which the Buddha was born (see, e.g., the eleventh-century *bKa'chems bka' khol ma,* the history written by Buton, and the fourteenth-century *rGyal rabs gsal ba'i me long;* for a review of the relevant sources, see Sørensen's translation of the latter, Sørensen 1994:138).

5. Chopel Sangpo was the court chaplain of the Gungthang kings (see chapter 1).

6. This passage can be read in several ways, for it highlights the agency of the deity, of the princess, and of her mother while diminishing the role of the chaplain and of ritual conventions. This view might be related to the extraordinary nature of the princess but might also be related to the particular position of the court chaplain in the kingdom's religious politics; see folio 101b.

7. Three in the text. I have consistently rendered age following English conventions.

8. Possibly an evocation of the healing practice called *jip* by which a healer sucks out the illness of a sick person (see chapter 4).

9. Langpokhar (Glang po mkhar) was one of the main fortresses in the Kyirong area, at times also a royal residence (see Everding 2000:412).

10. The princess is often indicated with different names and epithets; in some cases I've added the name Chokyi Dronma for clarity. This is the name she received after ordination and the name under which she is best known (see chapter 4).

11. Deden Yangtse (bDe ldan yang rtse) was presumably a building in the compound of the royal palace (see Everding 2000:544).

12. Tenma are a well-known group of twelve ancient goddesses protecting Tibet (see Nebeskyi 1993:181ff.). Considered to have been subjugated by Padmasambhava when he traveled through the area of Mangyul-Gungthang on his way to central Tibet, they are particularly associated with this region and appear, for example, in the biography of Milarepa and in many local oral traditions.

13. *Byang chub sems dpa' spyod pa la 'jug pa.* The *Bodhisattvacaryāvatāra* (Entering the Path of the Bodhisattva), composed by the Indian scholar Śāntideva in the eighth century, was a Buddhist text of the Mahāyāna tradition particularly popular and influential in Tibet (see TTP cat. 5272).

14. Gangkar (sGang dkar) is the capital of the Dingri area, currently marked on maps as Old Dingri.

15. Shag in upper Mangyul (see Everding 2000:316). Monastery ruins are still visible on the Shag hill, south of Trakar Taso and west of Longtse.

16. A real or divine family related to a locality in the region (Bong tshogs? see Everding 2000:214; or even sPo/sPong tshogs? i.e., the Porong confederation). The "three brothers from Bongdzog" (*Bong rdzog mched gsum*) are mentioned in relation to Chokyi Dronma's brother in the biography of Bodong Chogle Namgyal (311). Bongchu is the local name for the river that crosses the Dingri plain and becomes the Arun in Nepal.

17. This is Thri Namgyal De, often called Chenneba (gCen ne ba), meaning brother. This identification is made evident later in the text. The term "Chenneba" as a name defining this king is also used in the biography of Bodong Chogle Namgyal, 310–311.

18. The fact that Chokyi Dronma's mother had only two daughters is also confirmed by the biography of the court chaplain Chopel Sangpo (folio 4b). This contradicts the genealogical record given in the *Gung thang rgyal rabs* (see chapters 1 and 4).

19. Guge was one of the kingdoms established in western Tibet by the descendants of the ancient Tibetan emperors (see, for example, Petech 1988:369ff.).

20. This region is much lower than Gungthang, is green and lush in winter, and borders Nepal (see chapter 1).

21. Minkyu Drima Dzong (sMin dkyus gri ma rdzong), one of the six famous fortresses associated with Milarepa and described by Peter Aufschnaiter (see Everding 2000:337). It lies immediately east of Trakar Taso. The landscape in this area is very steep, with deep gorges, and the terrain is very loose and prone to landslides.

22. Situ Lhatsen Kyab (Si tu Lha btsan skyabs) was a ruler of Southern Lato in the fifteenth century (see chapter 1).

23. Protector of the Sakya tradition.

24. There are numerous epithets that include in various form the term "Palmo" (dPal mo) meaning magnificence, prosperity or glory. This term indicates also "she that has sprung from the ocean of milk" and refers to female tantric energy connected with Avalokiteśvara (Das 2000 [1902]:791). It is used to translate the Sanskrit Lakṣmī and may in this case imply a reference to the *mahāsiddha* Lakṣmīṅkarā, considered to be a spiritual ancestor of Chokyi Dronma (see chapters 3 and 5).

25. Although the notion of *rten 'brel* (lit. support-relation) can be glossed as "fortune," the underlying ideas are rather different, for it refers to the way all phenomena are interlinked and goes back to the causal nexus of interdependent origination.

26. Porong Palmo Choding, the seat of Bodong Chogle Namgyal (see chapter 1). This is located east of the Palkhu Lake, and the path that leads from Gungthang to Shekar passes nearby.

27. Lopa (Glo pa) indicates here the people inhabiting the area in northwestern Nepal called Lomangthang, currently known as Mustang.

28. The Palmo Palthang between the Palkhu Lake and the Himalayan range (Mount Shishapangma and Gang Ponchen in particular). Yau and Yeola are on the ancient way to Shekar, between Porong and Surtsho.

29. A *zhang* is a Bonpo ritual instrument still used in the region by local priests, called *aya,* who worship the local mountain deities (see Diemberger and Hazod 1997:272).

30. "May the gods win" (*lha rgyal lo*) is a common invocation at the end of propitiatory rituals.

31. According to the *Shel dkar chos 'byung* (folio 7a), Tsencham Gyalmo was the daughter of the lord of Northern Lato, Namgyal Dragpa (1395–1475), whereas according to the *Byang pa gdung rabs* (folio 8b), she was his sister.

32. Literally the woolen turban (*bal gyi thod*). Priests of local ancestral cults, such as *lha bon, aya,* etc., often wear impressive woolen headgear.

33. The ancient Tibetan emperors were considered to be incarnations of *bodhisattvas.*

34. It must have been a collection of translated commentaries produced during the Sakya period but not the canonical set, as it was assembled and edited at Narthang in the early fourteenth century.

35. Bumedegon (1253–1280) was the founder of the kingdom and appears repeatedly in the *Gung thang rgyal rabs* (see Everding 2000:391ff.).

36. *dbyar mchod gung mchod* were the most important religious events in the ritual calendar of Shekar monastery; see *Shel dkar chos 'byung* folio 42b.

37. The fourth month in the Tibetan calendar, considered particularly holy because of the anniversaries of Buddha's birth, enlightenment, and death.

38. Figurines made of clay that are consecrated and may contain the ashes of deceased people.

39. Probably the hot springs in the vicinity of Dingri Gangkar, which are the best known and most visited in the region. However, there are also little hot springs just behind the Shekar mountain, which would be closer but are not particularly known as a destination for healing and relaxation.

40. *rGya cher rol pa'i mdo* (*Lalitavistara*) is a popular work narrating the deeds of the Buddha.

41. The illness is indicated as a disorder of the "pneuma" or wind element (*rlung*) in the human body, conventionally translated as melancholia or depression. However, this has to be taken only as a rough indication, for Tibetan diagnoses are based on different premises than those of Western medicine. Given the description of Tshewang Tashi's behavior, I glossed this term with manic depression. His mental condition, and perhaps his early death, might also have been associated with the goiter. This ailment due to iodine deficiency is widespread in the Himalayan regions.

42. This was possibly Geshe [Palden] Sangye, the teacher of Tsunpa Choleg (Everding 2000:223).

43. For the future ordination ceremony.

44. The headman (*mi dpon*) of the Nyag (sNyag) area.

45. Probably a Tibetan rendering of Śāriputra, one of the chief disciples of the Buddha.

46. The secretary of Chogle Namgyal (see chapter 3).

47. Presumably Loden, one of the closest attendants of Chogle Namgyal, who became a follower of the princess after his death.

48. "Hor" indicates Mongols or other people of Central Asia.

49. Śrīri is the holy mountain chain of Tsibri that was particularly important for Buddhist masters active in this area, including Phadampa Sangye, Gotshangpa, Gyalwa Yangonpa, etc. This was also the scene of many Buddhist deeds of the rulers of Southern Lato (see *Shel dkar chos 'byung* passim).

50. The famous statue that is considered to have emerged spontaneously from one log, together with three "brothers," at the time of King Songtsen Gampo. This statue was kept at Kyirong Phagpa Lhakang until 1959 (on this statue and its cult, see Erhard 2004).

51. Presumably Jampal Dragpa ('Jam dpal grags pa), a senior scholar of the time who belonged to the inner circle of the people around Chogle Namgyal. Together with the attendant Loden, he is mentioned in the colophon of the biography of Bodong Chogle Namgyal as an inspirational figure (Biography of Bodong Chogle Namgyal 414).

52. Chodzema, the Lady of the Dharma, appears repeatedly in the biography; this could be both her title and her name. She was a woman from the ruling house of Tagtse (sTag rtse sde pa), residing at Laru Gedzong Karpo, north of the Palkhu Lake and south of the Brahmaputra River. This family had been closely linked to the Gungthang royal house since the early days of the kingdom (Everding 2000:411, 544).

53. rGyal ba'i yab yum or enlightened couple.

54. I.e., the fully ordained woman from the Śākya lineage, which is the original lineage of the historical Buddha.

55. Narratives and verses concerning the great twelfth-century *yogin* were already popular in the region where he was born and had spent most of his life. A few years later the famous *Life and Songs of Milarepa* were compiled by Tsangnyon Heruka (1452–1507) (see Smith 1969; Erhard 2000:17–18).

56. This is the *gcod* practice introduced by the famous twelfth-century *yoginī* Machig Labdron.

57. The great-great-uncle of Chogle Namgyal (see chapter 1).

58. This passage sounds slightly defensive and has some resonances with an episode described in the biography of Chogle Namgyal in which the master initially opposed the teachings of Machig Labdron's spiritual master, Phadampa Sangye, but after a mystical experience accepted them (Biography of Chogle Namgyal 98–100).

59. Torma (*gtor ma*) are dough figures used in rituals as offerings and as a support for the temporary embodiment of deities on an altar.

60. This master is mentioned both as Shakya pa and as Sha kha pa and seems to be from the region. He was a tantric practitioner, possibly of the Nyingma tradition. He might be the famous scholar with this name from Yolmo (which is just south of Mangyul-Gungthang). His dates are not certain, but unless he had a very long life, these events are too early for him (see Everding 2000:559).

61. Presumably the *rNying ma rgyud 'bum,* the most important and comprehensive collection of *tantra* of the Nyingmapa school.

62. Pal Chime Drupa (dPal 'Chi med grub pa) was the disciple of Chokyi Dronma who followed her in the later part of her life and took care of her second reincarnation (see chapter 5). In chapter 3 I suggest him as the most likely biographer of Chokyi Dronma.

63. *Chos kyi phung po brgyad khri bzhi stong,* all conceivable aggregates of mental, moral, and material substances, name of a classic Buddhist work.

64. Presumably a representative of the monastery Gendun Shar, in Northern Kyirong (see Everding 2000:641).

*Part II. Translation of the Biography*

65. Presumably this was the site of the famous debate between Sakya Paṇḍita and Harinanada and other prominent Hindu masters, probably Śivaites, in Kyirong around the year 1238 (Tucci 1949:626; Everding 2000:353).

66. The "spontaneously arisen" union; on the notion of Sahaja see Kvaerne 1975:88–135.

67. The constellations (*rgyu skar*) on the ecliptic that are used in Tibetan time-reckoning systems.

68. This expression indicates royalty. Formulae such as "the orders of the king are more precious than gold and heavier than a mountain" are still used in some Tibetan areas with this connotation (e.g., in Bhutan). Chokyi Dronma's royalty is also highlighted here by the use of the title *lha sras* for her (see chapter 1).

69. These are four verses in the middle of the prose that might have been quoted (see chapter 3).

70. This is the first quote in which she is publicly declared the embodied Vajravārāhī (see chapter 4).

71. This episode might correspond to the one described in the biography of Chogle Namgyal in which the spiritual master intervened as a mediator and spiritual guide for the Gungthang royal house, sorting out conflicts between father and son and tensions within the leadership of the kingdom (Biography of Bodong Chogle Namgyal 310–311).

72. For the sake of clarity, I refer to him simply as "prince." In fact, Thri Namgyal De Palsangpo is often called Chenne (*gcen ne*) or Chenneba, meaning "brother," in the text (see also folios 11b and 68–69). Apparently this term was a sort of title for him; he was the eldest son/brother of the royal house even though he was the younger brother of Chokyi Dronma. Such household-centered kinship terminology is common in the Himalayan regions (see chapter 4).

73. Changsungpa (Byang gzung pa) was part of the core group of disciples around Chokyi Dronma and Chogle Namgyal.

74. Gyalse Thogme (rGyal sras thogs med) was a famous Sakyapa lama (1295–1369).

75. This is an ancient and very popular metaphor for the religious and temporal legal orders. It appears, for example, in the *dBa' bzhed* folio 25b, *Nyang Chos 'byung* 446, referring to ninth-/tenth-century imperial Tibet.

76. This passage makes it clear that Chenneba and Thri Namgyal De are the same person.

77. Migmang is near the northern shore of the Palkhu lake (there are still ruins there). The nunnery was apparently established observing rules and regulations of the *Vinaya,* the part of the Buddhist canon that deals with monastic discipline. However, the biography does not say whether the specific rules that had originally been established for the female monastic community were observed (see Karma Lekshe Tsomo 2004:45ff.).

78. In this meditational practice used for sustenance, the practitioner was able to extract the essence from things and thus live with little or no food. This practice is also associated with those for longevity.

79. Dung sgra mThong smon.

80. Chos kyi sgron me, in the text.

81. Both the mind of Chokyi Dronma and the mental continuum of the deity that she embodied.

82. This is the distinctive dark red special woodwork, made of very thin sticks, usually found in monasteries and other religious buildings as decoration and insulation.

83. As in other similar passages, Chokyi Dronma is deliberately described as one with the deity, so that through her deeds, the deity acts in the human world.

84. Changchub Sangmo (Byang chub bzang mo) apparently became an important nun in Ngari and appears among the disciples of Tsunpa Choleg who requested this master to write the account of his life (Everding 2000:223).

85. Tharpa Sangmo, together with Deleg Chodren and Changchub Sangmo, seems to have been part of the core group of Chokyi Dronma's disciples; she appears repeatedly, carrying out tasks of some responsibility. Tharpa Sangmo followed Chokyi Dronma in her journey to Ngari.

86. The area in southern Tibet where the Yamdrog Lake and the Samding monastery are located.

87. See the biography of Bodong Chogle Namgyal, 362–363.

88. The present Kyamgo village near the western shore of the Palkhu lake. The ancient route coming from the Gungthang Pass to Kamgo proceeded to Koron (presumably Gurmu village on the northern shore of the lake) and then to Palmo Choding.

89. Even though they are mentioned only by title, not by personal name, it is clear that these are the attendant in charge of food and provisions (*gsol dpon*), Loden, and the attendant in charge of the sleeping quarters (*gzims dpon*), Osang, who appear several times in Chokyi Dronma's biography.

90. The visit by the King of Gungthang and Chokyi Dronma, who would then stay with the master until his death, is also reported in the biography of Bodong Chogle Namgyal (376–391), where it is described in detail.

91. Throughout the passage concerning the death of Chogle Namgyal, Chokyi Dronma's name is mentioned as Chos kyi sgron me, not as Chos kyi sgron ma. I have continued to use Chokyi Dronma to avoid confusion; however, this discrepancy is interesting in a closer analysis of the text (see chapter 3).

92. The text mentions the verb *bris,* meaning to write, take notes. However it is also possible that this is an orthographic mistake for *dri ba,* to ask.

93. According to the biography of Bodong Chogle Namgyal (see Diemberger, Pasang Wangdu, Kornfeld, and Jahoda 1997:87–88), this took place on the twenty-ninth sliver of moon of the third month, i.e., April 30, 1451. He was then cremated on the first day of the fourth month, May 5, 1451.

94. The crowd of followers of Chogle Namgyal apparently comprised both religious and secular personalities.

95. Distinctive *tsha tsha* are still produced in the Bodongpa monasteries.

96. Chogle Namgyal's robes, shoes, hat, and ritual items are among the precious relics preserved at various Bodongpa monasteries (especially Samding, Bodong E, and Palmo Choding).

97. The God of Wealth (see Nebesky-Wojkowitz 1993 [1975]:68ff.).

98. The presumed biographer.

99. Changchubkyi Sung (Byang chub kyi gzungs) is the same religious practitioner previously mentioned as Changsung. He belonged to the inner circle of Bodong Chogle Namgyal's disciples.

100. *Yikeba* means scribes, and may refer to the people copying texts of a manuscript edition or the people involved in copying texts in the process of production of a printed edition. The *Gung thang rgyal rabs* speaks explicitly of a printed edition. However, until extant block prints become available, it is difficult to make any definitive statement about the production of a print edition of this massive collection at Chokyi Dronma/Thri Lhawang Gyaltshen's time. The technology was definitely available, since it is well attested that printing became increasingly important during the reign of Chokyi Dronma's brother, Khri Namgyal De (see Ehrhard 2000:12–13). Whether Chokyi Dronma initiated an actual print edition or just promoted it indirectly, it is certain that from then on the reproduction of texts gained momentum in Gungthang.

101. The secretary had also written a set of notes on Chogle Namgyal's life that were later used by Amoghasiddhi Jigme Bang and by Mikyo Dorje for the compilation of their biographies of Bodong Chogle Namgyal.

102. Palden Sangye (dPal ldan sangs rgyas) (1391–1455) was one of the leading spiritual masters in Gungthang at that time. He belonged to the Bodongpa tradition and even though Chogle Namgyal's nephew took over as abbot at Dzonkha Chode, he seems to have been one of the guiding figures in the monastery, which had been split into two colleges a few years before. He was the teacher of Tsunpa Choleg (see Everding 2000:521–522; Erhard 2000:203; 2004:93, 403).

103. The mother of her father (see chapter 1).

104. This was possibly one of the earliest examples of printed work in Tibet (see chapter 4).

105. This is one of the passages mentioning the core group of nuns around Chokyi Dronma. Changchub Sangmo also became a disciple of Tsunpa Choleg and was instrumental in the compilation of his biography (Biography of Tsunpa Choleg folio 2b).

106. Presumably the same teacher mentioned before, who taught her the *rGyud 'bum*.

107. Presumably the Kathmandu Valley, famous for its Newari craftsmen.

108. Presumably a *siddha* from Palmo Ganden (Dpal mo dga' ldan), a locality in the vicinity of Palmo Choding where Chogle Namgyal had tried to build a water channel (Biography of Bodong Chogle Namgyal 152).

109. Presumably a misspelling for Phyag rgya chen mo, i.e., Mahāmudrā.

110. Earlier (around the wood hare year, i.e., 1435), Thangtong Gyalpo had visited Gungthang when Chopel Sangpo (1371–1439), the chaplain of the Gungthang royal family, was still alive. According to the biography of Thangtong Gyalpo (173–175), the latter had tried to poison him. Following this real or alleged murder attempt, Thangtong Gyalpo had kept some distance from Gungthang (Everding 2000:518–519). Thangtong Gyalpo was a follower of the tradition of Rindzing Godem and was linked with the Phagmodrupa rulers, whereas Lama Chopel Sangpo had close ties with Sakya. It is thus plausible that the difficult relationship between these spiritual masters was not only a matter of personal jealousy, as suggested by the text, but reflected the wider context of Gungthang's divided political and religious allegiances (see chapter 1).

111. This is Chung Riwoche (gCung Ri bo che), the site that became famous for the wonderful *stūpa* built by Thangtong Gyalpo during this period, 1449–1456 (see Vitali 1990:123ff.).

112. Chagsam Khar (lCags zam khar) was apparently a locality in the vicinity of the iron bridge of Chung Riwoche.

113. In the letter he used a particular form of her ordination name, Adrol Chodron (A grol chos sgron), that appears several times in contemporary and later sources (see chapters 3, 4, and 5).

114. Presumably the *bCom ldan 'das ngan song thams cad yongs su sbyong ba kun rig rnam par snang mdzad chen po'i dkyil 'khor cho ga,* by Sonam Namgyal (1401–1475), a disciple of Chogle Namgyal and peer of Chokyi Dronma.

115. Onpo Tingdzin (dBon po Ting 'dzin) appears earlier as one of the main editors of the collected works and was one of the members of her retinue.

116. Ngawang Gyaltshen, the successor of Chogle Namgyal, compiler of one of his biographies (see chapters 3 and 5).

117. This is presumably Shakya Sangpo, the same master from whom she had received the teachings of the *rGyud 'bum* and who had been appointed as caretaker of Chogle Namgyal's shrine at Dzonkha.

118. Chogle Namgyal had already tried to build a water channel in this location, which is in the vicinity of Palmo Choding and is also called Palmo Ganden. He had invited monks from Shekar and Gungthang to do the work, but a flash flood had destroyed the construction (Biography of Bodong Chogle Namgyal 152–153).

119. The divination is made by putting different responses inside each of three balls and placing them in a bowl. This is rotated until one of the balls falls out and gives the response. This practice is still used.

120. Labla (Blab la) is a pass on the way toward Northern Lato above Bormo village in Porong.

121. Ritual offering with items and gestures that evoke a mountain in the middle of a *maṇḍala.*

122. Sog was listed among the areas belonging to Ngari and was apparently located between Gungthang and Northern Lato, in the vicinity of the Brahamputra River.

123. Onmo Palkar (dBon mo Dpal dkar) could be either her niece or a woman from a local ruling family. The term *on* (*dbon*), meaning nephew, can also be a title for a local ruler (see Uebach 1980:301–310). In this case, the woman might have been related to the family of the Porong princes, who had the title *je on* (*rje dbon*) (see chapter 1).

124. The Buddhist canon translated into Tibetan. This had first been assembled at Narthang between 1310 and 1320 and had started to circulate as a corpus.

125. These are the buddhas of the cardinal directions as they appear in a *maṇḍala*. The identification of a religious hierarch with Amithāba had been used, for example, for Lama Phagpa (see Tucci 1949:627).

126. This was probably the rainy season of 1453.

127. Machig Labdron, the famous twelfth-century *yoginī* (see chapters 1 and 4).

128. Kabshiba Namkha Sabgpo (bKa' bzhi pa Nam mkha' bzang po) was a local scholar proficient in the four main subjects.

129. A description evocative of the female mMahāsiddha Lakṣmīṅkarā (see chapter 3).

130. Chogden Legpe Lodro (mChog legs pa'i blo gros) was a teacher of Thangton Gyalpo (see Stearns 2007).

131. Thangtong Gyalpo is indeed considered to have died in an extraordinary way in 1485; his death was kept secret, and his remains were eventually enshrined in a precious *stūpa* (see Stearns 2007). If the biography was actually completed shortly after Chokyi Dronma's death, Thangtong Gyalpo was probably still alive. I wonder whether the passage announcing his extraordinary demise may refer not only to the trope of the physical body miraculously disappearing, or almost disappearing, in the rainbow body but also to practices of death through self-starvation, popular among Jains but not unknown in Buddhist circles (possibly related to processes of self-mummification in dry climates).

132. The nephew of Chogle Namgyal residing there.

133. Mutre (Mu skrad) is the name of a monastery she had previously visited, where she was generously hosted. It was located in the area between Gungthang and Northern Lato.

134. This is possibly Chopel Sangpo, the court chaplain who had made the relationship between Thangtong Gyalpo and the Gungthang royal house difficult and who allegedly tried to poison him during his visit in 1435 (see Everding 518–519; Biography of Thangtong Gyalpo 173–175).

135. According to the biography of Thangtong Gyalpo, the work was completed in 1456; this must have happened some time before (see Vitali 1990:123ff.).

136. *ja sbyor gcig* = the length of time used for drinking tea.

137. Bya, Dags, rKong, areas in southeastern central Tibet.

138. Glo kha khra, Mi nyag, Chu rug mon atsara, areas in southeastern central Tibet and eastern Tibet.

139. This monastery was one of the seats of Thangtong Gyalpo and was located near the iron bridge on the Brahmaputra River, not far from Lhasa.

140. If the reconstruction of dates for the period between Chogle Namgyal's death in 1451 and her meeting with Vanaratna in 1454 is accurate, this must be the autumn of 1454.

141. The ruler of Northern Lato at that time; he was born in 1395 and died in 1475. He was not only a political personality but also a famous scholar in medicine, astrology, and the *kālacakra* practice. He was either the father or the brother of Chokyi Dronma's mother-in-law (see folio 17b and relevant notes); it is therefore not surprising that she avoids visiting him.

142. Samdrubtse (bSam grub rtse) is the fortified palace in the center of Shigatse, the residence of the local rulers. At that time the lords of Rinpung, after seizing power over Tibet from the Phagmodrupa rulers, had established their seat here (see chapter 1).

143. Narthang (sNar thang) is a famous monastery in the vicinity of Shigatse, where the Tibetan Buddhist canon was first assembled and edited between 1310 and 1320.

144. Ngorchen Kunga Sangpo (Ngor chen Kun dga' bzang po) (1382–1456), first head of the important Sakya monastery of Ngor.

145. Norbu Sangpo (Nor bu bzang po) was the son of the Rinpung ruler Namkha Gyalpo and was the de facto ruler of Tibet (see chapter 1). He would die a few years later, in 1466.

146. Norbu Sangpo was also a donor of Chogle Namgyal.

147. Lhacho, the Lady of Dragkar (Brag dkar dPon mo Lha chos), was a daughter of the Rinpung Ruler Norbu Sangpo and was polyandrously married to two brothers of the local ruling family. This was named after its original residence at Dragkar in Upper Kyisho; see Sørensen and Hazod forthcoming.

148. Around 1436, in Gungthang, during Vanaratna's second journey to Tibet. The second meeting took place in Ranga (present Ramba) on the ancient route between Rinpung and Yamdrog, at one day's walk from Rinpung town.

149. The pass that leads from the Yamdrog area to the Brahmaputra valley and eventually to Lhasa.

150. This locality is famous for the Droma Lhakhang temple, where Atiśa passed away.

151. The Iron Hill (lCags po ri) at Lhasa, where the traditional school of medicine and a Thangtong Gyalpo temple used to be located.

152. The Tshal Gungthang monastery of the Kagyupa school, founded by Lama Zhang (1123–1193).

153. The Nepa (sNe pa) were local officials (*rdzong dpon*) who served the Phagmodrupa rulers and acted as donors of Thang-stong rgyal-po; *TS I* 193–99, 207, 215–219, 243–245 (see Sørensen and Hazod forthcoming).

154. The Ushangdo ('U shang rdo) was built in the ninth century by the Tibetan emperor Thride Tsugtsen, alias Ralpacen, as his personal tutelary temple (see Sørensen 1994:413–414).

155. These are further defined by the terms *ljags, spyil, shen* (?).

156. He was a disciple of Thangtong Gyalpo and the first abbot of the Menmogang monastery, established by Thangtong Gyalpo, at New Tsari (Biography of Thangtong Gylapo 239).

157. The text mentions *ras pa*, i.e., a cotton-clad ascetic. This could possibly be read as *ral pa*, an ascetic with dreadlocked hair, making for a closer correspondence with the brief description of the same event given in the biography of Thangtong Gyalpo (284).

158. Alias dBa' ru rnam tshal. This was another monastery established by Thangtong Gyalpo in Kongpo (see Biography of Thangtong Gyalpo 121), later transformed into a Gelugpa monastery (see *Vaiḍūrya Ser po* 229).

159. The first and historically most important Buddhist monastery in Tibet, established in 779 by the Tibetan emperor Thrisong Detsen.

# Part III
## 5. Succession and Spiritual Lineage: Meaning and Mysteries of Chokyi Dronma's Reincarnation

1. The theme of the pearl seems to point to a non-Tibetan origin of the story (Kapstein 2000:39ff.), which does not affect the overall argument of Anne Marie Blondeau concerning death rituals and reincarnation.

2. Bell refers to comparable Tibetan popular beliefs and practices (Bell 1994 [1928]:198–199). The Bhutanese scholar Karma Phuntso told me about specific incidents in his village in Central Bhutan in which claims to objects or personal relations were informed by links from previous lives. I have often heard this kind of narrative in Tibet, but I never came across an actual transfer of rights over people or property in the name of links from previous reincarnations, except in the case of reincarnated lamas.

3. The term "Shamanic Buddhism" is confusing for the multiple connotations that can be attributed to it. However, Geoffrey Samuel's distinction—and synthesis—between "Clerical Buddhism" and "Shamanic Buddhism" as that between scholarly learning and spiritual attainment associated with ritual practice is important and distinctive of Tibetan Buddhism (Kapstein 2000:18).

4. Chokyi Dronma's life and the process of identification with the deity Dorje Phagmo present remarkable similarities to the way a woman, but potentially also a man, is recognized as an oracle: she usually undergoes disruptive life experiences that are subsequently identified as divine illness; this is healed through the acknowledgment of the religious call and is followed by the revelation of a master narrative that reframes the woman's life by merging the identity of the human being with that of a particular god or goddess, usually a mountain or lake spirit (see also chapter 3).

5. Even though the text uses the word "servants" (*phyag yog*), it seems to indicate the closer retinue that was taking care of the young girl, probably including Deleg Chodren. *Yog* may indicate a category of people but also a caring and assisting function that can be taken on by anyone.

6. The ritual of transfer of the principle of consciousness, which leaves the body after death.

7. It is disputed whether in this case "Maryul" (Ladakh) may have been a misspelling of "Mangyul" (Everding 2000:551).

8. Probably Mongols in western Tibet.

9. Riwoche, the main seat of Thangtong Gyalpo where he built his *stūpa* (see chapter 4).

10. For example, I am familiar with a case in which there have been controversies concerning the education of a young reincarnated lama and whether the father had a say in this.

11. The story of the Lawudo Lama in the Everest region provides a modern example of the tensions between transmission by kin and by reincarnation, which referred not only to the spiritual heritage but also to the ownership of cave, houses, and fields (Wangmo 2005:138).

12. Ondor Gegeen and Lamatan, respectively the reincarnation of the Sixth Dalai Lama and Desi Sangye Gyatsho, became the spiritual leaders of Baruun Heid monastery.

13. For example, Palden Sangye, one of the religious figures mentioned when the new edition of Bodong Chogle Namgyal's collected works was celebrated, was Tsunpa Choleg's teacher. The nun Chanchub Sangmo, a member of Chokyi Dronma's retinue, was one of the main instigators for the compilation of Tsunpa Choleg's biography and a supporter of his deeds (see Biography of Tsunpa Choleg folios 2b, 147b; Everding 2000:223–225).

14. According to Gyurme Dechen's account (Biography of Thangtong Gyalpo 174–175), after Thangtong Gyalpo was presented with iron donations in Kyirong, he stayed in Gungthang. At that time Chopel Sangpo sent his consort to see him with an offering of poisoned *chang*. Thangtong Gyalpo drank; he became ill and his skin turned dark, but thanks to his spiritual power he survived. Stories of poisoning are very common, especially in southeastern Tibet and in the Himalayan regions, and are part of a range of popular beliefs (see Da Col forthcoming). Sometimes they may refer to actual intentional poisoning, sometimes to unexplained illnesses and deaths interpreted against ill feelings in the community. In the case of Thangtong Gyalpo, although an intentional poisoning cannot be excluded, a coincidental case of arsenic poisoning related to the processing of the iron is plausible. An illness could have been read against the background of Gungthang religious and political factionality.

15. This marriage seems to be part of an interesting shift in political and religious allegiances during the reign of Chokyi Dronma's brother Thri Namgyal De (see also

Everding 2000:543). He also became one of the main supporters of Tsangnyon Heruka, who, like Chokyi Dronma, was close to Thangtong Gyalpo and had a strained relationship with the nephew of Bodong Chogle Namgyal (Biography of Tsangnyon Heruka folios 32–33).

16. The spiritual legacy of Bodong Chogle Namgyal was actually distributed among a great number of disciples belonging to different traditions, who referred to specific aspects of his comprehensive teachings. Later, some spiritual masters were also considered to be his reincarnations, most prominently the Jorra Tulkus (Guru Tashi's History 726).

17. Some fifteen years after having acted as a translator on Vanaratna's third trip to Tibet (on which occasion the latter met Chokyi Dronma in Rinpung) (Ehrhard 2004:245–265).

18. Lochen Sonam Gyatsho was in touch not only with the rulers of Yamdrog but also with a number of other disciples of Bodong Chogle Namgyal, including Zimpon Osang, one of the attendants who had followed Chokyi Dronma to Northern Lato, where Thangtong Gyalpo was based, and Taglung Thangpa Ngawang Dragpa (see chapter 3).

19. See Stearns 2007.

20. *gsang ba'i mdzod* is apparently a reference to the secret teachings and ritual practices. This term is used in the biography with a similar connotation.

21. Ache Droma Chokyi Dronme (A ce sgrol ma Chos kyi sgron me) was the full name that she was given when she was ordained as a novice (see chapter 4).

22. Phagmodrupa Dorje Gyalpo (1110–1170) was the chief disciple of Dagpo Lhaje, who founded the Phagmodrupa Kagyupa tradition. In fifteenth-century sources, he was considered to be an incarnation of Indrabhūti (see *Blue Annals* 1988:553). A *ḍākinī*, incarnation of Vajravārāhī, was prophesied as a suitable tantric partner for him (see *'Brug pa chos 'byung* 406).

23. That is to say the training in moral discipline, the training in concentration, and training in wisdom.

24. *kyed rang skyes ba gsum du byas kyi slad / tsa ri'i phyogs su skyes ba bshes mdzod.*

25. The author of the *Bo dong chos 'byung* follows the Tibetan convention that counts as many as three Indrabhūtis and Lakṣmīṅkarās that go back to a time between the eighth and the eleventh century. The dating of these figures is still uncertain; see English 2002:9–10.

26. Chenngaba Tsunthrim Bar (1038–1103) was a master of the Kadampa tradition.

27. Dromton Gyalbe Jungne (1003–1063/4) was an important master of the Kadampa tradition who had been recognized as incarnation of Avalokiteśvara by Atiśa (Van der Kuijp 2005:21).

28. Dagpo Lhaje (1079–1153 A.D.), disciple of Milarepa.

29. One of the six monasteries that were main centers for philosophical studies before the foundation of the great Gelugpa monasteries.

30. As he was considered to be an incarnation of Indrabhūti (see *Blue Annals* 1988:552ff.), Phagmodrupa Dorje Gyalpo's consort, Sonam Drenma, was considered to be an incarnation of Dorje Phagmo and a reincarnation of Lakṣmīṅkarā.

31. Tashi Tsering at the Library of Tibetan Works and Archives has a biography of Sonam Paldren that is currently being translated by Susanne Bessenger.

32. Area in southeastern Tibet in the vicinity of the river Nyangchu.

33. In this text Pal Chime Drupa is often mentioned as Palden Chime Drupa.

34. Loro is an area in southern Tibet to the east of Lhodrag.

35. Lhodrag is an area in southern Tibet close to the border with Bhutan.

36. Yamdrog is an area between U and Tsang where the famous Lake Yamdrog is located.

37. Traditional definition of western Tibet, indicating the "three circles of Ngari" ruled by descendants of the ancient Tibetan kings.

38. To-Hor indicates an area inhabited by some Mongolian troops living in western Tibet.

39. This seems to be a brief reference to the episode mentioned in the brief biographical outline of Kunga Sangmo reported in the Biography of Thangtong Gyalpo by Gyurme Dechen (see above).

40. Mar Kham is a locality in Kham (eastern Tibet).

41. The monastery of Yasang was founded in Yarlung at the beginning of the thirteenth century by Chokyi Monlam. His teacher was Kalden Yeshe Sengge, a disciple of Phagmodrupa, and his tradition was known as the Yasang Kagyupa.

42. The ruler of Phagmodrupa.

43. Yarlung Sheldrag is a monastery located in Yarlung.

44. Karma Chodrag Gyatsho (1454–1506), the Seventh Karmapa.

45. This Taglung, also called "Northern Taglung," is located north of Lhasa and was the main seat of the Taglung subsect of the Kagyupa tradition.

46. Taglung Ngawang Dragpa was a scholar abbot of the Taglung monastery and a disciple of Bodong Chole Namgyal (see chapter 3).

47. This approximate dating is based on the ages of the Dorje Phagmos and their partners as given in the *Bo dong chos 'byung*. By and large, this corresponds to Tashi Tsering's reckoning (Tashi Tsering 1993).

48. THDL—A List of Recognized Reincarnations (made in about 1819). Input and adapted by Dan Martin. http://www.thdl.org/collections/history/texts/tulku_list .html.

49. In chapter 3 I referred to a short text attached to Chokyi Dronma's *thangka* of the White Cakrasaṃvara that mentions "Chokyi Dronma's skull with special features." Like the prophecy mentioned in the *Bo dong chos 'byung* (see above), this may link Chokyi Dronma to the narrative of the skull of Phagmodrupa's consort at Tsari and to the relevant spiritual ancestry. A reference to this skull can be found in the *'Brug pa chos 'byung* (406), according to which Phagmodrupa Dorje Gyalpo was told that a girl with

special features (*mtshan ldan bu mo*) was the incarnation of Dorje Phagmo and that if he had taken her as a consort he would have acquired the rainbow body. However, as he neglected her twice, she died. Eventually, during the funerary rituals, "from her skull a voice was heard: 'I (*kho mo*) shall go to my place!' Hence it was ordered that her skull had to arrive at Tsari. . . . Buddha Cakrasaṃvara was Phagmodrupa, the special girl was the real Vajravārāhī (Dorje Phagmo)."

50. This spiritual master whose disciples promoted the spread of ascetics in the three major Tibetan holy places identified with the Indian *pīṭas* of Cāritra, Devikoṭa, and Himavat, i.e., Tsari, Lapchi, and Kailash (Petech 1988:357; Huber 1990:121ff.), had been particularly instrumental in shaping the Buddhist sacredness of Tsari.

51. This merging of genealogical narratives may account for the discrepancies in relation to who was the first Dorje Phagmo: Chokyi Dronma seems to be reckoned as the first, the third, or an indefinite successor of the Indian Mahāsiddha Lakṣmīṅkarā; some later traditions ignore her and refer instead to Nyendra Sangmo, who was a close disciple of the Karmapa and a foundational figure of the tradition based at Nyemo; or to Dechen Thrinley Tshomo, the first Dorje Phagmo after the reform of the institution at the time of the Fifth Dalai Lama. These discrepancies undoubtedly reflected the political circumstances and the viewpoint of the compiler of the genealogical account.

52. According to this tradition, the deity was taken from India to Tibet in the hat of the great-great-uncle of Bodong Chogle Namgyal, Pang Lotsawa, and became the protector of the Bodongpa tradition (see *Shel dker chos 'byung* 37b).

53. Shortly after 1620 the young Samding Dorje Phagmo was established on the abbatial seats that had been under the control of the nephew line of Bodong Chogle Namgyal. This was not entirely a novelty: Namkha Dorje, the last abbot related by kin to Bodong Chogle Namgyal on the seats of the Bodongpa monasteries mentioned in the *Shel dkar chos 'byung*, was followed by spiritual masters who had a close relationship with the Nyemo monastery (*Shel dkar chos 'byung* folio 53b).

# 6. "Lady of the Lake": The Dorje Phagmo at Samding

1. "Shabdrung" is an honorific title for a religious and temporal leader. For example, it was used for the local rulers of Nakartse at the time of the Fifth Dalai Lama (*Autobiography of the Fifth Dalai Lama* 448) and was used for the rulers of Bhutan before the monarchy.

2. The expression *mi la phab* indicates literally "make into human being." It is remarkable that the verb is related to *'bab*, used for a god taking possession of a medium.

3. I noticed ritual recitations that seem comparable among the Lhabon priests in the Arun Valley in northeastern Nepal (Diemberger 1997:287).

4. In his analysis he observes that "popular religion includes some elements of both Buddhism and imperial cults, more of Daoism, but it is identifiable with none of them.

In fact 'religion' here is simply a category not a singular thing . . . its content is an imperial metaphor, which stands in relation to the rest of its participants' lives, politics and historical events. . . . The performance and imagery of local temple rites and festivals are sufficiently different to present a sense of place and of power which is a supplementary power to that of the ruling orthodoxy" (Feuchtwang 2001:vi–vii).

5. The oral account of a relative of the woman, who had died in 1966, was not precise on this point. The identity of spirits possessing oracles is often a matter of delicate negotiation (see Diemberger 2005:130–132).

6. An adaptation and reconstruction of a divine heritage leading back to imperial Tibet was part of an ambitious national project, which implied the revitalization of key sites and drew inspiration from similar ideas and programs of earlier innovative visionaries such as Drigung Rinchen Phuntshog and Thangtong Gyalpo. The Gelugpa saw themselves in continuity and of an identical nature (*srog gcig*) with the Phagmodrupa rule (Sorensen and Hazod 2005:33). From this point of view, the integration of the Samding Dorje Phagmo with its Phagmodrupa-related genealogy was consistent with the broader political and religious vision.

7. This view is expressed in local oral tradition and in some Tibetological works, where it is claimed that she established the monastery in 1440 (Dorje Phagmo and Thubten Namgyal 1995:35). I endorsed this statement in the book *Feast of Miracles,* but the biography casts serious doubts on it, as in 1440 she was in her marriage in Southern Lato.

8. The Tsari protectors, Shinkyong Yabyum, are protectors of the Cakrasaṃvara tradition to whom the Fifth Dalai Lama was particularly devoted; he refers to them appearing in his secret visions (Karmay 1988:29) and composed prayers for them (Huber 1997:245).

9. The ruling family of Nakartse descended from the ninth Sakya Ponchen Aglen, to whom the myriarchy had been entrusted in the thirteenth century. Before that, parts of the area had been bestowed to the Phagmogrupa hierarchs "in order to defray the expenses of the ritual lamps to bkra shis 'od 'bar at gDan sa mthil" (Petech 1990:58; Hazod 1998:68).

10. "Rationalist" is how Anne Marie Blondeau defines him and his position in her article on the sources about Padmasambhava's life (1980:48).

11. See, for example, *Blue Annals* 1988:829, where it appears as a meditative monastery (*sgrub sde*) hosting hermits.

12. The Golden Vase implied the use of tally sticks with the names of the candidates, drawn by a qualified religious and political authority.

13. *rGyal yum rdo rje phag mo'i khrungs rabs gsol 'debs byin rlabs char rgyun zhes bya ba.* The last name mentioned in the genealogy is that of Jetsun Choyin Dechen Tshomo, who died in 1853 (see Tashi Tsering 1993:31–32, 40); this text seems thus to go back to the second half of the nineteenth century.

14. *rJe btsun rdo rje phag mo'i rnam thar gsol 'debs mi rim byon dang bcas pa byin brlabs bdud rtsi char 'bebs shes bya ba.*

15. Waddell organized the transfer of 200 mule-loads of Tibetan texts and religious items to England (Waddell 1912:1–35), which included some texts from the Bodongpa tradition. These are currently at the British Library, the Bodleian in Oxford, and the Cambridge University Library.

## 7. Dorje Phagmo in the Twentieth Century: Embodied Divinity and Government Cadre

1. For a sequence of the successive reincarnations and relevant tentative dating, see Tashi Tsering 1993, Dorje Phagmo Dechen Chodron and Thubten Namgyal 1995, and Diemberger, Pasang Wangdu, Kornfeld, and Jahoda 1997.

2. There are several birth dates given for her, ranging from 1937 to 1942. The year of the tiger 1938 is the date that I was told by her sister and by the Samding monks. The Dorje Phagmo's birth date is controversial since sometimes it is argued that she was born in 1937, before the Eleventh Dorje Phagmo died (Tsering and K. Dhondup 1979).

3. I am referring here to the general policy shift that followed the Third National Forum on Work in Tibet, Beijing, July 20–23, 1994.

4. My sources for this investigation include a short interview with the current Dorje Phagmo; a long oral account of her life by her sister, Kesang Dronma, and subsequent conversations with her over a number of years; a few brief conversations with the Dorje Phagmo's husband; and extensive conversations with the abbot of Samding, Thubten Namgyal, who died in 2000, and other members of the Bodongpa monastic community. In addition, there are several sources published in China, including an important article by Thubten Namgyal and the Twelfth Dorje Phagmo on the lineage to which I have already referred several times (Dorje Phagmo Dechen Chodron and Thubten Namgyal 1995); an interview with her published in Tibetan in 1991 (Wangdu 1999); a film on the flight and return to Tibet of the current Dorje Phagmo (*Niu huofu* 1985); and various pieces and fragments published in Chinese journals. Two articles written by K. Dhondup and Tashi Tsering (1979) and by Tashi Tsering (1993) from the perspective of the Tibetan exile community in Dharamsala provide invaluable information on the lineage and history of the Dorje Phagmo, on the current incarnation, and, most importantly, on Tibetan views about her. Finally, the book published by Silvain Mangeot (1979), with the account of the life of the Manchurian who acted as the secretary of the Buddhist Association in the 1950s and was involved in various ways with the Samding Dorje Phagmo, is a source of additional information (although this is difficult to use and verify, given the nature of the publication and the use of pseudonyms).

5. This is often considered to be a distinctive feature of the Dorje Phagmo. The current Bhutanese Dorje Phagmo (see chapter 3) is also considered to be an exceptionally "hairy girl."

6. Paradigmatic is the change in the interpretation of the Panchen Lama, who was considered a Chinese puppet before his engagement for Tibetan issues became fully known (Barnett 1997).

7. The revolt had started in the east, for in those areas a series of radical reforms had already been implemented, alienating a great deal of the local population. There the guerrilla organization was first established (see Shakya 1999:165ff.).

8. The famous hat of the Dorje Phagmo (see chapter 5).

9. This 1986 film became an important turning point in film production for its peculiar "transitional style" (see Barnett forthcoming) that combined Communist epic motifs with exoticizing religious themes.

10. The full text is given in Chinese and in English in Barnett 1997.

11. The block print is preserved in the British Library. It is one of the earliest works printed in Tibet, and the blocks were carved by the Lords of Yamdrog in the fifteenth century. The print came to England with the texts taken by Waddell during the Younghusband military expedition. Apparently there is a different version of the same text contained in the published collection of works of Bodong Chogle Namgyal, but this block print is indeed unique and particularly meaningful for the people in Yamdrog. Thanks to Burkhart Quessel and Gene Smith, it was retrieved.

12. The Party Secretary who was in charge of the Tibet Autonomous Region from 1992 to 2000 and is renowned as an extreme hard-liner (see Barnett 2001a).


## 8. The Living Tradition and the Legacy of the Princess

1. A forthcoming work by Jill Sudbury maps out the reconstruction of the Bodongpa tradition both inside Tibet and in exile.

2. This recommendation came especially from senior religious figures linked to Samding monastery; in fact, the monastic community of Samding underwent various training sessions with Gelugpa scholars from Sera monastery, which might explain the tendency to conform to Gelugpa standards.

3. This interview goes back to September 2004.

4. The center of the Avalokiteśvara cult introduced by Lakṣmīṅkarā (see Ehrhard 2004:294, 448–449).

5. The famous nun of Shugseb called Jetsun Lochen Rinpoche (1865–1951); see Havnevik 1999.

6. Probably in connection with the 1959 uprising.

7. It had been mentioned to me as a surviving nunnery in the first interview with Thubten Namgyal.

# BIBLIOGRAPHY

## Tibetan Sources

Autobiography of the Fifth Dalai Lama = *Ngag dbang blo bzang rgya mtsho'i rnam thar* (3 vols.). 1989. Lhasa: Bod ljong mi mang dpe skrung khang.

Autobiography of Nawang Tendzin Norbu = *Dus mthar mchos smra ba'i btsun pa ngag dbang bstan 'dzin nor bu'i rnam thar 'chi med bdud rtsi rol mtsho'i glegs pa ma gnyis pa zhes bya ba*. Block print of 496 folios printed at Rongbuk monastery.

*dBa' bzhed* = *dBa' bzhed*. Facsimile and translation of the Tibetan text by Pasang Wangdu and Hildegard Diemberger. 2000. Vienna: Österreichische Akademie der Wissenschaften and the Tibetan Academy of Social Sciences.

Biography of Bodong Chole Namgyal = Amoghasiddhi 'Jigs med 'bangs, *Bo dong pan chen gyi rnam thar*. 1990. Lhasa: Bod ljongs bod yig dpe rnying dpe skrun khang.

Biography of Bodong Chogle Namgyal by the Eighth Karmapa = Mi bskyod rdo rje, *rJe btsun phyog las rnam rgyal ba'i zhal lnga nas kyis rnam thar ngo mtshar gyis rgya mtsho*. Manuscript of 71 folios.

Biography of Chokyi Dronma = *Ye shes mkha' 'gro bsod nams 'dren gyi sku skyes gsum pa rje btsun ma chos kyi sgron ma'i rnam thar*. Incomplete manuscript of 144 folios.

Biography of Chopel Sangpo = *Bla chen chos dpal bzang po'i rnam thar*. Manuscript of 41 folios, compiled by *Chos 'khor lo tsa ba Manjusri Dznyana* in 1466 in Gungthang. Scan kept privately at Porong Shabkha.

Biography of Thangtong Gyalpo = 'Gyur med bde chen, *Thang rgyal rnam thar*. 1982. Chengdu: Si khron mi rigs dpe skrun khang.

Biography of Thangtong Gyalpo by Monpa Dewa Sangpo = Mon pa bDe ba bzang po, "Bla ma Thang stong rgyal po'i rnam thar gsal ba'i me long 1–589 [ = 1b1–294a3]." In *The Collected Works of Grub-chen Thang-stong rgyal-po*. Vol. II. 1984. Bhutan.

Biography of Thangtong Gyalpo by Sherab Palden = Shes rab dpal ldan, *rJe grub thob chen po lcags zam pa'i rnam par thar pa ngo mtshar rgya mtsho* 1–565. 1984/85. Thimphu: National Library of Bhutan.

Biography of Tsangnyon Heruka = rGod gTsang ras pa sna tshogs rang grol, *The Life of the Saint of Gtsan*. Ed. Lokesh Chandra. 1969. New Delhi.

Biography of Vanaratna = 'Gos Lo tsa ba gZhon nu dpal, *mKhas pa chen po dpal nags kyi rin chen gyi rnam par thar pa*. 1985. Thimphu: National Library of Bhutan.

*Bod kyi gnas yig bdams bsgrigs* = *Bod kyi gnas yig bdams bsgrigs*. 1995. Lhasa: Bod ljongs bod yig dpe rnying dpe skrun khang.

*Bo dong chos 'byung* = *dPal de kho na nyid dus pa las bo dong chos 'byung gsal byed sgron me zhes bya ba dPal thams cad mkhyen pa 'Chi med 'od zer gyis mdzad pa* (sixteenth century). Manuscript of 35 folios by 'Chi me 'Od zer, kept at Bodong E monastery.

*Bod rgya tshig mdzod chen mo* = *Bod rgya tshig mdzod chen mo*. 1985. Beijing: Mi rigs dpe skrun khang (The National Press).

*'Brug pa'i chos 'byung* = 'Brug pa Pad ma dkar po, *'Brug pa'i chos 'byung*. 1990. Lhasa: Bod ljongs bod yig dpe rnying dpe skrun khang.

*Bu ston chos 'byung* = Bu ston Rin chen grub, *Bu ston chos 'byung*. 1988. Tshongon: Krung go bod kyi shes rig dpe skrung khang.

*Byang pa gdung rabs* = *gYas ru Byang pa'i gdung rabs*. Manuscript of 24 folios kept in the Beijing National Library.

Chokyi Dronma (Chos kyi sgron ma). *Untitled*. In *Supplemental Texts to the Collected Works of Thang stong rgyal po Series* (*Grub chen thang stong bka' 'bum gyi rgyab chos*), 2:240–248. 1984. Thimphu: National Library of Bhutan.

*Collected Works of Bodong Chogle Namgyal* = *dPal de kho na nyid 'dus pa*. Edition of the collected works of Bodong Chogle Namgyal, 119 vols. 1973. New Delhi: Tibet House Library.

*Deb ther dmar po gsar ma* = bSod nams grags pa, *Deb ther dmar po gsar ma*. Ed. and trans. G. Tucci, 1971. Roma: IsMEO. Also 1989. Lhasa: Bod ljongs mi dmangs dpe skrun khang.

*Deb ther sngon po* = 'Gos lo tsa ba gZhon nu dpal, *Deb ther sngon po*. June 1985. Chengdu: Si khron mi rigs dpe skrun khang. *The Blue Annals*. 1988 [1949]. Trans. G. Roerich. Delhi: Motilal Banarsidass.

Demo 1970 = Demo Ngawang Deleg. *Three Karchacks*. 1970. Including a survey of printing blocks in Central Tibet, *Gangs can gyi ljongs su bka' dang bstan bcos sogs kyi glegs*

bam spar gzhi ji ltar yod pa rnam nas dkar chag spar thor phyogs tsam du bkod pa phan
bde'i pad tshal 'byed pa'i nyin byed. New Delhi.

Dorje Phagmo and Thubten Namgyal. 1995. rDo rje phag mo bde chen chos sgron dang
grwa Thub bstan rnam rgyal = "Bsam sdings rdo rje phag mo'i 'khrungs rabs dang|
sku phreng rim byong gyi mdzad rnam| yar 'brog bsam sdings dgon gyi dkar chag
bcas rags tsam bkos pa|." Krung go'i bod kyi shes rig. Nr. 2, pp. 31–58.

dPal rdo rje phag mo'i sgrub thabs rdo rje rnam par sgeg ma zhes bya ba. Trans. Vanaratna
and Lochen Sonam Gyatso of the Vajravilāsinīnāma Vajravarāhīsādhana. (TTP4681;
Derge vol. phu folio 43–45).

Gung thang rgyal rabs = Gung thang rgyal rabs by Rig 'dzin Tshe dbang nor bu, Bod kyi
lo rgyus deb ther khag lnga. 1990. Lhasa: Bod ljongs bod yig dpe rnying dpe skrun
khang.

Guru Tashi's History = Gu ru bKra shis, Guru bKra shis chos 'byung. 1990. Krung go'i bod
kyi shes rig dpe skrun khang.

rGya bod yig tshang = dPal 'byor bzang po, rGya bod yig tshang chen mo. 1985. Chengdu:
Si khron mi rigs dpe skrun khang.

rGyal rabs gsal ba'i me long = rGyal rabs gsal ba'i me long. 1981. Beijing: Mi rigs dpe skrun
khang.

rGyal yum rdo rje phag mo'i khrungs rabs gsol 'debs byin rlabs char rgyun zhes bya ba.
Manuscript of 10 folios kept at Samding monastery.

rJe btsun rdo rje phag mo'i rnam thar gsol 'debs mi rim byon dang bcas pa byin brlabs bdud
rtsi char 'bebs zhes bya ba. Ritual text of 8 folios kept at Samding monastery.

mKhas pa'i dga' ston = dPa' bo gtsug lag phreng ba, Dam pa'i chos kyi 'khor los bsgyur pa
rnams kyi byung ba gsal bar byed pa mkhas pa'i dga' ston. 1986. Beijing: Mi rigs dpe
skrun khang.

bKa' thang sde lnga = bKa' thang sde lnga. 1986. Beijing: Mi rigs dpe skrun khang.

rLangs kyi po ti bse ru = Phag mo gru Byang chub rgyal mtshan, rLangs kyi po ti bse ru
rgyas pa. 1986. Lhasa: Bod ljongs mi dmangs dpe skrun khang.

TTP = Catalogue and Index to the Tibetan Tripitaka, Peking edition. 1962. Ed. D. T.
Suzuki (Otani University, Kyoto). Tokyo: Suzuki Research Foundation.

Shel dkar chos 'byung = Ngag dbang skal ldan rgya mtsho, Shel dkar chos 'byung. History of
the "White Crystal." Religion and Politics of Southern La stod. Trans. and facsimile edition of the Tibetan text by Pasang Wangdu and Hildegard Diemberger with Guntram
Hazod. 1996. Vienna: Österreichische Akademie der Wissenschaften and Tibetan
Academy of the Autonomous Region Tibet.

sTag lung chos 'byung = sTag lung chos 'byung. 1992. Lhasa: Bod ljong bod yig dpe rnying
dpe skrun khang.

Tashi Tshering. bKra shis tshe ring "bSam sding rdo rje phag mo sku phreng rim byong
gyi mtshan dang 'khrungs gshegs kyi lo khams star chags su 'god thabs sngon 'gro'i
zhib 'jug mdor bsdud." 1993. In gYu mtsho 1 (1) (20–53).

*Vaiḍūrya ser po* = sDe srid Sangs rgyas rgya mtsho, *dGa' ldan chos 'byung Vaidurya ser po*. 1989. Beijing: Bod kyi shes rig dpe skrun khang.

Wangdu. 1999. "bSam sding rdo rje phag mo bde chen chos kyi sgrol ma" by dBang 'dus. In *Bod don gleng ba*, 109–119.

## Sources in English and Other Languages

Abu-Lughod, L. 1990. "The Romance of Resistance: Tracing Transformations of Power Through Bedouin Women." *American Ethnologist* 17 (1): 41–55.

Aufschnaiter, P. and M. Brauen. 2002. *Peter Aufschnaiter's Eight Years in Tibet*. Hong Kong: Orchid Press.

Aziz, B. 1976. "Reincarnation Reconsidered: or the Reincarnated Lama as Shaman." In J. T. Hitchock and R. L. Jones, eds., *Spirit Possession in the Nepal Himalayas*. London: Aris and Phillips.

——. 1978. *Tibetan Frontier Families: Reflections of Three Generations from D'ing-ri*. New Delhi: Vikas.

——. 1988. "Women in Tibetan Society and Tibetology." In H. Uebach and J. Panglung, eds., *Tibetan Studies*. Munich: Bayerische Akademie der Wissenschaften.

Bacot, J., F. W. Thomas, and Ch. Toussaint. 1940. *Documents de Touen Houang relatifs a l'histoire du Tibet*. Paris: Annales du Musee Guimet.

Barnett, R. 1996. *Cutting Off the Serpent's Head: Tightening Control in Tibet, 1994–1995*. London: Tibet Information Network and Human Rights Watch/Asia.

——. 1997. *A Poisoned Arrow: The Secret Report of the 10th Panchen Lama*. London: Tibet Information Network and Human Rights Watch/Asia.

——. 2001. "The Chinese Frontiersman and Winter Worms: Chen Kuiyuan in the T.A.R. 1992–2000." In A. McKay, ed., *Tibet and Her Neighbours*. London: Curzon.

——. 2001. "'Violated Specialness': Western Political Representations of Tibet." In T. Dodin and H. Raether, eds., *Imagining Tibet*. Boston: Wisdom.

——. 2005. "Beyond the Collaborator-Martyr Model: Strategies of Compliance, Opportunism and Opposition Within Tibet." In B. Sautman and J. Dreyer, eds., *The Tibet Question*. New York: M. E. Sharpe.

——. 2005. "Women and Politics in Contemporary Tibet." In H. Havnevik and J. Gyatso, eds., *Women in Tibet*. New York: Columbia University Press.

——. Forthcoming. "Female *sprul-sku:* Tibetan Cinema and the Filming of the Dorje Phagmo." Paper given at the 11th conference of the IATS, Bonn, 2006.

Barth, F. 1963. *The Role of the Entrepreneur in Social Change in Northern Norway*. Oslo: Norwegian University Press.

Battaglia, D. 1995. *Rhetorics of Self-Making*. Berkeley: University of California Press.

Beckwith, C. 1987. "The Tibetans in the Ordos and North China: Considerations on the Role of the Tibetan Empire in World History." In C. Beckwith, ed., *Silver on Lapis: Tibetan Literary Culture and History*. Bloomington: The Tibet Society.

Bell, C. 1994 [1928]. *The People of Tibet*. Delhi: Motilal Banarsidass.

Bellezza, J. 1997. *Divine Dyads: Ancient Civilization in Tibet*. Dharamsala: Library of Tibetan Works and Archives.

Beyer, S. 1988 [1973]. *Magic and Ritual in Tibet: The Cult of Tārā*. Delhi: Motilal Banarsidass.

Blondeau, A. M. 1997. "Que notre enfant revienne! Un ritual meconnu pour les enfants en bas age." In S. Karmay and P. Sagant, eds., *Les habitants du toit du monde*. Volume in Honour of Alexander Macdonald. Paris, Nanterre: Société d'Éthnologie.

———. 1980. "Analysis of the Biographies of Padmasambhava According to Tibetan Tradition: Classification of Sources." In M. Aris and Aung San Suu Kyi, eds., *Tibetan Studies in Honour of Hugh Richardson*. Warminster: Aris and Phillips.

Bramley, S. 2005. *Leonardo Da Vinci, Artista, Scienziato, Filosofo*. Milano: Mondadori.

Brockmeier, J. 2000. "Autobiographical Time." In M. Bamberg, M. McCabe, and A. McCabe, *Narrative Identity* Special Issue 10 (1): 51–73.

Brockmeier, J. and R. Harre. 2001. "Narrative: Problems and Promises of an Alternative Paradigm." In D. Carbaugh, ed., *Narrative and Identity: Studies in Autobiography, Self and Culture* (Studies in Narrative). Amsterdam and Philadelphia: John Benjamins.

Burke, P. 1999 [1986]. *The Italian Renaissance: Culture and Society in Italy*. Cambridge: Polity Press.

Butler, J. 1990. *Gender Trouble: Feminism and the Subversion of Identity*. London: Routledge.

Candler, E. 1905. *The Unveiling of Lhasa*. London: Nelson.

Cartsen, J. 2000. *Cultures of Relatedness: New Approaches to the Study of Kinship*. Cambridge: Cambridge University Press.

Chayet, A. 1985. *Les Temples de Jehol et leurs Modeles Tibetains*. Paris: Éditions Recherche sur les Civilisations.

———. 1994. *Art et archéologie du Tibet*. Paris: Picard.

———. 2002. "Women and Reincarnation in Tibet: The Case of Gung ru mKha' 'gro ma." In A. Cadonna and E. Bianchi, eds., *Facets of Tibetan Religious Tradition and Contacts with Neighbouring Cultural Areas*. Firenze: Olschki Editore.

Clarke Warren, H. 1984. *Buddhism in Translations*. New York: Atheneum.

Cook, J. Forthcoming. "In What Ways Do Hagiographic Narratives Create Possibilities for Buddhist Nuns?" Paper given at MIASU Research Seminar, November 2006.

Cueppers, C. 2004. *The Relationship Between Religion and State* (chos srid zung 'brel) in *Traditional Tibet*. Proceedings of a seminar held in Lumbini, Nepal, March 2000. Lumbini: Lumbini International Research Institute.

Da Col, G. Forthcoming. "Learning to See and Store Moralities: Moral Imagination, Nature and the Economies of Fortune Around Kha ba dkar po, a Tibetan Sacred Mountain in Northwest Yunnan (China)." Ph.D. thesis, University of Cambridge.

Das, S. C. 1988 [1902]. *Lhasa and Central Tibet*. Delhi: Mehra Offset Press.

Davidson, R. 2005. *Tibetan Renaissance: Tantric Buddhism in the Rebirth of Tibetan Culture*. New York: Columbia University Press.

Derrida, J. 2000. "What Is a 'Relevant' Translation?" Trans. L. Venuti. In L. Venuti, ed., *The Translation Studies Reader*. London: Routledge.

De Certeau, M. 1988. *The Writing of History*. New York: Columbia University Press.

De Silva, R. 2004. "Reclaiming the Robe: Reviving the Bikkhuni Order in Sri Lanka." In Karma Lekshe Tsomo, ed., *Buddhist Women and Social Justice*. Albany: State University of New York Press.

Diemberger, H. 1996. "Political and Religious Aspects of Mountain Cults in the Hidden Valley of Khenbalung: Tradition, Decline and Revitalization." In A. M. Blondeau and E. Steinkellner, eds., *Reflections of the Mountain: Essays on the History and Social Meaning of the Mountain Cult in Tibet and the Himalaya*. Vienna: Verlag der Oesterreichischen Akademie der Wissenschaften.

——. 1997. "Beyul Khenbalung, the Hidden Valley of Artemisia: On Himalayan Communities and Their Sacred Landscape." In A. Macdonald, ed., *Maṇḍala and Landscape*. New Delhi: Printworld.

——. 1998. "The Horseman in Red: On Sacred Mountains of La stod Lho (Southern Tibet)." In A. M. Blondeau, ed., *Tibetan Mountain Deities, Their Cults and Representations*. Vienna: Verlag der Österr. Akademie der Wissenschaften.

——. 2002. "The People of Porong and Concepts of Territory." In K. Buffetrille and H. Diemberger, eds., *Territory and Identity in Tibet and the Himalaya*. Leiden: Brill.

——. 2005. "Female Oracles in Modern Tibet." In H. Havnevik and J. Gyatso, eds., *Women in Tibet*. New York: Columbia University Press.

——. 2006. "Gender Politics: Three Women Rulers in the Mongolian-Tibetan Borderlands, 1916–2000." In D. Sneath, ed., *Technologies of Governance*. Washington: Western Washington University Press.

——. 2007. "Leaders, Names and Festivals: the Management of Tradition in the Mongolian-Tibetan Borderlands." *Proceedings of the 10th Seminar of the International Association for Tibetan Studies*, Oxford University.

Diemberger, H. and G. Hazod. 1997. "Animal Sacrifices and Mountain Deities in Southern Tibet: Mythology, Rituals and Politics." In S. Karmay and P. Sagant, eds., *Les habitants du toit du monde*. Volume in Honour of Alexander Macdonald. Paris, Nanterre: Société d'Éthnologie.

——. 1999. "Machig Zhama's Recovery: Traces of Ancient History and Myth in the South Tibetan Landscape of Kharta and Phadrug." In T. Huber, ed., *Sacred Spaces and Powerful Places in Tibetan Culture: A Collection of Essays*. Dharamsala: Library of Tibetan Works and Archives.

Diemberger, H. and C. Ramble. Forthcoming. "Rethinking Tibetan Kinship." *Inner Asia*.

Diemberger, H. and Pasang Wangdu. Forthcoming. *The Life of Chokyi Dronma and Other Materials from the Bodongpa Tradition: Tibetan Texts and Annotated Translations.* Vienna: Verlag der OeAW and Tibetan Academy of Social Sciences.

Diemberger, H., Pasang Wangdu, M. Kornfeld, and C. Yahoda. 1997. *Feast of Miracles: The Life and the Tradition of Bodong Chole Namgyal (1375/6–1451 A.D.) According to the Tibetan Texts "Feast of Miracles" and "The Lamp Illuminating the History of Bodong."* Clusone: Porong Pema Choding Editions.

Dhondup, K. and Tashi Tsering. 1979. "Samdhing Dorjee Phagmo: Tibet's Only Female Incarnation." *Tibetan Review* (August):11–17.

Dhondup, Y. and H. Diemberger. 2002. "Tashi Tsering: The Last Mongol Queen of 'Sogpo' (Henan)." *Inner Asia* 4, no. 2: 197–224.

Dreyer, J. 1972. "Traditional Minority Elites." In R. Scalpino, ed., *Elites in the People's Republic of China.* Seattle: University of Washington Press.

Dreyfus, G. 1994. "Proto-Nationalism in Tibet." In P. Kvaerne, ed., *Tibetan Studies.* Oslo: The Institute for Comparative Research.

Dudjom Rinpoche. 1991. *The Nyingma School of Tibetan Buddhism.* Trans. Gyurme Dorje and M. Kapstein. Boston: Wisdom.

Eisenstein, E. 1993. *The Printing Revolution in Early Modern Europe.* Cambridge: Cambridge University Press.

Empson, R. 2007. "Enlivened Memories: Recalling Absence and Loss in Mongolia." In J. Carsten, ed., *Ghosts of Memory: Essays on Remembrance and Relatedness.* Oxford: Blackwell.

English, E. 2002. *Vajrayoginī: Her Visualizations, Rituals and Forms.* Boston: Wisdom.

Erhard, F. K. 2000. *Early Buddhist Block Prints from Gung-thang.* Lumbini: Lumbini International Research Institute.

——. 2002. *A Buddhist Correspondence Lo-chen bsod-nams rgya-mtsho.* Lumbini: Lumbini International Research Institute.

——. 2002. *Life and Travels mo Lo-chen bSod nams rgya-mtsho.* Lumbini: Lumbini International Research Institute.

——. 2004. *Die Statue und der Temple des Aria Va-ti bzang-po.* Wiesbaden: Ludwig Reichert Verlag.

——. 2004. "Spiritual Relationship Between Rulers and Preceptors: The Three Journeys of Vanaratna (1384–1468) to Tibet." In C. Cueppers, ed., *The Relationship Between Religion and State (chos srid zung 'brel) in Traditional Tibet.* Proceedings of a seminar held in Lumbini, Nepal, March 2000. Lumbini: Lumbini International Research Institute.

Everding, K. H. 2000. *Das Koenigreich Mang yul Gung thang,* vols. 1 and 2. Bonn: VGH Wissenschaftsverlag.

Ferme, V. 2002. *Tradurre e tradire.* Ravenna: Longo Editore.

Ferrari, A. 1958. *mK'yen brtse's Guide to the Holy Places of Central Tibet.* Roma: IsMEO (Istituto Italiano per il Medio e l'Estremo Oriente).

Feuchtwang, S. 1992. *The Imperial Metaphor.* London, New York: Routledge.

Geertz, C. 1983. *Local Knowledge.* New York: Basic Books.

——. 1993. *The Interpretation of Cultures.* London: Fontana Press.

Gell, A. 1998. *Art and Agency.* Oxford: Clarendon Press.

Gellner, D. 1992. *Monk, Householder and Priest.* Cambridge: Cambridge University Press.

——. 1994. "Priests, Healers, Mediums and Witches: The Context of Possession in the Kathmandu Valley, Nepal." *Man* 29 (1): 27–48.

Germano, D. and J. Gyatso. 2000. "Longchenpa and the Possession by the *Ḍākinīs.*" In D. G. White, ed., *Tantra in Practice.* Princeton and Oxford: Princeton University Press.

Goldstein, M. and M. Kapstein. 1998. *Buddhism in Contemporary Tibet.* Berkeley and Los Angeles: The Regents of the University of California.

Goody, J. 1991. *The Interface Between the Written and the Oral.* Cambridge: Cambridge University Press.

Gyatso, J. 1985. "The Development of the *gCod* Tradition." In B. N. Aziz and M. Kapstein, eds., *Soundings in Tibetan Civilization.* Delhi: Manohar.

——. 1998. *Apparitions of the Self.* Princeton: Princeton University Press.

——. 2003. "One Plus One Makes Three: Buddhist Gender, Monasticism, and the Law of the Nonexcluded Middle." *History of Religions* 43 (2): 89–115.

Gyatso, J. and H. Havnevik. 2005. *Women in Tibet.* New York: Columbia University Press.

Hamayon, R. 1990. *La chasse à l'âme.* Paris: Société d'éthnologie.

Harrison, P. 1994. "In Search of the Sources of the Tibetan *bKa' 'gyur:* a Reconaissance Report." In P. Kvaerne, ed., *Tibetan Studies.* Oslo: The Institute for Comparative Research in Human Culture.

Al-Hassan, A. Y. and D. R. Hill. 1986. *Islamic Technology: An Illustrated History.* Cambridge and Paris: Cambridge University Press and UNESCO.

Havnevik, H. 1990. *Tibetan Buddhist Nuns.* Oslo: Norwegian University Press.

——. 1994. "The Role of Nuns in Contemporary Tibet." In R. Barnett and S. Akiner, eds., *Resistance and Reform in Tibet.* London: Hurst.

——. 1999. "The Life of Jetsun Lochen Rinpoche as Told in Her Autobiography." Ph.D. thesis, University of Oslo.

Hazod, G. 1998. "bKra shis 'od 'bar. On the History of the Religious Protector of the Bo dong pa." In A. M. Blondeau, ed., *Tibetan Mountain Deities: Their Cults and Representations.* Vienna: Verlag der Oesterreichischen Akademie der Wissenschaften.

Herrmann-Pfandt, A. 2001. *Ḍākinīs: Zur Stellung und Symbolik des Weiblichen im Tantrischen Buddhismus.* Marburg: Indica et Tibetica Verlag.

Huber, T. 1990. "Where Exactly are Cāritra, Devikoṭa and Himavat? A Sacred Geography Controversy and the Development of Tantric Buddhist Pilgrimage Sites in Tibet." *Kailash* 16 (3–4): 121–164.

——. 1994. "Why Can't Women Climb Pure Crystal Mountain? Remarks on Gender, Ritual and Space at Tsa-ri." In P. Kvaerne, ed., *Tibetan Studies*. Oslo: The Institute for Comparative Research in Human Culture.

——. 1997. "Ritual and Politics in the Eastern Himalaya: The Staging of Processions at Tsari." In S. Karmay and P. Sagant, eds., *Les Habitants du Toit du Monde*. Paris, Nanterre: Société d'Ethnologie.

——. 1999. *The Cult of the Pure Crystal Mountain*. Oxford and New York: Oxford University Press.

Humphrey, C. 1992. "The Moral Authority of the Past in Post-Socialist Mongolia." *Religion, State and Society* 20 (3 & 4): 375–389.

——. 1994. "Shamanic Practices and the State in Northern Asia: Views from the Center and Periphery." In N. Thomas and C. Humphrey, eds., *Shamanism, History, and the State*. Ann Arbor: University of Michigan Press.

——. 1995. "Chiefly and Shamanist Landscapes." In E. Hirsch and M. O'Hanlon, eds., *The Anthropology of Landscape: Perspectives on Place and Space*. Oxford: Oxford University Press.

——. 1996. *Shamans and Elders*. Oxford: Oxford University Press.

——. 1999. "The Fate of Earlier Social Ranking in the Communist Regimes of Russia and China." In R. Guha and J. Parry, eds., *Institutions and Inequalities*. Oxford: Oxford University Press.

Humphrey, C. and J. Laidlaw. 1994. *The Archetypes of Actions of Ritual*. Oxford: Oxford University Press.

——. Forthcoming. "Sacrifice and Ritualization." In E. Kiriakidis, ed., *The Archaeology of Ritual*. Los Angeles: Cotsen Institute of Archaeology UCLA Publications.

Jackson, D. 1996. *A History of Tibetan Painting*. Vienna: Verlag der Oesterreichische Akademie der Wissenscaften.

Jamyang Wangmo. 2005. *The Lawudo Lama*. Kathmandu: Vajra.

Kahlen, W. 1993. "Thang-stong rgyal-po: A Leonardo of Tibet." In C. Ramble and M. Brauen, eds., *Anthropology of Tibet and the Himalaya*. Zurich: Ethnological Museum of the University of Zurich.

Kapstein, M. 2000. *The Tibetan Assimilation of Buddhism: Conversion, Contestation and Memory*. Oxford: Oxford University Press.

——. 2001. *Reason's Traces*. Boston: Wisdom.

——. 2006. *The Tibetans*. Malden, Oxford, Victoria: Blackwell.

Karma Lekshe Tsomo. 2004. *Buddhist Women and Social Justice*. Albany: State University of New York Press.

——. 2004. "Is the Bhikṣuṇī Vinaya Sexist?" In Karma Lekshe Tsomo, ed., *Buddhist Women and Social Justice*. Albany: State University of New York Press.

Karma Thinley. 1980. *The History of the Sixteen Karmapas of Tibet*. Boulder: Prajna Press.

Karmay, S. 1980. "The Ordinance of Lha bLa-ma Ye-shes-'od." In M. Aris and Aung Suu Yi, eds., *Studies in Honour of Hugh Richardson*. Warminster: Aris and Philips.

——. 1987. "L'âme et la turquoise." *L'Éthnographie* XXXIII:97–130.

——. 1988. *The Great Perfection (rDzogs-chen): A Philosophical and Meditative Teaching in Tibetan Studies*. Leiden: Brill.

——. 1994. "Mountain Cults and National Identity in Tibet." In R. Barnett and S. Akiner, eds., *Resistance and Reform in Tibet*. London: Hurst.

——. 1996. "The Tibetan Cult of Mountain Deities and Its Political Significance." In A. M. Blondeau and E. Steinkellner, eds, *Reflections of the Mountain—Essays on the History and Social Meaning of the Mountain Cult in Tibet and the Himalaya*. Vienna: Verlag der Oesterreichischen Akademie der Wissenschaften.

——. 1998. "The Fifth Dalai Lama and His Reunification of Tibet." In S. Karmay, ed., *The Arrow and the Spindle: Studies in History, Myth, Rituals and Beliefs in Tibet*. Kathmandu: Mandala Book Point.

Klimburg-Salter, D. 2004. "Lama Yidam Protectors." *Orientations* 35 (3): 48–53.

Kvaerne, P. 1975. "On the Concept of *Sahaja* in Indian Buddhist Tantric Literature." *Temenos* II:88–135.

Laidlaw, J. and H. Whitehouse. 2004. *Ritual and Memory*. Oxford: Rowman and Littlefield.

Lobsang Lhalungpa. 1979. *The Life of Milarepa*. St. Albans and London: Granada Publishing Limited.

Lobue, E. 1994. "A Case of Mistaken Identity: Ma-gcig Labs-sgron and Ma-gcig Zha-ma." In P. Kvaerne, ed., *Tibetan Studies*. Oslo: The Institute for Comparative Research in Human Culture.

Lopez, D. 1988. *Buddhist Hermeneutics*. Honolulu: University of Hawaii Press.

Lucantiz, C. 2006. "The Eight Great Siddhas in Early Tibetan Painting." In R. Lingrothe, ed., *Holy Madness*. New York: Rubin Muesum of Art.

Macdonald, A. 1971. "Lecture des Pelliot tibétains 1286, 1287, 1038, 1047 et 1290—Essay sur l'emploi des mythes politiques dans la réligion royale de Srong btsan sgam po." In A. MacDonald, ed., *Études à la memoire de Marcelle Lalou*. Paris: Adrien Maisonneuve.

——. 1997. *Maṇḍala and Landscape*. New Delhi: Printworld.

Mahmood, S. 2001. "Feminist Theory, Embodiment, and the Docile Agent: Some Reflections on the Egyptian Islamic Revival." *Cultural Anthropology* 16 (2): 202–236.

Mangeot, S. 1974. *The Adventures of a Manchurian: The Story of Lobsang Thudup*. London: Collins.

Makley, C. 1999. "Gendered Practises and the Inner Sanctum: The Reconstruction of Tibetan Sacred Space in China's Tibet." In T. Huber, ed., *Sacred Spaces and Powerful Places in Tibetan Culture*. Dharamsala: Library of Tibetan Works and Archives.

——. 2005. "The Body of a Nun: Nunhood and Gender in Contemporary Amdo." In H. Havnevik and J. Gyatso, eds., *Women in Tibet*. New York: Columbia University Press.

Martin, D. 2005. "The Woman Illusion? Research Into the Lives of Spiritually Accomplished Women Leaders of the 11th and 12th Centuries." In H. Havnevik and J. Gyatso, eds., *Women in Tibet*. New York: Columbia University Press.

McKay, A. 2001. "'Truth,' Perception, and Politics: The British Construction of an Image of Tibet." In T. Dodin and H. Raether, eds., *Imagining Tibet*. Boston: Wisdom.

Meyer, F. 1988. *Gso-ba rig-pa, le Système médical tibétain*. Paris: Presses du CNRS.

Middleton, D. and D. Edwards. 1990. *Collective Remembering*. London: Sage.

Moore, H. 1994. *A Passion for Difference*. Cambridge: Polity Press.

Mumford, S. R. 1989. *Himalayan Dialogue: Tibetan Lamas and Gurung Shamans in Nepal*. New York: Macmillan.

Nebesky-Wojkowitz, R. de. 1993 [1975]. *Oracles and Demons of Tibet: The Cult and Iconography of the Tibetan Protective Deities*. Kathmandu: Tiwari's Pilgrims Book House.

Obeyesekere, G. 1984 [1981]. *Medusa's Hair: An Essay on Personal Symbols and Religious Experience*. Chicago: University of Chicago Press.

——. 2002. *Imagining Karma: Ethical Transformation in Amerindian, Buddhist, and Greek Rebirth*. Berkeley: University of California Press.

Ong, W. J. 1982. *Orality and Literacy: The Technologizing of the Word*. London: Methuen.

Onians, I. 2002. "Tantric Buddhist Apologetics or Antinomianism of Norm." Ph.D. thesis, University of Oxford.

Ortner, S. 1989. *High Religion: A Cultural and Political History of Sherpa Buddhism*. Princeton: Princeton University Press.

Pasang Wangdu. 1996. "A Chinese Inscription from the Tang Dynasty in Northern Kyirong." *Tibetan Studies* 3:56–63.

Pasang Wangdu and H. Diemberger. 2000. *dBa' bzhed: The Royal Narrative Concerning the Bringing of the Buddha's Doctrine to Tibet*. Vienna: Österreichische Akademie der Wissenschaften and Tibetan Academy of Social Sciences.

Paul, D. 1985 [1979]. *Women in Buddhism*. Berkeley: University of California Press.

Perdue, P. 2000. "Culture, History, and Imperial Chinese Strategy: Legacies of the Qing Conquests." In H. Van de Ven, ed., *Warfare in Chinese History*. Amsterdam: Brill.

Petech, L. 1988. *Selected Papers in Asian History*. Roma: IsMEO.

——. 1990. *Central Tibet and the Mongols*. Roma: IsMEO.

Phuntsho, Karma. Forthcoming. "Gangtey's Untold Treasures." In P. Sorenson, K. Phuntsho, et al., *Written Treasures: A Mirror of the Past and a Bridge to the Future*. Thimphu: National Library.

Pommaret, F. 1989. *Les revenants de lau-delà dans le monde tibétain*. Paris: CNRS.

Ramble, R. 2002. "The Victory Song of Porong." In K. Buffetrille and H. Diemberger, eds., *Territory and Identity in Tibet and the Himalaya*. Leiden: Brill.

Ricca, F. and E. Lo Bue. 1993. *The Great Stupa of Gyantse*. London: Serindia.

Richardson, H. 1974. *Ch'ing Dynasty Inscriptions at Lhasa*. Roma: IsMEO.

Robinson, J., trans. 1979. *Buddha's Lions: The Lives of the Eighty-Four Siddhas by Abhaya-datta.* Berkeley: Dharma Publishing.

Roerich, G. 1988 [1949]. *The Blue Annals.* Translation of *Deb ther sngon po.* New Delhi: Motilal Banarsidass.

Rosaldo, M. Z. 1983. "The Shame of Headhunters and the Autonomy of the Self." *Ethos* 11:135–151.

Sagant, P. 1990. "Les Tambours de Nyi-shang (Nepal)—ritual et centralisation politique." In *Tibet Civilisation et Societé.* Paris: Editions de la Fondation Singer Polignac.

Samuel, G. 1993. *Civilized Shamans: Buddhism in Tibetan Societies.* Washington: Smithsonian Institution.

Sanders, E. P. and M. Davies. 1989. *Studying the Synoptic Gospels.* London: SCM Press.

Sanderson, A. 1988. "Śaivism and the Tantric Traditions." In S. Sutherland, L. Houlden, F. Hardy, and P. Clarke, eds., *The World's Religions.* London: Routledge.

Schaeffer, K. 2003. "A Royal Nun in Fifteenth-Century Tibet." Paper given at the at the American Academy of Religion Annual Meeting, November 20, 2003.

——. 2004. *Himalayan Hermitess.* Oxford University Press.

Schein, G. and S. Strasser 1997. *Intersexions, Feministische Anthropologie zu Geschlecht Kultur und Sexualitaet.* Vienna: Milena Verlag.

Schicklgruber, C. 1992. "*Grib:* On the Significance of the Term in a Socio-religious Context." In S. Ihara and Z. Yamaguchi, eds., *Tibetan Studies.* Narita: Naritasan Shinsoji.

Seyfort Ruegg, D. 1988. "A Karma bka' brgyud Work on the Lineages and Traditions of Indo-Tibetan dBu ma (Madhyamaka)." In G. Gnoli and L. Lanciotti, eds., *Orientalia Iosephi Tucci Memoriae Dicata.* Roma: IsMEO.

——. 1997. "The Preceptor-Donor (yon mchod) Relation in Thirteenth-Century Tibetan Society and Polity, Its Inner Asian Precursors and Indian Models." In H. Krasser, T. Much, E. Steinkellner, and H. Tauscher, eds., *Tibetan Studies.* Vienna: Verlag der Oesterreichischen Akademie der Wissenschaften.

——. 2004. "The Indian and the Indic in Tibetan Cultural History, and Tsong kha pa's Achievement as a Scholar and Thinker: An Essay on the Concepts of Buddhism in Tibet and Tibetan Buddhism." *Journal of Indian Philosophy* 32:321–343.

Schuh, D. 1973. *Untersuchungen zur Geschichte der tibetische Kalenderrechnung.* Wiesbaden: Franz Steiner Verlag.

Schwartz, R. 1994. *Circle of Protest. Political Ritual in the Tibetan Uprising.* London: Hurst.

Shakya Tsering. 1999. *The Dragon in the Land of Snows.* London: Pimlico.

——. 2002. "Blood in the Snows—Reply to Wang Lixiong." *New Left Review* 15 (May–June): 39–60.

Sharlho, Tseten Wangchuk. 1993. "China's Reforms in Tibet: Issues and Dilemmas." *The Journal of Contemporary China* 1 (1): 34–43, 55–60.

Shaw, M. 1994. *Passionate Enlightenment.* Princeton: Princeton University Press.

Simmer-Brown, J. 2002. *Ḍākinīs Warm Breath: The Feminine Principle in Tibetan Buddhism*. Boston and London: Shambala.

Smith, G. E. 1969. "Preface." In *The Life of the Saint of Gtsaṅ*. Delhi: Sata Pitaka Series.

Sneath, D. Forthcoming. *The Headless State: Aristocratic Orders, Kinship Society, and the Misrepresentations of Nomadic Inner Asia*. New York: Columbia University Press.

Snellgrove, D. 1987. *Indo-Tibetan Buddhism*. Boston: Shambala.

Snellgrove, D. and H. Richardson. 1995 [1968]. *A Cultural History of Tibet*. Boston: Shambhala.

Sørensen, P. 1994. *The Mirror Illluminating the Royal Genealogies*. Translation of *rGyal rabs gsal ba'i me long*. Wiesbaden: Harrasowitz Verlag.

Sørensen, P. and G. Hazod. 2000. *Civilization at the Foot of Mount Sham-po*. Vienna: Verlag der Oesterreichischen Akademie der Wissenschaften.

——. 2005. *Thundering Falcon: An Inquiry Into the Histroy and Cult of Khra-'brug Tibet's First Buddhist Temple*. Vienna: Verlag der Oesterreichischen Akademie der Wissenschaften.

——. 2007. *Rulers on the Celestial Plain: Ecclesiastic and Secular Hegemony in Medieval Tibet: A Study of the Tshal Gung-thang*. Vienna: Verlag der Österreichischen Akademie der Wissenshaften.

Sperling, E. 1992. "Miscellaneous Remarks on the Lineage of Byang La-stod." *China Tibetology* Special Issue: 272–277.

Sponberg, A. 1992. "Attitudes Towards Women and the Feminine in Early Buddhism." In I. Cabezon, ed., *Buddhism, Sexuality and Gender*. New York: State University of New York Press.

Stearns, C. 1980. "The Life and the Teachings of the Tibetan Saint Thang-stong rgyal-po, 'The King of the Empty Plain.'" M.A. thesis, University of Washington.

——. 2007. *Tangtong Gyalpo: King of the Empty Plain*. Ithaca: Snow Lion.

Stein, R. A. 1959. *Recherches sur l'épopée et le barde au Tibet*. Paris: Bibliothèque de l'Institut des Hautes Études Chinoises.

——. 1961. *Une cronique ancienne de bSam-yas: sBa-bzhed*. Paris: Institut des Hautes Études chinoises: Textes et documents, I.

——. 1972. *Tibetan Civilization*. London: Faber and Faber.

——. 1988. *Grottes-matrices et lieux saints de la déesse en Asie orientale*. Paris: École Française d'Extrême Orient.

Steinkellner, E. 2006. "The Buddhist Tradition of Epistemology and Logic (*tshad ma*) and Its Significance for Tibetan Civilization." In A. Gingrich and G. Hazod, eds., *Der Rand und Die Mitte*. Vienna: Verlag der Österreichischen Akademie der Wissenshaften.

Strathern, M. 1987. "An Awkward Relationship: The Case of Feminism and Anthropology." *Signs* 12 (2): 276–293.

——. 1988. *The Gender of the Gift*. Berkeley and Los Angeles: University of California Press.

Tambiah, S. J. 1970. *Buddhism and the Spirit Cults in Northeast Thailand*. Cambridge: Cambridge University Press.

———. 1984. *The Buddhist Saints of the Forest and the Cult of Amulets: A Study of Charisma, Hagiography, Sectarianism, and Millennial Buddhism*. Cambridge: Cambridge University Press.

Tashi Tsering. 1994. "Introductory Notes on the Biographical Sketches of Six Incarnations of Gungru Khandroma." *g. Yu mtsho* 1:27–47.

Tatun Wangpo. 2006. "Gender Bender: The Myth of Gender Equality in Tibetan Society." October. http://www.phayul.com.

Taylor, C. 1989. *Sources of the Self: The Making of the Modern Identity*. Cambridge: Harvard University Press.

Tenzin Gyatsho. 1995. *The World of Tibetan Buddhism*. Trans. Geshe Thupten Jinpa. Boston: Wisdom.

Tsepak Rigzin. 1993 [1986]. *Tibetan-English Dictionary of Buddhist Terminology*. Dharmasala: Library of Tibetan Works and Archives.

Tsuda, S. 1978. "A Critical Tantrism." *The Memoirs of the Tokyo Bunko* 36:167–231.

Tucci, G. 1969. *Rati-Līlā: An Interpretation of the Tantric Imagery of the Temples of Nepal*. Geneva: Nagel.

———. 1987. *To Lhasa and Beyond*. Ithaca: Snow Lion.

———. 1999 [1949]. *Tibetan Painted Scrolls*. Bangkok: SDI.

Uebach, H. 1980. "Notes on the Tibetan Kinship Term *dBon*." In M. Aris and Aung Suu Yi, eds., *Studies in Honour of Hugh Richardson*. Warminster: Aris and Philips.

———. 2005. "Ladies of the Tibetan Empire (Seventh to Ninth Centuries CE)." In H. Havnevik and J. Gyatso, eds., *Women in Tibet*. New York: Columbia University Press.

Uray, G. Forthcoming. "The Personal Names in the 7th–8th Century Tibetan Sources and the Study of Tibetan History." Paper given at the 2nd Hungarian Conference of Onomastics, Budapest, 1969 and published in Hungarian in 1970. To be published in English in the forthcoming *Collected Works of Geza Uray*.

Van der Kuijp, L. 1993. "Two Mongol Xylographs (*hor par ma*) of the Tibetan Text of Sakya Paṇḍita's Work on Buddhist Logic and Epistemology." *Journal of the International Association of Buddhist Studies* 16 (1993): 279–98.

———. 2005. "The Dalai Lamas and the Origin of Reincarnate Lamas." In M. Brauen, ed., *The Dalai Lamas: A Visual History*. Zurich: Ethographic Museum Zurich and Serindia.

———. 2006. "On the Composition and Printing of *Deb gter sngon po* by 'Gos lo tsā ba gzhon nu dpal (1392–1481)." *Journal of the International Association of Tibetan Studies* 2. http://www.thdl.org/collections/jiats/02/.

Vasari, G. 1550. *Vite de' più eccellenti architetti, pittori, et scultori italiani, da Cimabue insino a' tempi nostri* (first edition). Firenze: Editore Ducale Lorenzo Torrentino. Original kept at the Cambridge University Library.

Venuti, L. 2000. *The Translation Studies Reader*. London and New York: Routledge.

Vitali, R. 1990. *Early Temples of Central Tibet*. London: Serindia.

——. 1996. "Nomads of Byang and mNga'-ris-smad: A Historical Overview of Their Interaction in Gro-shod, 'Brong-pa, Glo-bo and Gung-thang from the 11th to the 15th Century." In H. Krasser, M. Much, E. Steinkellner, and H. Tauscher, eds., *Tibetan Studies*. Vienna: Verlag der OeA.

Vitebsky, P. 1995. *The Shaman: Voyages of the Soul—Trance, Ecstasy and Healing from Siberia to the Amazon*. London: Macmillan.

Waddell, A. 1912. "Tibetan Manuscripts and Books, etc., Collected During the Young-husband Mission to Lhasa." Reprint from the *Asiatic Quarterly Review* (July): 1–12.

——. 1988 [1905]. *Lhasa and Its Mysteries*. New York: Dover.

Wang Yao. 1994. "Hu Yaobang's Visit to Tibet, May 22–31, 1980: An Important Development in the Chinese Government's Tibet Policy." In R. Barnett and S. Akiner, eds., *Resistance and Reform in Tibet*. London: Hurst.

Weintraub, K. J. 1978. *The Value of the Individual*. Chicago: University of Chicago Press.

Willis, J. 1985. "Nuns and Benefactresses: The Role of Women and Philosophic Innovation in the Development of Buddhism." In Y. Haddad and E. Findly, eds., *Women, Religion, and Social Change*. Albany: State University of New York Press.

——. 1989. *Feminine Ground: Essays on Women and Tibet*. Ithaca: Snow Lion.

Wylie, T. 1978. "Reincarnation: A Political Innovation." In L. Ligeti, ed., *Proceedings of the Csoma de Koros Memorial Symposium*. Budapest: Akademiai Kiado.

Yanagisako, S. 1997. "Geschlechter, Sexualitaet und andere Ueberschneidungen." In G. Schein and S. Strasser, eds., *Intersexions, Feministische Anthropologie zu Geschlecht Kultur und Sexualitaet*. Vienna: Milena Verlag.

Yurchak, A. 2003. "Soviet Hegemony of Form: Everything Was For Ever, Until It Was No More." *Comparative Studies in Society and History* 45 (3) (July): 480–510.

# INDEX

Namgyal's revival, 133, 194; contemporary revival, 9, 292, 300, 316, 316–319, 320–321, 359n3, 360nn6, 7; and creative innovation, 327–329n2; diffusion of, 9, 29–30; Drugpa Kagyu tradition, 336n26; and imperial legacy, 161, 342–343n4, 344n33; India as source of, 30, 265; Kadampa tradition, 45, 80; Kagyupa tradition, 46, 50, 51, 131; and landscape mythology, 269–270, 271–272; Mahāyāna, 113, 145, 181, 205, 241, 242, 271, 343n13; patronage in, 41–44; Phagmodrupa Kagyupa tradition, 95, 337n36, 355n22; political support by, 32–33; Sakyapa tradition, 45, 47, 50, 131, 160, 346n54; on self, 142, 143, 250; "Shamanic," 246, 353n3; Shangpa Kagyupa tradition, 46; and textual authority, 5; and Tibetan calendar, 345n37; and Tibetan Renaissance, 32–33, 113, 327–328n2; Yasang Kagyupa tradition, 356n41. See also Bodongpa tradition; Gelugpa (dGe lugs pa) tradition; Karmapa lineage; Nyingma tradition; tantra; Vajrayoginī/Vajravārāhī cults; women's status in Buddhism; *specific teachers and monasteries*

Buddhist Association, 302, 308

Bumdegon Nagpo (Bum lde mgon nag po) (founder of Gungthang kingdom), 34, 161, 345n35

*bume*, 10, 13

Burke, Peter, 33, 331n10

Buton, 133. See also Buton Rinchen Drub

Buton Rinchen Drub (Bu ston rin chen grub) (Tibetan scholar), 42

Cakrasaṃvara (deity), xiv, 30, 49, 50, 51. See also twin reincarnation line

*cakravartin* role, 43

campanilismo, 33, 331n9

Candler, Edmund, xv

Cāritra (place), 333n33, 337n36, 357n50

Carsten, Janet, 117, 340n16

Chagmen (Chag sman), 177

Chagpo ri (lCags po ri), 230, 233, 352n151

Chagsam Chubori (lCags zam chu bo ri), 68, insert p. 9

Chagsam Khar (lCags zam mkhar), 207, 350n112

Chamdrin Lhakang temple (Byams sprin lha khang), 331n14

Changchubkyi Sung (Byang chub kyi gzungs) (disciple of Bodong Chogle Namgyal), 108, 200, 349n99

Changchub Sangmo (Byang chub bzang mo) (nun), 192, 339–340n11, 348n84, 349n105, 354n13

Changchub Tsemo (Byang chub rtse mo) (Tibetan scholar), 45–46

Changsem (CD's grandmother), 36, 55, 202, 349n103. See also Changsem Sangye Wangmo

Changsem Sangye Wangmo (Byang sems sang rgyas dbang mo) (Jamyang) ('Jam dbyangs), 35, 36, 331n16

Changsungpa (Byang gzung pa) (disciple of Bodong Chogle Namgyal), 186, 197, 212, 347n73, 350n121. See also Changchubkyi Sung

Chang Targo (Byang rTa mgo) (mountain), 273

Chayet, Anne, xiv, xvi, 114, 253

Chekar monastery. See Nyemo Chekar (sNye mo Bye dkar) monastery

Chengnga Tsultrim Bar (sPyan snga ba Tshul khrims 'bar) (reincarnation of Cakrasaṃvara), 325. See also Chenngaba Tsunthrim Bar

Chen Kuiyuan, 312, 315

Chenneba (gCen ne ba). See Thri Namgyal De

Chenngaba Tsunthrim Bar (Tibetan scholar), 257, 355n26

Chenpo Namrin (Chen po Nam rin), 185

*chidar (phyi dar)* (later diffusion), 9, 30

Chime Drupa. See Pal Chime Drupa

Chime Oser ('Chi med 'od zer) (Tibetan scholar), 261, 325. See also Bo dong chos 'byung

Chime Palsang ('Chi med dpal bzang) (Tibetan scholar): and Chime Oser, 261; images of, 27, insert p. 3; and Karmapa lineage, 262, 263; and Nyemo Chekar monastery, 340n13; and Pal Chime Drupa, 336n22; and Taglung Thangpa Ngawang Dragpa, 82, 259, 336n21; and twin reincarnation line, 259–260, 325

Chinese People's Political Consulting Conference (CPPCC), 290–291, 292

Choding (Chos sdings) monastery. See Palmo Choding (dPal mo chos sdings) monastery

Choding Breboche (Chos sdings Bre bo che) (place), 193

Chodingpa (people of Choding; followers of the Bodongpa tradition). See Palmo Choding (dPal mo chos sdings) monastery

Chodrag Yeshe (Chos grags ye shes) (Fourth Red Hat Karmapa), 263

Chodron Wangmo (Chos sgron dbang mo) (Seventh Dorje Phagmo), 326

Chodzema (Chos mdzad ma) (lady of Tagtse), 177, 178, 213, 220, 346n52

*cho (gcod)*, 140, 182, 346n56

Chogden Dorje (mChog ldan rdo rje) (Kunga Sangmo's father), 258

Chogden Legpe Lodro (mChog ldan legs pa'i blo gros), 217, 351n130

Chogle Namgyal. See Bodong Chogle Namgyal

Chogyal Nasathro (Chos rgyal Na bza' 'phrod), 257

Chokyi Dronma: as begging nun, 61, 109, 177–182; birth of, 53, 121, 151–152, 333n1; and bridge-building projects, 52, 69, 113; brother of. See Thri Namgyal De; Buddhist scripture influence on, 154, 343n13; childhood of, 54–55, 90, 152–156, 239; commitment to women, 9–11, 12, 61–62, 123; and crazy *yogin* tradition, 60, 66, 140; as dance master, 109, 194–195; death of, 8, 47, 52, 69, 76, 80, 89, 97, 236, 258, 334nn5, 9; elite

325–326; as dynasty, 2, 327n1; feminist perspectives on, 13–14, 15; and Gelugpa rule, 278–282; images of, 8, 25–28, 111, 262–263, insert p. 2, insert p. 3; and imperial legacy, 145, 275; importance of, 2; international scholarship on, 15–16; and Karmapa lineage, 261–263, insert p. 3; possible new emanation, 322–323, insert p. 16; and Qing empire, 282, 358n12; reckoning system of, 95, 263–264; ritualization of, 282–284, 289, 358n12; significance for women, xiv, 9, 99; symbolic nature of, xv; textual construction of, 2; Tibetan exile perspectives on, 14; and Yamdrog rulers, 278–279. *See also* Dorje Phagmo lineage establishment; twin reincarnation line

Dorje Phagmo lineage establishment, 8, 240–241; and Amoghasiddhi Jigme Bang, 82, 253, 254–255; and Bodong Chogle Namgyal's lineage, 252–253, 255–257, 355n23; and *Bo dong chos 'byung*, 252, 255–261, 355n25; and CD biography, 5, 18, 95, 250–251; and CD's skull, 98, 263–264, 356–357n49; and Chokyi Dronma as embodiment of Dorje Phagmo, 251; and oracles, 246, 353n4; and Pal Chime Drupa, 47; and Taglung Thangpa Ngawang Dragpa, 76; and Thangtong Gyalpo, 47, 251–252; and Thangtong Gyalpo biographies, 243, 244, 246–247, 251; and Tibetan reincarnation context, 241–246; and twin reincarnation line, 256–257, 259–260, 261; and Yamdrog rulers, 50, 253–254, 259, 334n1. *See also* Dorje Phagmo, Second (Kunga Sangmo)

double reincarnation line. *See* twin reincarnation line

dough ball divination, 211, 350n119

*dPal de kho na nyid 'dus pa* (Bodong Chogle Namgyal): and Bodongpa tradition, 45, 115; as CD biography source, 72–73; current studies of, 133, 342n30; as influence on CD, 59, 168; and Namkha Sangpo, 82, 336n25; repatriation of, 288–289, 314, 321, 360n11, insert p. 15; women's full ordination in, 133. *See also* Bodong Chogle Namgyal collected works project

Dragkar (Brag dkar), 226, 352n147

Dragpa Gyaltshen (Grags pa rgyal mtshan), 45–46

Dragpa Jungne (Grags pa 'byung gnas), 47

Drangsong Sinpori (Drang srong srin po ri) (mountain), 230

*drelba ('brel ba)*, 340n16. *See also* relatedness

Dremotsho ('Dre mo mtsho) (demoness lake), 268, 269–270

Dreyfus, G., 39, 332n22

Drigung Rinchen Phuntshog ('Bri gung rin chen phun tshogs), 358n6

Dritsangshagpa (Dri gtsang zhag pa), 287

Drog Gangding monastery ('Brog sgang sdings), 337n40

Droma Lhakhang (sGrol ma lha khang) temple, 54, 352n150

Dromton Gyalbe Jungne ('Brom ston rGyal ba'i 'byung gnas) (Kadampa master), 257, 355n27

Dron Nyerpon ('Gron gNyer dpon), 220

Drowa Sangmo ('Gro ba bzang mo) (consort of Gotshangpa Gonpo Dorje), 240, 260

Drugpa Kagyu ('Brug pa bka' brgyud) tradition, 336n26

Drugpa Kuleg ('Brug pa kun legs), 100

Drungchen Kyabma (Drung chen sKyab ma), 160

Dudjom Rinpoche (bDud 'joms Rin po che), 322

Dudul (bDud 'dul) (craftsman), 194

Duldzin Ngawang ('Dul 'dzin Ngag dbang) (lama), 182

Dumotsho (bDud mo mtsho) (demoness lake), 268, 269–270

*Dunhuang Annals*, 269

Dusum Khyenpa (Dus gsum mkhyen pa) (First Karmapa), 242

Dzamling Gyalmo (rDzam gling rgyal mo) (CD's sister), 55, 65, 166, 169, 171, 210–211, 340n19

Dzatrul Ngawang Tendzin Norbu (rDza sprul Ngag dbang bstan 'dzin nor bu), 126

Dzongkha (rDzong kha/dkar) (place), 35, 192, 194–195, insert p. 4

Dzongkha Chode monastery (rDzong kha/dkar chos sde), 176, 182, 209, 349n102

Dzungar (Mongolian group), 281–282

Edward, Derek, 85

"Eighty-Four Thousand *Dharmaskanda*" (*Chos kyi phung po brgyad khri bzhi stong*), 183, 346n63

Eisenstein, Elizabeth, 16

Empson, Rebecca, 245

English, Elisabeth, 49–50

Everding, Karl-Heinz, 36, 40, 41, 111

*Feast of Miracles (ngo mtshar gyi dga' ston)*, 71–72, 73, 101, 334nn1, 3. *See also* Bodong Chogle Namgyal biographies

female infanticide, 123

*Female Living Buddha (Niu Huofu)*, 308, 360n9

Ferme, Valerio, 328n7

Feuchtwang, Stephan, 274, 314, 357–358n4

Four Rivers Six Ranges (Chushi Gangdrug; *chu bzhi sgang drug*) uprising, 303–304, 306, 360nn6, 7

Gadong (dGa' gdong) (oracle), 298

Gampa-la pass (Gam pa la), 228, 352n149

Ganden (dGa' ldan) (Palmo Ganden), 211, 349n108, 350n118

Gangkar (sGang dkar) (place), 154, 343n14

Gangkar Gyalpo (Gangs dkar rgyal po) (deity), 274

Gang Ponchen (Gangs bon/dpon chen) (mountain), 344n28

Garpa Donyo Dorje (sGar pa don yod rdo rje), 259

Geba (dGe ba), 179

Geertz, Clifford, 143

Gell, Alfred, 114

Pal Riboche (dPal Ri bo che) (place), 206, 350*n*III.
  *See also* Chung Riwoche (gCung Ri bo che)
  *stūpa*
Palsang Dronme (dPal bzang sgron me), 221
Palti (dPal sde). *See* Yamdrog (Yar 'brog) Lake
*Pañcakrama* (Nāgārjuna), 146
Panchen Lama, 20, 46, 278, 302, 308, 311, 360*n*6
Panchen Lama, First (Khedrubje Geleg Pal Sangpo)
  (mKhas grub rje; dGe legs dpal bzang po), 46,
  278
Pang Lotsawa Lodro Tenba (dPang lo tsa ba Blo gros
  brtan pa) (great-great-uncle of Bodong Chogle
  Namgyal), 46, 181, 264, 357*n*52
Pañjaranāth (Gur kyi dgon po) (deity), 156, 344*n*23
patronage, 38, 41–44, 109, 187, 251, 331*n*10, 347*n*75
Pawo Chuden (dPa' bo bchu ldan) (father of Urgyen
  Tshomo), 260
Pawo Lhundrub (dPa' bo lhun grub) (father of
  Nyendra Sangmo), 260
Pawo Tsuglag (dPa' bo gtsug lag) (scholar), 74,
  336*n*21, 340*n*13
Phadampa Sangye (Pha dam pa Sangs rgyas) (Indian
  Buddhist master), 100, 345*n*49, 346*n*58
Phagchog Sonam Dar ('Phags mchog bSod nams
  dar) (scholar), 337*n*40
Phagmodrupa (Phag mo gru pa) rulers: CD's refusal
  to meet, 234; and Dorje Phagmo lineage, 358*n*6;
  Phagmodrupa Changchub Gyaltshen, 31–32, 39;
  and Phagmodrupa Dorje Gyalpo, 255, 355*n*22;
  and Rinpung rulers, 331*n*8; and Second Dorje
  Phagmo (Kunga Sangmo), 252, 259, 356*n*42; and
  Thangtong Gyalpo, 47, 113
Phagmodrupa Changchub Gyaltshen (Phag mo gru
  pa Byang chub rgyal mtshan), 31–32, 39
Phagmodrupa Dorje Gyalpo (Phag mo gru pa rDo
  rje rgyal po): ancestral line of, 338*n*45, 356*n*30;
  and CD biography, 95; and CD's skull, 356–
  357*n*49; and Dorje Phagmo lineage establishment, 255, 257, 264; importance of, 95, 337*n*36;
  and Phagmodrupa rulers, 255, 355*n*22
Phagmodrupa Kagyupa tradition, 95, 337*n*36, 355*n*22
Phagpa (Phags pa), Lama, 31
Phagpa Lhakang (Phags pa lha khang; Phags pa Wa
  ti bzang po) temple, 331*n*14, insert p. 4
*Phags pa wa ti* (Self-Generated Great Compassionate statue), 176, 345*n*50
Phari (Pha ri) (place), 306
Pholhane Sonam Tobgye (Pho lha nas bSod nams
  stobs rgyal), 280–281, 282
*phowa ('pho ba)* (practice), 242–243
Phuntshog (Phun tshogs), 224
Phuntshogling (Phun tshogs gling) bridge, insert
  p. 9
Phurbagyal (Phur ba rgyal) (horse-keeper), 170, 171
Phurburagpa (Phur bu rags pa). *See* Tashi Ombar
*piṭas* (Indian holy places), 51, 337*n*36, 357*n*50
Ponmo Chogyal (wife of Tshewang Tashi), 171–172,
  345*n*44

Ponmo Lhacho (dPon mo lHa chos) (noble
  woman), 226, 352*n*147
Ponmo Lodro Gyalmo (dPon mo Blo gros rgyal mo)
  (nun), 192
Ponmo Sangring (dPon mo Sang ring) (nun;
  supervisor of craftsmen), 202
Ponne Simadar (dPon ne Srid ma dar) (official),
  156–157
Ponpo Lama (dPon po bla ma), 167
Porong (sPo/sPong rong), 38, 57, 332*n*21, insert p. 6
Porong Palmo Choding monastery. *See* Palmo
  Choding (dPal mo chos sdings) monastery
pre-Buddhist cults. *See* territorial cults
printing technology: and Amoghasiddhi Jigme
  Bang, 82, 336*n*25; and Bodong Chogle Namgyal
  collected works project, 64, 108–109, 336*n*25,
  339*n*9, 349*nn*100, 104; and Gungthang, 107,
  108–109; and Tibetan Renaissance, 1, 7, 16, 33,
  64, 107, 108–109, 329*nn*19, 20
prophecies: and CD's birth, 152; and CD's skull, 97,
  98, 236; and Dorje Phagmo lineage, xv;
  Thangtong Gyalpo, 66, 73, 76, 79, 97, 334*n*5;
  and treasure literature, 40–41, 332*n*23

Qianlong (Qing emperor), 282
Qing empire, 282, 291, 358*n*12
Qinwang Tashi Tsering (bKra shis tshe ring)
  (princess), 341*n*22

Ralpacen (Thride Tsugtsen) (King of Tibet), 30, 68,
  230, 352*n*154
Ramble, Charles, xx, 330*n*5, 340*n*21
Rangung Dorje (Rang byung rdo rje) (Third
  Karmapa), 242
recently recovered texts, 20, 329–330*n*24, 338*n*1
red color, 41, 332*n*28
Red Hat Karmapa, 27, 111, 262, 263, insert p. 3
regret (*'gyod pa*), 17, 125, 329*n*21
reincarnation: controversies about, 248, 264–265,
  299–300, 354*nn*10, 11, 360*n*5; and imperial
  legacy, 145, 342*n*36; and narratives of origin, 85–
  87; political implications of, 20, 242, 330*n*25;
  Qing reforms, 282, 358*n*12; and religious belief,
  264–265; and territorial cults, 244–246, 353*nn*1,
  2; Tibetan context, 241–246. *See also* Chokyi
  Dronma as embodiment of Dorje Phagmo;
  Dorje Phagmo lineage
relatedness: and Chokyi Dronma, 116–120, 340*n*16;
  and gender, 120–123; and reincarnation, 248. *See
  also* kinship
Ren Rong (TAR Party secretary), 311
Reting Rinpoche (Rwa sgreng rin po che), 330*n*25
*rGyal rabs gsal ba'i me long*, 55, 333*n*3
Ribo Gandenpa (Ri bo dga' ldan pa) tradition, 258.
  *See also* Gelugpa (dGe lugs pa) tradition
Richardson, Hugh, 104
Rigsum Gonpo (Rigs gsum mgon po) (lama), 51–52,
  68, 231–233, 235–236, 334*n*5, 353*nn*156, 157

389

*Index*

Vasari, Giorgio, 104, 116
Venuti, Lawrence, 328*n*7
*Vinaya* (monastic rules), 132–133, 134, 138, 189, 347*n*77

Waddell, Austin, 284–285, 290, 321, 359*n*15
water channel projects. *See* irrigation projects
Weber, Max, 283
Wencheng, 29, 55, 330*n*5
Whitehouse, Harvey, 249
Williamson, Margaret, 286
wisdom *stūpa*, 145, 191–192, 193–194, 198, 348*nn*82, 87
women: Buddhist religious life as transcending limits on, 11, 123, 328*n*9; and CD biography authorship, 83, 87, 336*n*26; CD's commitment to, 9–11, 12, 61–62, 123; historical effacement of, 3; low status of, 10, 11, 123, 328*n*9; and Tibetan Renaissance, 108, 339–340*n*11; Tibetan terms for, 10, 13. *See also* women's status in Buddhism
women's full ordination, 329*n*23; and Bodong Chogle Namgyal's Buddhist revival, 133–134; and Buddha, 132, 341*n*26; and CD biography limited circulation, 19, 20; Chokyi Dronma, 7, 12, 60–61, 132, 133–134, 177, 183–184, 346*n*54; current debates, 15, 132–133, 329*n*18, 341*n*28; female participation requirement, 132, 133, 341*n*27; and sexuality, 137, 342*n*32
women's status in Buddhism: and biographical models, 17, 329*n*22; and Bodong Chogle Namgyal, 60, 62, 127–128, 132, 133, 134; and Bodong Chogle Namgyal's lineage, 253; and CD biography, 87–88; CD's contributions to, 10–11, 61–62; and Communist China, 319; and enlightenment, 132, 185–186, 253, 341*n*25; and Fifth Dalai Lama, 279–280; international scholarship on, 15–16; and madness, 60; nuns' social position, 10–11; and patronage, 44; and resistance to Chokyi Dronma, 11–12; soteriological inclusiveness, 11, 328*n*10; and Tsari shrine, 51, 96; and Vajrayoginī/Vajravārāhī cults, 51. *See also* women's full ordination
Wu (Chinese Empress), 341*n*22
Wu Jinghua, 311
Wylie, Turrell, 241, 242, 246, 283

*yab-se (yab sras)*, 119
*yab yum*, 120

Yamdrog (Yar 'brog), 192, 258, 348*n*86, 356*n*36; and CD biography authorship, 82; and landscape mythology, 267–275; and Tibetan uprising, 303, 306. *See also* Samding (bSam sdings) monastery; Yamdrog (Yar 'brog) rulers
Yamdrog (Yar 'brog) Lake, 268, 289–290, insert p. 10
Yamdrog (Yar 'brog) rulers: background of, 358*n*9; and Dorje Phagmo lineage establishment, 50, 253–254, 259, 334*n*1; and Samding monastery, 259, 276, 278–279
*yangdar* (yang dar) (further diffusion), 9, 292, 300, 316–319, 320–321, 359*n*3, 360*nn*6, 7
Yarlha Shampo (Yar lha sham po) (mountain/deity), 273
Yarlung Sheldrag (Yar lung shel brag) monastery, 234, 259, 276, 335*n*12, 356*n*43
Yarsib (Yar sribs), 228
Yar To (Yar stod) (place), 259
Yasang (g.Ya' bzang) monastery, 259, 356*n*41
Yasang Kagyupa (g.Ya' bzang bka' brgyud pa) tradition, 356*n*41
Yau (gYa'u) (place), 158, 344*n*28
Yeola (dBye 'o la) pass, 158, 344*n*28
Yeshe Tshomo (Ye shes mtsho/gtso mo) (Fifth Dorje Phagmo), 265, 267, 279, 325
Yeshe Tsogyal (Ye shes mtsho rgyal) (consort of Padmasambhava), 100
*yondag*, 42
Younghusband expedition, 280, 284–286, 321, 359*n*15
*Yuganaddha (zung 'jug)*, 146
*yullhas (yul lha)* (mountain deities), 271
Yumbudo (Yum bu do) (island), 289–290
Yumtsho Chugmo (Yum mtsho phyug mo). *See* Yamdrog (Yar 'brog) Lake
*Yumtso (Yum mtsho)* (journal), 13, 14, 267
Yungdrung Lingpa (gYung drung gling pa) (master), 163
Yurchak, Alexei, 292, 313

Zhou Enlai, 307
Zimpon Osang (gZim dpon 'Od bzang) (disciple of Bodong Chogle Namgyal), 355*n*18
*zung 'jug* (Yuganaddha), 146